COMPLETE
HORSE
RIDING
MANUAL

COMPLETE
HORSE
RIDING
MANUAL

William Micklem

LONDON, NEW YORK,
MELBOURNE, MUNICH, AND DELHI

Managing Editor Deirdre Headon
Managing Art Editor Lee Griffiths
Senior Art Editor Joanne Doran
Senior Editor Simon Tuite
DTP Designer Louise Waller
Production Controller Mandy Inness

Commissioned photography by Kit Houghton

Produced for Dorling Kindersley by

13 SOUTHGATE STREET   WINCHESTER   HAMPSHIRE   SO23 9DZ

Design Dawn Terrey, Helen Taylor
Editorial Kate Hayward, Laura Seber

First published in 2003 by
Dorling Kindersley Limited
80 Strand, London WC2R ORL

Penguin Group

2 4 6 8 10 9 7 5 3 1

Copyright © 2003 Dorling Kindersley Limited
Text copyright © 2003 William Micklem

A CIP catalogue record for this book is available
from the British Library

ISBN 0 7513 6444 4

Colour reproduction by Colourscan, Singapore
Printed and bound by Mohndruck, Germany

Discover more at
www.dk.com

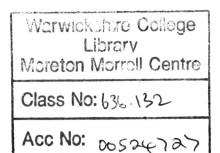
CONTENTS

SHOWJUMPING TRAINING AND COMPETITION 184

CROSS-COUNTRY TRAINING AND COMPETITION 254

FOREWORD

I first met William Micklem in 1971 at a training clinic in Massachusetts when I was 13 years old. It was exciting for me to learn classical dressage from someone whose passion was eventing, and it was apparent, even then, that William's teaching philosophies were ahead of their time. Later that year, William introduced me to the champion British eventer, Lucinda Green. He told Lucinda to remember my name because I would win an Olympic medal one day. I never forgot that moment: William was the first person outside my family who believed in me. His teachings became the foundation for my riding. He taught me that you must always show a horse what to do and never use force. I learned about the partnership one has with your horse and how sacred it is.

William has studied horse and human behaviour all his life and has mastered the relationship between the two. His unique eye for a talented horse is unprecedented. Over the years, he has found many great Irish-bred horses for me, including Biko and Mr Maxwell. For my husband, David O'Connor, William is responsible for the purchase of his two great Olympic horses, Gilt Edge and Custom Made. William's horsemanship continues to be the flagship of our training programme.

I feel very privileged to have spent so much time under William's tutelage. He has shaped my career, as he has so many others. Now, for the benefit of us all, he has put pen to paper in the *Complete Horse Riding Manual* to share his knowledge throughout the world. Enjoy this timeless contribution to the horse world.

Karen O'Connor.

Karen O'Connor, Olympic medallist

INTRODUCTION

One of the many benefits of horse riding is that men and women can compete on equal terms, and that both the young and the more mature can ride successfully. Unlike so many other sports, you can continue riding and improving for a lifetime. It is both a sport for all and a sport for life.

It is important to be well taught initially. If you establish the core skills early on, everything else falls into place automatically. Rather like a snowball rolling down a hill, which becomes bigger and bigger as it gathers more layers of snow, every ride will bring new knowledge and help you develop your expertise.

With the right foundation stones, you may well be one of the tens of thousands of ordinary people who find that horses and horse riding allow them to do extraordinary things. It is my intention that this book will be an integral part of your riding education and will complement the work you do with your coach, as well as inspire you to do more with your riding.

A CONSISTENT APPROACH

In horse riding, there are many ways of doing things, for example, two riders may use differing aids to ask a horse to canter. Although this will achieve what is required, it is important to recognize that simplicity and best practice are the keys to success. Some techniques or pieces of equipment may have been accepted for many years, but it is important to be flexible enough to allow a good idea to give way to a better idea and make any necessary changes to your approach.

EXPLORING THE COUNTRYSIDE Gentle hacking is good exercise, as well as being beneficial to the human spirit. It allows you to enjoy beautiful countryside, away from busy roads.

As far as possible, my aim is to find methods that work for all horses and all riders, in all activities and at all levels. It is a difficult task, but using consistent methods has benefits for all riders and is a fundamental advantage when producing a complete book of riding, rather than concentrating on one activity alone. This book is laced together with key skills that work for the beginner rider and the more advanced rider, for the dressage rider and the showjumping rider, for the younger rider and the older rider.

Even the journey to Olympic level can be based on easy steps if your training is well structured. You will find that the specialist chapters in this book on dressage, showjumping, and cross country are all interlinked. Showjumpers will need to refer to the dressage chapter as well as the showjumping chapter, because so much of their work is based on dressage. Similarly, the eventing rider will need to concentrate on all three activities.

In each of these chapters, the prerequisite skills for the rider and for the horse are outlined, before the practical exercises that lead to competition work are explained. The competition work is divided into four progressive levels and you are encouraged not to be too modest in your aims. By setting yourself achievable targets, you will have a structure for your training and you can work towards meeting your long-term goals.

COACHING YOUR HORSE

This book will also go a long way to giving you a best-practice model that will make you a good trainer, or coach, to your horse. The whole idea of a learner also being a coach is unique to equestrian sports. It is an essential dimension of riding and an essential part of a rider's education, because if you ride, you influence your horse, for good or for bad. The horse is very adaptable and willing to respond to any consistent stimuli, so, if your horse makes progress, it is easy to become deceived into believing that you must be training in the right way and, worse still, into assuming you are a good trainer. The chapter on basic horse training gives you advice on how to train your horse in the best way. There are two keys to good training: your methods must always be consistent and progressive, and you must always work

within the horse's capabilities. Examples of Olympic horses, such as Biko, Custom Made, and Gilt Edge, with their brilliant riders Karen and David O'Connor, are included in the book because they show the importance of good training. Together with my brother John, we spotted the potential of these young horses, but it was their early training that gave them the foundation for their future success.

HORSE AND RIDER PARTNERSHIP

Our relationship with the horse has always been based on more than pure performance targets. It is important to realize your responsibility to

EASE AND EFFICIENCY If a riding exercise is done well, it will be easy. There is no need for great physical strength, just good training of both the horse and rider.

the horse and to guard this special relationship. This book is based on the philosophy of treating each horse as an individual and developing the horse's natural outline, paces, and abilities. It demands both an educated and humane approach: for example, the use of force or mind-numbing repetition of an exercise until you achieve a particular result is unacceptable.

With good training, the horse will retain his spirit and individuality, and will become a responsive and willing partner in the long term. Over a period of time, many people find their partnership with their horse becomes the most satisfying aspect of all their equestrian activities.

ENJOYING YOUR RIDING

Every rider is an individual and has particular needs, and this concept forms part of the philosophy of this book. This is why it is important not to be too fixed on the idea of the perfect position or the perfect progression to an exercise. As there is such a huge number of variables in horse riding, the words "correct" or "perfect" are rarely used. Best practice includes keeping your focus on what you and your horse can do and working from this point, rather than focusing on what you cannot do.

If your aim is a personal best then enjoyment must be part of this endeavour. Learning must be a mixture of effort and delight. This is the basis for quality work, which is not only the aim of competition riders but also the route for a long and happy life for any horse.

CAPTURING THE DREAM

The partnership between horse and rider can be inspiring and motivating. We can all benefit and achieve more as a result of our work with horses. You will be invigorated by the amount of freedom, courage, and success horse riding

CHAMPIONSHIP COMPETITION Not every rider wants to compete at a high level, but horses make it possible for ordinary riders to do extraordinary things. If you aim high, you could achieve great success.

can bring you, and this can motivate you to give more in other aspects of your life, too. If you believe in yourself, it is possible to achieve extraordinary results.

William Micklem

William Micklem

CHAPTER ONE

THE BEGINNER RIDER

Once you have found a suitable riding school and instructor, learning the basics of riding is not difficult, and you will be surprised at how quickly you progress. At the end of your first lesson, it should be possible for you to control your horse in walk and in trot in the riding arena, and even to be led out on a short hack. Once you have established the basics – getting on and off, starting, stopping, and steering – you can learn how to balance in rising trot and to canter. Having mastered these initial riding skills, it is only a small step to your first jump.

You may feel nervous at first, but there are ways to combat your fears. The simple techniques outlined in this chapter will provide the foundation for your progression to riding activities and equestrian sports at all levels.

GETTING STARTED

Learning to ride is not difficult, and with the guidance of a good coach, you can progress quickly and safely. The first step is to find a riding school that has good teaching facilities, suitable horses, and the necessary safety equipment. Start off having individual tuition for your first few lessons, before joining a group session.

Your hat should fit comfortably and be fastened with a three-point chin strap.

FINDING A RIDING SCHOOL

You will find riding schools advertised in riding magazines and listed by equestrian organizations, but a recommendation from a friend who rides is ideal. A good school does not have to be big, but it must have a small, enclosed arena for novice lessons. The horses and students should look relaxed and happy in their work. Equipment should be in good condition; leather tack, for example, should be soft and flexible because if it is brittle it could snap and cause an accident.

Bridle

Bit

WHAT TO WEAR

It is not necessary to spend a fortune on gear for riding, but there are some essential items: trousers or riding breeches in a soft, stretchable fabric; a comfortable shirt or sweater that will not restrict your movement; footwear that supports your ankles and has a small heel; elasticated half chaps (leggings covering the lower leg); and riding gloves.

Protective headwear should always be worn. A good hat that conforms to safety standards will be provided by the riding school. A hat should have a three-point chin strap so that it cannot slip out of place while

Reins

Gloves

THE COACH

Look for a qualified and registered coach who is experienced in teaching novice riders. A good coach will answer all your questions about riding and, when you start lessons, will allow you to progress at a rate that suits you. Above all, he or she will encourage and motivate you, no matter what age or level you are.

The coach

Half chaps

Footwear should have a good heel so that your feet cannot slip through the stirrups.

you are riding. At a later stage, as you begin riding outside the arena and jumping, a body protector (a reinforced, sleeveless jacket) is also advisable.

A SUITABLE HORSE

The best horse for a novice rider is quiet and well-trained, responding easily and consistently to both the coach and rider.

The monkey strap is a loop on the front of the saddle for the novice rider to hold on to.

Breastplate

General-purpose saddle

Girth

Stirrup

Saddle cloth

COACH, HORSE, AND RIDER
Your coach will select a suitable horse for you to ride, advise you on what to wear, and introduce you to all the horse's equipment.

Front brushing boot

Hind brushing boot

Older horses are ideal because they are generally calm and laid-back, and small horses are less intimidating and easier to get on and off. For most adults, an obedient cob (see p.378) between 10 and 25 years old is perfect.

Your coach will advise you on which horse will be suitable for you and appropriate for your height and weight. You will discover very quickly that your horse is your partner, and the relationship you develop with him is often the most rewarding aspect of riding.

INTRODUCING THE TACK

Before you are ready for your first lesson, your coach will introduce the main pieces of the horse's equipment, or tack. The reins are attached to the bit, which is held in place in the horse's mouth by the bridle. The stirrups are attached to the saddle, and your coach will adjust them to the appropriate length before you get on the horse. As a beginner rider, you will be using a general-purpose saddle, which is shaped to give great support and comfort. The saddle has a strap called a breastplate attached to the front. This is the strap that stops the saddle from slipping back out of place, but it also serves as a secure point for you to hold on to in your early lessons when you are still getting used to being on horseback. In addition, the saddle has a loop called a monkey strap attached to the front arch, which you can hold on to for security.

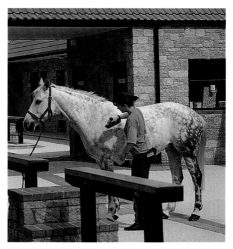

VISITING A STABLE
When you visit a riding school, look for welcoming staff and well-maintained facilities.

GROUP AND INDIVIDUAL LESSONS

There are a number of different types of lesson for the beginner rider, but they will always take place in the safety of a small, enclosed arena.

Group lessons allow you to watch and learn from others as well as to gain confidence from riding with people of a similar ability to yourself. You may learn with three to five other riders, and then, as you improve, with up to twice this number if space allows. Lessons will be up to an hour and a half in length.

Your first lessons, however, should always be one-to-one. In these sessions, you will ride by yourself under the direction of your coach, getting used to the movement of the horse, establishing balance, and practising starting, stopping, and steering. Depending on your level of confidence, your coach may suggest you have two or three individual lessons before you join a group session.

LEAD AND LUNGE LESSONS

Individual lessons tend to take two forms. In a lunge lesson, the coach stands in the centre of the arena and controls your horse via a long rope attached to his bridle. You and your horse move around the coach on a circle of approximately 15 m (49 ft) in diameter. This is an extremely effective way of learning, because it allows you to progress gradually without being daunted by the thought that you must be in charge of the horse.

You will start off in walk and will move in both directions around the arena. You can hold on to the breastplate or the monkey strap for security – depending on the length of your

arms, you might find the monkey strap easier to reach than the breastplate. You will quickly develop your balance and gradually learn how to communicate with and control the horse yourself. Soon, you will be ready for the lunge rope to be detached and progress to riding independently in the same controlled space under the supervision of your coach.

Some beginners benefit from having an individual lead lesson. In these sessions, your coach will lead your horse around the arena in walk and possibly a little trot, while instructing you on what to do. A useful development of this is for the coach to be on horseback, leading your horse in trot.

USEFUL RIDING TERMS

There are some riding phrases that you will find useful to understand before you start your first lessons:

INSIDE AND OUTSIDE When you are riding around an arena, your inside leg and hand are the ones on the inside of a bend, and your outside leg and hand are the ones on the outside of a bend. These terms are also used to refer to the horse's legs.

RIGHT REIN AND LEFT REIN If your right hand is on the inside, you are riding on the right rein. If your left hand is on the inside, you are riding on the left rein.

OUTSIDE TRACK AND INSIDE TRACK If you are riding around an arena close to the fence, you are riding on the outside track. If you are riding nearer to the centre of the arena, leaving room for a horse to ride on your outside, you are riding on the inside track.

Alert other riders before entering the arena

Keep a safe distance between you and others

Pass another rider with left-hand shoulder to left-hand shoulder

AT THE RIDING SCHOOL

In a riding arena, there are certain rules to be aware of. Always be vigilant when entering or leaving the arena, and make sure that all the other riders are aware of your presence. Ask someone to help you open and close the gate – you should never leave the gate open while there are horses in the arena.

If you are walking, halting, or dismounting, do this away from the outer edge – the outside track – so that you do not get in the path of other riders who may be trotting or cantering around the arena. By following these simple rules, everyone can enjoy safe riding.

HACKING OUT

Once you have had your initial lessons and feel comfortable and confident in the saddle, a good equestrian facility will be able to offer you the opportunity to hack out (ride in the countryside) on tracks and bridleways, without the necessity of riding on open roads.

Hacking is a superb way to spend time in the saddle and practise the basic skills you have learnt in the arena until they start to become instinctive. The freedom of riding in the countryside in the company of other riders, and the gradually increasing ability to go up and down hills and jump small obstacles, make this a wonderful exercise. For some people, this is what being able to ride is all about.

OUT ON A HACK While you are still learning to ride, your coach may attach a lead line to your horse's bridle and lead your horse so that you can ride out on a hack at an early stage of your training, for between 15 minutes to an hour.

A FIRST LESSON

It is possible to learn the basic techniques of riding in a short session, such as this 1-hour programme. During this type of programme, your coach will lead you through the basic riding skills, including getting on and off, sitting, walking, trotting, steering, and stopping. Before you start, your coach may suggest you practise some of the techniques on a stationary wooden horse for 15 to 30 minutes, so you can get a feel for the saddle, hold the reins, and even practise the rising trot before you are introduced to your horse.

INTRODUCTION Your coach will take 5 minutes to get to know you and find out if you have had any previous riding experience. He or she will check your hat and footwear before introducing you to your horse and the main pieces of equipment.

GETTING ON AND OFF During the next 10 minutes, your coach will demonstrate how to get on and off. The horse will be held as you practise getting on with the aid of a large, solid mounting block. You will be shown how to sit naturally in the saddle and then you will dismount and repeat the exercise. (See pp.20–21)

WALKING AND TROTTING Your horse will be attached to a lunge rope, and for the next 15 minutes will remain in the full control of your coach. This will allow you to concentrate on your balance and comfort in walk and trot without worrying about controlling your horse. You will not be holding the reins, but will hold on to the breastplate or monkey strap. (See pp.22–23)

STARTING, STEERING, AND STOPPING This 15-minute phase is carried out on the lunge, while you practise the techniques for controlling and communicating with the horse. Your coach will teach you how to hold the reins, and show you the simple signals you can make to guide your horse. (See pp.24–25)

REVISION AND PRACTICE When you feel comfortable and relaxed in the saddle, your coach may take you and your horse on a lead rope on a 15-minute hack, so you can practise and enjoy your new riding skills.

A LUNGE LESSON During a lunge lesson, focus on keeping in harmony with the horse's movements. Hold on to the front arch of the saddle for security, but avoid resting your weight on your arms because this will unbalance you. In later lessons you will try taking your feet out of the stirrups and practise keeping your balance without their support.

GETTING ON AND OFF

Before you get on the horse, your coach will adjust the length
of the stirrups and provide you with a large, solid mounting
block to stand on. Practise getting on and
off until it feels natural. Once the method
shown here has been mastered, you can quickly
progress to mounting with the aid of a leg-up.

Hold the breastplate and the
end of the reins.

GETTING ON

Step on to the mounting block and turn to face
the rear of the horse (**1**). Hold the end of the
reins and the breastplate in your left hand. Hold
the right-hand side of the stirrup in your right
hand, twist it towards you, and place the ball
of your left foot in it (**a**). Let go of the stirrup
and grasp the right-hand
side of the front arch of
the saddle (**b**). Hop
round to face the same
way as your horse (**2**),
keeping your left toe
away from the horse's
side. Using your right
arm to help support
your weight and
balance, spring up and
swing your leg over
the horse's back (**3**).

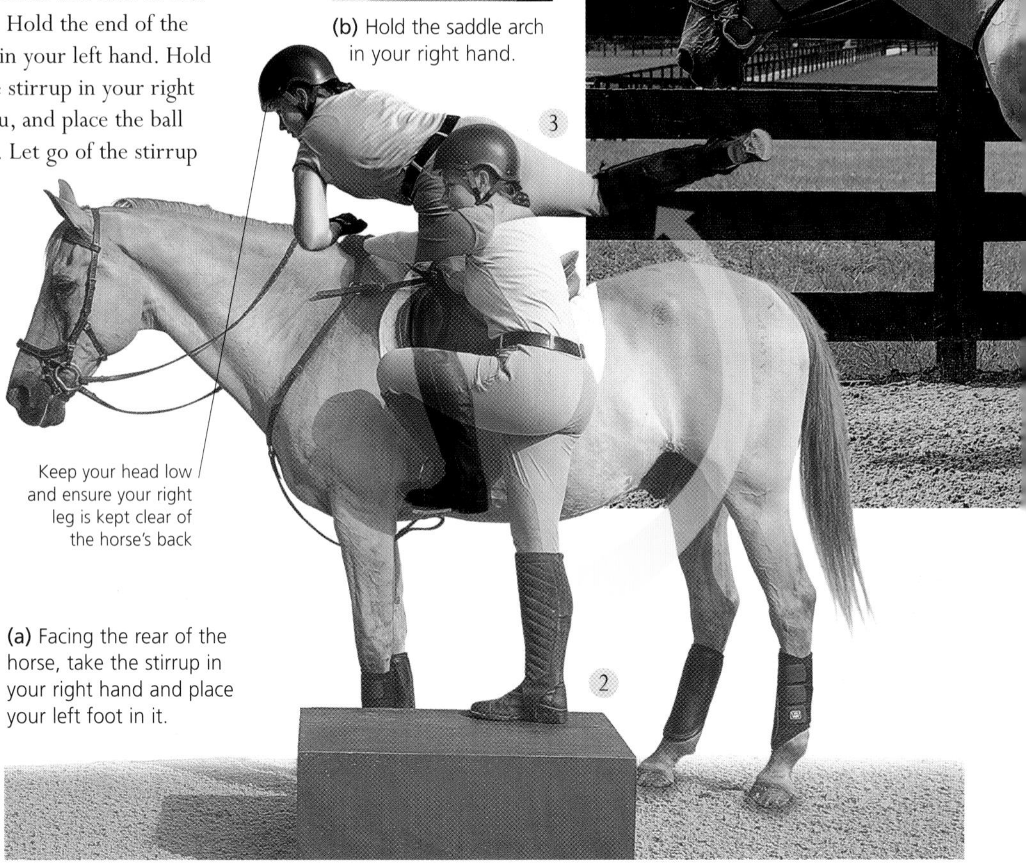

(**b**) Hold the saddle arch
in your right hand.

3

Keep your head low
and ensure your right
leg is kept clear of
the horse's back

(**a**) Facing the rear of the
horse, take the stirrup in
your right hand and place
your left foot in it.

2

AT A GLANCE

1   2   3   4   5   6   7

Relax your shoulders and breathe naturally

Keep your shoulder in line with your hip

Wriggle down into the saddle

Keep your knee in line with the ball of your foot

THE SITTING POSITION

Gently lower yourself into the saddle and place the ball of your right foot in the off-side stirrup (**4**). Sit naturally in the saddle. It can help your balance and security if you imagine a vertical line running from your shoulder to your hip and another from the middle of your knee to the ball of your foot (see left). Hold on to the breastplate with both hands and the end of the reins in one hand, and look in the direction you want to go.

SITTING SECURELY

When sitting centrally in the saddle, your lower legs should be vertical and touching the horse's sides.

Take both feet out of the stirrups.

Keep the stirrup on the ball of your foot.

GETTING OFF

Hold the breastplate and the end of the reins in your left hand and hold the front arch of the saddle with your right hand. Take your feet out of both stirrups (**5**) and lean forwards a little. Then, swing your right leg over the horse's back (**6**) and either drop down lightly on to your toes without touching the horse (**7**), or slide down more slowly. Make sure that you land lightly, with bend in your knee and ankle joints, and facing in the same direction as the horse.

Bend your knees to absorb the impact on landing

WALKING AND TROTTING

Once you are sitting in the saddle, the next step is to get used to the movement of the horse in walk and trot before you learn how to hold the reins and control the horse yourself. Your coach will attach the horse to a lunge rope, and control him from the ground. Hold on to the breastplate to help maintain your balance; sit into your saddle; and let yourself go with the motion of the horse, first in walk, and then in trot. You will quickly learn how to rise in time to the trot.

WALKING ON THE LUNGE

As the horse starts to walk on the lunge, the first thing you will be aware of is the movement under your buttocks, or your seat. Hold on to the breastplate and breathe normally **(1)**. You will find that your seat naturally moves slightly backwards and forwards with the swing of the horse's back. It is a regular, steady movement that is comfortable to go with.

LEARNING TO TROT

Once you are comfortable in walk, your coach will signal to your horse to increase his speed to a trot for just a few steps at a time. You will stay in contact with the saddle – this is called the sitting trot and it will feel like you are in a car going over some small bumps spaced at regular intervals.

The rising trot is a technique that enables the rider to be comfortable in the trot and avoid these bumps. The aim is for your seat to rise out of the saddle in time with the horse's movement. With the horse's upwards movement, rise out of the saddle **(2)**. Keep your weight through your legs and your heels lower than your toes.

On the horse's downwards movement, lower your seat into the saddle again **(3)**, letting it lightly touch the saddle before it rises again. Keep your seat rising and lowering in time with the horse's movement **(4)**.

PROGRESSING FROM WALK TO RISING TROT
Your coach will signal to your horse to walk and then speed up to a trot. The key to the rising trot is keeping your weight in your legs, not on your seat.

1

In walk, hold on to the breastplate and let your seat go with the gentle swing of the horse's back

2

As your horse starts to trot, let your seat rise upwards and forwards with the movement of the horse

Lunge rope

Keep your weight down through to your heels

PRACTISING RISING TROT

Many riders find it helpful to practise the rising trot movement off the horse. Since your weight is kept largely through your legs for rising trot, it works well to practise it standing up:

(a) Stand upright with your feet approximately 60 cm (2 ft) apart. Keep your shoulders square.

(b) Close the angle of your knees until your lower legs are parallel to each other. Try to keep a little more weight on your heels than on your toes.

(c) Keeping your knees still, with a vertical line between the middle of your knee and the ball of your foot, drop your seat a few centimetres. Your upper body will incline forwards slightly to keep your balance.

PRACTISING RISING TROT
Practise the rising trot technique off the horse – this is a good way to learn how to keep your balance and rhythm without being distracted by the horse's movement. It helps your muscles become accustomed to the movement.

(d) From this position, and keeping your knees still, open your knee and hip joints a little. This will have the effect of bringing your seat forwards and upwards as though it is swinging under your shoulders.

(e) Lower your seat down again by closing the knee and hip joints and keeping your weight evenly on your feet. Then repeat this opening and closing and gradually speed it up, until you are rising and falling in a steady rhythm.

(a)   (b)   (c)   (d)   (e)

FRONT VIEW   SIDE VIEW

3

Lower your seat back into the saddle in time with the horse before rising again

Keep holding the breastplate but avoid using your arms to balance yourself

4

Look in the direction you want to go

START, STOP, AND STEER

When you have got used to the movement of the horse in walk and trot on the lunge, you are ready to take the reins and start controlling the horse yourself. The way you handle the reins and use your legs forms the basis of how you communicate with your horse through signals, or aids. Learn the basic aids to ask your horse to walk on, stop, and change direction. Then, practise your steering aids by guiding your horse through a course of obstacles.

CONTACTS AND AIDS

The reins are attached to a bit in the horse's mouth, so by holding the reins, you are making contact with the horse's mouth. When you are sitting in the saddle, your stirrup leathers should be parallel to the girth (the strap around the horse's middle that holds the saddle in place) so that your legs are close to the sensitive part of the horse's sides. Once you have established these leg and rein contacts, you can signal to the horse by nudging his sides with your lower legs – this is the leg aid – or by momentarily increasing the pressure on the reins – this is the rein aid.

Always make sure your aids have a definite beginning and end, because if you exert continuous pressure, your signals will not be precise and your horse will start to ignore them.

STARTING AND STOPPING

When you want to move forwards, one nudge on the horse's girth with your calves is usually sufficient. If necessary, repeat this aid with a little more strength. Keep the rein contact soft and allow your horse to walk forwards. Let your legs and hands move with the horse, so that your contacts remain the same and do not send him confusing signals. Allow your seat to move with the horse.

When you want to slow down, say "Whoa" and tweak the reins – that is, exert a small increase in pressure by momentarily squeezing your fingers. If your horse does not respond, try turning your wrists in a little, or bringing your arm back a little. Repeating the action will bring the horse to a halt.

STEERING

Use your rein aids to signal to your horse the direction you want to ride in. Tweak the right rein to go to the right, and the left rein to go to the left. To help you practise changing direction, your coach will set up a course for you to steer through, using obstacles such as cones (see right).

HOLDING THE REINS Thread the reins between your third and fourth finger and up and out between your thumb and first finger (a). Make a fist of your hands without clenching your fingers (b). The reins should be close to the base of your fingers so that they become an extension of your arms and allow you to maintain a steady contact when the horse is moving. Your elbows should be a little bent and your hands turned slightly in.

(a) Thread the reins through your fingers.

(b) Keep your hands level and your wrists facing slightly inwards.

Look in the
direction you
want to go

PRACTISING STEERING As you approach the first cone, gently tweak your left rein so that your horse turns his neck in this direction. His body will bend around your inside leg. Then, to steer around the next cone, tweak your right rein to signal to your horse to bend to the right. Your outside leg will naturally move a little further back from the girth **(a)** – this outside leg guides the direction of the horse's hindquarters and helps to retain the bend. Continue steering alternately left and right through the course.

(a) Allow your outside leg to move back.

Keep your inside stirrup leather parallel to the girth as you turn

Tweak your inside rein to encourage your horse to turn to the left

NECK REINING

If a horse is not responding to your turning aid, or is not bending sufficiently on the turn, neck reining is very effective. Without pulling backwards on the reins, just move both your hands to the side you wish to turn towards and then back again to their original position. Repeat as necessary. This puts extra pressure on the outside of the horse's neck and mouth, which encourages him to turn.

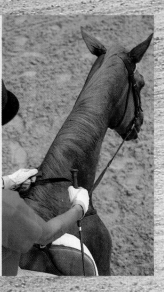

BEYOND THE BASICS

Having learnt the basic techniques, you can begin to enjoy riding with friends for the first time. This is an exciting and rewarding phase for you as a rider as you start to improve your abilities. In the saddle, you can become more accustomed to the movement of your horse, refine your rising-trot skills, and progress to cantering. Out of the saddle, concentrate on developing your physical fitness and gaining a better understanding of horses.

DEVELOPING FEEL

Time spent in walk is invaluable. It allows you to get used to your horse physically and develop an awareness, or feel, for how he is moving and responding, so that you can react sensitively and appropriately. You will start to notice the swing of the horse's back and the motion of his head and neck, and you will begin to recognize those movements that feel more comfortable and those that feel stilted. The movements of each of the horse's legs will start to become obvious, too.

RISING TROT DIAGONALS In rising trot, you need to rise and lower your seat in time with the horse's inside hind leg (highlighted in red, below). Your balance should stay the same throughout with your weight in your legs and your lower leg staying in the same position, both as your seat rises and lowers back into the saddle. Keep the rein contact soft and allowing so your horse is not restricted.

DEVELOPING THE RISING TROT

When a horse trots, his legs move in diagonal pairs. The inside hind leg moves in parallel with the outside foreleg and the outside hind leg moves in parallel with the inside foreleg. These are known as the diagonals.

It is possible to rise to the trot on either diagonal, but if you are riding on a circle it is more comfortable and beneficial for the horse if you ride in time with his inside hind leg. In order to find the diagonal you are on, glance down at the horse's shoulders and see which one you are moving in time with.

If you rise up as the horse's outside shoulder moves forwards, and you lower back into the saddle when his outside shoulder moves back, then you are riding in time with the inside hind leg. If you are rising and lowering in time with the inside shoulder, then you need to change diagonals.

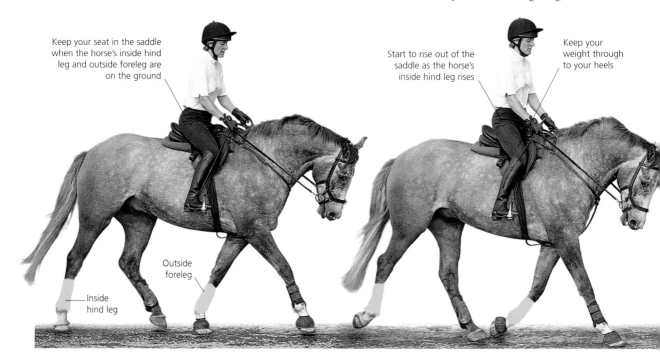

Keep your seat in the saddle when the horse's inside hind leg and outside foreleg are on the ground

Outside foreleg

Inside hind leg

Start to rise out of the saddle as the horse's inside hind leg rises

Keep your weight through to your heels

EMERGENCY AIDS

If your horse does not respond to your normal forwards aids, take your heels away from his sides and use them in an inward motion close to the girth, with a little extra strength than your normal aid. If necessary, repeat, but slightly stronger. Likewise, if your horse does not listen to your normal slowing-down aids, tighten the reins slightly and let your seat sink into the saddle. Put your weaker hand into the horse's mane, pull back on the reins with your other hand, and use your voice to encourage him to slow down.

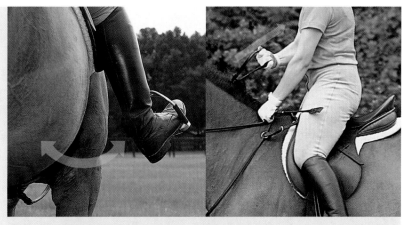

EMERGENCY FORWARDS

EMERGENCY STOP

In order to change diagonals, stay in the saddle at the moment when your seat is lowered for one extra beat – this will feel like a small bump – and then rise again. You will then have successfully changed diagonals. You will need to do this if you are changing direction in trot.

HACKING OUT

Going on a hack with other riders is a good opportunity to practise your new riding skills. Horses enjoy riding out in the company of other horses, although they can become excitable, and they do have a tendency to follow each other's lead. You will find that some horses are more responsive than others, but the ideal is to keep your aids and rein contact as soft as possible. Get a feel for how responsive your horse is before you start a hack, while you are still in the arena.

Use your voice to calm your horse if he becomes over excited. If your horse is reluctant to move forwards or to stop, for example, when his attention has been distracted by other horses, you may have to use your emergency forwards or emergency stop aids (see box, above).

Lower your seat as the inside hind leg begins to return to the ground

Let your seat touch the saddle as the horse's inside hind leg touches the ground

LEARNING TO CANTER

At this stage of your training, you are ready to learn how to canter. You can go faster in canter than in trot and it can be an extremely comfortable pace, but it may feel a little strange to begin with because the movement is not symmetrical, as it is in the walk and trot. This is because the horse canters with his inside legs slightly in advance of his outside legs, and his body therefore naturally bends a little to the inside. For this reason, it is easier, and more comfortable for the horse, if you start the canter by riding in a circle, so that he can canter off – or strike off – with the inside foreleg leading.

Your first cantering lesson should take place in a small, enclosed arena. Your coach will ask you to begin in rising trot and then to close your seat to the saddle and nudge the horse's girth with both legs at the same time. If the horse you are riding is well trained, he may respond to a single aid, normally a nudge from your outside leg behind the girth. This is where your coach's knowledge of an individual horse will guide you. Let your weight sink down into your heels, and keep a soft rein contact.

CANTERING ON BOTH REINS

When the horse canters to the right, his right foreleg will be leading, and this is known as cantering on the right rein. When the horse canters to the left, his left foreleg will be leading, and this is known as cantering on the left rein.

CANTERING Once you are in trot, use your aids to signal to your horse to canter. Let your hands go with the movement of the horse's mouth.

A BALANCED POSITION

The same secure balance that the novice rider learns for the rising trot will also serve well for cantering and jumping. If you compare the rider's position during trotting, cantering, bucking, and jumping (see right), you will see strong similarities. In all cases, the rider pushes her weight into her heels, not into the saddle, and there is a vertical line from the middle of the knee to the ball of the foot. The angle of the upper body is similar. This position allows the rider to accommodate the movement of the horse and still keep her balance. Riders are often told to lean back with their weight in the saddle when a horse bucks, but this is as ineffective as trying to ride a bicycle down a bumpy road sitting full on the seat. On a bicycle, you need to stand on the pedals so that your buttocks do not bump up and down on the saddle and throw you off balance. Likewise, on horseback, you need to keep most of your weight in your stirrups to keep your balance and remain secure.

TROTTING

CANTERING

BUCKING

JUMPING

Most horses have a tendency to be better at cantering on one rein, but it is good training to practise cantering on both reins.

TIME OUT OF THE SADDLE

Even when you are not riding, there are things you can do to help improve your riding skills. In particular, you need to maintain a good level of fitness and there are specific exercises you can do to help you improve your posture, suppleness, strength, and balance (see pp. 332–51). However, one of the most important things you can do is spend time with horses, becoming more aware of their unique nature and needs. Stable-management work is extremely valuable in the development of a good relationship with a horse. It is often possible to help out at an equestrian facility, and this is a good way to get to know your horse's daily needs and routines.

UNDERSTANDING HORSES
Most horses like company and will benefit from regular contact and care from their riders. Getting to understand horse behaviour and habits will also improve your ability as a rider.

COPING WITH NERVES

Horses are basically gentle creatures, but they can also be frightening animals, particularly if your first experiences as a rider are without the guidance of a good coach. By avoiding unnecessary risks and always riding within your current level of ability, there should be no need to feel intimidated about trying something new. A common cause of nerves is the fear of falling off, and it can be reassuring and beneficial to learn how to fall safely.

BEING REALISTIC

There is no such thing as a fearless person – everyone has their limits. Fear is a basic human response that ensures our survival by limiting what we do. With horse riding, it is sensible to treat an animal, weighing over 450 kg (1,000 lbs) and measuring approximately 1.5 m (5 ft) at the withers, with great respect. It is totally understandable that such an animal may frighten you initially.

As fear is mentally and physically paralysing, to a greater or lesser extent, it is vital that riding exercises are not undertaken in this state of mind – even if a bad coach is trying to bully you. Always talk to your coach if you are nervous about a riding exercise so that you can get to the root of your anxiety and resolve it. There are two main types of fear: the fear of the unknown and the fear of the known.

FEAR OF THE UNKNOWN

Some people are frightened that they may be asked to do something that they do not have the ability to do. By going to a riding coach with a good track record, and by watching and talking to other beginner riders who are progressing successfully, you can overcome this. In addition, a good coach will always demonstrate and explain every step, so nothing will be unexpected. Overcoming a fear of the unknown is a matter of keeping a positive mental attitude and making sure you are prepared. Role playing is a very successful technique to help you improve mental attitude (see p.357).

FEAR OF THE KNOWN

Some people are frightened of a particular aspect of horse riding, for example, the fear of falling off. You may have already had a bad experience yourself, or seen someone else in trouble, or you may have just imagined a disaster about to happen. The fact that this is only imagined makes this fear no less real than the others.

Once again a good coach can help enormously. By proceeding one small step at a time, using best practice techniques, by continual revision, and by establishing the basics of balance, security, and understanding, you will become braver. This is because you will always feel fully in control, knowing that you are easily achieving the desired result at each stage. A good coach will also encourage you to surround yourself with riders and trainers who are obviously doing good-quality work. Spend time observing the best riders in action because you will find them inspiring; you will learn from their techniques; and their standards and confidence will rub off on you.

PREPARING FOR A FALL If a steeplechase rider knows they are about to take a fall, they kick their feet free of the stirrups, and start to roll, pushing themselves away from the horse.

VAULTING COMPETITION In a vaulting competition, the horse is controlled on a lunge rope. Using the momentum of the horse's movement, the vaulter springs up on to the horse.

work until it feels natural. When it is natural, you do not have to worry about your responses to situations, because they will be automatic. This is the best way to avoid accidents and the fear that often follows.

A valuable technique to help overcome your fear of falling is to learn how to vault on and off a horse – this method allows you to spring up on to a horse, without the aid of a mounting block or a leg-up, and to spring off a horse when it is cantering. Knowing that you can get on and off a horse even when it is moving will help you feel more in control and less afraid of taking a tumble.

KNOWING HOW TO FALL

The fear of falling off a horse can also be reduced by learning what to do should you ever be in that situation. This is a positive strategy that will benefit the vast majority of riders because all riders do have falls – albeit more infrequently if you are better trained. If you do have a fall, the key is to get your feet out of the stirrups and allow yourself to be thrown away from the horse. Then, put your chin on your chest, curve your back, tuck up your legs, and be ready to roll.

It is a real advantage to practise techniques to help you learn how to fall (see box, below). Knowing that you can land safely and avoid injury will make you less nervous about riding. Of course, regardless of this preparation, every effort should be made to avoid falls in the first place by the use of safe exercises, by riding horses with good temperaments, and by following rules and exercising self control.

FEAR OF FALLING

The best way to cope with fear is not to generate it to begin with. A good coach will do their best to ensure you largely avoid bad experiences. They will do this by continuously assessing your performance and building on your achievements progressively. At every stage you should practise good-quality

PRACTISING FOR A FALL

It can be helpful to carry out exercises that simulate what you should do in the event of a fall. The main prerequisite for learning how to fall is the help of a qualified trainer: do not attempt this exercise without professional supervision. Make sure you have plenty of space, and use an exercise mat so that there is no risk of you slipping.

FORWARDS ROLL: Start the forwards roll in a squat position with your hands and arms parallel to each other. Pull your chin in against your chest and put the back of your neck and shoulders on the ground. Finish the exercise in squat. Once you can easily carry out this exercise, repeat it from a walk, and then a run.

Bend your legs as you roll over

Keep your weight equally balanced on your shoulders

Finish in the squat position

AN INTRODUCTION TO JUMPING

Jumping on horseback is a wonderfully liberating experience, and most riders and horses enjoy it. It is important, however, that you are introduced to jumping carefully and progressively, and only once you have already achieved a good rising trot balance. Start by walking up and down a slight hill, to get accustomed to the movement of the horse and the necessary change in your position. Soon you will progress to jumping up and down little banks, and jumping over small fences.

RIDING UP AND DOWN HILLS

The key to successful jumping is maintaining the right balance throughout the ascent and descent. This is not only for your own safety, but it is also so that you do not interfere with your horse's natural movement. Begin your jumping training by practising riding up and down a gentle slope. The beauty of this method is that it mirrors the ascent and descent of a jump, but, because you are in walk, it gives you sufficient time to practise adjusting and achieving the right balance.

For rising trot and for jumping, your weight needs to be kept through your legs. This means that the lower leg should remain vertical, with the knee in line with the ball of the foot. If you do this, it should be possible to maintain your balance during both the ascent and the descent of the hill, even if your legs are not in contact with the horse's sides. Do not make the mistake of using strong inward pressure with your legs in an attempt to stay balanced. If you try to grip the horse's sides as he moves up the hill, then your lower leg will no longer be vertical but will stay at a right angle to

RIDING UPHILL
As you learn how to keep your balance going up- and downhill, it may take quite a physical effort to keep your seat out of the saddle, but as you improve your balance, this will happen naturally.

Hold on to the breastplate with one hand for security

Keep your lower leg vertical

Ensure your heel is lower than your toes

JUMPING A SMALL BANK

For the beginner rider, jumping small banks is a real confidence booster. It splits the phases of a jump into two. You therefore have the opportunity to get used to the first half of a jump – going up the bank – and then the second half of the jump – going down the bank. Initially, hold on to the breastplate. Keep a long rein, so that your horse is free to move, and concentrate on keeping a consistent balance with your weight through your legs and your heels staying lower than your toes. Practise jumping up and down the bank, and repeat this until you feel secure in the saddle.

JUMPING UP A SMALL BANK   JUMPING DOWN A SMALL BANK

the bodyline of the horse – it will be too far forwards. Likewise, as you walk down the hill, your lower leg will be too far back. The effect of this will be both restriction to the horse's movement on the ascent and insecurity to your seat and balance on the descent.

MAINTAINING YOUR BALANCE

As you walk up and down the slope, concentrate on staying in harmony with the movement of the horse, and keep your weight through your legs and your heels down. Maintain a steady, soft rein contact, allowing your horse's head to move freely. Once you are able to keep your balance in walk up and down the hill, repeat the exercise in trot and canter – everything will happen more quickly and will be more similar to the speed of an actual jump. Then, progress to jumping up and down a little bank (see box, above) as a good preparation for jumping your first fence.

Strides tend to lengthen as the horse walks downhill

RIDING DOWNHILL By keeping your lower leg vertical, regardless of the angle of the horse's body, you will remain secure and will not fall forwards.

Keep your knee and the ball of your foot in line with each other

Let your hands move to allow the horse to use his head and neck

INTRODUCING FENCES

When you learn to jump fences, it is always worth starting with an exercise that is slightly too easy than with one that is too difficult. If you work through these progressive exercises (see box, below), you will quickly advance from trotting over planks to jumping a small course of fences.

PROGRESSING TO YOUR FIRST FENCE

Your coach will set up the exercises so that they are at suitable distances for the size of your horse. The first exercise involves riding over two planks on the ground **(1)**. The purpose of this exercise is to develop a steady speed and to encourage your horse to take even strides. Start by walking over the planks, then trot over them in rising trot. When you can keep a consistent trot and a secure balance, you are ready to progress further.

The next exercise involves two poles placed on the ground in a funnel shape, and a plank on the ground in front of a small fence **(2)**. The use of the funnel of poles in front of the fence helps to guide your horse, so that he jumps in the middle of the fence. The plank on the ground acts as a guide for the horse's take-off point over the fence. Approach in a steady trot and keep a soft position. The horse will do the jumping — all you need to do is concentrate on retaining your balance and keeping your weight through your legs. If your rising trot balance is good, you will have no problem jumping the fence. On landing, use your leg aids to prompt your horse to canter away from the fence.

WORKING TOWARDS A SET OF FENCES

The next exercise uses two poles in a funnel shape on the ground and two planks on the ground. The planks should be at a distance that requires your horse to take two or three strides between them **(3)**. Approach in canter and stay cantering at a steady speed from start to finish. Focus on your horse's strides and how close or far away his forelegs are from

---

PROGRESSIVE JUMPING EXERCISES

These are simple, progressive exercises to help you learn to jump – you will start by trotting over planks on the ground, lead on to jumping little fences, and finish by jumping a small course of fences. Your coach will lead you step-by-step through exercises 1 to 6. Alternatively, if you are a little nervous, you can do exercise 1, 3, and 5 by themselves. These exercises involve trotting or cantering over planks, so, although they do not include any fences, they will help you develop a feeling for distances and take-off points before you move on to jumping a small fence. Your coach will make sure you progress steadily. Start each exercise by walking through it first, to get a feel for what is required (see below).

WALKING THROUGH EXERCISE 4

1. Walk, then trot over two planks on the ground.

2. Trot through funnel poles and over a plank and a fence. Land in canter.

3. Canter through funnel poles and over two planks on the ground two strides apart.

4. Trot through funnel poles, over a plank and a fence, land in canter. Take two strides to a fence.
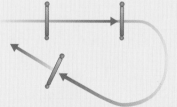

5. Canter over a short course of three planks.

6. Canter over a short course of three small fences.

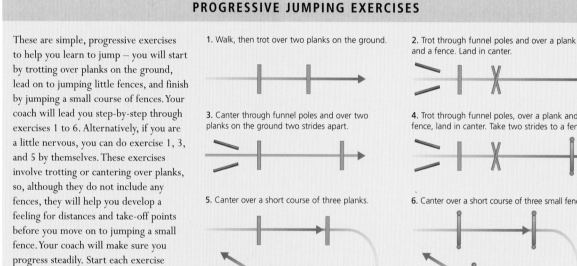

USING TROTTING POLES

If your horse does not take off at the same point each time, even when you use a plank before the fence as a guide, then place three square poles in front of a fence, 1.25–1.45 m (4–4½ ft) apart. The take-off point should be halfway between the last pole and the fence. Start by walking over them without jumping a fence.

the planks. Each time your horse finishes a stride in canter, count out loud. The place where your horse's canter stride ends in front of each plank will, in effect, become the take-off point for each jump when fences are added to the exercise.

The next exercise is the same as exercise 2 but with the addition of a second, slightly larger fence (4). Jump the first fence and land in canter. Because of your preparation, you need only concentrate on maintaining a good balance as you jump the second fence in canter – let everything happen naturally.

JUMPING A SMALL COURSE

In this exercise, you will ride over three planks on the ground, set up in the shape of a small course (5). Use your aids to steer the horse around the course, keeping a consistent speed. Once you can do this, you can advance to a course of three small fences (6). Concentrate on maintaining even strides, and keep a soft rein contact so that your horse can jump easily and naturally, without being held back.

JUMPING A FENCE This is the second fence in exercise 4. The poles resting on the barrels help to guide the horse. The beginner rider here has an excellent balance. If you took her off the horse and put her on the ground in this position she would not fall over. It is very similar to her position using the trotting poles (see box, above).

Keep your weight through your legs, with the middle of your knee in line with the ball of your foot

Maintain a good posture and look where you want to go

Hold on to the breastplate or mane. Keep the reins long enough so your horse can use his head and neck

RIDING ACTIVITIES

Even when you are a relatively new rider, there is a vast range of equestrian activities to suit every age, taste, and ability. In many cases it is possible for the same horse or pony to take part in different activities, and it is excellent for your training to try various riding disciplines. Riding clubs run introductory competitions in all the main activities – dressage, showjumping, and cross country are the most popular, but there are many more to choose from.

GETTING GOING

For the beginner rider, riding clubs are a good place to find out about the individual and team activities that are available. You do not have to own your own horse and the emphasis is on good sport and good company, not high level work. Alternatively, you may wish to contact the national organization of the particular activity that interests you. In general, the equestrian community is welcoming and keen to share its knowledge and love of horses with others.

COMPETITIONS AND EVENTS

If you enjoy turning out a horse to a high standard and are interested in good conformation and manners in a horse, then showing could be the right activity for you. There is a wide variety of classes to enter, which cover a range of abilities and allow for all shapes and sizes of horse – a larger rider may, for example, enjoy the opportunity to show a heavyweight horse. There are also equitation classes, where competitors are evaluated for the way they ride, as well as for achieving a clear round of fences. Shows also have introductory showjumping and dressage classes, which will allow you to practise your skills and discover which type of competition you enjoy.

CARRIAGE DRIVING

Competitive carriage driving is another way to join the show circuit. It can be as demanding as three-day eventing (see p.306) and is based on this sport. A dressage test is followed by a marathon drive, and the final phase is the equivalent of the showjumping course, with cones to be avoided rather than poles to be jumped. Even if you are not interested in showing, there are many people who take up carriage driving just for pleasure and there are many horses that both ride and drive.

TEAM GAMES

For riders who like more exciting activities and a greater physical demand, polocrosse and horse ball may be the answer. Like polo, they are both played in teams, and, similarly, they require rapid acceleration and changes of direction. Polocrosse riders use a net on a stick to catch and pass a small ball as they seek to score a goal. Horse ball involves a larger ball with several handles attached, which participants pass to each other, again with the aim of reaching the goal. The goals in both cases are raised nets at the end of the grounds, which may vary in length from 40 m (130 ft) to 100 m (330 ft). Both games are fast and exciting but they can be very demanding on the horses, who therefore must be very fit and well prepared.

GOING TO SHOWS In showing, there are classes for all types of horse and pony. Getting ready for a show sets you good training targets, and you get to enjoy the company of other riders with similar interests.

TRAIL RIDING

Long-distance riding is making a major impact on the world equestrian stage. It is one of the six sports now included in the World Equestrian Games, where riders have to complete a 160-km (100-mile) ride at 21 km/h (13 mph). Long-distance riding can take many forms, with competition rides ranging from distances from 15 km (9 miles) to 80 km (50 miles), as well as an increasing number of shorter fun rides.

Trail riding is not just about long distances. One development is Le Trec. It involves three phases: an orienteering exercise on horseback, a test of the rider's control of the horse's paces, and a cross-country course. The latter is composed of fences, hazards, and set tasks, such as dismounting and leaving your horse in a circle for a short time.

WESTERN RIDING

People interested in trail riding often also like Western riding. This type of riding is based on the skills needed by those who used to spend all day in the saddle working on the ranch. The Western saddle is large and shaped to give great support, which makes it safe, secure, and ideal for the beginner rider. The rider's position in Western riding is very similar to that used in dressage, so if you like this type of riding, you should also try dressage.

POLOCROSSE The rider holds both reins in his left hand and holds the net on a stick in his right hand. The aim is to pick up the ball and get it into the goal at the end of the grounds.

TRAIL RIDES It is possible to enjoy trail rides in locations all over the world. This is not only a sociable way to enjoy wonderful scenery, it is also a great way to improve your fitness.

CHAPTER TWO

UNDERSTANDING THE HORSE

Riding differs from other sports in that you are responsible for the coaching of another: your horse. In order to do this successfully, you need to understand the unique nature of this animal.

In this chapter, you will see how the horse's physical structure dictates what you can and cannot expect him to do. Knowing what he can see, hear, and smell will help you predict his behaviour. Regard the horse as your student: be aware of how he learns, of what his instincts tell him to do, and of his individual personality. In order to put this knowledge to practical use, you must develop your coaching skills: even the novice rider's actions will have an effect on the horse for better or worse. Being able to shape your horse's behaviour in a positive way will make your time with him even more satisfying.

THE STRUCTURE OF THE HORSE

In order to progress as a rider it helps to have a basic knowledge of the horse's unique structure, particularly the mechanics of the spine. The way a horse uses his back is fundamental to all riding theory because it is the basis for how he carries the rider and how we train him to perform athletically and effectively. Even a light burden can cause discomfort to an untrained horse, and to perform well the trained horse has to be able to arch and bend his back efficiently.

AN EXTRAORDINARY ANIMAL

The horse is an extraordinary animal. Weighing in at over a ton, he is capable of jumping an obstacle over 2 m (7 ft) high and over 6 m (20 ft) long, of travelling at over 64 km/h (40 mph) for a mile, and over 16 km/h (10 mph) for a hundred miles. He is all the more extraordinary because he can do all this while carrying a human being weighing up to 20 per cent of his own body weight. No other creature comes close to this performance in harmony with man, which is why the horse has played such a major part in our history.

It is uncanny how suited the horse is to being ridden. The saddle goes on the narrowest part of the horse and where the rider's calves or heels rest there are motor nerve connections to the horse's hind legs, so the horse naturally goes forwards when the rider's legs are used in this area.

The horse is also happy to accept the rider as leader of the herd (see pp.42–43) despite his massively superior strength.

It is important to remember, however, that even though the horse is well suited to the purpose, he was not designed to carry a human being, and our challenge is to find ways to allow this burden to be carried easily. The key to the ridden horse's comfort lies in an understanding of how he is built.

THE STRUCTURE OF THE SPINE

The horse's spine is a fairly rigid structure, which is necessary to support the heavy body and cope with the huge forces exerted through the hind limbs. The vertebrae under the horse's croup are fused, and those from the withers to the croup are capable of only limited movement. However, the small arching and lateral movement that is possible in the

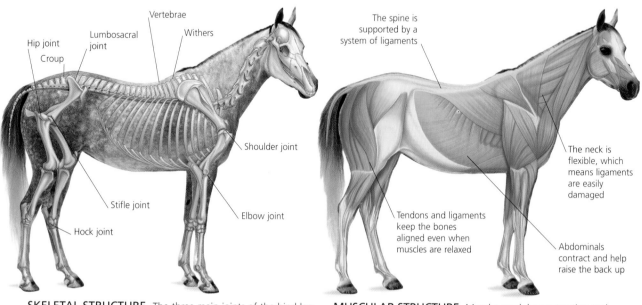

SKELETAL STRUCTURE The three main joints of the hind leg – the hip, hock, and stifle – combined with the lumbosacral joint bring the hind legs forwards to generate power and lift the back. The neck vertebrae do not follow the line of the neck.

Hip joint
Croup
Lumbosacral joint
Vertebrae
Withers
Shoulder joint
Stifle joint
Elbow joint
Hock joint

The spine is supported by a system of ligaments
The neck is flexible, which means ligaments are easily damaged
Tendons and ligaments keep the bones aligned even when muscles are relaxed
Abdominals contract and help raise the back up

MUSCULAR STRUCTURE Muscles work by contraction and relaxation. The contraction of muscles, acting on tendon cables, bone levers, and joint hinges make motion possible. One group of muscles bends or flexes a joint and an opposing group extends it.

USING THE BACK

The athletic horse's back will arch upwards by approximately 6 per cent of his height at the withers. A typical, well-trained 16-hand horse will have a back arched almost 15 cm (6 in) higher than that of a similar-sized horse whose back has been allowed to dip, or lock. It is vital for a horse to develop an arched back if he is to be comfortable and perform efficiently when carrying weight. This arching is achieved when the horse is ridden correctly, so that he is encouraged to use his stomach muscles, engage the hindquarters, and to arch and stretch his head and neck forwards.

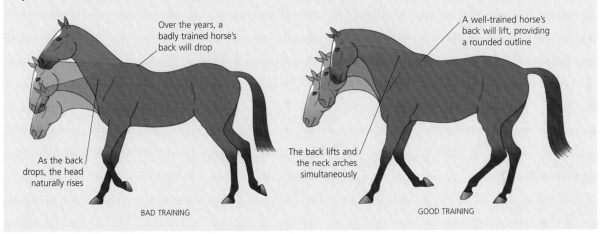

Over the years, a badly trained horse's back will drop

As the back drops, the head naturally rises

BAD TRAINING

A well-trained horse's back will lift, providing a rounded outline

The back lifts and the neck arches simultaneously

GOOD TRAINING

area under and just behind the saddle is all important. The chain of ligaments and muscles stretching from the poll to the dock work like a suspension bridge with a main support at the lumbosacral joint (see diagram, far left) and a subsidiary support point where the neck meets the withers.

The floor of this bridge is slightly curved and a pull at either end of this muscular chain will have the effect of raising the back. By far the most important pull is provided by the horse bringing his hind legs forwards underneath him – known as engaging the hind legs. This, combined with a contraction of the muscles of the belly, creates a ring of muscles to bring the back up to form the desired arch.

The effect of the forwards movement of the head and neck on the back is reduced because the horse has no collarbone. Therefore his spine is not connected to his forelegs by bone. Instead, it is held in a cradle of muscle that allows the withers to drop easily or move from side to side.

DEVELOPING THE ARCHED BACK

Training the horse to adopt a rounded outline is important because it helps him to bear the weight of the rider without placing excessive stress on his spine (see box, above).

If the horse's back is not arched, his useful life will be shortened and his mental attitude may be harmed. It is impossible for the horse to fulfil his athletic potential or provide a comfortable ride if his back is locked in a hollow position. Getting on the back of a horse that has never been ridden before is not difficult, but preparing a horse so that the rider's weight can be carried without his back collapsing requires real skill (see pp.72–73).

Many horses show muscle wastage either side of the spine, particularly where the saddle sits. This can result from lack of use or damage to the nerve supply, which in turn is often created by an ill-fitting saddle and by horses carrying weights that are too heavy for them. For the same reason, both older and younger horses can develop dipped backs, caused by slackening of the ligaments and muscles that support the vertebrae from the withers to the croup.

LATERAL MOVEMENT

Vertical movements between the vertebrae of the back can be classified as either flexion (arching) or extension (dipping). The horse can also make lateral (sideways) movements of the spine, to the same degree that he arches his back. (A horse may appear to be able to bend further than this. This is because of his ability to bend laterally in the lumbarsacral area and because of movement in the ribcage.)

Bending laterally is fundamental to dressage, in which every movement is based on a circle or part of a circle. The requirement is for the front and hind legs to be on the same track, with an even bend from poll to croup, so lateral movement must be developed in training.

THE HERD INSTINCT

To understand a domestic horse's behaviour we must consider how his ancestors behaved in the wild. Their instinctive behaviour relates directly to survival. The horse is a herd animal that enjoys company, and is prey rather than predator, which explains his instinct to flee if he perceives any real or imagined danger. Horses communicate largely through body language within a herd. Understanding the signals horses make can be extremely useful for the rider.

SOCIAL ANIMAL

As a herd animal, the horse is a team player. In the wild, herds used to travel hundreds of miles in search of new grazing, and while some herd members rested, others watched for predators. To play his role in the herd and stay alive, the horse has a rare combination of strength, docility, and sensitivity, and this forms the cornerstone of his relationship with humans. Understanding the herd instinct can be invaluable in training. For example, if a young horse is reluctant to enter a horse box for the first time, allowing him to follow a more experienced horse will usually allay his fear. The same applies to jumping, when a young horse follows the lead of another.

SELF-PRESERVATION INSTINCTS

In order to survive in the herd, horses have developed very acute senses (see pp.44–47). They have extraordinary athletic ability, and notably great speed and endurance, which enables them to flee from predators. They have fantastic memories — if something harms a horse as a youngster he will remember it for years and be slow to change his opinion about it.

HERD HIERARCHY Despite popular belief, it would usually be an older mare rather than a dominant stallion that led the herd. The herd would follow the leader over long distances if needed, while the stallions would keep watch for predators.

EQUINE BODY LANGUAGE

The language of a horse includes a few sounds and a huge variety of signals from the body. Each horse develops his own language based on his own experience – if a horse finds that a particular signal works, he will keep using it. There are many universal equine signals, however, that can be recognized (see chart, below). We can greatly improve our communication with the horse and enhance our partnership with him by studying his body language and understanding his particular needs and moods.

INSTINCTIVE REACTIONS

The Quarter Horse is instinctively predisposed towards his work on the ranch, in which he separates – or cuts – an individual animal from a herd. This is similar to a wild stallion separating horses from another herd to be part of his own herd. When this behaviour is combined with training, a partnership is born.

INTERPRETING A HORSE'S MOOD THROUGH HIS BODY LANGUAGE

MOOD	MOVEMENT	HEAD AND NECK	EARS AND EYES	NOSE AND MOUTH	BODY AND TAIL
SUBMISSIVE	Takes slow steps sideways.	Keeps head and neck slightly lowered.	Moves ears and eyes to side.	Chews and gives a soft nicker.	Slackens muscles and tail.
AGGRESSIVE	Moves backwards; turns rear to face you.	Keeps head and neck lowered.	Keeps ears back and looks backwards.	Bares teeth, snorts, and flares nostrils.	Tightens muscles and swishes tail.
EXCITED	Gallops, stops and starts, and swivels.	Raises head and neck.	Moves his eyes and ears from side to side.	Squeals and blows. Flares nostrils.	Remains firm, with tail up.
FRIGHTENED	Moves away.	Raises head and neck slightly.	Keeps ears back and looks backwards.	Takes shallow, rapid breaths. Whinnies.	Shakes and keeps tail down. Sweats.
STARTLED	Stops or moves sideways.	Raises head and neck slightly.	Pricks his ears towards a noise.	Holds breath.	Tightens muscles and clamps tail.
ANGRY	Moves towards you and paws ground.	Keeps head and neck lowered.	Keeps eyes forwards and ears back.	Bares teeth and snorts.	Tightens muscles and clamps tail.
SUSPICIOUS	Stands still and watches.	Raises head and neck.	Points ears and eyes forwards.	Smells and blows.	Has tail down.
SLEEPY	Stands still.	Keeps head and neck lowered.	Points ears and eyes loosely upwards.	Breathes slowly and deeply.	Has a slow pulse and keeps tail down.
DEPRESSED	Stands still.	Keeps head and neck lowered.	Points ears down and sideways.	Takes slow, shallow breaths.	Low temperature, weak pulse, tail down.
CONFIDENT	Remains resolute and unflinching.	Raises head and neck slightly.	Pricks ears forwards or to one side.	Breathes normally.	Has a normal pulse and carries tail.
SICK	Has a weak, motionless posture.	Keeps head and neck lowered.	Points ears down and sideways.	Takes fast, shallow breaths.	Weak, raised pulse and temperature.

A HORSE'S SENSES

As well as using body language to communicate with other horses, the horse relies on his senses of touch, smell, and hearing to exchange information and establish relationships. Although it is largely through the sense of touch that humans signal to the horse when riding, an understanding of all the senses is beneficial for effective horsemanship. The horse's hearing is far superior to that of a human, and his eyes work in a very different way to our own.

TOUCH

The horse has a heightened sensitivity to touch, and a rider makes special use of this. The most obvious conventional signal is the use of the leg in the area near the girth to ask the horse to go forwards. However, it is possible to train a horse to recognize any consistently used touch as a signal for him to respond to. For example, we teach the horse that a small leg movement behind the girth is a signal for him to canter, but we could equally pull on the horse's mane to achieve the same result (this, in fact, can be the canter aid applied by disabled riders who have no use of their legs). Watching horses nuzzle each other's backs – particularly along the crest – it is obvious that they find this action pleasurable. We can reproduce this action as a reward for good behaviour by gently rubbing the area in front of the saddle. The common

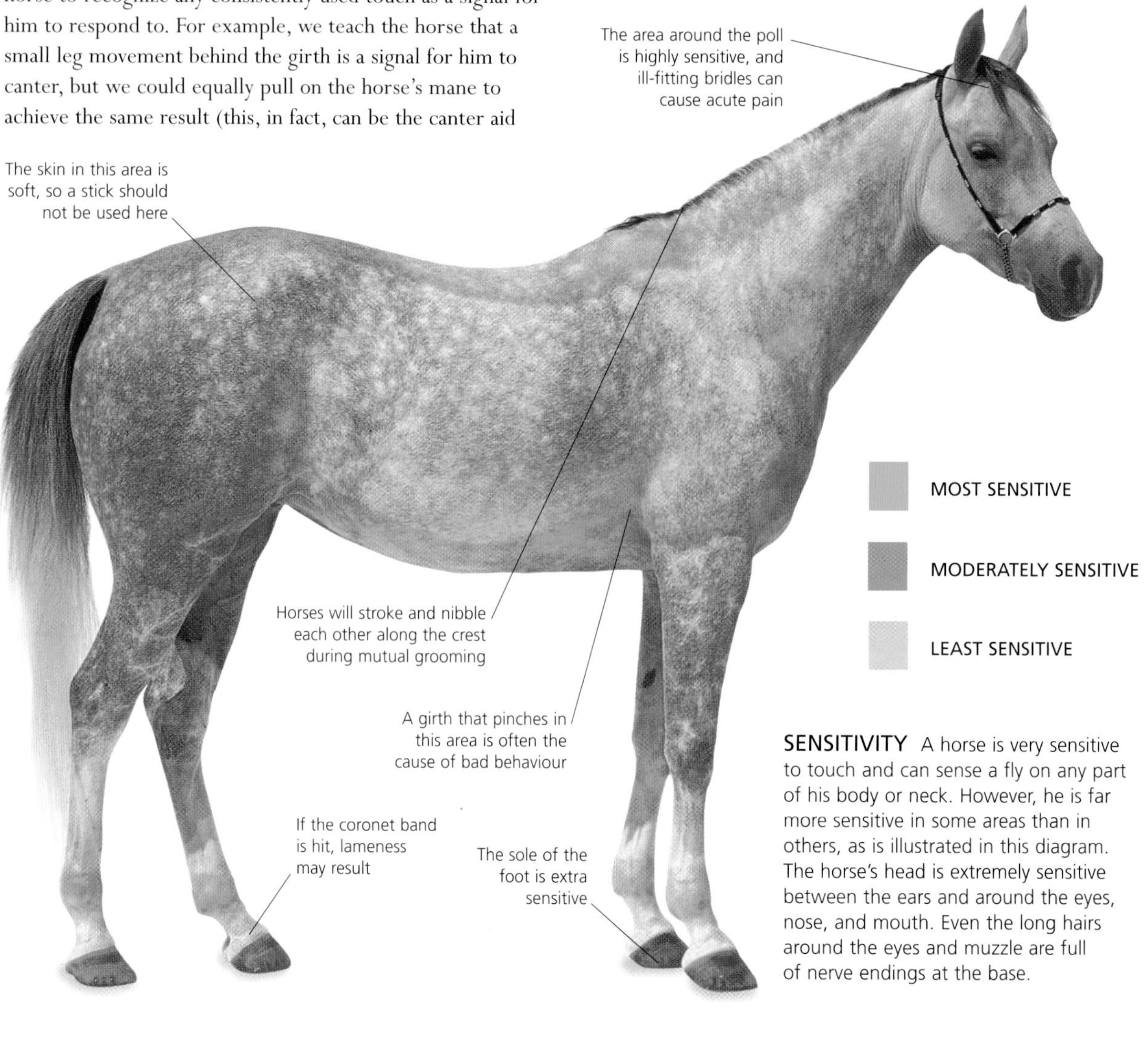

The area around the poll is highly sensitive, and ill-fitting bridles can cause acute pain

The skin in this area is soft, so a stick should not be used here

Horses will stroke and nibble each other along the crest during mutual grooming

A girth that pinches in this area is often the cause of bad behaviour

If the coronet band is hit, lameness may result

The sole of the foot is extra sensitive

MOST SENSITIVE

MODERATELY SENSITIVE

LEAST SENSITIVE

SENSITIVITY A horse is very sensitive to touch and can sense a fly on any part of his body or neck. However, he is far more sensitive in some areas than in others, as is illustrated in this diagram. The horse's head is extremely sensitive between the ears and around the eyes, nose, and mouth. Even the long hairs around the eyes and muzzle are full of nerve endings at the base.

USING THE EARS

Pricked ears are typical of a horse that is startled or interested in something. If a horse has his ears forwards when he is doing an exercise, such as jumping a fence, it shows that he is interested and happy in his work. When being lunged, he will often have the outside ear forwards as he looks or listens and the inside ear sideways as he looks at and listens to the lunger. When a horse is frightened, angry, depressed, or in pain, he will flatten his ears backwards.

EXPRESSING INTEREST   LISTENING   SHOWING RELUCTANCE

practice of rewarding a horse with a hard pat on the side of the neck is probably difficult for the horse to understand. With young horses, it is well proven that a gentle rubbing with the hand or a cloth over the whole of the body helps to build up initial trust and acceptance of human contact.

SMELLING AND TASTING

The horse has a highly developed sense of smell. In the wild, this sense is vital for finding fresh food and water, and for sensing the presence of predators before they can be seen or heard. The sense of smell is particularly important to mares and stallions in the breeding season, but it is important to all horses as a means of recognizing members of their own herd; horses have communal rolling areas so that the herd has a single scent. It has been suggested that a horse can smell fear, although he is more likely to be picking up on a rider's nerves.

Horses will spontaneously reject bitter-tasting food by spitting it out. This reaction is a defence mechanism to help prevent them from swallowing poisonous plants (which often have a bitter taste). Conversely, horses enjoy sweet foods, and we can use sugar lumps, mints, and carrots as rewards in training. If you give a horse too many sweet treats, however, it can encourage him to nip.

A HORSE'S HEARING

In humans below the age of 25, the range of hearing extends from approximately 20 Hz to 20 kHz. In contrast, horses have a range from 55 Hz to 35 kHz, which means that they are able to hear many higher frequency sounds that we cannot hear. This is why horses can become distracted for what appears to be no good reason. In addition, they can rotate their ears to more than 180 degrees, pinpointing the source of sounds from a great distance. Generally speaking, the ears show where the eyes are looking, but they also signal a horse's emotional state (see box, above). Horses are sensitive to voice tones and can distinguish between harsh tones of anger and gentle tones of praise. The voice should not be underestimated as a riding aid.

SMELLING HIS FOOD
The horse's taste buds are less well developed than our own. Horses always smell their food before tasting it to check what it is. We can use sweet-smelling additives to encourage horses to eat food that they would otherwise not be keen on.

THE HORSE'S EYESIGHT

Whereas a human's field of vision (through circular pupils) is circular, the horse's field of vision (through more elongated pupils) is much wider and less deep. The horse's eyes are placed at the side of his head, and he has a lateral field of vision of 160–170 degrees on either side of him. This means that when the horse is grazing he can see almost everything around him, except the area directly behind his hindquarters.

The horse can use both eyes independently (this is known as monocular vision) or both eyes together (known as binocular vision). Binocular vision allows him to judge distances but means he can see only in a relatively narrow field of vision (see right). In addition, the horse has areas of blurred vision below his binocular field.

Research has shown that horses are dichromates, which means that they have limited colour vision. They can distinguish between light and dark, and between reds and blues, but not between greens and greys. This is why you will not find green or grey poles used in a grass showjumping arena.

HOW THE HORSE FOCUSES

It has been shown that horses' eyes naturally focus monocularly on distant objects when they are calm, which makes sense when you consider their evolution as prey animals living on open plains. To see objects at a short distance, a horse must focus the lens. It used to be thought that a horse could not change the shape of his lens in order to adjust focus between near and distant objects (a process known as

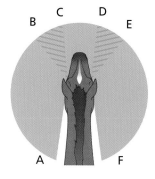

FIELD OF VISION

The horse's field of vision extends around almost his entire body. With monocular vision, he can see on either side of him (**A** to **C** and **D** to **F**), but he cannot see directly in front of him. Using binocular vision, he has a relatively narrow field of vision (**B** to **E**).

HEAD AT 45 DEGREES With the head at this angle, the horse can clearly see the area in front of him (**2**) when using his eyes binocularly. Above and below this area (**1** and **3**) is an area of blurred vision and, higher up, there is a blind spot (**4**). If he uses his eyes monocularly, he will not see the small area immediately in front of him – he will see clearly to either side.

HEAD VERTICAL With the head in this position, typical of dressage, the blind spot (**4**) and the blurred area (**3**) are obscuring the view straight ahead, but the horse can see clearly immediately in front of his feet (**2**). If he uses his eyes monocularly, he can clearly see to either side (**1**). To focus on a fence, he will have to change the angle of his head.

THE PROPRIOCEPTIVE SENSE

In a human, the proprioceptive sense is that which enables us to judge the position of our hands and legs even in the dark, and exactly how far the ground is beneath our feet when we run upstairs. It is often confused with co-ordination, but it is not the same thing. The horse is built so that his four legs are mostly out of his line of vision, so the proprioceptive sense is especially important to him. It is particularly valuable when moving at speed, over undulating ground, or when jumping fences. Messages conveyed to the horse's brain tell him when he is moving in a well-balanced way and when he needs to make corrections. Early in training, the horse should experience undulating and changing ground in order to develop this sense.

accommodation), which is something humans do with great ease. Instead, it was thought that he had to move his head up and down to focus. A recent study has shown that the horse does, in fact, have a limited accomodation, but we now know that the reason he has to lift his head up and down is that his binocular vision is in a zone that is down his nose and not straight ahead. So, with his head at the vertical, a horse focuses on the ground about 2 m (6½ ft) in front of him. Only with the head held higher can he focus immediately ahead (see far left).

MOVING THE HEAD TO SEE

The majority of photographs of horses approaching fences show the horse raising his head and neck. If a rider prevents a horse from raising his head as he approaches a fence, the horse will tend to panic and go faster or tilt his head at the pole in an effort to see. In showjumping, it is both unfair on the horse and possibly dangerous to the rider to approach a fence using any of the restraints that fix the head in the vertical position.

Also, when a horse has his head at or close to the vertical, as in dressage, he cannot see immediately in front of him, but is looking at the ground instead. If you can imagine yourself in the place of the horse, it is obvious that he has to show considerable acceptance and trust of his rider in order to do this, and still ride forwards willingly. It is also not surprising that most horses immediately want to raise their heads when they are disturbed by sounds outside their binocular field of vision, so horses should be given the benefit of the doubt in these types of situations.

Horses that have the movement of the head restricted by the use of various gadgets tend to tilt their heads and may exhibit various signs of tension and frustration, including excessive chewing of the bit and grinding of their teeth.

USING YOUR KNOWLEDGE

An appreciation of the limitations of the horse's vision can help us care for horses in a more understanding way and avoid accidents. For example, if a person approaches a horse from behind and startles him, the horse may well kick out in what he sees as self defence. Similarly, if you startle a horse, he may gallop away while looking backwards, using his monocular vision, and this may lead to him injuring himself, for example, he may crash into a fence. Conversely, if his attention is taken by something in front of him, he may step sideways into a ditch.

The best way to approach a horse in the stable or field is to walk diagonally towards his head so that, whether he is using his monocular or binocular vision, he will see you. You should also make your presence known by using your voice on approach. The clearest indication of where your horse is looking is the position of his ears: the horse will normally point the ears in the direction he is looking – so, as you approach, note the position of his ears so that you can avoid surprising him when his attention is on something else.

Many horses suffer eye damage or defective vision, so it is important to have your horse's eyesight examined regularly. A horse that goes blind in one eye can still perform successfully, but he must be allowed to carry his head slightly to one side so that he is able to use his good eye.

HORSE'S VISION APPROACHING A JUMP

If a horse is to see and judge the distance as he approaches a showjumping fence, he must be allowed the freedom to raise his head and direct his binocular vision at the fence.

If the horse is prevented from lifting his head on approaching a fence, the fence will fall in his blind spot. This is why it is so important that a rider avoids keeping a fixed rein contact and preventing the horse from using his neck. Instead, the rider must maintain a soft, allowing rein contact. The higher the fence, the more the horse will want to be able to change the angle of his head to see the top of the fence.

If a horse is allowed flexibility, he will be able to see the fence clearly when he is within one stride of it (see area within the red lines, below), although his vision of either side of it and above it will be blurred.

HOW A HORSE LEARNS

Horses have strong instincts and, in training, it is an advantage to work with, rather than against, their natural behaviour and responses. However, they are also very adaptable and quick to learn from their experiences. It is possible to teach a horse to respond to quite subtle signals, and even to overcome their natural instincts, such as fear of an unfamiliar object or sound. Given the right training, a horse can become a willing and responsive equestrian partner.

INSTINCTIVE AND LEARNED BEHAVIOUR

It is undoubtedly easier to teach a horse to respond to a signal when the desired behaviour comes naturally. A horse will readily move forwards to a squeeze from the leg but he will be reluctant to respond to a signal to move backwards when he cannot see what is behind him. By understanding the natural behaviour of the horse, we can use and develop his strengths, rather than work against them. Similarly, we should always work to develop the natural shape and paces of the horse, rather than attempting to force him into an unnatural gait or posture.

Although the horse will respond to situations instinctively, he can also learn responses based on his own observation and past experience. We can make the most of his quickness to learn and his ability to remember how to deal with particular situations, such as remembering how he successfully jumped a difficult fence on a previous occasion.

As well as learning through his own experience, he can be taught how to respond to particular signals. A conditioned response is one that is established by training to a stimulus that is not natural. When a young horse walks forwards of his own accord – perhaps following another horse – some trainers

(a) Use your rein aid to turn your horse away.

SHYING FROM AN OBJECT Instinctive behaviour, such as shying from a strange object, can be corrected by good training. If your horse shies, turn his head away from the object **(a)** – this will help to calm him and distract his attention away from the source of his anxiety. Reward him for keeping calm **(b)**. If this technique is repeated over time, your horse will become familiar with the object, and will no longer shy from it.

(b) Praise your horse for coping well.

STABLE VICES

Horses can develop repetitive habits – or stable vices – when they live in restricted environments or in social isolation. Typical stable vices include weaving (moving the head from side to side); crib biting and wind sucking (taking hold of something with the teeth and sucking in air); and stable or field walking (pacing up and down or around in small circles). Practising stable vices produces a release of endorphins, a naturally produced pain killer, and horses can become hooked on this effect, creating a vicious circle.

Over a long period of time, these habits will damage a horse physically. For example, if a horse crib bites, his incisor teeth will be worn down, and this will mean his teeth will wear out more quickly. Some horses are genetically predisposed to stable vices but boredom or poor quality of life are major causes. You rarely see such repetitive behaviour in horses that have a natural regime with space, companionship, and opportunities to eat little and often. By having good stable management from the start you can prevent these vices ever occurring.

CRIB BITING

work, notice the relaxed position of his ears, the calmness in his eyes, his regular breathing, and the ease of his movement. These signs are all symptomatic of a contented horse who accepts his rider, enjoys his work, and uses his back.

A horse must understand what is required of him, however, and understand his part of the bargain. Anything less than this is not acceptance but submission – the difference between a horse that knows he could react differently but chooses not to, and a horse who knows that there is no option. If a horse merely submits to his rider, he will not be performing to the best of his abilities.

EFFECTIVE TRAINING

Well-trained horses show real intelligence. They are sensitive creatures, capable of great attentiveness and will power. They are able to vary their behaviour in response to different situations, requirements, and past experiences, and this is to the benefit of the horse and rider partnership. In the state of captivity in which a horse is held, it is up to the rider or the trainer to assume the responsibility for developing a horse's mental ability and to influence the degree to which he can become independent and find more enjoyment in his work.

Many of the equine reactions that could be called stupid are probably no more stupid than the reaction of a child who is afraid, and we should never assume that a horse is being deliberately slow or stubborn. Of course there are horses that are slow learners – and certainly stupidity often masquerades as good temperament and docility – but there are probably more who are badly trained. If a rider is poor at equine communication, even the brightest of horses will find it difficult to know what is expected of him.

COMPARING DAILY ROUTINES

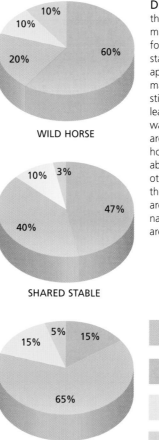

WILD HORSE

SHARED STABLE

SEPARATE STABLE

DIFFERENT ROUTINES In the wild, a horse spends the majority of his time looking for food and grazing. In stables where horses are kept apart, a horse will spend the majority of his day standing still and little time eating. This leads to stress and muscle wastage. If domestic horses are kept in loose boxes, however, where they are able to touch and see each other, and feed on hay when they choose, their routines are not too dissimilar to their natural behaviour and they are more content.

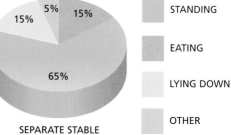

STANDING

EATING

LYING DOWN

OTHER

HAVING REALISTIC EXPECTATIONS

With good training, it is possible to improve a horse's state of mind and develop him mentally so that he can achieve his highest potential. However, your expectations need to be relevant to your horse's age and level of training.

The most one can expect from a young horse is that he is steady and animated. Such a horse is likely to have a good temperament and to be a pleasure to train. It is important to distinguish between these horses and those that are passive and mechanical; the latter will always be difficult to ride and do not have good temperaments.

A novice horse that is encouraged to become positive and sure about what he is asked to do will develop into a willing equestrian partner. As he learns to trust and understand his rider, he will enjoy the work required of him.

A fully trained horse is confident and responsive. He is also knowledgable and brave because he has experience and judgment and is able to apply these sensibly. It is a rewarding sight for a trainer to see a horse galloping over cross-country fences that neither horse nor rider have seen before, with the horse taking sensible decisions. The same can be said for watching an advanced dressage horse responding precisely to a rider's aids as he does an intricate exercise in front of an audience of 20,000 people. This takes great bravery and shows that the horse has been well-prepared mentally.

RESOLVING TRAINING PROBLEMS

Whatever the level of your horse's training, you may find your horse is unsettled in his work. All horses that have a difficult temperament or show a sudden change in mental attitude should have a thorough veterinary examination. With the majority of difficult horses, pain is found to be at the root of the problem. Often, the cause is something very easily resolved, such as badly fitting tack, or sharp teeth requiring the attention of an equine dental technician. Sometimes the problem is of a more long-standing or insidious nature, such as foot or back pain resulting from injury or a pinched nerve; to address these problems, an ongoing programme of treatment will be necessary.

If the vet and farrier give the all-clear, there are a number of ways you can resolve some of the typical problems. Generally, it helps to turn your horse out for most of the time and let him have company, although you should keep an eye on the horses that he is turned out with: watch for any signs of bullying that may be causing your horse to be fretful or unhappy. The more confined a horse is, the more regular exercise he will need. Many stables use a horse walker – a revolving machine in which the horse has to keep walking or trotting in a circle – to supplement daily exercise.

VETERINARY CHECK If your horse exhibits a sudden change in behaviour, such as an unwillingness to jump fences or move forwards at the leg aid, ask your vet to examine him for signs of pain. Your vet will check for heat or swelling, and will also watch the horse moving at walk and trot to determine whether there is any lameness.

In addition, most horses benefit from regular grooming sessions and other close contact with their rider on a regular basis. Lungeing work (see pp.68–69) is particularly good for improving a horse's mental attitude and to help him become more relaxed and steady. It is also a useful way to develop communication between the horse and rider.

PINPOINTING BEHAVIOUR TRAITS

It is worthwhile to assess your horse's character traits (see chart, opposite), not only so that you can devise a suitable stable-management regime, but so that you can judge his suitability for an activity and plan a training programme that will take account of any behavioural problems.

When assessing your horse, do not forget to look at your own attitudes and behaviour to see if they may be adversely affecting the horse. For example, some people associate ugliness in horses with stupidity; if a horse is treated as though he is stupid and unresponsive, however, he is likely to fulfil the handler's expectations.

DEVISING SUITABLE PROGRAMMES

Once you have pinpointed a particular behavioural issue, plan a programme to help resolve the problem. In many cases, this will mean going back to basics so that you can encourage and reinforce good behaviour. In all cases, follow common-sense methods and structured routines.

• An excitable horse needs a structured approach, a calm environment, and long, slow work. He will work best if he is turned out all the time and is always ridden by the same, patient rider. Often, this type of horse can benefit from travelling to competitions and being ridden around but not competed – this habituates him to these kinds of surroundings. Given time and an advanced rider, many excitable horses settle completely.

• A nervous horse needs a sympathetic rider. He may also be happier in a more restricted environment. The key to dealing with a young, nervous horse is to begin training him as soon as possible. As the training progresses, he will show dramatic improvement, becoming calmer as he begins to trust his rider.

• If a horse is depressed, it may be because of pain, sickness, boredom, or bullying from humans or other horses. If the horse is bored, a stimulating environment and plenty of communication are needed. A spirited rider with a kind heart can motivate many dull or depressed horses to good effect.

• A horse that has suffered pain or discomfort in his early lessons or experiences will often be inherently suspicious. Taking your horse through lower level exercises in a controlled environment will help to build trust and consistency. It is also worth having his eyesight examined – horses with very suspicious natures often have defective vision.

• If an aggressive horse is not actually suffering pain, it may be that he has learnt aggression as a suvival habit. The typical example of this is the stallion that learns to be aggressive in a herd situation and carries this type of behaviour into the stable yard. In this situation, take some steps backwards in the training process, so that you can form an unthreatening, trusting relationship.

ASSESSING YOUR HORSE'S CHARACTER

Behaviour traits can manifest themselves in a positive or negative way. For example, calmness is a desirable quality in a young horse, but taken to one extreme it can mean slow-wittedness or doziness; the opposite extreme of this trait is, of course, fear or neurosis.

The aim of corrective training is to make extreme behaviours become less so by, firstly, identifying the behaviour, and, secondly, by devising effective training programmes that specifically work to increase or lessen the trait, whichever is required.

	EXTREME BEHAVIOUR	LESS DESIRABLE BEHAVIOUR	DESIRABLE BEHAVIOUR	LESS DESIRABLE BEHAVIOUR	EXTREME BEHAVIOUR
YOUNG HORSE	Frightened	Nervous	**Calm**	Sleepy	Dormant
	Aggressive	Headstrong	**Docile**	Meek	Passive
	Excitable	Fragile	**Stable**	Laid-back	Tranquilized
	Hyper	Unsettled	**Alert**	Lethargic	Mechanical
	Sexual	Frisky	**Sociable**	Shy	Introverted
	Over-the-top	Fresh	**Healthy**	Sore	Sick
NOVICE HORSE	Racing	Free-wheeling	**Willing**	Reluctant	Stubborn
	Exuberant	Eager	**Enthusiastic**	Apathetic	Idle
	Silly	High-spirited	**Happy**	Serious	Sad
	Suspicious	Questioning	**Trusting**	Unquestioning	Sheep-like
	Refusing	Resisting	**Accepting**	Resigned	Subservient
	Angry	Irritated	**Peaceful**	Indifferent	Detached
TRAINED HORSE	Bossy	Cocky	**Confident**	Diffident	Confused
	Hyper-sensitive	Sensitive	**Responsive**	Dull	Unresponsive
	Erratic	Inconsistent	**Adaptable**	Set in his ways	Wooden
	Loopy	Eccentric	**Intelligent**	Slow	Stupid
	Unpredictable	Impetuous	**Brave**	Cautious	Cowardly
	Dangerous	Complacent	**Contented**	Glum	Depressed

THE RIDER AS COACH

Every rider is a coach to their horse, to a greater or lesser extent. The first step in your partnership is to establish a solid foundation from which to work by gaining your horse's trust and treating him with respect. Then, build on your horse's strengths and develop good communication between you. Adopt flexible methods that you can continue to use at every stage of your training, and make sure that you and your horse are well prepared to meet your long-term goals.

ESTABLISHING A PARTNERSHIP

As you develop your riding skills, you will naturally improve the communication and understanding between you and your horse – your aids will become more refined as your horse becomes more accustomed to what your signals mean, and your feel for the horse's movement and responses will improve. You and your horse are therefore learning and training together and, as a rider, you are effectively a coach to your horse. In order to be successful in this role, you need to be steady and consistent. You need to treat your horse humanely, as well as have an understanding for how he sees the world.

BEING STEADY

Good training begins with patience and consistency, because learning takes place more easily in a non-threatening environment, with trustworthy teachers, and a familiar timetable. Horses thrive on consistency and a calm, authoritative approach, and successful training will be possible only once the horse has learnt to trust his rider. It is important to have rules, but this does not mean you have to break a horse's trust to enforce them. It is not acceptable for a horse to push you around in the stable, nor is it acceptable for him to ignore communications. The solution is not to use strength or punishments, but to deal with small problems on a daily basis before they become bigger ones. For example, do not hit your horse to stop him walking into you; instead, teach him to lead and to halt, and make sure he knows what "no" means. When he rubs his head on you, stop him the instant it becomes slightly too vigorous, not when he is trying to head-butt you. This way, you will gain the horse's respect, but you will not have to resort to harsh discipline. It is like being a good teacher of children. You must always be in control and be polite, but at the same time you must set clear limits.

A YOUNG HORSE Even a young horse will be calm and responsive with a rider on his back if he has had good, progressive training.

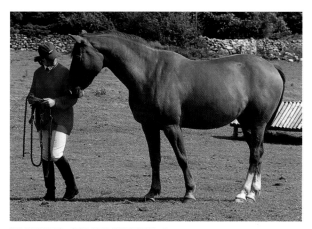

LEARN TO COMMUNICATE If you are steady and humane in the care and training of your horse, you will have a contented and willing equestrian partner. As you learn to listen to him, he will listen to you and respond to you as his rider and leader.

BEING HUMANE

The equestrian world is full of physically talented riders who do not fulfil their potential because they lack self control. It only takes one bad experience for a horse to see humans in an unfavourable light, and they do not forget such experiences. As the famous 17th-century French riding master, Antoine de la Baume Pluvinel, said, "We shall take care not to vex the young horse, or cause it to abandon its affable gracefulness in disgust. For this is like the fragrance of blossoms, which never returns once it has vanished." The vast majority of riders have no wish to be cruel but some people become frustrated as they face up to the difficulties of working with a live animal.

Of course, for most riders, understanding your horse and communicating effectively with him can be the most rewarding and stimulating aspect of horse riding. Nuno Oliviera (a leading Portuguese trainer of the 1960s to 1980s) said, "The horse must not be trained to be a soldier at our command. Instead we must have a communion of two minds."

DEVELOPING EMPATHY

Even though you are working in partnership with your horse, it is important never to make the mistake of projecting human characteristics on your equine friend – this is known as anthropomorphism, and it leads to poor communication and misunderstandings. The best riders at all levels have the ability to see the world from the horse's perspective – to empathize with the horse. With young horses in particular, you have to act like a horse and prove yourself unthreatening but able to stand up for yourself. For example, if a horse becomes pushy, and tries to assert his own dominance, be quick to stand your

ground. If he tries to bite you, it is quite acceptable to give him a sharp smack on the nose. If you assert yourself on a daily basis, the horse will accept you as part of the herd and you will be seen as the herd leader.

Empathy means that you neither overlook the needs or gifts of individual horses nor ask too much of your horse mentally or physically. This is the basis for a horse doing things voluntarily. Many riders can get a horse to perform, but the good riders get a horse to perform because the horse wants to. When this stage is reached, it is amazing how hard a horse will try to understand and do what is required.

On a daily basis, always listen to your horse and be aware of his body language (see pp.42–43). Learn to tell the difference between a frightened horse and a naughty horse, a confused horse and an unco-operative horse, a horse that is accepting and a horse that is submissive.

The best place to begin to communicate with the horse is not on his back but on the ground. A horse responds primarily to an audio visual world and so, initially at least, he needs to see and hear you. As you enhance your mutual understanding on the ground you can gradually develop ridden communication with your horse through the normal leg and rein aids. It is said that a good horseman can hear a horse talk, but a great horseman can hear him whisper. This is how the so-called magical powers of horse whisperers originated, but it is not magic; they just understand horses and how to communicate with them.

HUMAN CONTACT Spending time grooming and caring for your horse will allow you the opportunity to study his body language and character, as well as his likes and dislikes. You can also identify any particularly sensitive areas of his skin.

ESTABLISHING PRIORITIES

Your coach will help you pinpoint the training priorities. For example, it is generally agreed that work has to be based on the natural shape and paces of the horse so that he uses his back well. It should be a priority that your horse is calm, accepting of his rider, moving forwards willingly, and using both sides of his body equally well.

It is also agreed that the rider needs a consistent balance and must develop a good feel for the movement of the horse, together with a mental partnership with him. By putting the essential ingredients in place, there is a good chance of doing quality work. This is vital because practice makes permanent, not necessarily perfect, and if you practise poor quality work this is what you will establish.

Of course, in the process of establishing the training priorities, you will make some mistakes. This is inevitable. However, it is a valuable part of the learning process, as long as you use what you learn to help you refine your actions and improve your techniques.

REWARD YOUR HORSE When your horse has done good work, and after every exercise session, always stroke him and let him know that he has done what was expected of him. This will encourage him to repeat his good performance the next time.

BUILDING ON STRENGTHS

Horse training needs to be based on assessment and proven methods. If you start training without identifying strengths and weaknesses, you will delay your progress. Ask someone to video you and your horse while you are working so that you can make an accurate assessment of your own strengths and weaknesses, as well as those of your horse. Even when you have mastered your basic riding skills, keep working with a coach so that you can receive guidance and advice on how to refine your basic methods and develop further.

BEING POSITIVE

As you and your horse progress with your training, the key is to be positive in your approach, as well as to keep communication simple. Neither humans nor animals respond well to a negative approach, and simplicity is fundamental to a partnership between two individuals who use different languages.

The training phrase, "Ask for much, be content with little, and reward often" neatly sums up the positive philosophy required for training horses. Being positive means working

with your horse's strengths rather than with his weaknesses, so that you build his confidence and form the foundations for achieving more.

It might be tempting to focus on problem areas during your training sessions, but the result will be confusion and a lack of co-operation on the part of the horse. By allowing your horse the chance to do work that he is comfortable doing, and letting him feel relaxed and confident, you can then move on to progressively related exercises and gradually extend his abilities and understanding.

For example, your horse may find the walk and canter easier than the trot; riding on the left rein easier than the right rein; and keeping a slow speed easier than maintaining a fast speed. If you focus on these strengths during a training session, your horse will find that he can respond successfully to your requests and will be more willing to respond positively to new challenges. There are so many different equestrian sports and it is possible to find a role suited to the talents of the vast majority of horses, particularly if they have been well trained.

The meaning of the word "aid" should not be forgotten — to aid means to help. Unfortunately, it is easy to put the emphasis on our own needs when it should be on the horse's needs. Good riding involves helping your horse understand you and respond to you. Work hard at communicating with small, positive aids that tell the horse exactly what to do, rather than attempting to manipulate him physically with big, negative aids that tell him what not to do.

BEING SIMPLE

When you are training, always ask yourself, "Is this easy to do and easy to understand?" The key is not to confuse a horse by being complicated, using too many words, or introducing numerous signals. This will encourage a horse to ignore your signals, just as a human switches off from someone whose chatter is incessant and meaningless. Simplicity is the hallmark of a good rider.

If you use simple communication from the beginning, this will eventually enable you to do high-level work. A beginner rider learns the basics of communication with the horse in a matter of minutes: the legs used in the normal position mean go forwards; the inside rein indicates the direction; a soft use of the voice can suggest slowing down; and a sharper use of the voice means go forwards. These basic signals are used at all levels of riding.

Remember that your horse, in most respects, should be treated as a young child. This emphasizes the huge benefits of a simple approach for both communication and the progression of training exercises. Making things more simple leads to gains in efficiency and eventually allows you to do more with your horse.

WORKING WITH A COACH Whatever stage you have reached in your riding training, it is always beneficial to work with a coach. A good coach will prevent you from picking up bad habits, and will keep you focused on long-term goals.

HAVING LONG-TERM GOALS

The activities you pursue and the level you ride at will be greatly restricted if your training is based on meeting short-term goals, and is not wide enough in scope to allow you and your horse to develop your skills in new, challenging directions. If you want to achieve the highest levels as a rider, be flexible in your approach and form long-term aims to work towards. Even if you start riding merely for pleasure, you may soon aspire to become, for instance, an international-level dressage rider. Similarly, you may find that a horse has a much longer useful life and greater value if the training you have given him means that he is proficient at various different types of equestrian activities.

BEING FLEXIBLE

Flexible training is not about using all and every type of technique. It is about using methods that will work at both the lower and the higher levels of riding and, as far as possible, for all activities.

It is more difficult to adopt an entirely new technique than to refine an established one, so flexible methods should be used from the start. For example, when you learn to mount and dismount, it is more valuable to use

a method that can stay basically the same for the more advanced progression, which is having a leg-up and vaulting on and off. When you learn an aids system for the first time, you want these aids to be the same aids you will use in the competition arena several years later. Similarly, a good, general-purpose riding position is the foundation for either a dressage or jumping position. Let yourself be guided by your coach, who will choose riding techniques on which you can build, and who will recognize any bad habits that need to be ironed out. Any rider will gradually become effective if they are consistent in their methods.

Consistency, however, must not be followed slavishly at the expense of restricting a horse's potential. If a training method or programme is causing problems or is effective in reaching only short-term goals, you must be prepared to reassess and adopt alternatives. For example, some methods of training young horses break their spirit to a greater or lesser degree, or produce a horse that habitually evades the bit, and some methods produce an unnatural outline in the horse and restriction in the use of his back. It may be necessary to go several steps back in the training process to help iron out problems and teach the horse new, more effective methods (see pp.60–89).

BEING PREPARED

Horses are relatively easy to train and many people try to progress without lessons but, in all cases, riders will benefit enormously from watching the best riders at any level.

During your early days of training, you will be totally dependent on your coach, but as you progress, you will gradually take responsibility for a greater proportion of the training decisions. Then, as you complete each stage or level, you will assume sole responsibility for what you are doing. This is so that, when you go into a competition, you are accustomed to being in charge and making decisions. The sign of a good coach is not how

QUALITY WORK Even if your main interest is showjumping, every exercise session should include good-quality flatwork, which will help develop your horse's strides and the use of his back, as well as allow you to develop your own fitness and co-ordination.

much they do for their student but how little they have to do. The same attitude should apply to the training of your horse.

A well-trained horse responds automatically when he is asked to do an exercise. The key to good preparation is regular, structured sessions that train both you and your horse to react to various situations without conscious effort. This means that when you are competing you are free to concentrate on a few vital elements, like maintaining the right speed and direction, rather than being under pressure to ride brilliantly in order to achieve the right response from your horse.

The preparation for a competition starts at home. All the competition exercises can be broken down into small units for you to practise separately and build on. Practise putting a series of training exercises together like a mini competition. It will give a focus to your training and help you and your horse learn to make decisions quickly. For many of these decisions it is not a question of the right or wrong answer, but of balancing conflicting demands and choosing from a number of options.

Think ahead to all the potential difficulties you might encounter, such as, "What happens if my horse stops in the practice ring? What if my horse naps by the entrance of the arena? What happens if I lose my way?" In this way, you are prepared and ready to deal with all eventualities.

DOING PROGRESSIVE EXERCISES Grid work, in which a series of fences is set up at particular distances, is excellent for encouraging your horse to take responsibility for making his own decisions and to respond to situations in specific ways.

ASSESSING YOUR STRENGTHS AND WEAKNESSES

If you are going to be a good coach to your horse, you need to be aware of your own strengths and weaknesses. A horse will thrive under the care of a steady, calm rider who creates a structured routine for him to work in. Your role is to be positive and communicate simply. In this way, you will be in a position to gain the best results from your horse, by being well-prepared and adopting flexible training methods. Ask yourself a series of searching questions, so you can assess your qualities and look at areas you could improve on. This will also help you to identify patterns in your behaviour that may be affecting your horse's training or his response to you. For example, you may find that you are naturally positive, but are less able to be flexible. There are no right or wrong answers and no one is perfect all the time, but role playing can help you improve in areas that you find difficult (see p.357).

BEING STEADY AND HUMANE

- Are you good at following a routine?
- Are you methodical?
- Do you stay calm in difficult situations?
- Are you observant?
- Are you compassionate?
- Are you intuitive?
- Can you cope with imperfection?
- Do you have priorities other than winning?

BEING POSITIVE AND SIMPLE

- Are you a good communicator?
- Do you focus on possibilities rather than limitations?
- Is partnership a top priority?
- Are you optimistic?
- Are you precise?
- Are you analytical?
- Are you good at prioritizing?
- Do you learn from failure?

BEGING FLEXIBLE AND PREPARED

- Are you open minded?
- Are you creative?
- Do you value efficiency?
- Do you use lateral thinking?
- Do you set yourself goals?
- Are you decisive?
- Do you have good judgment?
- Do you seize the moment?

CHAPTER THREE

BASIC HORSE TRAINING

Horse training is not a suitable activity for someone new to horses, but knowing how it is done will help the novice to understand the horse better, particularly if behavioural problems arise as a result of poor early training. If, at any stage or age, a horse becomes confused or begins to develop a bad habit, the trainer should return to these basics before resuming normal training.

   The progression of exercises in this chapter teaches the fundamentals of good horse training, including familiarizing a foal to human contact, leading and lungeing, introducing saddlery, and preparing a horse to accept a rider on his back for the first time. It also outlines how to teach the basics of dressage and jumping work in readiness for more advanced training to begin.

TRAINING EQUIPMENT

Much of the horse's early education is received on the lunge, so the main items of equipment required for training purposes are a lunge cavesson, a lunge rein, and a whip. A roller and saddle pad are also needed to accustom the horse to the feel of the saddle and girth, while side reins introduce your horse to a rein contact. The correct type of bit is crucial to the horse's comfort, as is access to suitable training facilities.

HANDLER'S CLOTHING

You must be able to move easily and quietly when working with young and inexperienced horses, whose behaviour is less predictable than that of trained horses. Half chaps and soft clothing are ideal. Body warmers are especially useful; these sleeveless, padded jackets allow great freedom of movement so that you can react quickly when necessary. Even when lungeing, head protection should always be worn, and strong gloves are essential to avoid friction burns from the lead rope or lunge rope if the horse suddenly pulls away.

CAVESSONS AND BRIDLES

It is of paramount importance that the horse, too, remains as calm and comfortable as possible at all times during initial training, so all equipment must fit snugly without pinching or rubbing. A vital piece of training equipment is a drop-noseband lunge cavesson (a special headcollar with a padded, reinforced noseband, with the bottom strap going under the bit), which should fit snugly. The cavesson has a centrally positioned ring to which a lunge rope can be attached. It must also have a back strap to prevent the cheekpiece sliding up against the eye. Soon after introducing the

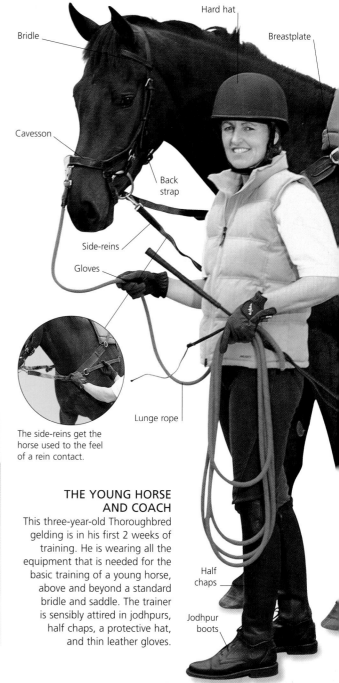

Bridle

Hard hat

Breastplate

Cavesson

Back strap

Side-reins

Gloves

Lunge rope

The side-reins get the horse used to the feel of a rein contact.

THE YOUNG HORSE AND COACH

This three-year-old Thoroughbred gelding is in his first 2 weeks of training. He is wearing all the equipment that is needed for the basic training of a young horse, above and beyond a standard bridle and saddle. The trainer is sensibly attired in jodhpurs, half chaps, a protective hat, and thin leather gloves.

Half chaps

Jodhpur boots

HEADCOLLAR

The headcollar should be introduced as early as possible to facilitate easy handling of a young horse. It will also accustom the horse to the feel of a bridle. When putting the headcollar on, undo the side buckle so that the headpiece does not go over the horse's ears – a browband is not used initially.

horse to the cavesson, you would add a browband to secure the headpiece and accustom him to the browband of a bridle.

One of the major problems encountered when working young horses is finding a bridle or lunge cavesson that is sufficiently robust yet comfortable for the horse. The major

Always start with the roller done up loosely. An elasticated insert in the roller helps prevent a horse from being frightened by the sudden tightening associated with a fixed roller.

Roller

Saddle pad

Lunge whip

Brushing boots

discomfort for many horses occurs inside the mouth, whether or not there is a bit being used. Discomfort is caused primarily when the sensitive tissue inside the cheeks is squashed between the teeth and the noseband because the upper jaw is wider than the lower jaw (see p.64). This can cause the horse to toss or tilt his head or neck. A newly developed multibridle, which doubles as a bridle and a lunge cavesson, solves the problem – the noseband is designed to avoid direct contact with the sensitive area of the jaw (see p. 390).

LUNGE ROPE AND LUNGE WHIP

A soft rope or lunge rein, approximately 9 m (30 ft) long, is attached to the cavesson's ring to control and guide the horse when lungeing. The great advantage of a rope over traditional webbing lunge reins is that it does not flap or catch in the wind. The lunge rope controls the size of the circle the horse is on while a lunge whip is used to encourage him to go forwards. The lunge whip is light and should be used gently on the back of the horse's quarters. Once you have used it once or twice, you will only have to raise it and the horse will understand. The solid part of the whip should be long so that the lash stays away from your feet.

ROLLER AND PAD

The purpose of a roller, which is usually used with a saddle pad, is to familiarize the horse to the feel of a girth strap and saddle. Since so many equine behaviour problems can be traced back to the point at which the saddle is first introduced, it can be argued that the roller is the most important piece of training equipment.

The roller has a breastplate that prevents it from slipping back when it is done up loosely in the initial few days of training. The roller should only be tightened gradually over a period of days because sudden pressure from the girth can cause the horse to become extremely distressed. Even if a girth is not done up tightly it can feel very tight if the horse is suddenly alarmed: a distressed horse involuntarily expands his ribcage and holds his breath. So, as an added precaution, there should be an elasticated insert in the roller, and the lower part of the roller should be made of a soft material, such as candlewick. Once the roller can be tightened sufficiently without distressing the horse, a soft foam pad can be placed underneath it to emulate the feel of a saddle.

SIDE-REINS

The roller has another important function in that it bears the rings to which side-reins are attached. Side-reins are the adjustable straps used to introduce the horse to the feel of rein contact, and to stop his neck bending too much to the inside or outside. They must never be so short that they stop the natural positioning of the horse's head.

Side-reins are generally made of leather but should have an elasticated insert to allow a small amount of play. The side-reins should be neither so light that the contact is inconsistent nor so heavy that their weight annoys the horse. A standard pair of side-reins will be about 90–120 cm (3–4 ft) in length from the roller to the bit and must be adjusted carefully as training progresses (see pp.72–73).

CHOOSING THE CORRECT BIT

A correctly fitting bit is, of course, vital to the horse's comfort and therefore essential if the horse's experience of bitting is to be a positive one. Bear in mind that no bit should be fitted without first having the horse's teeth checked. Sharp teeth will cause discomfort and interfere with the bit's action. Wolf teeth (vestigial premolars), which are present in some horses, should be removed as they can cause pain.

A horse that is calm and not stiff in his back will have a white mouth – that is he will produce a natural, not excessive, amount of saliva. This is desirable because it shows that the horse is comfortable not only with the bit but with the way he is going. A white mouth is possible even with a bitless

FIXED-RING
JOINTED SNAFFLE

D-RING JOINTED SNAFFLE

TRAINING BITS For the majority of horses, at whatever stage in their development, all that should ever be needed is a plain fixed-ring jointed snaffle, which should be about 1.25 cm (½ in) wider than the horse's mouth. The D-ring snaffle is a slightly different version of the fixed-ring with slightly more length against the horse's cheek.

bridle, as long as the horse is going well. This is confirmation that complicated bits or strange attachments are not necessary to produce a white mouth. The answer to most young horse mouth problems is not a new bit, but a new way of going; with an older horse that has an established way of going, alternative bits may be necessary.

THE ACTION OF A SNAFFLE

A fixed-ring jointed snaffle acts primarily on the tongue and the bars of the mouth. The larger the tongue in relation to the lower jaw, the greater the pressure on the tongue, because the bit will tend to press against the tongue. The more a horse moves his head forwards away from the vertical, the more the bit acts on the corners of the mouth instead of on the tongue and bars.

The loose-ring snaffle produces a different action from that of the fixed-ring, particularly when a little extra rein pressure

THE HORSE'S SKULL AND JAW

The upper jaw of a horse's skull is much wider than the lower jaw. This is why tight, traditional lunge cavessons or cavesson nosebands can be so uncomfortable – the sensitive tissue inside the mouth gets trapped between the outer edge of the upper molars and the

noseband. The mouthpiece of the bit rests on the bars, which lie between the incisors (the front teeth used to crop grass) and the molars (the back teeth used to masticate). The bars are shaped like a blunt knife and covered by a layer of tissue that is easily damaged.

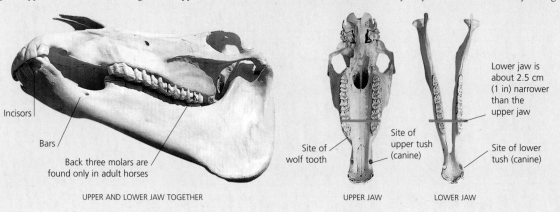

Incisors

Bars

Back three molars are found only in adult horses

UPPER AND LOWER JAW TOGETHER

Site of wolf tooth

Site of upper tush (canine)

Lower jaw is about 2.5 cm (1 in) narrower than the upper jaw

Site of lower tush (canine)

UPPER JAW   LOWER JAW

is applied. As the bit rings are drawn back, the mouthpiece is drawn up and there is downward pressure on the cheek pieces, which puts pressure on the horse's poll. This is the action of the gag snaffle. The larger the ring, the stronger the action of the snaffle.

A jointed snaffle is preferable to a straight-bar mouthpiece because the latter tends to squash the tongue and encourages the horse to escape the pressure by lifting his tongue over the bit, and this is a difficult fault to correct. If a horse does have a tendency to lift his tongue, a hanging snaffle (a Baucher or a Fulmer) can be used to hold the mouthpiece higher in the mouth. The bit can also be attached directly to the nosepiece of a multibridle to reduce pressure on the tongue.

BOOTS

Brushing boots should be used on all four of the horse's legs to protect the joints and tendons from brushing injuries: these occur when a foot hits the opposite leg on the ankle (fetlock) or just above. This happens mostly when the horse is shod but rarely happens in an unshod horse, particularly if he is a good mover. A variety of boots is available but brushing boots are the best for all-round training purposes.

Brushing boots start just below the knee and finish just below the fetlock joint on the inside of the leg and just above the fetlock joint on the outside of the leg. For additional protection they have a reinforced pad along the inside. The hind boot should be longer than the fore boot to protect the full length of the hind cannon bone.

AN IDEAL ARENA

The ideal young horse arena is approximately 20 x 30 m (65 x 100 ft). It should also be part of a larger arena (see below), which can be used as training progresses. The young horse area should have rounded corners to make it easy to steer your horse when lungeing. It should have a fence 2 m (6½ ft) high, but it should not be a solid fence. In this way, your horse can get used to the look of the bigger arena before he is introduced to it.

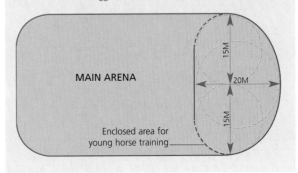

MAIN ARENA

15M

20M

15M

Enclosed area for young horse training

TRAINING FACILITIES

It is not possible for everyone to have their own training arena, but for safety and efficiency it is necessary to find somewhere that has appropriate facilities for your young horse. Large stables are often safest because they give both you and your horse sufficient room to move, and a small yard outside the stable is ideal. The most important facility is a small arena to enable you to lunge easily and possibly even to work your horse without a lunge rope or any attachment— this is known as loose schooling. This is an excellent way to develop good communication with your horse from the ground, and it means the horse has nothing to fight or pull against.

In addition, it is desirable to have a small field, surrounded by good fencing, and a quiet area for hacking. A young horse cannot be considered to have finished his basic training until he is happy to hack and work in company.

ADDITIONAL SPACE A small yard attached to a stable gives a horse extra room to move around, which will help to keep him relaxed. Ideally it should be a round space. Such a yard is also useful as a place to introduce training equipment before going into the arena.

HANDLING A YOUNG HORSE

An experienced trainer can handle a young horse from the day it is born to accustom him to human contact. The focus of early handling is to establish communication and trust. Foals and yearlings need to be taught to lead and to stand quietly while being groomed or having their feet attended to by the farrier. This can usually be achieved in a week of training. When the horse is 2 years old, it is useful to teach him how to lunge, and this can usually be done in five to ten brief sessions.

IMPRINTING

There is no doubt that, like humans, horses can learn more (and learn more quickly) when they are young. When foals are first born they have a particularly sensitive period when their behaviour can be influenced substantially. If a human spends time with a newborn foal within the first 3 hours of his life and then regularly over the next 3 days, it is possible to form an extremely strong bond with the foal – significantly stronger than is normally possible in a relationship between two different species. This bonding process is known as imprinting. During this period, the foal should be handled gently all over the head, neck, body, and legs, and can even be introduced to grooming implements.

FITTING A HEADCOLLAR

To begin with, you will need a special foal headcollar, called a foalslip, which can be fitted soon after the foal is born and used when you are handling the foal. The foalslip will allow him to be handled more easily, which is particularly important when he is due a visit from the vet or farrier. Generally speaking, do not leave a foalslip or headcollar on a young horse unless they are difficult to catch. This is because, if the headcollar becomes caught on something, the horse's natural tendency is to pull backwards strongly, and this can cause damage to the neck. If a horse is difficult to catch, introduce him to lungeing early in his training (see p.84).

The foalslip must be soft, and it must fit the foal's head closely so that it cannot catch on anything. Never be tempted to use a bridle on a foal, no matter how difficult he may be; introducing a bit to his highly sensitive young mouth may cause pain and possibly severe damage and a lifelong aversion to the bit.

LEADING

The starting point of all training is communication. Therefore teaching a horse to lead forwards and stop is more important than teaching him to stay still to be groomed, which does not have the same need for direct communication.

Begin to establish communication early on by asking the foal to lead a step or two in the stable on the left rein and then halt. If he is reluctant, bend his neck gently towards you, taking a step backwards to encourage him to follow you. Reward the first step. Work quietly until it is easy to walk and halt

LEADING YOUR HORSE
When leading a horse, always wear gloves. Stay close to your horse's shoulder and lead him alongside a fence to help prevent him moving away from you. Carry a solid stick that is long enough to reach his quarters: you can then gently touch the quarters (but do not frighten him) to encourage forwards movement. Immediately reward him when he walks forwards.

on one rein. This may take 5 or 10 minutes. Later in the day, repeat this on the other rein. Stay on the inside. Do this again on the second day. Gradually progress to a small, enclosed area outside the stable, and then to the arena if your foal is obedient. In 2 or 3 days, your foal will be good at leading. If you are not leading him to the field as part of your routine, repeat these lessons every few weeks.

GROOMING

During this training you can groom your horse for the first time and pick up his feet for inspection, although this should be attempted only if you have established communication and trust. Out of fear of the unknown, a young horse may be very wary of grooming.

Once comfortable with human contact, most horses will enjoy gentle grooming. Progress slowly and always be aware of the horse's reactions, especially when touching sensitive areas such as the belly and around the face. Always keep your free hand in contact with the horse so that you feel any reaction more quickly. If there is any sudden tensing, take a break and reassure him before progressing.

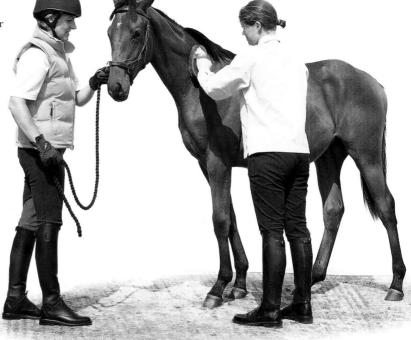

GROOMING A YOUNG HORSE Initially, do not tie your horse up for grooming; instead, have him held by an assistant, who can also reassure the young horse. Your horse should be encouraged to stand still and to move over when asked. Use a soft body brush and keep your free hand in contact with his body.

PICKING UP THE FEET

The farrier will trim your horse's feet regularly, even as a foal, so it is important to prepare the horse for having his feet touched and picked up. Do not attempt to pick up the feet if you are inexperienced, or until the horse is settled and has been taught to lead and accept basic grooming. Eventually, all four feet should be checked every day.

FRONT LEGS An experienced person should hold the horse. Stand facing the horse's quarters, then run your inside hand along the horse's shoulder and down towards his leg. This will avoid startling him and ensure you stay with him even if he moves, which is safer.

Continue running your hand down the front of the leg and take hold behind the knee (a). Then clasp the pastern with your outside hand (b). Pull gently forwards at the knee and lift the foot up (c). Keep your inside shoulder against the horse to keep your balance (by moving with the horse) as you examine the foot.

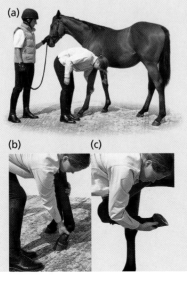

HIND LEGS Starting at the shoulders, keep your hands in contact with the horse's body so that you stay close to him if he moves and so he knows where you are. Move to the horse's quarters (d). Stand close to the horse so that he can only push you, rather than kick you.

Talk soothingly to the horse to reassure him and to keep his attention. Run your inside hand down the thigh and then down the front of the leg. With your fingers placed round the inside of the leg, pull forwards gently just below the hock and pull a little to begin raising the leg (e). Take hold of the pastern with the right hand as the leg is lifted (f).

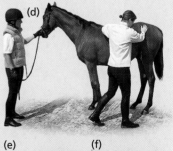

INTRODUCING LUNGE WORK

In addition to building communication and trust, lungeing helps you assess the horse's way of going and attitude of mind but a 2-year-old horse is too immature physically to do any serious work. If you are not very experienced, you must practise using the lunge rope and whip with an older, very quiet horse before lungeing a young or inexperienced one.

The horse's introduction to lungeing is a natural progression from leading (although, with horses that have learnt to be unruly, it is often easier to lunge before teaching them to lead because this will help to establish communication). In a small enclosed arena the vast majority of horses can be taught to lunge well in just two or three short sessions. There should be no need for either you or your horse to work hard. All that is required of a 2-year-old is that he understands you, stops and starts on demand, and goes willingly in both directions in walk, trot, and possibly a little canter. Use a circle of around 15–20 m (50–65 ft) in diameter. When lungeing in walk, or experiencing difficulty in controlling the horse's speed, it may be useful to reduce the size of the circle temporarily.

For the first lunge session, the only equipment that is required is a cavesson, a lunge rope, and a lunge whip. Make sure you protect the horse's legs with brushing boots (see p.65). During these first 2 or 3 days of lungeing it will also be possible to introduce the roller, but it is not helpful to introduce a bit at this stage. Be sure to limit each session to approximately 10 minutes in either direction or you will over-exert the horse.

THE LUNGE POSITION Seen from above, the lunge position forms a triangle. The first side of the triangle travels from your inside shoulder through the outside shoulder and along the lunge whip to the horse's quarters; the second side is from the quarters to the horse's nose, and the third side runs from the nose along the lunge rope to your hand and inside elbow.

HOLDING THE ROPE

When working on the left rein, the lunge rope is in the left hand, the whip in the right. If the horse gets strong you can use your whip hand to grasp the rope in front of the lunge hand. This will exert more pressure on the rein and bring the whip away from the horse's quarters, thus placing the trainer in front of the horse's movement and encouraging him to slow down.

CHANGING THE REIN

Here, the horse has been on the right rein and so the whip is in the left hand. To change the rein, reduce the size of the circle and halt the horse by the fence. Transfer the whip to your right hand by bringing it behind your back (a) – let the lash end point to the ground. Walk out to your horse (b) keeping a light contact on the lunge rope (c). As you reach the horse (d), the whip will be in the right position for leading him to the middle of the circle (e) and for rewinding the rope ready to work on the left rein.

HOW TO LUNGE

Many people are taught to lunge with their shoulders parallel to the horse's body but this is inefficient and unsafe, because it makes it easy to trip up over your own feet. Nor is it possible in this position to walk with your horse or lunge him over a fence. Instead, face the way the horse is going so that your outside shoulder and your whip arm are brought closer to the horse and the arm holding the lunge rope is positioned more or less as it would be if you were holding the rein when riding.

If you have any difficulty keeping the horse moving forwards, move yourself nearer the quarters so that you reduce the angle between him and the lunge rope. This position will oblige you either to walk faster in order to keep the same size of circle or to let out more rope. If you have difficulty slowing the horse down you can move yourself in the opposite direction, opening up the angle and placing yourself more forwards in relation to the position of the horse.

VOICE AIDS

The voice is the main aid while lungeing, supported both by the use of the whip and the positioning of the handler. The downward transitions are asked for using a low, soft voice; the upward transitions are requested with a slightly higher, more staccato voice. The following are the conventional aids, although they may vary slightly from one trainer to another. These are also the same voice aids that are used when your horse is ridden for the first time, so they are doubly important:

Upward transitions:
• halt to walk: "walk on"
• walk to trot: "trr - ot"
• trot to canter: "ca - an - ter"

Downward transitions:
• canter to trot: "trott - ing"
• trot to walk: "a-n-d - walk"
• walk to halt: "a-n-d - whoa"

USING A LUNGE WHIP

As you lunge, keep moving the whip round, with the end of the whip near the ground so that the horse becomes familar with it rather than frightened by it. Moving it more assertively behind the horse's quarters will reinforce the message given by the voice aids. If there is no response you may initially be obliged to apply the whip to the horse, but soon you will not need to touch him at all because he will associate a movement of the whip with going forwards. To help the horse distinguish between the aids, raise your whip hand as you ask for canter.

USING THE BACK

Lungeing work begins a process of ensuring the horse lifts and uses his back (see pp.40–41) in preparation for being ridden. It has never been fundamentally difficult for a rider to get on a horse's back, but what can be difficult is ensuring that the horse uses his back well in preparation for carrying a rider.

To carry the weight of the rider easily, the back needs to be arched like a bridge. To do this all the muscle groups from his quarters to his poll need to be connected like a chain. When the hind legs are brought under the body, they are said to be engaged. The neck arches forwards, the back lifts and swings, and the horse has impulsion – power and energy created by the hindquarters. This process is the origin of the equestrian terms "having the horse connected" and "coming through the back".

As part of this process, the horse needs to be forwards thinking. This forwardness primarily refers to the horse being willing to go forwards without the rider having to continually kick. A stiff rider or a dropped back quickly kills the forwardness in many horses.

INTRODUCING RIDING TACK

Once communication and trust are established, the introduction of riding tack is simply a matter of following a progression that is at once safe for the coach and pleasant and comfortable for the young horse. New equipment should be introduced slowly and calmly, and only when the horse is settled. The horse should be allowed to get used to each new piece of equipment in turn. Before moving on to a new item, it is wise to revise earlier steps.

TIMETABLE

Every horse is different but most can have all riding tack – and even a rider (see p.76) – introduced in under a week. Beyond this it may take anything between a week and 3 months before your horse is ready to be worked with a rider on his back; the precise timing will depend on how the horse uses his back and the way he lunges. All equipment should be introduced in a small enclosed yard or in a small arena. It must not be introduced in a stable because of the risk of injury to both humans and horses if something goes wrong. Two 20-minute sessions per day are better than one long period.

THE PROGRESSION

The horse shown in the sequence below is a 3-year-old who is having equipment introduced for the first time. A lunge rope can be used from the beginning but the handler must always wear gloves. First, introduce the bridle without a bit and without the browband (1). The horse should already be

SADDLE PAD Let the horse both look at and smell each new piece of equipment. Here, the horse examines the saddle pad.

AT A GLANCE

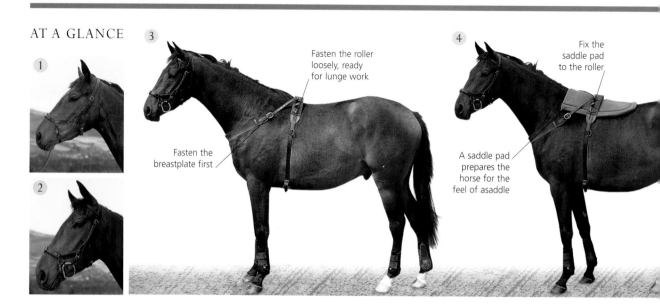

1

2

3   Fasten the roller loosely, ready for lunge work

Fasten the breastplate first

4   Fix the saddle pad to the roller

A saddle pad prepares the horse for the feel of asaddle

PUTTING ON THE BRIDLE

When inserting the bit in the horse's mouth for the first time, you must put it into the mouth after the rest of the bridle has been put on. Once the horse has got used to having the bit in his mouth, you can put the bridle on with the bit already attached. Firstly, put the bit in the mouth. Then, gently lift the headpiece over the horse's ears. Finally, do up the bottom straps of the bridle.

familiar with a headcollar, so the bridle itself should not be a surprise. The introduction of the bit **(2)** is rarely a problem if you use a well-fitting, plain-jointed eggbutt snaffle. Make sure nothing is attached to the bit until the horse is accepting the bit quietly without chewing.

Secure the bit to one side of a multibridle, or ordinary bridle, then ease the mouth open by pressing with a thumb under the lips of the upper jaw and quietly put the bit in the mouth and attach. If you encounter any problems, always have the horse's teeth checked.

Over a period of days, it is possible to introduce the roller and breastplate **(3)**. Always fasten the breastplate before the roller (and undo the roller before the breastplate) so that the roller does not slip back. Only tighten the roller very slowly and always lead the horse around for a few minutes before tightening it by even one extra hole. Then work the horse on the lunge with the roller until he is happy, before introducing the saddle. This process may need to take place over 3 or 4 days.

INTRODUCING THE SADDLE

Add the saddle pad as soon as the roller can be done up fairly tightly **(4)**. If the pad is added with a loose roller, it may flap around and frighten the horse. At this stage, side-reins can be introduced on the lunge (see p.72). The roller and breastplate is substituted by a saddle and breastplate, using the same saddle pad as before **(5)**. Ideally, the saddle should be very flat. It should have no stirrup irons at this stage, and a surcingle – a strap that goes round the whole horse – should be fitted around it to stop the flaps from moving and spooking the horse. The girth and the surcingle should have elastic inserts to allow give.

Finally, remove the surcingle and add the stirrup irons and reins **(6)**. When lungeing, the reins can be twisted and put in the top strap of the bridle. Initially, the stirrups should be secured so that they do not frighten the horse (see inset, below), but gradually they can be moved down. Begin by adjusting them so that they are no lower than the saddle flap. Tie them together with a piece of soft cord running from one stirrup iron to the other under the belly. By degrees you can lower them down to a suitable length for riding.

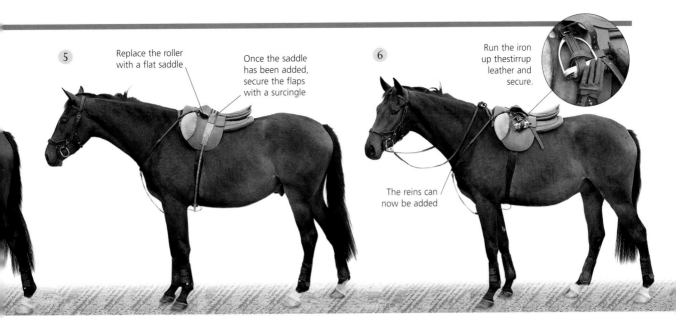

5

Replace the roller with a flat saddle

Once the saddle has been added, secure the flaps with a surcingle

6

Run the iron up the stirrup leather and secure.

The reins can now be added

PREPARING FOR A RIDER

Horses should be prepared physically to carry a rider, so, once the horse is accustomed to the feel of the saddle and bridle, the primary aim is to get the horse to lift and use his back. A few horses will do this naturally but most will need to be worked on the lunge in order to achieve this. If the horse has sufficient energy and engagement of the hind legs, while remaining calm and moving forwards willingly, he is said to have impulsion and to be connected through his back.

INTRODUCING SIDE-REINS

Side-reins are attached from the girth to the bit and are used to introduce the horse to some weight on the bit and to stop the neck bending too much. They must be introduced carefully. If in doubt, always make them a hole longer than you think necessary. At the start of a lunge session the horse may give a few little bucks in his enthusiasm so it is better to begin by attaching the end of each side-rein to the D-rings on the saddle rather than risk damaging his mouth by attaching the reins to the bit. Once the horse has settled, you can then attach the side reins to the bit. If you use a multibridle or a Wels cavesson, you can attach the bit directly to the front of the noseband so that any heavy pressure will be taken on the nose and not the mouth.

NOT CONNECTED Here the horse is calm and thinking forwards but he is not yet engaging his hind legs. He is therefore not yet ready to carry the rider, although the rider can be introduced in halt and a little walk.

CONNECTED This 3-year-old horse has connected use of his back for the first time, after 2 weeks of training, starting from the unhandled stage.

Take the time to let your horse settle and go quietly forwards in walk, trot, and canter on both reins. If your horse is reluctant to go forwards then use several short periods of canter, and be both assertive with your aids and quick to reward good responses. Until the horse becomes happy with the lunge rope's contact, the side-reins should be attached fairly high on the saddle so that they do not hang down and trip the horse up. They should also be fairly loose.

As the horse's work improves, the side-reins can be lowered at the girth until they are parallel to the ground. In walk, they have to be long enough to allow the natural nodding motion of the horse's head and neck. In trot, when the head is naturally held more still, they can be a little shorter. When the side-reins are a little shorter in trot, the very minimum of walk should be requested. If you want to spend more time in the walk, the side-reins should be lengthened or they should be undone and attached once more to the D-rings on the saddle. Also, because of the small bend to the inside on the lungeing circle, it is common practice to have the outside side-rein a hole or two longer than the inside one.

Just as most people are left- or right-handed, horses tend to be one-sided in that they have a preference for working on one particular rein. The side that they feel least comfortable with is called their stiff side. With the lunge rope attached to the front of the noseband, however, there is no increase in pressure on the inside of the mouth, even on the horse's stiff side. This is one of the advantages of lungeing over riding at this stage, especially when training horses that have become desensitized in the mouth on their stiff side. Good lungeing will immediately make your horse more even on both reins.

CONNECTING THE BACK

Over a few days, the horse will become responsive to your forwards aids and slowing-down aids and will understand what a reward is – by now he will have become familiar with your voice softly saying "Gooood" when he is going well. At this stage, when he is accepting both you and the equipment, and going forwards in a calm manner, he will be ready to be put between the aids for the first time – this is when he is responding to the aids and connecting through his back. The horse will be increasingly happy to work into a light contact of the side-reins. As this happens, you can gradually shorten the side-reins so that in trot there is a light contact with the mouth. You should not need to shorten the side-reins beyond the length shown in the main photograph (see left).

Put your horse on the rein on which he is most comfortable and in the pace at which he is going best (this will normally be the trot). Then slow the speed of the trot down. As long as the steps are remaining regular, add a little extra energy by using your voice and the swing of the whip if necessary. If the horse goes faster then immediately slow him down and repeat the process. He will soon respond by engaging his hind legs: he will have a rounder topline, he will have an increased swing in his back, he will breathe more regularly and look contented, and there will be a small amount of saliva at the corner of his mouth. The horse will also begin to reach forwards to seek contact with the bit; this stretches the muscles along the neck, back, and hindquarters and encourages the rounded outline that is desirable. (You can test whether the horse is coming through his back by loosening the side reins: the horse's shape should not change dramatically but become a little longer and lower in the head and neck.) Then change the rein and repeat.

When the horse is comfortable, introduce the canter as well. When he has worked successfully for 2 or 3 weeks he will be ready to carry a light rider while going in the same manner, although most horses will not be physically mature enough to do serious work for another year or so.

LONG REINING

Long reining is a technique where you drive a horse forwards using two ropes, one on each side. It is a traditional preparation for training a horse for carriage driving, but it is occasionally useful for encouraging the horse to go forwards and for getting him used to rein aids. Unfortunately, long reining is very difficult to perform well because it is difficult to keep the rein contact light enough. It should therefore be practised only with the greatest care, and only by a very experienced trainer. As a consequence of poor long-reining technique, many horses have mouth problems or tend to unnaturally shorten their necks.

When teaching a horse to long rein, start with someone leading the horse on his left-hand side while you attach one long rein to the same side. Once the horse is settled, the rein can go through the ring on the side of the roller, which stops it dropping down too far. Then remove it and do the same thing on the other side before introducing both reins. Long reins should be approximately 10 m (33 ft) long and lighter than the normal lunge rope, with no handles on the end. If a horse gets loose when being long reined, the two ropes tend to "chase" and frighten him.

JUMPING WITHOUT A RIDER

Horses love jumping, and humans love to watch them jump. Negotiating fences on the lunge or totally loose is a useful means both of introducing your horse to jumping and of assessing his natural style. To begin, you should set up a simple grid of fences that can be made a little more challenging as the horse gains confidence. It is especially important to check his speed on the approach and landing. The golden rules are not to ask too much of the horse and to jump him on both reins.

JUMPING ON THE LUNGE

The prerequisites for jumping on the lunge are that the horse already lunges well and is sufficiently physically mature to cope. Use extra-light poles and ensure that the surface he jumps off is firm. Nothing damages a young horse's confidence more than a slippery or loose surface that moves away from the hind legs as he tries to jump. The lunger has to be agile and proficient at shortening and lengthening the lunge rope.

PREPARING FENCES

Start with just two planks on the ground, 2.75–3 m (9–10 ft) apart, then replace the second plank with a small cross-pole fence – use a pole at the base to act as a ground line. Initially, establish a 10–12 m (32–40 ft) circle in trot before the horse

jumps the first fence, then carefully let out the rope as he jumps the grid. Try not to run but give the horse plenty of freedom through the lunge rope. When the horse is landing over the cross poles in a steady canter then another ground plank can be introduced 10 m (32 ft) away. This can gradually be converted into a second small fence – a small vertical with a ground line – and eventually into an oxer (see pp.190–91). Special attention should be paid at all times to the speed and

(a) Before jumping a second fence, check the distance is right by lungeing your horse over a pole on the ground.

JUMPING ON THE LUNGE This 3-year-old is jumping on the right rein. Many people are more comfortable lungeing on the left rein, but it is very important that the horse is jumped in both directions. Only light poles should be used, and the fences should have no fillers, so it is made as easy as possible for the horse. Before adding fences, always check that they are at the right distance for your horse **(a)**. The aim of this grid exercise is to assess the jumping technique, not to jump as high a fence as possible.

The hind legs should be half-way between the placing plank and the cross poles

The horse has good natural use of the neck

The canter on landing must be consistent before adding a second fence

The horse should show confidence but look at the fence

length of stride of the canter so that the horse is always given an appropriate distance between the fences (see pp.210–11). An introduction to a very small oxer is probably enough to do in one session; a bigger oxer of 90–120 cm (2 ft 9 in–3 ft 9 in) can be introduced on the third or fourth jumping session.

The exercises in each jumping session should be repeated on the opposite rein in the next session. This should be enough to complete the introduction and assessment. There should be no need for a horse to jump more than ten fences in any one session.

ASSESSING JUMPING STYLE

Most horses will jump better without the rider particularly because they are not being restricted by the rein contact. When the horse jumps, he should be calm and be moving forwards willingly. He should take off half-way between the placing plank and the cross poles. If he is closer to the cross poles, the speed of the trot on approach is probably too fast. If he is too far away, slightly reduce the distance between the placing plank and the fence. The horse should land over both fences in a steady canter. If he wants to trot, he is not thinking forwards sufficiently or he is being asked to jump too big a fence. If he goes too fast then he is not ready to jump and requires more work on the flat before being asked to jump again.

The horse's hind legs should be together on take-off. If they are not, change the rein and see if the same leg stays in front on take-off. If it does, stop jumping and work the horse on the flat until his action becomes more even on both reins. If the other hind leg is now in front then the legs will probably come together as the fences become more demanding. Always look to see the neck stretch forwards and down as the hind legs leave the ground. The shoulders and elbows should come forwards and the forearm be parallel with the ground over the top of the fence.

LOOSE JUMPING

Loose jumping is when you jump a horse without any lunge rope. Using a suitable arena (see p.65), you can loose school a horse with just one handler. Otherwise, you may need two assistants. Many horses jump straighter when loose jumped because they are not being distracted by the trainer moving alongside them, as they are when they are being lunged over a fence. You must not loose jump a horse if he is unsettled, but otherwise everything can be very similar to lunge jumping. If necessary, add an extra placing fence of cross poles 6 m (20 ft) before the placing fence, and add approximately 60 cm (2 ft) to the distance before the oxer, because the horse will be cantering, not trotting, to the middle fence. When you see how well most horses jump when they are loose it emphasizes the importance of a rider keeping a consistent, balanced position when jumping and the need to make only the smallest changes so that the horse is encouraged to take responsibility for the jump.

The horse jumps with great ease and shows good spring off the ground

The lunge rope must be long enough to give the horse freedom

The canter after the fence should be the same as in front of the fence

BACKING

Backing – placing a rider on a horse for the first time – is a safe activity if the horse is prepared thoroughly and there is an experienced handler in charge. It can be accomplished with just two people, but three is ideal – a rider, a handler, and an assistant. As with the introduction of a new piece of equipment (see pp. 70–71), backing must be achieved in stages: lying across, mounting, leading, and lungeing. The horse can then be ridden off the lunge in an arena and then on a short hack.

PREPARATION

Backing can take anything from 1 day to 1 week, or even longer with spoilt horses. At every stage the coach must be prepared to go back to an earlier exercise if there is any loss of obedience or confidence. The process should be carried out in a small yard or small arena. It is very important that the people handling the horse have no loose clothing that may flap around and distract or frighten the horse. It is also important that their footwear allows them to move easily. Head protection is required, but do not use any type of detachable covering as it could fall off and spook the horse.

The rider should be a light person who will start by springing up and down lightly on the horse's left side (see right), with hands positioned as they would be for mounting and dismounting: the right hand holding the front arch of the saddle and the left hand holding the breastplate and the end of the reins. The hands should stay in this position for all the steps of the backing (but be reversed when the process is repeated on the horse's other side). The horse should be held throughout; the handler should stand in front and slightly to the side. All

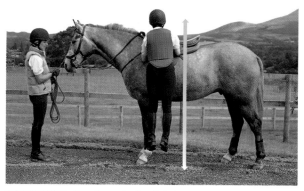

BOUNCING Start by springing lightly up and down a few centimetres off the ground on the left-hand side. Gradually bounce higher off the ground as the horse relaxes. Change to the right-hand side and repeat the process.

three people should stay on the same side of the horse, and there should be approximately 3–5 m (10–16 ft) between the fence and the horse so that the rider's head is well away from the fence when she lies across the horse.

LYING ACROSS

The assistant should carefully lift the rider up (as though giving the rider a leg-up) and then back to the ground, going a little higher each time until the rider is lying across the horse with the horse supporting most of the rider's weight. This action is then repeated on the other side (with the horse facing the other way so that he stays between the fence and the people). If all goes well, the horse can be led in walk with the rider lying across, first to the left and then to the right (see left). This exercise is repeated until the horse is almost bored by it. Then he is ready to be mounted for the first time.

MOUNTING

The rider is given a leg-up from the left. Taking her weight in her right hand she should swing her leg over the horse, without coming down into the saddle, and then return to the ground. This step is then repeated two or three times. If the horse is happy then the rider can lower into the saddle,

LEANING OVER ON THE MOVE The handler leads the horse in a 15 m (49 ft) circle. As the horse relaxes, the rider will begin to move about a little. With an athletic rider, the assistant will not be needed.

LEADING The horse is gradually walked and halted repeatedly on both reins. The rider holds on to the breastplate and the front arch to begin with, then just to the breastplate. The rider starts to use the aids as soon as possible and takes over from the handler.

putting her feet straight into the stirrup irons as they are lowered. If a problem arises the rider can either keep a light seat or vault off the horse.

It is easier for the horse to adjust to the rider's weight while moving, so the handler should now ask the horse to walk one or two steps forwards (see above) and then stop. When the horse has done this a few times, the assistant can leave. Using the same

voice aids that were used during lunge work, the rider should gradually take over control of the horse from the handler.

LUNGEING

The horse's way of going as he is lunged with a rider for the first time is a real test of your preparatory work. From the beginning, the horse should accept the rider and engage his hind legs in walk and trot. The rider will have got the horse used to movements of her body and legs when they were being led. This process is continued on the lunge and gradually control of the horse is passed over to the rider until the horse is happy to walk and halt independently of the lunger. At this stage, the rider is in the best position to judge when to ride loose for the first time (see below). The rider will have the normal leg and rein contacts at this time and the horse will be beginning to understand the normal leg and rein aids.

RIDING LOOSE When the rider feels that the horse is ready to be ridden loose, the handler can remove the lunge rein. Initially, however, the rider should continue to circle the handler to maintain extra control.

The handler continues holding the lunge whip to encourage the horse until he responds well to the rider's aids

The rider keeps a normal contact on the reins while the horse circles the handler

RIDING AWAY

When first riding off the lunge, it is a good idea to have the company of an older horse. This will help to give your horse confidence as well as get him used to company, and the older horse can give a lead whenever it is required. In this way, progress on the flat can be made very quickly. Your horse will soon understand your leg and rein aids to the extent that you will not have to use the voice except to reward. By this time, you can introduce a short stick, which the horse should not be afraid of. It is used to back up the leg aids and is a good introduction to the use of a dressage stick. Firstly, get the horse used to quiet movement of the stick as you change it over from one side to the other. Rub the stick down the horse's shoulder and behind your leg. Then use the stick by flicking the wrist and giving a tap just behind your leg or occasionally on the horse's shoulder. Always reward the desired response so that the horse understands what is required.

As he progresses, the young horse should be asked to trot and canter on both reins. Use only big circles, going round the outside of the arena. Keep everything simple and take plenty of breaks. The horse should accept the rider and be calm, going forwards willingly, and using both sides of his body equally well. He should also be responding to the aids and using his back – he is then between the aids. It is important that any work you do is of good quality so that your horse gets into the habit of going well and using his back. Work sessions in the arena should last for about 20 to 30 minutes, and hacking should start as soon as possible. If the horse lacks physical maturity or deteriorates in his way of going, alternate working in the arena with work on the lunge. Three sessions per week in the arena is enough for most 4-year-olds.

WALK When a horse is first ridden in an arena, there should be plenty of rest periods when he is kept in walk on a long rein.

TROTTING This 4-year old shows how a young horse should go from the beginning, accepting the rider, using his back, being calm, and moving forwards willingly.

CANTERING Watch to see if there is a period of suspension in the canter. If there is not, try going a little faster. Otherwise, go back to trot and aim to improve the horse's impulsion.

RIDING OUTSIDE THE ARENA

When you begin to ride out of the arena, great care should be taken when introducing the horse to traffic. Let him spend time just watching traffic before he is asked to pass it on the road. Most horses will be very good in this situation but if they have a bad early experience it will take a long time to restore their confidence.

At this stage, a few slightly longer hacks of 1 to 2 hours are very beneficial for the horse mentally. In addition, the young horse should be ridden in the field and cantered uphill in straight lines. At all times, the horse should work well and be happy and comfortable. After approximately 2 to 4 weeks of riding in the arena and out hacking, the young horse will be ready to jump with the rider on his back for the first time.

CANTERING UPHILL Going uphill, the horse has to work too hard to misbehave very much. The rider keeps the horse's head a little high to prevent any possibility of it going down, which might encourage the horse to think of bucking.

HACKING OUT

On a hack, the young horse should be led out by an older horse. This will boost his confidence and help him get used to riding in company. For the first hack, an ideal start is a narrow lane leading uphill. In these early days, especially, make sure that someone knows where you are going and when you will return.

JUMPING WITH THE RIDER

All horses can jump if their training follows a logical progression and they are not frightened. If a jumping session is to be successful, the rider must be experienced and the correct preparatory work must have been completed on the flat. The key to any set of fences – a grid – is to build backwards so that the fence that is introduced at the start of a training session ends up as the final fence when the grid is built. It is vital that the horse is confident about jumping the last fence comfortably.

A SUITABLE RIDER

A rider who is going to jump a young horse should be experienced, lightweight, and athletic. Things can happen very quickly and you need to be so familiar with the situation that you respond automatically. An unexpected little trip or a small movement sideways is of little consequence to an advanced rider, but it can be the start of a chain of events that would put a novice rider in difficulties. Even an experienced rider needs to hold on to the mane or neck strap at times, particularly if a horse is feeling fresh. Nevertheless, a young horse with a good temperament may become suitable for a less experienced rider after 6 months to a year, if the horse continues to be trained with the help of a good coach.

DRESSAGE WORK

There is little point in jumping unless the young horse is calm and riding forwards willingly. If your horse is excitable, then progress must be delayed until he settles. If he learns to jump by rushing at fences or becoming tense, it will take a long time to re-establish calmness. If the horse is not thinking forwards, an occasional canter in a field up a slight hill is very

USING TROT PLANKS If the use of a single placing plank is not producing a consistent take-off point, then add two more planks 1.4 m (4½ ft) apart in front of the placing plank. This encourages your horse to take regular trot steps.

good for him mentally. If there are no inclines available, canter down the long side of the arena a number of times to achieve a similar result before jumping.

PRELIMINARY EXERCISES

Keep things as simple as possible and avoid distracting or confusing a young horse with too many poles on the ground. Ground planks are safer than poles, which are more likely to

JUMPING A BANK

This type of small, solid bank is ideal for young horses. Although this is the first bank this particular horse has seen, he jumps with the perfect combination of confidence and care that is vital for successful jumping. The approach should be in trot, and the horse should be given time to look at the fence and be clear about what he is being asked to do. Note that the two hind legs are together on take-off – this is ideal and will result in a straight and balanced jump. The rider's lower leg position keeps her secure.

move and cause injury if stepped on. Repeat the exercises that you introduced at the lungeing stage (see p.74) by first walking and then trotting over a pair of planks placed 2.7–3 m (9–10 ft) apart. Then replace the second plank with two poles on the ground and two barrels and wingstands at either ends of the poles. This set-up has a gap between the barrels for the horse to go through, which guides him through the middle of the fence. It also familiarizes the horse with the use of fillers, which can save time in the long run. If young horses get used to fillers from the beginning, rather than introducing them

later on, you will find it both saves time and gives something positive to work on when otherwise you might be tempted to raise the fences too quickly.

PREPARING FOR THE FIRST FENCE

Every time you jump, you must aim for a steady, straight approach. You must also ensure that although the horse approaches in trot he lands in canter and keeps moving forwards at a steady speed. This is required in preparation for the next stage when you will canter over a fence.

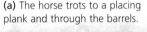

(a) The horse trots to a placing plank and through the barrels.

(b) A pole is added to create a sloping fence.

INTRODUCING A FENCE AND FILLER This 4-year old is doing this jump for the first time with a rider. He has previously been introduced to jumping on the lunge (see p.74) and has had a month of riding on the flat. First walk, then trot between two barrels with the placing plank 2.7 m (9 ft) in front (a). Then, add a pole and progressively raise it to the height of the barrel (b). Then, start making the gap between the two barrels smaller. Soon you can add a third barrel. This horse is jumping big and the fence should not be raised until the horse makes a smaller jumping effort, staying closer to the fence.

The horse makes good use of his back, but needs to take off closer to the fence. Using trot planks will help achieve this

Rider wears a body protector, a standard safety precaution when jumping all horses

The rider's rein contact allows the horse to use his head and neck

JUMPING OUT OF CANTER

Once the horse is comfortably jumping the barrel fence, a simple cross pole with a ground line and placing plank is set up about 10 m (33 ft) behind the barrels. The aim is to have the horse trot into the cross poles, land in canter, and take two canter strides before jumping his first fence in canter. Later on, the distance between fences can be reduced to one stride, but two or three strides gives more time for the rider to make any necessary alterations.

Finally, a back pole can be added to turn the barrels into an oxer (see pp.190–91). The highest point of the jump will now be over the middle of the oxer, which is the equivalent of lengthening the distance between the fences (see p.209). So the distance may have to be adjusted slightly.

The oxer will encourage the horse to make a good shape over the fence. As you carefully progress with this exercise over the following weeks, he will quickly gain confidence and strength. Once again, it is important to be aware if one particular hind leg is always in front of the other on take-off. If it is, the horse should cease jumping for a while and do more flat work to develop his weaker side and weaker hind leg (see pp.72–73). If this is not done, your horse will become habitually crooked over the fence. This is a common problem that takes a long time to improve unless it is tackled at an early stage.

LEFT AND RIGHT CANTER LEAD

The ability to land after a fence cantering on the right or left lead equally easily is a key foundation exercise for jumping. To strike off on the left leg on landing from a fence, the rider looks towards the left, moves both hands slightly to the left without pulling back, and puts a little more weight in the left stirrup. This is reversed when going to the right. If this is difficult in one direction, more flat work should be done. Eventually, just the rider's change of weight in the saddle should produce the desired canter lead even when cantering on a straight line after a fence.

BUILDING THE GRID BACKWARDS

First, jump the fence with the barrels, approaching in trot. Then add a placing fence two strides behind the fence and jump both fences. Building the grid backwards helps avoid giving your horse a bad experience.

Concentrate on controlling the direction

Maintain a soft, allowing rein contact in the last stride

USING LEFT AND RIGHT CANTER

If the rider does not direct the horse to land on a specific lead, the horse will tend to land on the same lead. This will gradually make your horse even more one-sided than he already is. By teaching a horse to canter left or right on landing (see box, left), and developing the flat work, your horse will eventually be able to land equally easily on the left or right canter lead while jumping on a straight line. If your horse continually wishes to stay on just one canter lead, then the other rein should be used more often. If the horse does not improve quickly, you will have to stop jumping and return to flat work. Even in a grid that is set up on a straight line, try to be aware of which canter lead your horse is on between fences. If he is always on the same lead, you will need to check on your balance and, again, return to the flat work.

INTRODUCING NATURAL FENCES

Once the horse is jumping well in the arena, he has reached the exciting stage where he can tackle small, natural obstacles in the countryside. Hacking is the introduction to cross-country work. Put yourself in the place of the young horse who may have spent his whole life up until now in a small number of paddocks or working in the arena: any trip out hacking is a great adventure, and it takes time for him to get used to the different sights and sounds. As he becomes steadier and calmer,

you can begin to go up and down gently sloping hills and over little banks, ditches, and logs that you may encounter on the hack. This is all excellent for developing the horse's confidence, co-ordination, and proprioceptive sense (see p.47). As the young horse begins to trust his rider, he will also begin to tackle obstacles that he would not attempt if he was riderless. The horse-and-rider partnership is beginning in earnest.

MAKING PROGRESS

From small, natural fences, you can progress to jumping a whole range of cross-country fences in miniature. There is a huge advantage to doing this with a young horse: if he has a pleasant experience he will always come back to cross-country work with confidence later on in life. Conversely, if a young horse does not jump cross-country fences, a later introduction will not be as successful. The only thing to be careful about is to be aware if one hind leg is always in front of the other on take-off. You will see this particularly when jumping banks from trot or a slow speed. If this is the case, you must wait a little while and your horse should do more flat work to develop his weaker side.

You will find that your young horse will naturally make flying changes in canter – go from one canter lead to the other – as you change the rein. This is good as long as you deliberately straighten the neck and then ask for the change with your new outside leg by drawing it back a little and then forwards again, combined with a tiny bend into the new direction. This will help teach the horse only to do a flying change when it is asked for.

Keep your weight through your legs and hold the mane

Allow the horse to jump naturally

ADDING THE BACK RAIL This young horse is jumping an oxer with a rider for the first time. The preparation has been done well, so the horse takes it in his stride.

TRAINING CHALLENGES

CHALLENGE	POSSIBLE CAUSES	SOLUTIONS
AVOIDING BEING CAUGHT	• Cheeky	• If you cannot catch your horse easily there is little point following him with a bucket of nuts that he largely ignores. The short-term solution is to find a way to herd him into the stable and then catch him, if necessary with the help of a second person. Then, once your horse is caught, give him a reward. The permanent solution involves either lungeing (see pp.68–69) or loose schooling. Loose schooling, where you work your horse without any tack, is particularly suitable for young horses who have not been introduced to tack, or older, spoilt horses who have got used to fighting against it. Ideally, you should initially work your horse loose in a round pen of approximately 15 m (50 ft) in diameter; in a small space, the horse soon realizes that he cannot run away. Open up communication and build up trust with the horse by asking him to go forwards in walk and trot, changing the rein, and halting. Eventually, he will start wanting to turn towards you and to follow you around. At this stage, catching him will be easy. If the exercise in the round pen is repeated a few times you will also be able to catch him in the field. The same results can be achieved with lungeing. If your horse has not been lunged before, however, he will probably be concerned about the lunge rope and it will take more skill and sensitivity to achieve the same result.
	• Afraid	• If your horse is frightened the same solutions apply, but it will take longer to achieve results.
REFUSING TO BE LED	• Fear	• If your horse is afraid, lungeing (see pp.68–69) or loose schooling should provide the quickest solutions. As soon as the horse understands that communication is possible, his fear tends to disappear – this will be obvious when he begins to breathe normally.
	• Lack of understanding	• If your horse simply does not understand what is required of him, go back to early training methods for teaching him to lead (see pp.66–67). Carry a thin but fairly rigid stick in your outside hand. Use this to touch the horse on the quarters when you want to encourage him to go forwards. Ask him to walk forwards one or two steps before halting and rewarding, rather than walking for sustained periods. Always try to stay close to his shoulder so that he does not tread on your toes.
	• Unwillingness	• If your horse does not want to be led, it is safest to teach him to be accepting in a round pen or small arena. Especially with a young horse, it is not a good idea to be too assertive about him going forwards when there is a person very close to his front end.

CHALLENGE	POSSIBLE CAUSES	SOLUTIONS
TURNING QUARTERS TOWARDS YOU	• Pain	• If your horse consistently turns his quarters towards you, try lungeing (pp.68–69) or loose schooling work. The origin of problems with most difficult horses lies in pain and bad experiences. If riding produces pain in the feet or back then it is understandable that the horse develops strategies to avoid being ridden. Always get your vet to check the horse over. When you are in a stable, never walk to the back to reach a horse's head. Always ask the horse to walk forwards on a half circle until he is facing you by the door.
	• Aggression	• The same strategy explained above applies.
TURNING AROUND ON LUNGE	• Fear	• If your horse is afraid on the lunge, he will tend to start walking backwards away from you as soon as you stop. If you develop good communication and reward the desired behaviour, this action will quickly disappear. Always make it obvious which direction the horse can go in by giving him space to move forwards. Then, reward with your voice.
	• Preference for one rein	• Some horses will turn on to their favourite rein during lungeing work because they have learnt that it will stop or disrupt the work session. Change your lungeing position so that you reduce the angle between the lunge rope and the horse. It is then possible to stay more behind the horse, and it is easier to keep him going on the one rein. With this type of horse, who is essentially being naughty, it is one of the very few times that a little smack with the lunge whip on the quarters may be appropriate. Always be very quick to follow up the desired behaviour with a verbal reward.
	• Submission	• If your horse has not yet developed a relationship with humans, it is normal, after a period of lungeing, for him suddenly to say, "I am going to join your team". At this stage it is natural for him to want to turn and face the lunger. In this case, he is not being bad mannered or difficult – in fact, he should be rewarded for this attitude. You do not want him to learn to evade working on the lunge, however, by stopping and turning his quarters to the outside, so this response has to be modified. Do this by facing more in the same direction as the horse. Move quietly to get closer to him before he halts. It is then possible for you and the horse to accept each other in halt without the horse moving towards you. From this it is an easy progression to halt the horse at the end of the lunge line without him moving. This is also good training for halting him under saddle when you want to get him in the habit of halting and staying still from the beginning.

TRAINING CHALLENGES

CHALLENGE	POSSIBLE CAUSES	SOLUTIONS
TOO MUCH BEND IN THE NECK	• Lungeing circle too small	• When you are in the middle of a lungeing circle, it is sometimes difficult to see that the size of the circle is creating a problem. Generally speaking, try to lunge on a circle of 15–20 m (50–65 ft). This will also reduce the forces on the horse's legs, avoiding unnecessary injury.
	• Pulling on the lunge rope	• If your horse is allowed to continually pull on the lunge rope he will invariably end up bending his neck so much to the inside that he falls to the outside of the circle. Initially you need to allow him to lunge on a bigger circle, closer to the arena fence. In this way, he will have nothing to pull against, which in turn means he will keep a straighter neck. Then, ask him to go forwards.
	• Not thinking forwards	• Encourage the horse to think forwards – for example, by assertively asking him to continue trotting or cantering even as he passes the arena gate. You will soon find that he stops hanging to the outside and bending his neck inwards. If your horse is doing the opposite, by bending his neck to the outside and falling in, this will also stop as he becomes calm and thinks forwards. For horses that are bending their necks excessively in one or both directions, using cross-reins (see p.387) will help control the bend in the neck without pulling the head in or shortening the neck unnaturally. Cross-reins are like side-reins (see pp.72–73) and are attached to the bit at each side. They go just in front of the withers where they cross over to the other side and attach to the roller (where you would normally attach the breastplate). Cross-reins are also ideal to use as a safe introduction to side-reins.
LIFTING HIS TONGUE	• Too much pressure on the tongue	• Many horses dislike pressure on the tongue and they will lift the tongue to try to push the bit away. Pressure can be caused by side-reins that are too tight, and by long reining with too heavy a hand (see p.73). Use a jointed snaffle that is slightly rounded in shape from one side of the mouth to the other to reduce pressure (straight-bar and French-link snaffles tend to do the opposite).
	• Habit	• Having learnt to lift the tongue, some horses continue to do it simply through habit and often without a reason. Working without a bit for a sustained period of time can cure the problem, but the greatest care must be taken to avoid strong pressure on the tongue thereafter. The straps that link the bit and the noseband on a multibridle are very effective at keeping pressure off the mouth.

CHALLENGE	POSSIBLE CAUSES	SOLUTIONS
HOLDING HEAD UP	• Fresh	• It is natural for a fresh horse to raise his head up to scan the horizon and for him to have exaggerated, bouncy steps. This is evidence of the horse's well-being – wait for him to settle and become calm. This may not happen in the first work session but, given sufficient time, and as long as the horse is not in pain or frightened, he will eventually relax and lower his head and neck.
	• Discomfort in the mouth	• If a horse is unhappy in the mouth, he will fight against the bit. Take the bit out of the horse's mouth; if he immediately improves, then you have confirmed that the bit is the problem. Check his teeth for sharpness or wolf teeth. Even if there are no teeth problems it is better to then work the horse for a period without a bit. If a horse works well on the lunge he will have a white mouth (see p.64) even without a bit. It is at this stage that the bit can be reintroduced (but without any pressure from the side reins). If, when you do attach the side reins, the horse becomes unhappy again, reduce the pressure on the tongue by attaching the bit to the front of the noseband. With horses that constantly have mouth problems, it is probably best to use a bitless bridle for 3 to 9 months before trying the bit again.
	• Lack of impulsion	• If your horse engages his hind legs and arches his back, he will naturally lower his head. This will in turn help to arch the back still further. If necessary, do lungeing work to encourage the horse to lift and use his back (see pp.72–73).

TRAINING CHALLENGES

CHALLENGE	POSSIBLE CAUSES	SOLUTIONS
TONGUE OVER THE BIT	• Habit	• Once a horse starts to lift his tongue, he will soon learn to put his tongue over the bit, and this can become a habit. In the majority of horses it starts because the horse is uncomfortable. Use the same approach as outlined in "Lifting his tongue" (see p.86).
	• Too much pressure on the tongue	• A mouthpiece that goes forwards and upwards from the bars of the mouth at an angle of 45 degrees takes pressure off the tongue. It also makes it difficult for the horse to put his tongue over the bit. Any bits with a gag action, such as a Dutch gag (a three-ring snaffle) have the same effect. An alternative remedy would be to tie the tongue down (as is done with many racehorses), but this is tackling the symptom rather than curing the problem.
NAPPING (ATTEMPTING TO RETURN HOME)	• Pain	• If a horse naps repeatedly, despite being asked to do things reasonably and clearly, you must arrange a veterinary examination to check that he is not in pain.
	• Fear	• If nothing is found in the veterinary examination, it may be that the horse is afraid. Like children, horses can be afraid of many things that we would consider silly. A shadow, a noise, or a movement in the hedge may all frighten a horse and cause napping. Punishment is therefore unlikely to be effective. A progressive training programme, working the horse either loose or on the lunge, is extremely effective. The company of older, more experienced horses can also work wonders in these cases.
	• Naughtiness	• If pain or fear does not seem to be the problem, napping may be a learnt behaviour. Excessive demands or the use of unclear or confusing aids can teach the horse first to ignore and then to resist his rider, and eventually to nap. In the process of correcting this it is vital to use simple exercises and give obvious rewards. After this, you should be gradually more assertive and tackle areas where there are minor resistances. It may be necessary, for example, to reinforce slight use of the leg with a stronger use of the leg and/or a smack of the stick on the horse's quarters. Careful consideration should be given before doing this, and at no time should the stick be used repeatedly or in anger because this is counter-productive. Dealing with this type of problem is difficult if your horse is over fresh. Turning him out more, reducing his feed, and using a horse walker (see p.52) will all be helpful.

CHALLENGE	POSSIBLE CAUSES	SOLUTIONS
REARING	• Trapped and frightened	• In the wild, horses naturally react to danger by turning and galloping away – they only learn to rear when they are feeling trapped. Your strategy to prevent rearing should be to push the horse forwards in any direction as he threatens to rear – horses cannot rear as they move forwards. As he moves, reward him with your voice and by gently rubbing your hand on his neck. Then, ask him to do easier exercises and slowly build up his trust.
	• Conditioning	• A horse will learn to rear if the rider makes excessive demands and gives him something to fight against. When the horse discovers that rearing is an effective way to avoid doing something his rider wants, he will continue to do it. Most horses, however, will forget about rearing if their work is enjoyable, particularly when riding in company. Horses always look for the most comfortable solution, and if they can immediately feel that life is easier when they comply, they are more likely to be amenable. Strong punishment is rarely effective and is especially counter-productive if used while the horse is rearing or just afterwards. The only time to be stricter is just before a horse rears, but this takes experience to predict.
BUCKING	• Fresh	• It is natural for a horse to buck and squeal a little when he is fresh so this is not something to worry about. With a young horse that is fresh, it is better to avoid putting the saddle on, otherwise he will learn to buck against the girth.
	• Reaction against the girth	• It is easy for a young horse to frighten himself as he tenses against a fixed girth: his natural reaction is to round his back and buck. The further back the girth is, the more this happens (which is why the loin strap on a rodeo horse is called a bucking strap). Use a breastplate and never have the girth tight to begin with. Make sure you use a girth with an elasticated insert, so that it gives a little with the horse's movement.
	• Conditioning	• If a horse learns that work stops as soon as his rider is thrown off he will quickly realize the merits of bucking. In this case, it is important to re-introduce an experienced rider as quickly as possible to help avoid this happening again. It may require additional lungeing work (see pp.72–73) and repeating some earlier training steps, but it can all be done in the same session.
	• Not ready to be ridden	• Do not hurry the process or leave out any steps, and always be guided by an experienced coach. Difficult horses need specialist expertise and your safety must always come first.

CHAPTER FOUR

BALANCED RIDING

Good balance is the key to successful riding. This chapter explains how to achieve a good, basic position in the saddle. Once you have achieved this, it will be easy to adapt it for different riding disciplines by lengthening or shortening your stirrups. For example, in dressage most of your weight will be in the saddle so you will need to ride with longer stirrups, but, for jumping, you will need to keep a light seat and your weight in your legs, so you must ride with shorter stirrups. The key is to stay in harmony with the horse's movements at all times, so that you are able to give effective aids and remain secure.

To become a better rider, you will also need to develop empathy with the horse, a feel for how he moves, an understanding of all the training exercises, and good communication skills. Practising all the skills explained in this chapter can turn you from a beginner into a proficient rider.

UNDERSTANDING BALANCE

You need to work at three balances when riding: your own balance, the balance of the horse, and the balance of you and the horse together. The position in which you can be deemed balanced will depend on the activity you are doing, such as dressage or jumping, and the balance of the horse will depend on his level of training. Understanding how balance works and how you as the rider can affect it is the key to an effective partnership with your horse.

THE HORSE'S NATURAL BALANCE

In a standing horse, the natural centre of gravity is situated approximately half-way between the withers and tummy – under the saddle flaps, close to the girth line. The horse puts approximately 60 per cent of his weight on his forelegs and 40 per cent on his hind legs, although with some heavily built horses the proportions may well be closer to 66 per cent and 33 per cent. It is also important to understand a horse's balance while he is in motion, not just when he is stationary. A horse's spine has a limited ability to change shape so his centre of gravity does not move as much as it can in some other animals. In a galloping racehorse, particularly at the finish line, the centre of gravity moves slightly forwards. In dressage, a well-trained horse is able to carry more than 50 per cent of his weight on his hind legs.

THE RIDER'S EFFECT ON BALANCE

With a rider in the saddle, the centre of gravity of the combined unit of the horse and rider is approximately 10 per cent higher than with the horse on his own, but it is in the same

DRESSAGE BALANCE In dressage, keep your balance through your seat. Maintain a vertical line between your shoulder, hip, and the back of your heel.

JUMPING BALANCE In showjumping, keep your balance by putting your weight through your lower legs. Maintain a vertical line from the middle of the knee to the ball of the foot.

vertical line. The proportional distribution of weight on the horse's front and hind legs should not be affected – if this were not the case, the horse's natural paces and way of going would be changed by having a rider on his back. If a rider keeps a light seat, most of their weight is dispersed through their legs to the stirrup irons and the part of the saddle under the stirrup leathers. These leathers are attached to the stirrup bars, which are just behind the front arch of the saddle, so most of the rider's weight will be here, near the horse's withers. A well-fitting saddle will spread the load a little, but the majority of the weight will still be forwards.

USING THE HINDQUARTERS

During a horse's training, the hind legs are encouraged to carry more of the burden so that there is equal weight on the hind- and forelegs, without restricting the natural paces. This allows the horse to carry the rider easily in sitting trot, even though this pace brings the rider's weight slightly back. As the weight distribution is adjusted by training, the horse's centre of gravity moves slightly backwards. At this stage, it is actually easier for the horse if the rider puts more weight in their seat, as in dressage, thus keeping their centre of gravity over the horse's centre of gravity. However, if the horse is jumping, the rider will have to put more weight through their legs in order to keep in line with the horse's centre of gravity.

When riding on a straight line, as well as being balanced over hind- and forelegs, the horse and rider must be balanced vertically, with equal weight on both sides. As a horse goes around a turn, however, he will put a little weight to the inside. The rider's weight should mirror this weight redistribution, so that the horse can maintain his balance (see box, right).

POSITION IN THE SADDLE

In order to maintain a good balance, both your seat and the saddle must be central. A crooked saddle position is caused either by an unbalanced rider or a loose girth. Even if a horse leans in around a corner, the saddle should remain central. Although putting a little weight temporarily to the inside will signal to the horse that you want to go in that direction, movement as great as that shown here will hinder the horse's balance and he will have to lean in the opposite direction to compensate.

SADDLE TO THE INSIDE

SADDLE TO THE OUTSIDE

SEAT TO THE INSIDE

SEAT TO THE OUTSIDE

LEVELS OF TRAINING

A novice horse can be trained to have equal weight on both his hind- and forelegs (see right) and to carry the rider in the sitting trot. With progressive training, he will be able to carry more weight on his hind legs, making him lighter in his front end so that he appears as if he is going uphill (see far right). Even a novice horse needs to carry more weight behind when taking off over a fence.

The horse's natural centre of gravity has moved back a little with training

NOVICE HORSE

The outline of this dressage horse is slightly shortened

ADVANCED HORSE

ADJUSTING YOUR STIRRUP LENGTH

The reasons for choosing a particular stirrup length are purely practical. In dressage, most of the rider's weight is in the saddle, so you balance on your seat. It is easier to do this if the stirrups are long and your leg is in a naturally extended position – this is known as riding long. However, your lower leg must remain in contact with the horse's sides because it is through this contact that the leg aids are given.

When jumping or riding cross country, the rider's weight is not always in the saddle, but through the legs. In order to keep your balance over the horse's centre of gravity as he jumps, you have to be able to keep your seat out of the saddle without losing the support of your lower leg. It is therefore necessary to ride short – by shortening the stirrups and balancing by keeping your weight in your legs. As you go faster and need more security, it is necessary to ride even shorter so that you adopt a position similar to squatting. This position increases your stability because it gives you a lower centre of gravity than you would have if you were more upright. From a showjumping length, you may shorten by two or three holes for cross country, and lengthen two or three holes for dressage. The amount you shorten and lengthen will depend on your size in relation to the width of your horse – a short-legged person on a wide horse will not need to adjust the length of stirrups by much.

GIVING AIDS

The point on the horse's body at which you apply the leg aid is important if the horse is to understand you. The leg aid to ask the horse to go forwards is always given in the same place on his side. When riding long, you give the aid with your calves. When riding shorter, you naturally give the aid lower down your leg. A short rider on a big horse may have to bring their leg a little forwards in order to use this same spot.

WRONG POSITION IN SHORT STIRRUPS

Whe you ride with shortened stirrups, your lower leg must provide a secure base for your balance. Here, the rider's knee is too far forwards and the heel too far back with the weight in the toes. This will have the effect of tipping the rider forwards and the leg aid will be given too far back for the horse to understand it.

RIDING WITH LONG AND SHORT STIRRUPS

DRESSAGE LENGTH The angle at the back of your knees should be around 120–130 degrees, with your knees and toes pointing forwards. If you ride longer than this, it is not possible to keep the lower leg in contact. If your horse is very wide, you will have to ride a little shorter.

JUMPING LENGTH The angle at the back of your knees should be around 105–115 degrees. This shorter position makes it easier to keep the balance through the leg in order to go with the horse's jump. If you are short and the horse is big, it may help to ride a little longer.

CROSS COUNTRY LENGTH The angle at the back of your knees should be around 90–100 degrees. The disadvantage of riding shorter is that there is more weight in the leg so it is more difficult to use the leg aids. The shorter you ride, the lower you should keep your heel.

MISCONCEPTIONS ABOUT BALANCE

There are two big misconceptions about balance that prevent many riders and horses from fulfilling their potential. The first is that it is possible for the rider to support the horse through the rein contact, thus preventing him losing his balance. It is important to remember that the horse carries us, not the other way round – it is physically impossible for the rider to support the horse's balance. We can, however, help the horse maintain his balance by encouraging him to have the right speed and level of impulsion.

The second misconception is that it is possible to improve the horse's balance by moving your weight further back in the saddle, regardless of the way the horse is going. In fact, this can prevent the horse from arching and using his back. If taken to the extreme, where the rider's weight is over the horse's hindquarters, this can cause the horse's hind legs to become overburdened and unable to function normally. The only way to get the hind legs to carry more weight is by gradual and progressive training. Developing the horse athletically and increasing impulsion will bring the weight of both horse and rider further back, as one unit (see p.93).

If a horse loses his balance, he naturally slows down to regain it. This is what the rider should encourage the horse to do in order to make his balance more stable. However, because the horse has four legs, it is remarkable how well he can balance, even when his weight is too far

forwards. Unfortunately, this also increases the strain on the front feet and forelegs, which can in turn increase the risk of injury.

As a horse learns to be more evenly balanced, this strain on his forelegs is reduced, which will extend his working life. The easy way to instantly reduce wear and tear on the forelegs and improve a horse's balance is to work him going up an incline. Small hills are an invaluable resource in helping a horse achieve a natural balance.

A NATURAL BALANCE

When toddlers squat, they naturally keep the knee over the foot, not in front of it. A jockey will use a similar position in order to keep his balance secure, despite the fact that his seat is out of the saddle. It means that he can keep his centre of gravity low and adjust his knee and hip joints to absorb the movement of the horse. Skate boarders and skiers also adopt this position to absorb the shock of bumpy ground. It is this lower leg position that you need to adopt when you shorten your stirrups.

RIDING SHORTER Even when riding as short as this steeplechase jockey, the lower leg position will remain the same. Although the stirrup iron may be behind the ball of the foot, the heel is still kept down. This helps to keep the leg functioning like a spring.

The jockey is keeping his hips level with his knee, giving him a very low centre of gravity

BALANCE AND FORM

To change your balance, you need to change the form – or shape – of your position in the saddle. The way you need to balance yourself depends on the demands of the activity you are practising but, once you have perfected the basic position, you can adjust it accordingly. In all cases, have a vertical line from the middle of the knee to the ball of the foot. This leg alignment allows you to always have your leg around the narrowest part of the horse and stay secure.

A FORM FOR ALL ACTIVITIES

The great advantage of a good basic riding position is that it allows for an easy, natural progression to riding with a longer length of stirrup (as for dressage) or shorter (as for cross country). The lower leg will move up or down the vertical line (see line A in all diagrams, right), but will remain alongside the girth. Whatever type of saddle you use, the girth goes in the same place – around the narrowest part of the horse's body. Keeping your leg alongside the girth means that, regardless of stirrup length, the lower leg is on or close to a sensitive area of the horse's sides, which is the ideal place to give leg aids.

For example, when riding dressage in a general-purpose saddle (1) the rider keeps their shoulders over their seat and a vertical line from the middle of their knee to the ball of their foot – in parallel with the line of the girth. This is the basic position used for novice riders, with the leg close to the sensitive part of the horse's sides. If you lengthen the stirrup leathers in this saddle, your legs will be around the wider part of the horse and the lower leg will not be able to stay in contact with his horse's sides. However, if you ride in a dressage saddle (2) you can ride with this longer length and still keep the leg around the narrow part of the horse. This is because the seat of a dressage saddle is further forwards. In this position, you will have a straight line between the shoulder, hip, and the back of the heel.

ADJUSTING YOUR STIRRUPS

When you shorten the stirrup leathers for jumping (3), your seat moves back a little and your shoulders forwards a little – the classic balance and position for showjumping. When the stirrup leathers are shortened even more for cross country (5), the angles at the knee and hip close further but the shoulders remain in the same line – approximately over the knee. From the horse's point of view, these two different positions are the same: the rider's weight will act in exactly the same place.

From the rider's point of view, the stirrup length can be more significant. The shorter you ride, the more difficult it is to keep balanced when you ride around tight turns and the more difficult it is to give leg aids. It is easier, however, to keep balanced as you jump, particularly on the ascent and descent, and you will also be more secure if your horse hits a fence. The reverse is true if you ride longer.

STEEPLECHASING This sport involves racing over a course of birch fences at speed. Since there are no tight turns to deal with, riders use very short stirrups to help them stay secure over fences.

A RANGE OF BALANCES

1. BASIC DRESSAGE POSITION This diagram shows a good basic position if you are riding in a general-purpose or jumping saddle. If you incline forwards a little and put more weight through the legs, you will have the balance for rising trot.

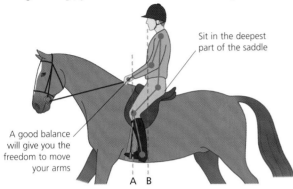

Sit in the deepest part of the saddle

A good balance will give you the freedom to move your arms

A   B

2. ADVANCED DRESSAGE POSITION The stirrups are long and the leg extended. The vertical line between the riders shoulder, hip, and back of the heel is maintained for all the work in a dressage saddle.

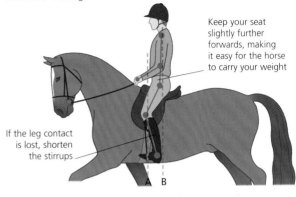

Keep your seat slightly further forwards, making it easy for the horse to carry your weight

If the leg contact is lost, shorten the stirrups

A   B

3. CLASSIC SHOWJUMPING POSITION In this position, the riders shoulders are over the knees, taking the weight off the seat and into the legs. It is sometimes called the two-point position.

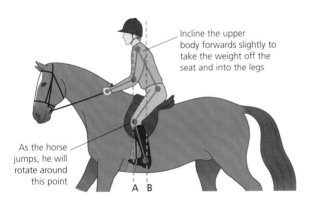

Incline the upper body forwards slightly to take the weight off the seat and into the legs

As the horse jumps, he will rotate around this point

A   B

4. SHOWJUMPING POSITION As your horse becomes more advanced and carries more weight in his hindquarters, you can put more weight in the saddle.

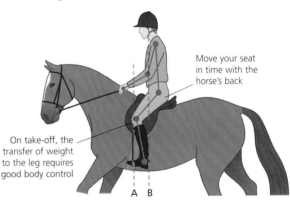

Move your seat in time with the horse's back

On take-off, the transfer of weight to the leg requires good body control

A   B

5. CROSS-COUNTRY POSITION The shorter length of stirrup is required to give the rider security over fences and to cope with drop fences (see diagram 6). It does not affect the vertical position of the lower leg.

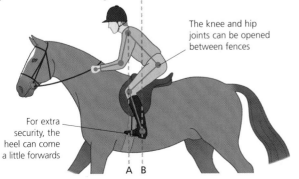

The knee and hip joints can be opened between fences

For extra security, the heel can come a little forwards

A   B

6. CROSS-COUNTRY SAFETY POSITION When going down a drop, open up the angles of the knee and hip to assume the equivalent of an advanced dressage position.

Keep your weight through to the heel, rather than the ball of the foot

Let the reins slip through the hands

A   B

MOVING WITH THE HORSE

It is only possible to keep a consistent balance in the saddle if you move in harmony with the horse. This physical unity is vital for allowing and encouraging the horse's natural movement, for giving aids, and for your security as a rider. If you are not in harmony with the horse, you will find that communication is compromised, and you may feel yourself being bumped out of the saddle. The degree of the horse's movement – and therefore your own – varies between the different paces.

MOVING IN WALK

In walk, you need to go with the movement of the horse's back, head, and neck. The back moves with the hind legs, so your seat will naturally swing slightly forwards and back twice every stride. Just let your seat move and you will soon feel the swing. At the same time, the horse's head nods forwards and back in time with each hind leg. Let your arms go with this movement by opening and closing your shoulder and elbow joints. If your arms stay static, the rein contact will vary and may restrict the horse, making his walk unnatural. To encourage a natural movement of the head, slightly lighten the rein contact.

MOVING IN TROT

In trot, there is less movement of the horse's head, so keeping a consistent rein contact is much easier. In rising trot, going with the horse is not difficult because you rise out of the saddle as the horse's back rises. To go with this movement in sitting trot, however, requires very good control of the lower back, and most novice riders will only be able to do a little sitting trot at a time. Many riders accommodate the movement of the trot by collapsing the small of their back as the horse rises, but this puts more weight on the horse's back just as his feet leave the ground. Other riders lean back to anchor their seat to the saddle, but this disrupts the trot. The better the trot is and the more the horse's back is softly arched, the more comfortable the sitting trot will be.

MOVEMENT IN WALK

MOVEMENT IN TROT

RHYTHM OF DIFFERENT PACES

There is a period of suspension between each trot step and between each canter stride that produces a wave motion in the horse's back. The rise and fall of this wave is quite small in trot, but quite large in canter. The rider has to accomodate this movement and allow the seat to rise and fall in time with the horse without their own weight in the seat changing.

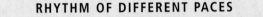

WORKING CANTER

3.7 m (12 ft) stride

WORKING TROT

1.4 m (4½ ft) step

MOVING IN CANTER

In canter, the rider has to go with the rise and lower of the horse as his feet leave and return to the ground. If the rider's seat goes with the horse it will improve the canter. So, as the horse's legs enter the period of suspension – the moment where all four feet are off the ground – let your seat swing upwards and forwards. Then move back again as the horse's feet touch the ground.

It is useful to learn how to do this on the lunge, holding on to the front arch of the saddle. Try to allow your seat to move under your shoulders so that the whole of your body does not swing. At the same time, the horse's head and neck will lengthen slightly into each period of suspension, so let your hands go with this movement as well.

MOVEMENT IN CANTER To move with the horse in canter, imagine that your seat is making a small, anticlockwise circle every stride, with the seat reaching the bottom of the circle just before the horse's leading foreleg touches the ground.

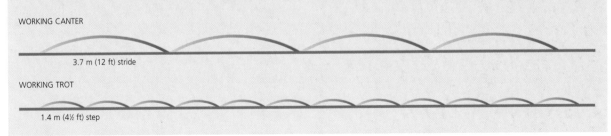

BECOMING A BETTER RIDER

You will be more comfortable in the saddle if you have a balanced, supple position and you feel secure. With a good position, you will also become more effective, because you will be able to use your leg and rein aids independently and evenly. As you develop your feel for both the movement of the horse and his state of mind, and as you begin to understand and work through the range of riding exercises, your riding skills will progress rapidly.

A SIMPLE PROGRESSION

Every novice rider needs to be shown how to sit in the saddle with a stable balance and how to take their weight through the legs, as is necessary in rising trot and when jumping. As soon as you have achieved a secure balance, you can start going with the movement of your horse, which means that you are in harmony with him. At this stage in your riding, you will immediately become more effective, because good

ACHIEVING A GOOD POSITION

KEEPING A GOOD SHAPE
Form refers to the shape of the rider's position – the body, legs, arms, hands, and fingers. Every activity requires a slightly different form, but a neutral alignment of the spine is essential for all (see p.336). This allows greater control and ease of movement as well as efficient breathing.

MAINTAINING YOUR BALANCE
A balanced position allows you to ride without gripping tightly or using great strength. It also leaves your legs and arms free to signal effectively to the horse. Your weight should be balanced solidly in your seat for dressage. As the stirrup leathers are shortened for jumping and cross country, your weight will be concentrated more through the legs.

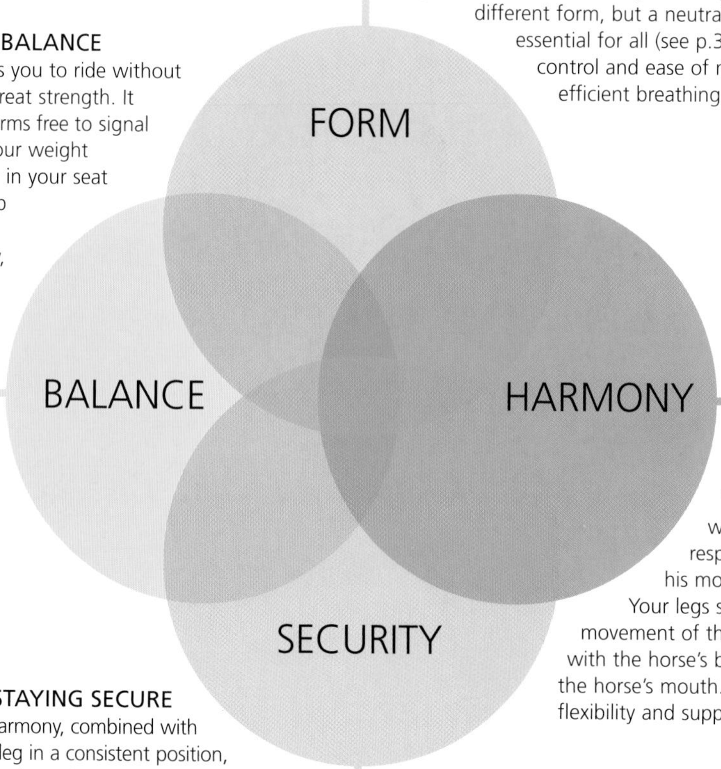

FORM

BALANCE

HARMONY

SECURITY

MOVING WITH THE HORSE
You must be in harmony with your horse if he is to respond to your aids without his movement being restricted. Your legs should go with the movement of the horse's sides, your seat with the horse's back, and your hands with the horse's mouth. This takes physical flexibility and supple joints (see p.342).

STAYING SECURE
Good balance and harmony, combined with keeping your lower leg in a consistent position, will aid your security in the saddle. It takes well-toned muscles to hold a good position for long periods, so building your strength and stamina will help you to remain secure as well as keep an even rein contact.

harmony allows both a good feel of what the horse is doing – such as being aware of which diagonal your horse is on in rising trot – and an ability to use small, more precise aids. You will be able to give the right aids at exactly the right time and really take charge of your horse. Conversely, a lack of harmony produces an inconsistent seat and uneven leg and rein contacts that only serve to confuse the horse.

As you progress, it is worthwhile working at the shape – or form – of your position. Aim to achieve a good alignment of your spine (see p. 336). You also need to be able to achieve a natural position of your arm, with a straight line between your elbow, your hand, and the horse's mouth, so that you can maintain a consistent rein contact.

You will feel even more secure in the saddle if you develop your stamina. If necessary, you may have to work at your general fitness off the horse's back (see pp. 332–51). As you ride and watch other riders, you will build up your knowledge of all the riding exercises, from simple school movements to special techniques. You will start to see how all the exercises complement and relate to each other. Continued experience and study will give you an empathy with the horse. As you start to see the world from your horse's perspective, you will make even greater progress.

BEING YOUR OWN COACH

Helping yourself to become a better rider requires a sense of mental well-being and self-confidence. Enthusiasm and a positive outlook are essential. Throughout your riding training, always remember that improvements happen gradually, and not without effort.

BECOMING MORE EFFECTIVE

BEING AWARE OF YOUR HORSE'S MOVEMENT
To do the right thing at the right time, you need to be able to physically feel what the horse is doing so that you can move in harmony with him. Practical experience gained from riding different horses and doing different activities will help you develop feel.

UNDERSTANDING YOUR HORSE
Empathy means being in tune with your horse so that he will perform with confidence and ease. Try to see your surroundings from your horse's perspective, and be aware of his state of mind so you can anticipate his reactions. A sound working knowledge of equine psychology and physiology is necessary if maximum progress is to be made.

FEEL

EMPATHY

EXERCISES

LANGUAGE

DOING EXERCISES
As you progress, you will do an increasing range of exercises in training and competition. At each level, an understanding of the purpose and relationship of these exercises, including their advantages and disadvantages, is essential if you are to achieve your full riding potential while developing your horse humanely.

GOOD COMMUNICATION
To communicate with the horse you use the voice, legs, and hands, as well as your weight. This language can invite, encourage, persuade, or, at times, demand that the horse does any of a multitude of exercises, according to his abilities and the courage of both horse and rider. Gradual refinement of this language will improve your partnership with your horse.

ACHIEVING A GOOD POSITION

A good position gives you the freedom to be an effective rider. You will have established a good position when you no longer have to think about it as you ride, but instead are able to respond automatically to changing circumstances. By using benchmarks against which you can measure your areas of strength and weakness, you can set precise goals to work towards to help you improve your position, whatever your level of riding skill.

DEVELOPING YOUR POSITION

In your first riding lessons, you learn to keep a safe position in the saddle by riding with the right length of stirrup and by keeping a vertical line from the middle of your knee to the ball of your foot. This position serves you well for walking, rising trot, and introductory jumping exercises (see pp. 32–35). If you are able to maintain a good balance in rising trot and over small jumps, you have already achieved a level of harmony with your horse's movements. You will feel secure enough in the saddle to ride a quiet horse in an enclosed arena without anxiety. As you start to progress through dressage and jump exercises, you will become more aware of your horse's movements and needs. You will continue to develop a better position in the saddle, which in turn will allow you to give clearer, more effective aids.

Using a saddle suitable for the work you are doing and for your size and shape is essential. Your coach can advise you about saddles and may also suggest lunge lessons to develop your position. This will allow you to concentrate on your

BEGINNER RIDER As a beginner rider, your main priority as far as your position is concerned is to achieve a secure balance in the rising trot. Using a well-padded, supportive saddle and wearing non-slip breeches will help. Once this has been achieved, your priority will be to let yourself move in harmony with the horse.

form and balance without having to control the horse. The more you practise, the easier it will become to hold a good position. However, it is also possible that you will unintentionally pick up some bad habits, which will block your path to future progress. Typical problems are round shoulders, a lack of control in the lower back, one-sidedness, and a lack of suppleness. One of the best ways to correct these is to do a series of exercises off the horse, aimed at improving your posture, suppleness, strength, and balance (see pp.332–51).

SETTING YOURSELF GOALS

The chart below can be used to assess your riding position and to identify your strengths and weaknesses. The levels of skill to be achieved are broadly based on competition standards and show a possible progression that can be a useful aid to goal setting and prioritizing. Every rider is an individual, however, and will develop at his or her own pace. The first goal is to be able to control a quiet, trained horse in an enclosed arena. Then the next stage is to ride the same horse outside in company and possibly jump a few small fences. Then you will begin to progress rapidly. It is important to feel positive and confident at every stage of your riding and to maintain a disciplined and pragmatic approach to your riding.

ADVANCED RIDER If you are an advanced rider, your position will have developed to such an extent that you hardly need to think about it. You will be able to adjust your position automatically to each situation, whether you are jumping uphill or going over a series of challenging fences.

POSITION BENCHMARKS

	INTRODUCTORY LEVEL OF COMPETITION	NOVICE LEVEL OF COMPETITION	INTERMEDIATE LEVEL OF COMPETITION	ADVANCED LEVEL OF COMPETITION
FORM	Sits equally on both seat bones without tucking the pelvis under or arching the back.	Achieves a neutral alignment of the spine while riding in a general-purpose saddle.	Attains a neutral alignment of the spine while riding in a dressage saddle.	Maintains a good form as habit, even at difficult moments.
BALANCE	Easily maintains a consistent balance in rising trot and over small fences.	Easily balances on seat bones in walk, trot, or canter – even without using the stirrups.	Easily balances with very short stirrups (such as a jockey does on a racehorse).	Is able to make minute changes to balance. Uses subtle weight aids.
HARMONY	Achieves good seat and leg contacts using a general-purpose saddle.	Achieves good seat, leg, and rein contacts in either a dressage or a jumping saddle.	Maintains good control of the lower back in the sitting trot.	Is able to stay as one with the horse when doing advanced dressage or showjumping.
SECURITY	Remains secure on a trained horse on a hack for periods of up to 2 hours.	Remains secure in the saddle on a fit competition horse for up to 3 hours.	Remains secure enough in the saddle to ride young or difficult horses for up to 4 hours.	Remains secure enough in the saddle to ride actively for up to 5 hours over varied terrain.

BECOMING MORE EFFECTIVE

Effectiveness has little to do with strength and a great deal to do with your ability to give clear aids. Good feel for the horse's movements will allow you to use your aids at just the right time. Being able to empathize with your horse will help you understand his reactions, as well as help you judge which exercises to attempt and how much to ask of him. Assess your current ability, and set yourself goals to work towards.

PHYSICAL EFFECTIVENESS

As you progress, you will gain a sufficiently good feel for the movement and speed of the horse to be able to identify his paces and keep in control. You will have done walking, trotting, and cantering exercises in an enclosed arena and have learnt to use your leg and rein aids to ask the horse to start, stop, and turn. You will also have started to gain an understanding of the horse's perspective on the world.

With these foundations in place, you can continue to develop your effectiveness as a rider by riding as many different horses as possible and doing as many different activities as you can. Spend time with your horse so you can see how he responds to particular situations. Learn about horse senses so you can start to see why your horse might react strangely to a particular fence or object (see pp.44–47). Do progressive exercises that help to build your own skills and communication with the horse, as well as deal with any problem areas that your horse may have. Your aim is to develop a trusting partnership, with a mutual understanding of the work required.

It is also important to ensure that you can use both sides of your body equally, so that you can work well on both reins. Everyone is one-sided to a degree, and horses are the same. To make your horse more even, you need to become more even yourself. Your co-ordination will be improved if

BEGINNER RIDER As a beginner you have to rely on your coach, but you can quickly develop the effectiveness of your leg and rein aids and start to have a feel for the horse's movements.

you do exercises off the horse's back (see pp. 332–51). As you gain more experience, your effectiveness will improve and you will progress to higher levels of riding. The broad competition levels shown in the chart below are a useful guide to monitor your progress and set yourself goals to work towards.

A good coach will be able to assess your progress and will know when you should be asking more or less of your horse. In addition, your coach will know what exercises you can do to improve your effectiveness.

MENTAL EFFECTIVENESS

Riding demands self-control and discipline, and you need to stay positive and confident if you are to achieve your goals and get the best results from your horse.

A working knowledge of mental preparation techniques will help you make the most of your physical ability (see pp. 352–71), both in your training and in your competition work. Furthermore, having an instinctive feel for your horse's movements and state of mind demands sensitivity and experience. Concentration and an ability to analyse what is happening are essential, and you may find you have to work at these off the horse. You also need a pragmatic but flexible approach in order to find the best way forwards.

ADVANCED RIDER As an advanced rider, your co-ordination will have developed to such an extent that real refinement of the aids is possible. Your horse will react to even the slightest change in position of your weight in the saddle. The key to effectiveness, however, will be a good relationship with your horse.

EFFECTIVENESS BENCHMARKS

	INTRODUCTORY LEVEL OF COMPETITION	NOVICE LEVEL OF COMPETITION	INTERMEDIATE LEVEL OF COMPETITION	ADVANCED LEVEL OF COMPETITION
FEEL	Is able to change diagonal in trot and recognize the canter lead.	Feels the regularity of the paces. Develops a feel for a horse's stride to within 60 cm (2 ft).	Feels the level of the horse's impulsion. Judges a stride to within 50 cm (1 ft 6 in).	Has instinctive feel for the horse's movements. Judges a stride to within 30 cm (1 ft).
EXERCISE	Is proficient at dressage and jumping level 1 exercises (see p. 161 and p. 231).	Is proficient at dressage, jumping, and cross-country level 2 exercises (see p. 161, p. 231, p. 297).	Is proficient at dressage, jumping, and cross-country level 3 exercises (see p. 161, p. 231, p. 297).	Is proficient at dressage, jumping, and cross-country level 4 exercises (see p. 161, p. 231, p. 297).
EMPATHY	Has an appreciation of the horse's herd instincts, and the basic needs and senses of the horse.	Understands how the horse learns through conditioning and reinforcements.	Remains in tune with the horse and understands his reactions to different situations.	Is able to keep a step ahead of the horse's responses and adapt accordingly.
LANGUAGE	Achieves an independent use of seat and legs and some co-ordination of the aids.	Achieves an independent seat, and leg and hand co-ordination. Puts the horse between the aids.	Is able to use several aids at once, and is able to control difficult horses.	Achieves refinement of aids, including use of the seat and lower back.

CHAPTER FIVE

DRESSAGE TRAINING AND COMPETITION

Dressage, or working on the flat, enhances not only the horse's strength and co-ordination but also his gracefulness of movement. The aim is to train both the mind and body of the horse so that he and the rider can achieve their long-term goals in any equestrian sphere. Dressage is the core of all riding activities, including jumping, but it can also be taken to an advanced level for its own sake.

In this chapter, you will become familiar with the horse's paces and transitions, and with the various school movements and exercises. From learning to ride circles, turns, straight lines, and bends, you can progress to the more intricate school movements, such as pirouette and half pass. You will also find advice for preparing for competition at all levels, and a troubleshooting section to help you deal with any challenges that arise.

INSPIRATIONAL DRESSAGE

The highest levels of dressage take years of training to achieve, but when it is done well, especially when performed to music, it is spectacular to watch. For the rider, it is a hugely challenging and rewarding sport. Even if you do not plan to compete, practising dressage will make your horse more pleasant and responsive to ride. It is the foundation for all riding, with the key elements being an absence of force in the rider, and responsiveness and athleticism in the horse.

ORIGINS OF DRESSAGE

The origins of dressage developed primarily from the classical riding of the Renaissance period, although its roots can be traced to the time of Xenophon (*c.* 435–354 BC), the Greek soldier, essayist, and historian, whose book, *On the Art of Horsemanship*, is one of the most famous works on equitation. Xenophon wrote: "If one induces the horse to assume that carriage which it would adopt … when displaying its beauty, then, one directs [it] to appear joyous and magnificent, proud and remarkable for being ridden."

ULTIMATE PARTNERSHIP The 1988 German Olympic champions, Nicole Uphoff and Rembrandt, formed a true partnership. Rembrandt was lightweight and small, but he was successful because his paces were correct and he created real impulsion.

The sport has continued to evolve; even within the last 100 years, dressage and dressage training have changed dramatically. For example, when it was first included in the Olympic Games in Stockholm, in 1912, the piaffe and passage (see p.157) were not performed; instead, competitors had to jump over five obstacles, the highest being 110 cm (43 in) and the last being a barrel, which was rolled towards the horse as the horse approached it.

In the modern era, dressage has risen to new levels of difficulty. The transitions now required, such as going directly to and from extended trot to passage, the number of piaffe and passage movements that must be performed, and the addition of riding to music, are just three of the factors that make today's top dressage competitions so demanding. What have remained constant, however, are the basic qualities of good dressage work.

A PAINSTAKING PROGRESSION

Good dressage cannot be achieved without years of progressive, patient training that develops the natural outline and paces of the horse. It cannot be achieved without a true partnership between a horse and rider, with both reaching heights of performance that depend on each other. It requires willingness and a sense of ease in the horse, and this, in turn, cannot be achieved without trained riders.

There is no such thing as an unimportant element in dressage. Attention to detail, self-control, consistency, and accuracy are all vital factors, especially as dressage is performed in the confines of a 60 x 20 m (65 x 22 yd) arena within which little escapes scrutiny.

ACHIEVING REAL BEAUTY

There is an ultimate test of good dressage. Does it make the horse more beautiful? The Olympic gold medallist Rembrandt, ridden by Nicole Uphoff (see picture, left), in full flight in extended trot; and Ahlerich, the 1984 German Olympic champion ridden by Dr Reiner Klimke, in full flight in piaffe, certainly were beautiful.

The sight of a dressage horse going well is unforgettable. The neck will stretch forwards into an arch as the back lengthens and widens, giving grace and elasticity to the horse's movement. The breathing is regular and the facial expression is one of contentment. For the rider, there should be a feeling of great ease and comfort, and of privilege at riding such a trained horse.

SPORT FOR ALL

Good dressage is enhancing and liberating, and it is not surprising that it has the highest growth rate of all equestrian sports. It is beneficial for all levels and types of horses, including ponies. Although ponies are at a disadvantage in terms of the size of movement they are able to perform, there are gains for the rider because of the relative increase in the size of the arena. There is no reason why a small horse cannot be competitive.

The first woman to win an individual Olympic medal was Denmark's Liz Hartel in 1952, the first year that women were allowed to compete in the Olympic dressage. Now, female competitors outnumber males, which emphasizes the fact that it is not a sport that depends on great strength.

SPANISH RIDING SCHOOL At the Spanish Riding School in Vienna – home of the famous Lipizzaner horses – the classical principles of dressage are maintained. The riders are some of the most sought after coaches in the world. They emphasize the need for simplicity, progressive training, and respect for the horse. Their stallions also perform the impressive classical leaps, or airs above the ground (levade, courbette, and capriole), which are not featured in competition.

EQUIPMENT AND ARENAS

Top hat and tails are synonymous with dressage attire, although a normal riding hat and jacket are worn for the lower levels. The dressage saddle is shaped to allow the rider to ride with a long leg, and, in competition, the more advanced horses are ridden in a double bridle, which has two bits: a small-ring snaffle and a curb. Dressage is performed in an arena that is marked with letters to help guide the rider through the various movements.

THE RIDER'S EQUIPMENT

The top hat, tailcoat, and spurs worn for top-level dressage are largely decorative, unlike the clothes worn for other disciplines, which tend to be functional. The tailcoat is worn either with a waistcoat, or with a mock waistcoat attached to the front of the coat. At the lower levels of competition, it is normal to wear a standard riding jacket and riding hat. These are usually black, although some riders wear blue or brown. A harness to secure the riding hat is not usually compulsory, but it is recommended for general use and for all novice riders in competition. The breeches must be white and need to be comfortable, so they are usually made from stretch cotton. A dressage whip is often carried in training – this is disallowed in the arena. The whip is approximately 120 cm (47 in) long and, like the spurs and double bridle, should be used to aid humane communication, rather than to physically manipulate the horse.

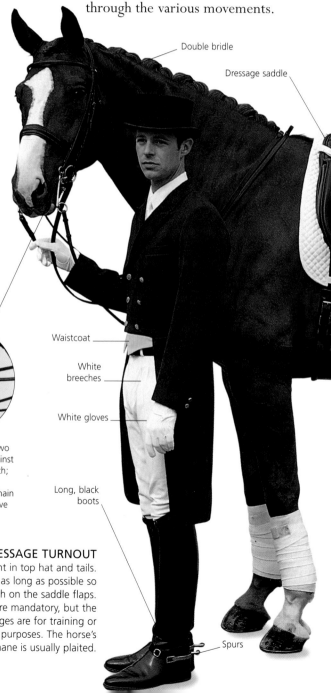

Double bridle

Dressage saddle

Waistcoat

White breeches

White gloves

Long, black boots

Spurs

SNAFFLE BRIDLE

The snaffle bridle is commonly used in lower-level dressage, with an eggbutt snap-jointed snaffle. The joint in the middle allows the bit to fit comfortably, and gives the rider independent use of each rein. Here, the noseband is a drop noseband, fitted with the front nosepiece a hand's breadth above the nostril.

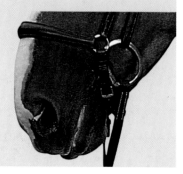

The double bridle has two bits. The snaffle fits against the corners of the mouth; the curb sits below the snaffle, with the curb chain resting in the curb groove behind the mouth.

DRESSAGE TURNOUT

All riders look elegant in top hat and tails. The riding boots are as long as possible so they do not catch on the saddle flaps. Gloves and spurs are mandatory, but the horse's leg bandages are for training or demonstration purposes. The horse's mane is usually plaited.

THE HORSE'S EQUIPMENT

A dressage saddle is designed so that the rider carries the greatest proportion of their weight in the seat rather than in the leg and stirrup. For this reason, the centre of a dressage saddle is a little further forwards than that of a jumping saddle (see pp.188–89). Since dressage requires you to ride with a long leg, the saddle flap is cut straight. However, you must be careful that the flaps are not so straight in the front that you ride too long, with your leg forced back, because this will lessen lower leg contact. The girth straps on the saddle are longer than normal so that the buckles of the short dressage girth can fasten near the horse's elbows. This allows a closer contact of the rider's leg. The stirrups are a little heavier than normal to keep them hanging down.

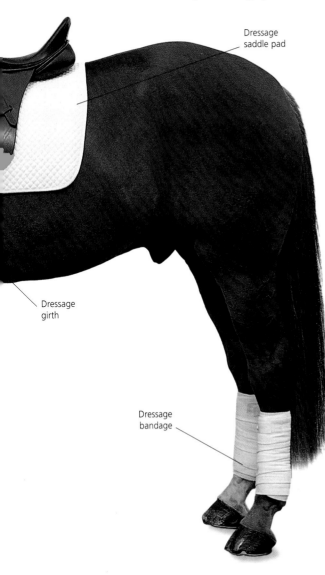

Dressage saddle pad

Dressage girth

Dressage bandage

DRESSAGE BANDAGING

Dressage bandages are usually used when riding dressage on any horse (unless it is raining, when boots are used instead). However, they are not used in competition. These soft bandages are similar to polo wraps and can be used by themselves or with a cotton lining underneath. Their purpose is to stimulate circulation, prevent rupture of the joint-fluid sacs, and protect from brushing. They must be applied carefully to avoid pressure points.

STEP 1 Start just below the knee. Place the end of the bandage just behind the cannon bone, and keep it smooth.

STEP 2 Taking care to keep an even tension on the bandage, bring it around once to secure the end.

STEP 3 Holding the bandage at a slight angle, work your way down the cannon bone in even turns: use your free hand to keep it smooth.

STEP 4 When you reach the back of the fetlock joint, angle the bandage upwards slightly. This will create a "V" at the front.

STEP 5 After making the "V", go around the leg once more before working your way back up with uniform turns and even pressure.

STEP 6 Finish where you started. The bandage should fasten on the outside of the leg, facing backwards.

DRESSAGE BRIDLES

A novice horse often wears a loose-ring jointed snaffle with a flash noseband. However, riders have begun to understand the discomfort that flash nosebands can cause. Therefore, increasingly, drop nosebands are used with an eggbutt snap-jointed snaffle (see p.110). This type of snaffle spreads direct contact between the tongue, the bars of the mouth, and the lips. It works well with a drop noseband because the lower strap fits neatly under the ring of the snaffle. With a loose-ring snaffle, there will be some gag action produced, where pressure on the reins will bring the bit up into the corners of the mouth. The larger the rings, the greater this gag action will be.

The double bridle is so called because it has two bits: the snaffle and the curb. The curb, which sits below the snaffle, has a curb chain, which passes around the back of the lower jaw and attaches either side at the top of the curb's shanks, or cheeks. The longer the cheeks of the curb, the stronger

the action of the bridle because pressure on the curb rein causes the curb chain to act as a fulcrum, resulting in pressure on both the tongue and the poll. The curb chain should not allow the cheeks to pivot back further than 45 degrees, otherwise the curb bit will rise up into the snaffle, causing discomfort. You should have slightly less weight in the curb rein than in the snaffle rein. Horses like double bridles, and generally work well in them, but they should be trained in a snaffle bridle, too.

THE DRESSAGE ARENA

There are two different sizes of dressage arena (see below). Alphabetical markers are placed about 50 cm (20 in) outside the arena, to guide the rider through their movements. The A

TWO DRESSAGE ARENAS The 60 x 20 m (65 x 22 yd) arena is the standard shape for higher level tests; the 40 x 20 m (44 x 22 yd) arena is used for lower levels. The quarter markers, F, M, H, and K, are all 6 m (19 ft 9 in) from each corner; otherwise, the markers are 14 m (46 ft) apart in the smaller arena and 12 m (39 ft 6 in) apart in the large arena.

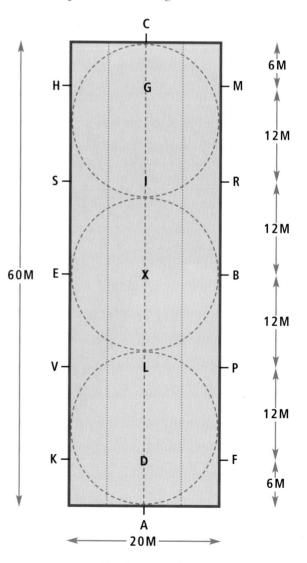

40 x 20 M (44 x 22 YD) ARENA

60 x 20 M (65 x 22 YD) ARENA

marker is set further back to allow room for you to enter the arena. Pegs are placed on the boards around the edges to show the precise spot denoted by the markers. The line from A to C is called the centre line; the line from B to E is the half-way line. The lines half-way between the long side and the centre line are called the three-quarter lines. When riding alongside the board, you are said to be riding on the outside track; when riding 2–3 m (6½–9½ ft) in from the boards, you are said to be riding on the inside track. An arena is surrounded by a continuous or intermittent barrier. If the continuous barrier is 25 cm (9½ in) or higher, you will be eliminated if your horse leaves the arena. In other cases, if you leave the arena, you will just be marked zero for that movement.

In competition and training, the international standard is for all dressage movements to be given in metric, but for ease of accessibility, they also appear in imperial throughout this book.

ARENA SURFACES

The type of surface on which you ride is of great importance because it affects your horse's way of going and the length of his working life. Too hard a surface will produce extra jarring and concussion of the legs and will discourage a supple step. Too loose a surface will reduce the spring in the horse's step, and the period of suspension that is so vital in trot and canter.

The arena surface can be a little softer for dressage than for showjumping because dressage is not subject to the extreme forces of take-off and landing. However, it should not be loose. The ideal is a surface that imitates good turf, such as a combination of sand and rubber pieces: there should be some give in the surface, but not so much that it does not spring back again quickly, and the horse's feet should not break through it.

COMPETITION ARENA This 20 x 60 m (65 x 22 yd) arena was set up for international competition at Goodwood House, England. The judges' boxes on either side at E and B can be seen; and there will also be three judges along the C end of the arena. The boxes are one of the distractions to which a horse must get used, but it is a wonderful feeling to ride in such an arena with your horse going well.

DEVELOPING FORM AND BALANCE

The form – or shape – of the dressage riding position is designed to enable the rider to achieve a balanced seat. It facilitates the rider's ability to go with the horse's movement, and have full use of the limbs, both of which are essential for effectiveness. All riders need to maintain a neutral alignment of the spine (see p. 336) so that they can ride with maximum suppleness. However, due to the widely differing shapes of riders and horses, everyone's form will be slightly different.

THE RIDER'S POSITION

The dressage rider should sit solidly on their seat with their spine in neutral alignment. If the spine is either hollow or rounded, the lower back will have limited ability to move. This will make a soft sitting trot almost impossible, as well as preventing the supple use of the legs and arms.

When viewed from the side, the rider's shoulders should be in line with the hip, and most of the rider's weight should be evenly distributed through the seat. Some of the weight of the leg will be taken in the thigh against the saddle, and there will be just enough weight in the stirrups to keep the foot and iron in contact. There should be equal weight on both sides of the foot, and the toes and knees will point in the same direction. The heel should be slightly lower than the toe, but not forced down too far.

If you keep your toe lower than the heel, either you are riding too long or you are not sitting deep enough into the saddle.

GOOD FORM Here (see photo and diagram **2**), the rider's spine is in neutral alignment. The rider neither hollows his back to sit on his fork (**1**), nor rounds his back to tuck his seat underneath (**3**). There is a straight line from the shoulder to the hip to the back of the heel, and another straight line from the elbow to the hand to the horse's mouth.

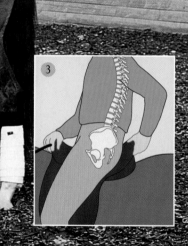

RIDER'S POSITION ON BROAD AND NARROW HORSES

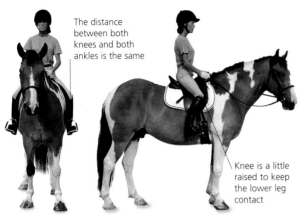

The distance between both knees and both ankles is the same

Knee is a little raised to keep the lower leg contact

POSITION ON A BROAD HORSE

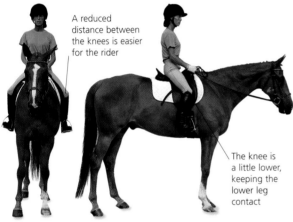

A reduced distance between the knees is easier for the rider

The knee is a little lower, keeping the lower leg contact

POSITION ON A NARROW HORSE

You cannot keep your leg entirely straight. This is because the knee has to have some bend if the lower leg is to hang vertically and be in contact with the horse's sides. The most common fault is riding too long, which prevents easy contact of the lower leg, tending to bring it too far back.

POSITION OF THE ARMS

To find the natural position of your arms and hands, do the following exercise:
• Drop your arms down by your side.
• Gently curl your fingers towards your palm, without tightening the hand, to form a 90-degree angle at the knuckles.
• Swing the lower arms up and forwards so that your hands are in front of you, approximately 10–15 cm (4–6 in) apart, with the front of your elbows almost in line with the front of your body (see picture, far left).
• The thumb and first finger will be on the top of your hand, although, as your upper body posture develops, the shoulders will become more erect, which will affect the carriage of the hands and bring the thumbs higher. The thumb should be slightly bent and the whole hand position should feel comfortable. The reins should be held by the pressure between the fingers and not by pressing the thumb down on top of the reins. In this way it will be easy to hold the two reins of the double bridle and keep a lighter feel in the curb rein (see box, below).

RIDING WIDE AND NARROW HORSES The wider a horse is, the shorter the stirrups must be. This is because, as the distance between the knees increases, the knee and the hip joint have to close to allow the lower leg to be in a vertical line and stay in contact with the horse's side. If you ride longer than this, your lower leg would lose contact with the horse's side.

HOLDING THE REINS

The snaffle rein (see right) goes into the hand between the third and fourth fingers; the little finger is under the rein. The rein comes out between the first finger and the thumb. With a double bridle (see far right), the snaffle rein stays in the same position but the curb rein goes in above it (between the second and third fingers) and comes out either with the snaffle rein (between the finger and thumb) or between the first and second finger. The latter position allows you to release pressure on the curb rein simply by opening the second finger.

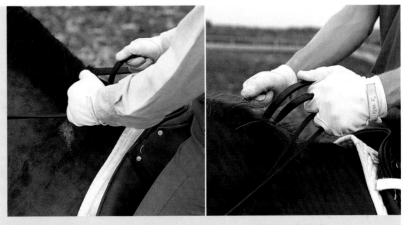

HOLDING A SINGLE REIN

HOLDING A SNAFFLE AND CURB REIN

HARMONY WITH THE HORSE

The rider has to stay in harmony with the horse's movement for three main reasons: to be comfortable, to encourage the movement, and to give small aids. In walk, the rider's seat and hands move with the horse's hind legs and head respectively. In trot and canter, the rider's seat and body go with the rise created by the horse's period of suspension and the subsequent lowering back to the ground. The need for harmony is the reason for developing a supple, soft position.

ACHIEVING HARMONY

The movement you require to stay in harmony with the horse will develop relatively easily if you are comfortable and improve your position slowly and progressively. If you do not develop this ability, you may find you grip with your legs, support yourself with the rein contact, and round your back. The rider in these sequences has these weaknesses. For her, and all riders like her, small improvements in harmony would greatly enhance comfort and performance.

SECURITY IN THE SADDLE

Harmony and security are inextricably linked: the more you can go easily with the movement of the horse, the safer and more secure you will be. Advanced riders are more secure than novice riders simply because they are in greater harmony with the movement of the horse. This enables them to ride safely for long periods of time, even when sitting on their seat.

MOVEMENT OF RIDER IN WALK The rider's seat moves in time with each of the horse's hind legs as they move forwards in walk. Here, the seat moves forwards (**1** and **2**) with the inside hind leg. It then moves back (just before and after **3**) ready to go forwards with the movement of the outside hind leg (**4** and **5**). The seat then moves back again (just before and after **6**). The horse's head and neck also move in time with his hind legs, so the rider's hands should move forwards with the movement of the horse's mouth, in time with the movement of the seat.

MOVEMENT OF RIDER IN TROT
In trot the horse reaches his highest point above the ground during the period of suspension (**1**). The opposite pair of diagonal legs push off the ground (**2**) and once again the horse takes off into a period of suspension (**3**). Each time a diagonal pair pushes off (**4**) into suspension (**5**), the rider's lower spine should go forwards (see inset, right) and then return to normal as the horse's legs come to the ground (**6**). This is why control of the lower back is necessary for harmony in trot.

MOVEMENT OF THE SPINE

MOVEMENT OF RIDER IN CANTER In canter, the horse begins the rise into the period of suspension as the outside hind leg (in this case, the left leg) leaves the ground (**1**) and continues as the diagonal pair (**2**) and then the leading leg (in this case, the right leg) leave the ground (**3**).The rider's seat comes down as the outside hind leg (**4**) and then the diagonal pair touch the ground (**5**).
Then the outside hind leg leaves the ground again (**6**) to start a new sequence. To go with this movement, the rider's seat must move in a circular motion (see inset, right).

MOVEMENT OF THE SEAT

DEVELOPING LANGUAGE AND FEEL

Riders communicate with horses using signals based upon the independent use of their voice, legs, hands, weight, and seat. These signals are known as the aids. When a rider develops feel – and is therefore in tune with the horse – the aids will be used at the right times. Eventually, they can be refined so that it becomes difficult for the observer to see the rider applying the aids at all. Simplicity is the goal, so that your horse can immediately understand what is required of him.

GOOD COMMUNICATION

The prerequisite for good communication is the rider maintaining a position that is in harmony with the horse. The more your seat, leg, and rein contacts go with the movement of the horse, the greater the possibility of your communicating in a way that can be understood by the horse. Good harmony also allows for good

feel, which is vital for giving precise aids. It is not difficult to learn which aids to use and how to use them, but it is difficult to learn when to use them, how much to use them, and in what combination. Essentially, good feel allows you to do the right thing at the right time.

This ability is often attributed only to advanced riders, but many novice riders are capable of good

PERFECT UNDERSTANDING The double bridle enables the rider to give the horse very subtle directions. However, its use, like that of the stick and spurs, should be to enhance communication, rather than to bully the horse.

Going with the horse helps to maintain forwards movement

The rider will feel the horse's movement through the seat

The rein contact is a communication point, not a support point

There should be a little less weight in the curb rein than in the snaffle rein

This is where the normal aids to go forwards will be given

REIN CONTACT

There are many faults that relate to the holding of the reins, which can make it difficult for the rider to go with the horse and give good rein aids. Some of these faults are illustrated here, and relate to the incorrect length of the reins, and the incorrect position of the hands, thumbs, and wrists. For a good position, you should hold the snaffle rein between the third and fourth fingers (see p.115), close to your knuckle so that the rein becomes an extension of it. The fingers should curl lightly around the rein as though you were holding a little bird in your hand (see top left). To find the right thumb position, turn your thumb out and in as far as you can, when rotating from the elbow, and find the mid-point. Similarly, if you round and then hollow the wrists, as far as you can, the mid-point will be the natural position, with the hands turned in very slightly. The hands should be at the mid-point of their range of lateral movement, with the upper arm angled slightly forwards.

GOOD POSITION   REINS TOO SHORT   REINS TOO LONG

HANDS TOO LOW   HANDS TOO HIGH   THUMBS OUT

HOLLOW WRISTS   ROUNDED WRISTS   THUMBS IN

feel if they have a supple position and are encouraged by their coach to be aware of how the horse is responding, and of what they can feel beneath their seat. When good harmony and feel are combined with a genuine wish to communicate with – rather than simply to make demands upon – the horse, you are well on your way to being an effective rider.

SIMPLE SIGNALS

The simpler our aids can be the better. The application of these aids involves a small increase of pressure followed by a release of pressure. Pulling continuously on the reins, or nagging with the legs, is not an aid. If a horse does not respond to a mild aid, it is normal to repeat it and then, if necessary, to use a stronger one, but always return to the use of the basic aid so that the horse does not become insensitive to the rider.

The use of the legs in the normal position – stirrup leathers parallel to the girth – means "go forwards". This message is the same whether the rider's legs are used together or individually. The movement that is initiated by the legs is controlled and directed by the reins. The inside rein is used for direction, and either the outside rein by itself or both together for slowing down.

ARTIFICIAL AIDS

The stick and spurs are refered to as artificial aids. They should be used as tools to help your horse understand the leg aids, not as tools for punishment. The spur should never be sharp or capable of injuring. It is applied by turning the toe out slightly so that the spur turns in towards the horse's side. The dressage stick is used with a flick of the wrist, while still holding the rein. It should touch the horse just behind the rider's leg.

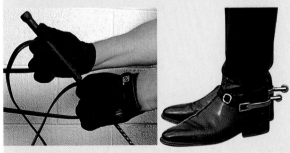

DRESSAGE STICK   SPURS

THE RANGE OF LEG AND REIN AIDS

The legs and hands can be used in different ways and in different places to extend the language of the aids. For example, the normal leg aid to go forwards is given with the leg in the usual position, but it can also be used behind this point (as when asking the horse to move sideways), or it can be used in a small backwards and forwards brushing movement (as when the outside leg asks for canter or a flying change). The legs can also be used either with a small increase and decrease of pressure, as when asking the horse to go forwards, or with continuous pressure, as with leg yielding (see pp.146–47).

The normal rein aid is given with an allowing rein contact – that is, with the hands going with the movement of the horse's head. The opposite of this is called a non-allowing rein, or rein of opposition. This is used in rein-back (see p.149), when you ask the horse to go forwards but the hands do not allow this to happen, so that the horse steps back.

There is also what is known as an open rein, when you move a hand away from the neck; this increases the inward pressure on the opposite side of the mouth and can be used for turning. The open rein is often accompanied by the opposite hand moving in the same direction, crossing over the neck (but not pulling back). This is called an indirect rein. The use of the open and indirect reins together is called neck reining, which is the main turning aid used in both polo and Western riding.

When this range of aids is combined with weight and seat aids, it is possible to find precise aids for both the individual elements of one movement and for individual exercises.

WEIGHT AND SEAT AIDS

The aim with your weight is to be as light and easy a load for your horse as possible. It is important that the horse's performance is not sacrificed by the desire to use weight aids. Therefore, any weight aids need to be almost invisible. The main weight aid is when the rider takes weight to the inside to indicate a turn to the inside (see p.93).

If the proportion of weight on the inside and outside of the saddle differs, for more than a moment, from the proportion of weight on the inside and outside legs of the horse, this ceases to be an aid and instead becomes a negative influence. Bringing the weight forwards may sometimes also be useful as an indication for forwards movement, but bringing the weight back to ask the horse to slow down is unhelpful.

The use of the seat is a different matter. The seat always moves with the swinging of the horse's back, and, as the rider builds a closer relationship with the horse, it is possible to stop or start a horse by stopping or starting the movement of the seat a fraction ahead of the horse's movement. The stopping is done by controlling or bracing the lower back. This should on no account be translated into leaning back, and it cannot be used unless the horse is actually rounding and swinging in his back.

REFINING THE AIDS

Once a horse understands the basic aids and is engaging his hind legs and working through his back, it can be said that he is between the aids. This is a more accurate and useful expression than its substitute, the commonly used "on the bit", which places too much emphasis on the neck and head of the horse when it should imply riding the horse from behind, from the leg to the hand.

At this stage, the use of the aids can be further refined so that you begin to use fewer, but more precise, aids. This will help to avoid misunderstandings. For example, the speed and impulsion required for medium trot and working canter (see pp.126–27) are so similar that it is necessary to have separate aids to enable the horse to distinguish between the two. In addition, if you have specific aids to start an exercise, it will have the effect of simultaneously ending the previous exercise, so you both have to concentrate on only one thing.

Your horse should be taught to remain in an exercise until you ask him to do something else. This is true whether it is a canter, medium trot, or half pass. This means that your aids can be used much less, just increasing them or omitting them as required. For example, in half pass the horse is doing a number of different things at the same time – bending to the inside, going forwards and sideways, and maintaining the required speed. Once positioned to start the half pass and instructed (by the rider's outside leg) to begin the movement, a well-trained horse should then continue in half pass – without needing any major additional aids – until the rider changes the aids to ask for the next exercise.

The difference in aid systems used by various trainers can create difficulties. A horse that learns to canter from an aid with the outside leg will not understand a canter aid from the inside leg, while a rider's effectiveness will be reduced if they have to keep changing aids. Although we must accept that there are different methods, it is important to keep everything as consistent and simple as possible. It can help to study the best riders because their aids will vary less and also work for all levels of dressage.

THE BASIC AIDS AND HALF PASS

Here, the 2002 World Champion, Nadine Capellman, of Germany, is asking her horse Farbenfroh to go sideways with her outside leg, while asking him to go forwards with her inside leg. Her inside rein controls bend and the outside rein controls speed.

INTRODUCING THE CONSTANTS

In all dressage work there are fundamental elements that must be present in your horse at all times. Called the constants, these are acceptance, calmness, forwardness, straightness, and purity. The five constants are interlinked and, when they are all in place, their combined effects exceed the sum of their individual parts. The degree to which you have established the constants dictates the quality of your work so, in training, the constants always take priority.

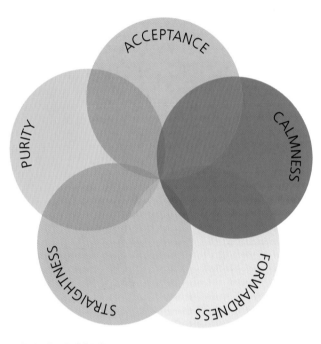

THE FIVE CONSTANTS These elements are constantly required in the dressage horse in order to perform good quality work. They must form the focus of your training, because they are the foundation stones for all dressage movements.

CONTROLLED IMPULSION

Impulsion, where the horse engages his hind legs and uses his back, consists of a combination of strength, suppleness, speed, and spring. Its presence makes the horse more athletic and more at ease with what he is doing, and it is therefore a major aim of all training. For controlled impulsion to be achieved, the horse must accept the rider and he must be calm. Good impulsion requires a willingness to go forwards, while for mechanical efficiency the horse should be straight and work as one co-ordinated unit. This requires purity in the paces and a natural outline.

ACCEPTANCE AND CALMNESS

The horse must accept – both physically and mentally – the rider's presence, weight, and leg, seat, and rein contacts. Acceptance leads to trust, partnership, and agreement, but it cannot be achieved instantly because the horse must first understand what is required of him. Your aim and responsibility is to create a mutual respect between you and your horse. Anything less than this is not acceptance but submission. The difference between acceptance and submission is the difference between a horse that knows he could react differently, but chooses not to, and a horse that knows there is no other option. This is quite a subtle distinction, but it makes a huge difference to the effort that a horse is prepared to put into his work.

The horse must be mentally calm in order to avoid the paralysing effect of mental tension. This will allow an unconstrained basis for his work and enable him to perform with confidence. Acceptance and calmness go hand-in-hand. The great enemy of calmness is a lack of time. So, if you make time for slow but steady, progressive training, as well as time for rest periods and his individual needs, calmness will become habitual in your horse's work.

FORWARDNESS AND STRAIGHTNESS

Forwardness refers to the horse responding to the forwards aids. He must ride forwards willingly, whatever his speed. Once again, it is an attitude of mind. Forwardness helps a horse to be focused, and when it is combined with acceptance and calmness, he will have the mental foundation for fulfilling his physical potential, and there will be nothing mechanical about his work. Many horses lack forwardness because they are in pain or because they are asked to do more than they are able. A rider's task is to show a horse what he can do, not what he cannot do, and always to finish with the horse able to do a little more. In this way, the forwards attitude will be maintained.

Straightness refers to the equal development of both sides of the horse in each pace and, in particular, to the precise positioning of the forehand, which together produce straightness. Straightness makes for symmetry in the horse's movement, and this maximizes the scope of the horse's work.

It seems contradictory that you have to bend him in order to make him straight, but riding a circle (see pp.140–41) is an essential training exercise for straightening. A straight horse will always keep his forehand and quarters following the same track – whether this is on a curve or on a straight line. However, almost nothing restricts a horse's paces so quickly as forcing straightness – the process has to be done with patience.

PURITY

Purity refers to the naturalness and correctness of the paces: the natural and rhythmic sequence of steps, including a period of suspension, combined with a natural outline and natural use of the body, head, and neck. Purity makes it possible for a horse to go close to perfection, but it is possible only if the various muscle groups function as an ensemble. Many young horses have innate purity and then lose it through inappropriate work or injury. To gain awareness of purity, you must work at your feel, and study and understand the horse's paces.

Achieving all five constants together produces a powerful synergy. It produces controlled impulsion (see box, below left) and makes the horse feel good, which is at the heart of accelerating progress and fulfilling potential.

ACHIEVING THE CONSTANTS Here, the horse is at ease, with all his muscle groups working together as an entity. He accepts the rider willingly and is calm, forwards, and straight. His way of going is natural and correct, with each diagonal pair of legs being synchronized in trot.

THE PURITY OF THE PACES

The horse has four main paces — walk, trot, canter, and gallop. Each pace should have an evenly repeated sequence of steps. With the trot, canter, and gallop paces, there should also be a period of suspension, where all four legs are off the ground momentarily. When badly ridden, many horses lose their natural sequence of steps and the period of suspension, and this destroys their natural pace. This must be rectified because purity of the paces is at the core of good dressage.

WALK There are four beats to the walk stride, and each beat should be evenly spaced. At least two legs are on the ground at all times, making it the most stable of the paces. An integral part of the walk is the motion of the horse's head and neck, which moves forwards and back in time with his hind legs.

Beat 1 – right hind leg touches the ground

Beat 2 – right foreleg touches, as the left hind leaves the ground

Both left legs are off the ground together

TROT There are two beats to the trot stride, with the legs moving in diagonal pairs and a period of suspension between each beat. If the period of suspension is reduced or lost, then the tempo (speed of the rhythm) becomes faster. The periods of suspension between each beat should be of equal duration.

Beat 1 – the right hind and left foreleg touch the ground together

The left hind and right foreleg move forwards together

Period of suspension occurs as all four feet leave the ground

CANTER The canter is often described as a three-beat pace, with one hind- and one foreleg acting as a diagonal pair, and with a period of suspension after the third beat. With a rider on the horse's back, the period of suspension can be lost. This is often mistaken for a four-beat canter, and occurs when the diagonal pair is split.

All four feet are off the ground

Beat 1 – the right hind leg touches the ground

Beat 2 – the left hind leg and right foreleg (diagonal pair) touch the ground

ANALYSING THE PACES

All the paces have a specific, rhythmic sequence of steps (see walk, trot, and canter, below), and it is helpful to analyse the differences. The canter becomes a gallop when the diagonal pair of legs split up, and the four feet begin to touch the ground separately. Therefore, the gallop has a four-beat sequence: the outside hind, inside hind, outside fore, inside fore, followed by a period of suspension. This type of standard gallop is called a transverse gallop. Sometimes, the hind legs are used in a reverse sequence: inside hind, outside hind, outside fore, inside fore. This is called a rotary gallop. It is possible for both the canter and the gallop to start with either hind leg but, when riding a circle they should start with the outside hind leg, which will make the inside fore the leading leg.

The rein back (see p.149), which could be seen as a backwards walk, is also considered a pace in its own right. However, unlike in walk, when the horse moves each leg separately, a horse in rein-back moves his legs in diagonal pairs. Each diagonal pair should touch the ground at the same time. If there is a high degree of collection (see pp.126–27) as the movement is performed, the hind leg may touch the ground before the foreleg.

Beat 3 – the left hind leg touches the ground

Beat 4 – the left foreleg touches, as the right hind leaves the ground

Both right legs are off the ground together

Beat 2 – the left hind leg and right foreleg touch the ground together

The right hind and left foreleg move forwards together

Period of suspension occurs as all four legs leave the ground

Beat 3 – the left foreleg (the leading leg for left canter) touches the ground as the right hind leaves

The diagonal pair (left hind leg and right foreleg) leave the ground together

The left foreleg leaves the ground to produce a period of suspension

VARIATION OF PACES

It is possible to vary the length of the stride within each pace, from shorter collected steps to longer extended steps. As you do this, it is vital that you preserve the purity, or correctness, of the pace and that the horse accepts the rider throughout and remains calm, forwards, and straight. The quality of the steps is more important than their size. Having first established the working paces, you can teach your horse to shorten a little, and then to lengthen.

NOVICE VARIATION

The novice horse starts off by performing what are known as working trot, working canter, and medium walk. After novice level, most school movements are performed in the collected or medium paces. At the next level, extended paces (the longest strides that a horse can take) are introduced. While training for the extended paces, you can start work at collection plus. This is needed for advanced level: in the canter half-pirouettes and for the Prix St George level, and in trot as preparation for piaffe and passage.

The horse therefore has five gears: collection plus, collection, working, medium, and extended. The precise length of each stride will be different for each horse, but strides should be equally spaced. To begin working paces, the horse must be between the aids (see pp. 130–31); he must be coming through the back, with good horizontal balance and good impulsion. Once this has been achieved, it is possible to start slowing down and shortening the steps a little, using smaller circles and shoulder-in (see pp. 148–49) to encourage him to take a little more weight on the hind legs. As your horse becomes comfortable with a little shortening and the change of balance, it is possible to start a little lengthening.

With continued work, the shortening will gradually become true collection, with the horse sitting more on his hind legs and taking rounder steps; the lengthening will gradually develop into the medium pace. The tempo should stay the same in both the shortening and the lengthening of the stride.

LEARNING TO LENGTHEN This horse is showing good lengthening of the stride. However, he needs to carry a little more weight on his hind legs, which would encourage him not to lean on the rein. The rider has slipped back a little and lost the neutral alignment of the spine, making it difficult for him to go with the movement of the horse's back.

The joints are more bent, and the quarters lower

The rein contact must be light

COLLECTION IN TROT Here, the horse is clearly lowering his quarters as he sits in collection. This is collection plus, which is required for the horse to take half steps in preparation for learning piaffe. Compared with working trot, the neck naturally rises and shortens and the steps become rounder and shorter, with more use of the knee. In collected walk, be careful not to lose the regularity of the steps.

COLLECTION IN WALK

The alignment of the spine stays the same as in collection

The lengthening of the neck is in proportion to the lengthening of the step

WORKING TROT This horse's steps are approximately 30 cm (12 in) longer than they are in collected trot, and approximately 30 cm (12 in) shorter than in medium trot. The hind foot will overtrack the print of the fore foot on the same side by about 25 cm (10 in). The horse's topline is longer than it is in collected trot. There is no working walk; instead there is a free walk on a long rein, which is good for developing the regularity of the walk.

FREE WALK

The horse extends his legs further than he does in working trot

The rein contact should remain comfortable and accepting

MEDIUM TROT In this pace, the horse should be at ease and as comfortable as he is in working trot. The angle of the cannon bones (bandaged area) of each diagonal pair of legs will be the same. This horse will overtrack by approximately 35 cm (14 in) in medium trot. Medium walk is the basic walk used in dressage tests. The extended walk (and other extended paces) should show a clear difference from the medium.

MEDIUM WALK

INTRODUCING THE VARIABLES

The variable elements – direction, speed, impulsion, balance, and timing – are necessary for all exercises but, unlike the constants, requirements change according to circumstances. With the exception of impulsion, all the variables are absolutes – they are either right or wrong. Impulsion, however, is dependent on the horse's stage of training. As long as an exercise is within the capabilities of the horse, the correct combination of variables will produce the right result.

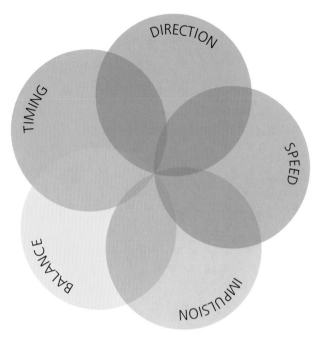

THE VARIABLES These elements are required in variable amounts for all dressage exercises and movements. Once the constants are in place, these variables must take priority in competition work, because they are the building blocks for each exercise and the keys to success.

DIRECTION AND SPEED

Once you have established the constants satisfactorily, the priority in any dressage test or showjumping round is to ensure you have the right direction and speed.

Achieving the right direction refers to the precise route you take, the rein you are on, and the bend that you achieve, and these will be dictated by the school movement or exercise you are riding. A horse is like a car with front-wheel steering and rear-wheel drive. You control the direction primarily by controlling the bend in the neck and the position of the forehand. At all levels, riders will find it easier to control the direction if they always look ahead to where they want to go: then the body will follow, enabling an accurate application of the aids.

The speed refers to going slower or faster from one movement to another, or within one pace, as in shortening and lengthening a stride. A decrease of speed leads to shortening, and an increase to lengthening; with the right level of impulsion, it can produce collection or extension.

TROT, HALT, AND CANTER Here, the horse is performing a trot-to-halt-to-canter transition on a straight line. This exercise requires a precise speed for the trot, a slower speed while preparing to halt, then a faster speed for the working canter. Impulsion is reduced for the halt and then increased for the canter.

Once your horse is attentive, start in working trot

Slow down and ask for a degree of collection before halting

Halt

ACHIEVING IMPULSION Impulsion begins in the hind legs. It should travel forwards through the horse's back to be controlled or directed by the rider's hands. Maintaining impulsion involves working the horse from his hindquarters to his front end, so that you are utilizing his full power.

RELATING THE VARIABLES TO JUMPING

During a showjumping round, most of the work is done on the flat between fences — the constants and variables apply just as much to jumping as they do to dressage. Controlled impulsion is essential for the jumping horse, and for this the five constants are required. But just as for the dressage horse, the first priorities are to achieve the right direction and speed.

With regard to direction, the showjumping track can be considered as a series of dressage movements with the jump being at the end of one movement and the beginning of the next. The speed will be more consistent in showjumping than in dressage because of the need to keep a 3.7 m (12 ft) stride. When the correct degree of impulsion is added to the right direction and speed, the right balance will begin to fall into place by itself. In addition the timing of the stride will become easier, and less important if your horse is not working to his maximum capability.

BALANCE AND TIMING

The horse can be balanced more on the forehand, as with a galloping racehorse or youngster, or he may be more horizontally balanced, as with a novice horse in the working paces. In collection, the horse lowers his hindquarters so that the forehand becomes raised. Eventually, this results in the sitting position required in advanced movements. Achieving the correct balance is primarily achieved through having the right speed and impulsion. The horse's natural way of regaining balance is to slow down.

Timing refers to the timing of transitions, the beginning and ending of movements, and the use of the rider's aids. It requires good use of the aids. When the first four variables are in place, good timing generally follows. If you work at timing in isolation, the result will be contrived and inefficient movement.

IMPULSION

Impulsion refers to the power that originates from the horse's hind legs to support him and propel him forwards, so that he is working as one co-ordinated unit. Controlled impulsion is the key element of performance, and the right speed and level of impulsion produce correct rhythm and good tempo.

The degree of impulsion required depends on the work you are doing. For example, more impulsion is needed for the extended paces and a high level of collection, and less is needed for the working paces.

At first, before the constants are in place, you will just achieve increased energy, rather than impulsion. Increasing and decreasing the energy levels to match the speed required will be a normal part of establishing the constants and putting your horse between the aids.

Ask the horse for working canter

Increase the speed to working canter, together with an increase in impulsion

Working canter is achieved

CONSTANTS AND VARIABLES

When you have established the constants (acceptance, calmness, forwardness, straightness, and purity) in basic work, the horse will be between the aids and have controlled impulsion. You can then select the key variables (direction, speed, impulsion, balance, and timing) for each progressive exercise, and series of exercises, in training or competition. Using the constants and variables in this way will help you adopt a systematic approach to all training.

GOOD BASIC TRAINING

No two horses are the same, so while training should be systematic, no two training programmes should be identical. With good basic training that takes account of the horse's individuality and uses the constants and variables together, the vast majority of young horses will quickly develop controlled impulsion and therefore be working between the aids.

Acceptance and calmness are the prerequisites for effective training, but it is not possible to improve either without controlling the two key variables, direction and speed. Even when leading a horse, you are asking your horse to calmly accept this activity while moving in a specific direction and at a particular speed.

Lungeing is superb for helping a horse to develop both acceptance and calmness, and for exercising precise control of direction and speed. It has the huge advantage that the horse is not burdened with weight when he has yet to connect through his back (see pp.72–73). Lungeing is also invaluable for achieving forwardness and the right level of energy necessary for the speed the horse is going. As the constants and variables become established, the horse will begin to use his back and offer real impulsion and thus to come between the aids.

PUTTING A HORSE BETWEEN THE AIDS

It may be possible to put the untrained horse between the aids when ridden if you have a good basic position and an allowing rein contact. The first step is to gain precise control of direction and speed within an enclosed arena. Walk around, changing the rein and bend, making minor changes to the speed, and getting the horse to respond to your forwards leg aids. As you do this, acceptance and calmness will improve.

Then work the horse on a 15 to 20 m (50 to 65 ft) circle on the rein that he is most comfortable with. Go as slowly as you can, without losing the forwardness, and then add a little energy at a time by using your leg aids, but without losing acceptance and calmness. If forwardness is lost, wait a moment and then ask again with the legs, without losing the acceptance and calmness. As you do this, the horse will come between the aids with genuine impulsion and accept the rein in this limited area of work. He will immediately start breathing more easily and using his neck more; your hands will be brought forwards, so your rein contact must be allowing. Gradually, you can work on the other, less comfortable rein, going a little faster, and using all the paces. The horse will increasingly lift his back and maintain controlled impulsion in the novice exercises.

Putting the horse between the aids in this way is humane, natural, and long-lasting. As a rider you can still be assertive when appropriate but it means you do not have to use force. The whole process is immensely rewarding.

USING GADGETS

Some riders may use strength, a strong bit, or various gadgets to bend and shorten the neck artificially; others may kick with their legs or fix their hands in the hope that the horse will lift his back. In either case, the greater likelihood is that, while the neck will shorten, the back will remain the same.

Such methods often cause the horse to produce large amounts of white saliva around his mouth because the shortening in the neck stops him from swallowing properly. This should not be confused with a wet or "white" mouth (see p.64), which indicates acceptance.

Anyone can use hands or bits and gadgets to lighten the horse in the mouth, but this leads to submission, not acceptance, and will be of no use unless the horse becomes light in the whole forehand.

Lightness in the forehand can occur only when the hind legs are engaged, the back is kept up, and there is genuine impulsion. Then acceptance of the bit will automatically be good and the horse will seek a contact with the rider's hands, which will lift the back further.

A horse going in this way will have a wet mouth even without a bit (as when ridden in a bitless bridle). Using a proliferation of special equipment ignores the crucial fact that acceptance of the bit is primarily related to the way a horse comes through his back with impulsion.

COMING BETWEEN THE AIDS If a horse is not between the aids, he will not have impulsion (a). In order to achieve this, you must have the constants and the right variables in place. Here (see main picture), the rider brings the horse between the aids by adjusting her speed and slowing down a little.

(a) The horse is not using his hind legs and back efficiently.

DEVELOPING THE CONSTANTS

Each constant – acceptance, calmness, forwardness, straightness, and purity – influences the others, so they should not be considered in isolation. Looking at them in pairs and groups will help you understand how they work, and enable you to give your training programme direction and structure. Establishing the constants is the initial aim of dressage training; they should then remain in place permanently. If they do not, you will need to go back a few steps in your work.

ACCEPTING AND CALM

Acceptance and calmness jointly underpin all the training. To achieve acceptance without calmness is worthless because the lack of calmness would indicate the presence of tension; to have calmness without acceptance means that the horse feels that he is in charge, which is unacceptable to the rider. Achieving acceptance and calmness together makes it possible for impulsion to become controlled.

The most obvious time to work at acceptance and calmness simultaneously is when a young horse is being worked for the first time. By asking the horse to accept things gradually, starting with leading and lungeing, and progressing to the introduction of the rider, it is possible for him to become both accepting and calm. If you force things without building up trust and understanding, then almost certainly calmness will be lost and the horse will be restricted both mentally and physically. Equally, if the young horse is apparently calm but refuses to lead, or to allow anyone to handle him, the training process will come to a dead end. So the two must go hand-in-hand.

CALM, FORWARDS, AND STRAIGHT

The novice competition horse should be calm, forwards, and straight. These qualities are continually identified as the supreme priorities. Calmness without forwardness will not get you off the starting blocks, while forwardness without calmness can lead to speed but never to impulsion.

The foundation for both calmness and forwardness is understanding. In part, this means that the rider should not ask the horse to do things that are beyond the horse's capabilities. It also means continuously assessing your horse and responding accordingly. For example, if you find that slow, regular work begins to increase calmness but your horse is also becoming a little backwards thinking, ride

LUNGE WORK Lungeing, when done well, is a superb way to develop all five of the constants. This young mare demonstrates a natural outline and step, and acceptance and calmness, all of which have been developed on the lunge without the use of gadgets. Lungeing makes it easy to send the mare forwards and to work her evenly on both reins to achieve straightness.

out in company and be more demanding. Then, if the calmness is being lost you can once again make the work less exciting. In this way, you can gradually progress with both calmness and forwardness. When forwardness is added to acceptance and calmness, the young horse will have everything required before you begin to improve the straightness.

As a horse goes forwards he will naturally tend to be a little crooked. Then as you work to straighten him, by bending work on smaller circles and using degrees of shoulder-in (see pp.148–49), it is likely that forwardness will decrease. So it is necessary to keep alternating between riding forwards and straightening, until you can ride forwards with a straight horse. This process may take months.

In the long term, you will have to continually return to repairing and improving straightness. Forwardness and straightness together make it possible for the whole horse to work as one unit with both sides being used equally.

PURITY

The purity of the paces, which is not just about regular steps but about the natural outline and the whole way of going of the horse (see pp.124–25), is the key to every movement and exercise. While working on any one of the constants, you have to be constantly aware of maintaining purity. At the start of training, rather than actively trying to improve purity, work on areas in which it already exists. Therefore, if your horse has no period of suspension in canter you should only do a minimum of canter to begin with (just sufficient to get the horse thinking forwards), otherwise you risk confirming the fault – practice makes permanent, not perfect. If the right tempo and regularity of steps exists only in the working paces then these are the ones you must work in initially.

Whatever you do to develop a particular constant, you must always maintain purity. The following training techniques are unacceptable because they result in the loss of purity: getting acceptance by using a gadget (because this may produce an unnatural way of going); getting forwardness by trotting fast with short hurried steps; getting straightness, but losing the regularity of the steps or the period of suspension.

If any of the constants are weak or missing, controlled impulsion immediately deteriorates. Continually revisit the constants in daily training. In every training session, start by re-establishing acceptance and calmness in the warm-up period, then go on to confirm forwardness and straightness in the suppling period before carrying all the constants into your main work. In competition, the variable components (see pp.128–29) take priority because the constants should automatically be in place without any action required from the rider.

IMPROVING THE CONSTANTS

ACCEPTANCE	Acceptance starts with handling in the stable and in other non-riding activities. Leading, lungeing, and grooming build up mutual respect and lead to communication and understanding. For riding, comfortable tack and a supple, soft position of the rider are essential. Then, as you engage the horse's mind, asking him to perform simple movements, changes of direction, and transitions, you gain basic acceptance.
CALMNESS	The basis for calmness is a secure environment that is as natural as possible, regular work, and adequate but not excessive feeding. You also need to give a young horse time to settle before you make new demands. Lungeing is useful because of its repetitive nature. Also beneficial are turning out, frequent rest periods, giving away of the rein, and being calm yourself. Never abuse the horse's trust or make demands beyond his abilities.
FORWARDNESS	Horses are very willing to do things for humans if they understand what is required and have confidence in their ability. This is the basis for forwardness. Lungeing shows the young or difficult horse that forwardness is what is needed. The same applies to riding in company, jumping and cantering with a light seat, and hacking. It is also true that nothing encourages forwardness more than a rider who is allowing and enthusiastic.
STRAIGHTNESS	Straightness in any quadruped is rare. It can be achieved only by continuously developing both sides of your horse, controlling the forehand, and considering the whole horse as one athletic unit. If you are uneven yourself or you demand too much of your horse, straightness will be lost. Circles, serpentines, and shoulder-in exercises are useful. When leading, make sure you turn in both directions and lead from alternate sides.
PURITY	To maintain purity of the paces, the horse must have a connected, swinging back. If he is stiff in the back, use lungeing, rising trot, and a light seat in canter, combined with simple exercises to engage the back and achieve impulsion. Once this is done, every exercise you do must develop and improve purity because you will not accept any work in which the regularity of the paces or natural outline and way of going are lost.

USING THE VARIABLES

The variables cannot be worked on in isolation because each one influences and is affected by the others. Each riding exercise requires its own specific set of variables, and, for the exercise to be good, each variable must be right. If you look at how the variables relate to each other in groups and how they are used, you will understand why they are the priority for successful competition work. You will also be able to relate them to the work you do to develop the constants.

DIRECTION, SPEED, AND IMPULSION

When riding a dressage test – or whenever you are under pressure – you should concentrate simply on getting the right direction and speed. If you do this everything else has a chance of falling into place. Because of the simplicity of this strategy, it is extremely effective for novice riders, yet it works even better at the higher levels because a well-trained horse will automatically give you the right level of impulsion for whatever speed you choose.

To begin with you may not have controlled impulsion because all the constants are not in place. Instead you will just have energy, and it is a fact that the faster you go the more energy your horse will need and vice versa. As the horse comes between the aids with real impulsion, however, it is possible to increase the impulsion without going faster, which is how piaffe is achieved (see p.157). For piaffe, impulsion is increased in walk until the horse first bounces and then trots on the spot. Nevertheless it is still true that the extended trot is the fastest trot in terms of speed and requires a very high level of impulsion, while the medium trot will require a little less impulsion and the working trot less again. So, while schooling your horse, it is often easier to slow down the speed to match the available impulsion than it is to add more impulsion.

The most obvious indication of a lack of impulsion will be an increase in the tempo (speed of the rhythm) and a decrease in the period of suspension in trot and canter. In the novice exercises, by achieving the right direction, speed, and impulsion, all the difficult work is done. Your horse will be between the aids, able to compete at this level, and ready to start training for collection and higher level work.

UNIQUE REQUIREMENTS A jumping exercise like this requires precise direction, speed, and impulsion in order to produce exactly the right stride length and take-off point. The dressage exercises need to be looked at in the same way: you need to identify which of the variables should be in place for each exercise.

IMPULSION, BALANCE, AND TIMING

Having the right impulsion and balance is what dressage is all about. Balance is variable in that it will be adjusted according to the stage of training and the exercise required. So, for example, developing collection requires a gradual change of the horse's balance so that he carries more weight on his quarters (see pp.156–57). In between this balance, which will eventually make it possible for the horse to sit on his quarters in piaffe, and the horizontal balance used for warming up, there is a range of different balances for different exercises.

The right balance will come primarily as a result of having the correct speed and impulsion – decreased speed and increased impulsion. To begin with, all you have to do is to slow down the speed in the working trot or canter but keep the same impulsion level so that, relatively speaking, you have more impulsion. Later on, as the horse becomes more athletic, you can add still more impulsion. If you work without sufficient impulsion you will invariably have the wrong balance. For example, it is possible to teach a horse to do a piaffe-like movement without the characteristic sitting on the quarters, but this is not a natural balance; in other words, the lack of impulsion prevents the horse from achieving the correct balance in piaffe. Similarly, to achieve a more advanced balance in collected trot or canter, there must be sufficient impulsion.

With the correct balance and impulsion, you lay the foundations for good timing. This is because, if your horse is also truly responsive and obedient to the aids, you can time the movements and transitions to perfection, producing a high-level performance. This is the natural and long-lasting way to train a horse, and it makes gadgets redundant.

GERMAN SCALES OF TRAINING

German trainers base all their dressage training on six fundamental factors, referred to as scales. These are *Reinheitergange, Losgelassenheit, Anlehnung, Schwung, Geraderichtung,* and *Versammlung. Reinheitergange* (or rhythm) means purity of the paces; *Losgelassenheit* means looseness, calmness, and cheerfulness; *Anlehnung* refers to the acceptance of the leg and rein contacts; *Schwung* means spring and an improved period of suspension; *Geraderichtung* refers to straightness; and *Versammlung* means collection. The scales are further broken up into three stages: the familiarization phase, when rhythm and *Losgelassenheit* take priority; the development of carrying power, when *Schwung,* straightness, and collection take priority; and the development of propulsive force, or impulsion, when all six factors must be present. The scales show there is a strong connection between the constant and variable elements.

IMPROVING THE VARIABLES

DIRECTION	Direction and straightness go hand-in-hand, so exercises in controlling one will improve the other. Precise control of direction stems partly from your attitude of mind: being prepared to accept a lack of precision makes it difficult to remedy it. Precise control does not require strength – you must think ahead and make the exercise easy enough to ensure you have consistent control. For example, consider every part of every circle you ride as important.
SPEED	Very small changes in speed can make an immediate difference to a horse's way of going. As with direction, it demands good communication and the use of clear language rather than physical manipulation. You have to develop an attitude of mind that says, "A precise speed is important and I shall consistently prioritize it." The first step is to change the speed regularly by tiny amounts and then feel and compare the result.
IMPULSION	With the five constants in place, controlled impulsion can be developed if you work your horse athletically: use the normal progression of exercises, including shortening and lengthening in all paces, and work your horse in a physically demanding way. Do this for very short periods of time, after the warming up and suppling exercises. Becoming effective with your forwards aids and being assertive in your attitude is essential.
BALANCE	This refers to different balances, rather than being out of balance or in balance. To change the balance, you must be able to easily increase and decrease both the speed and impulsion. Using small circles and shapes, transitions, lateral work, and regular rest periods will all help to control both the speed and impulsion. Athletic development of the horse using the progressive exercises will develop the impulsion and different balances.
TIMING	Good feel enables you to do the right thing at the right time, so it is the basis for good timing. Good feel comes from developing your ability to use your aids in a co-ordinated and co-operative way, and for this you need to practise using your legs and arms independently in your daily life. It is also helpful to experiment with using an aid a little earlier or later, starting an exercise a little earlier or later, or doing the exercises in a different order.

A TRAINING PROGRAMME

When devising a training programme, plan backwards from your long-term aims. You can then work out the best way to go forwards, in small daily steps, to achieve these aims. Establishing a suitable weekly programme is the basis from which you might eventually go forwards to compete at the highest level. Each horse is different, so it is important not to be too prescriptive; as you get to know your horse better, your expectations can become more precise.

LONG-TERM PLANNING

In the long term, extraordinary things are possible. Riding in the Olympic Games is a real possibility if you start with this aim, but is much less likely if you just take a day at a time. In international dressage, there are progressive classes from Prix St George to Intermediate I and II level, then Grand Prix, and Grand Prix Special, and the freestyle to music (kur). The freestyle tests have become the highlight of most championships, and dressage riders now have to design a unique programme, as well as find appropriate music, to prepare their horses for this. Riding at such a high level necessitates sacrifices because of the time commitment that is required and the financial implications, but riders are often surprised at what can be achieved with their horse once they have set their mind to it.

Having decided on your long-term aims, it is important that you then plan the goals that should be achievable in the next year. With a solid foundation, most horses and riders can progress by one level a year, so this should be part of your plan. You should also include performance goals for specific areas, which you can write down and agree with your coach. The fact that dressage test marks are always presented as percentages, and the collective marks are out of ten, helps to make it possible to set quantifiable goals. The collective marks (see p.159) are particularly important because the quality of the work must always take priority.

NOVICE LEVEL Preparing a novice horse well is probably both more difficult and more rewarding than moving on to the next stage. This is because it is at this novice level that the priorities for all the subsequent levels are set and the foundations for all future work are laid.

SHORT-TERM PLANNING

If your horse is to progress, he will need to be able to cope mentally with working in the arena four or five times a week. This work should be supplemented by hacks, jumping, and – once the horse has settled – as much work in company as possible. The most valuable thing you can do is consciously plan your daily rides. The rides can be broken up into four stages:
- Warming up and loosening.
- Suppling.
- Strong work.
- Cool down.

Warming up and loosening is for the benefit of both mind and body, and will take 15 to 30 minutes. Going for a hack is ideal, but lungeing is a good alternative if your horse is not established in the basic work.

As your horse warms up and begins to work more actively, use the rising trot or some short periods of canter. You should use canter if the period of suspension is better than in trot or if you want to go a little faster to get your horse thinking forwards. The canter is also better if your horse is tense and holding his breath because the pace forces

MEDIUM LEVEL The correct position of this rider, the good, balanced physical development of the horse, and the horse's acceptance of the rider, means the partnership is ready for the challenge of higher level dressage.

ADVANCED LEVEL
Even with higher level horses, it is sometimes important to go back to slightly lower level work. This horse has to learn how to lower the quarters before doing piaffe.

a horse to breathe with each stride. Otherwise, use large school movements and possibly a little leg-yielding.

The next stage of the session should be working at the suppling of your horse, which will take a further 15 to 30 minutes. For this, the horse has to be between the aids and coming through the back (see pp.130–31). Use circles and serpentines carried out in the working paces, combined with progressive transitions, a little shortening and lengthening, and shoulder fore and travers with a small angle (see pp.138–57). Do not introduce new lessons or ask for maximum effort. Even advanced horses will work with a less developed outline and balance at this stage of their work session.

With novice horses, or when retraining horses, this suppling stage is as far as you will go before cooling down. With other horses, you can then begin to work a little harder. For two to five short 4- to 5-minute periods, with 1- to 2-minute rest periods between, you should begin to take a horse closer to his physical maximum in whatever area you are working, as long as he remains accepting and calm. It is during this strong work stage that you will do the most collected work and ask for maximum impulsion. To finish the session, return to the loosening phase before doing an active cool down.

TRANSITIONS

A transition is a change from one pace to another. When you change from one pace to the next, such as from walk to trot, this is a progressive transition. If you omit an intermediate pace, such as from canter to walk, this is a direct transition. If this is followed by a return to canter, it is a simple change. Transitions can also be made within a pace, such as when moving from medium to collected trot. Seamless transitions require obedience and good-quality paces before and after the transition.

MAKING GOOD TRANSITIONS

Good transitions are valuable because they improve the horse's impulsion and connection with the rider. In order to perform a transition, the horse must be between the aids. Prepare for the transition by checking the quality of the pace you are in. Give your normal forwards aids for the required pace and expect an immediate response in the following stride. Just getting the right speed and impulsion for the pace, combined with the necessary movement of the seat (see p.117) will produce the transition you require. The paces before and after the transition must be good. For clarity, more specific aids can be introduced. For example, brushing your outside leg back and then forwards works well as a signal to canter. The opposite (brushing the leg forwards and then back) can be used to signal a transition to walk. If you use normal leg aids, the horse understands that this signals a transition to trot.

TROT TO CANTER In trot, the inside hind and outside foreleg go forwards together. Using his leg aid, the rider signals to the horse to strike off into canter with his outside hind – this is followed by the inside hind and foreleg, and, finally, the leading leg.

Start in trot

Signal to the horse to strike off into canter

Here, the canter stride is almost complete

SIMPLE CHANGE This sequence shows a simple change, which involves transitions from canter to walk (without trot steps in between), and directly back to canter again. It requires a degree of collection in the final canter stride before the transition is made. The canter finishes with the leading (inside) foreleg (1). The first step of walk is made with the outside hind leg (2). After completing one stride of walk (2, 3), the horse strikes off into canter with the outside hind (4) as normal.

Keep your body upright to help the back stay arched

A good round last stride will produce a good transition

Immediately allow the horse to use his head and neck in walk

1

2

HALF-HALT

The half-halt improves the horse's balance and attention to your aids. It involves a momentary, co-ordinated, and barely visisble use of aids. Get a little extra impulsion, using the leg, then use a non-allowing rein contact, which tells the horse not to go forwards. Then once again ask and, this time, allow him to go forwards. Think of the half-halt as a swift progression of go-whoa-go. You cannot perform a half-halt unless your horse is between the aids and you have the co-ordination to use these aids within the space of 1 or 2 seconds. Therefore, begin by performing the half-halt over a period of 10 to 15 seconds and gradually reduce the time it takes.

CANTER TO TROT It is important to finish the canter stride with the inside leading foreleg coming to the ground before giving the aid for trot. Then the first beat of trot is the outside hind leg and inside foreleg striking out together.

Start in canter

Complete the stride before signalling to trot

First step of trot stride

3 — Give the canter aid without pressing the leg inwards, so the horse stays straight

4 — Let your seat rise with the horse into canter

The steps are correct, but the horse here is a little tense into canter — 5

TURNS AND CIRCLES

The circle is the most important of all movements because every other school exercise is based on it. Work on circles is also the basis for improving the horse's straightness because it will help him learn to bend equally well in both directions. Since the aids for riding a circle can be used for all exercises, riding circles will help you to establish a system of aids that your horse finds easy to understand and that can be applied to the rest of your school work.

THE AIDS FOR RIDING A CIRCLE

When you ride a circle, the most important thing to do is to look where you want to go and ensure that neither your seat nor your saddle slip to the outside. To achieve this, place a little weight to the inside. Then, use the inside rein to ask for the bend while your outside leg prevents the horse moving to the outside. With the correct bend, the quarters will rarely swing out.

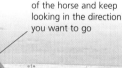

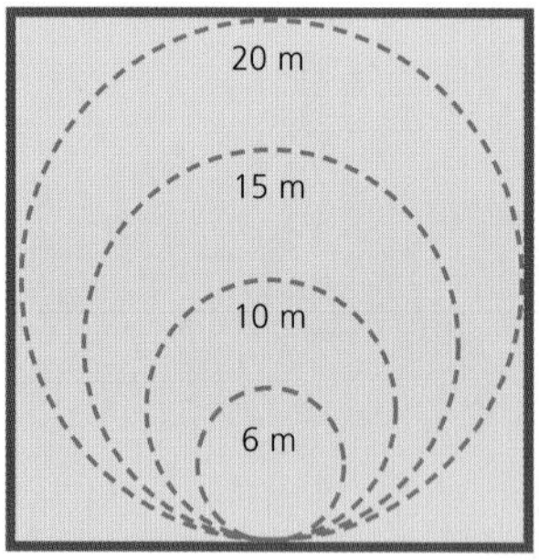

Go with the movement of the horse and keep looking in the direction you want to go

STANDARD CIRCLES

20 m
15 m
10 m
6 m

The inside fore foot should be on the same track as the inside hind foot

RIDING BIGGER AND SMALLER CIRCLES When you start novice work, you will ride mainly 20 m (65 ft) and 15 m (50 ft) circles in trot and canter with a few 10 m (32 ft) half circles in trot and walk (see diagram, above). Here (sequence, right), the rider is practising riding a 10 m (32 ft) circle, using cones to guide the horse. She uses her outside leg to control the bend **(a)**, and maintains an allowing rein contact **(b)**.

ACHIEVING THE RIGHT BEND

When riding circles, the line that you follow is of the greatest importance. Although following an imaginary line to your outside **(a)** is a natural thing to do in an arena, this carries the risk that you will make your horse crooked. This is because the horse is narrower in front than behind, which automatically puts his forehand slightly to the outside. To improve on this, many riders imagine that the circle line is underneath the spine of the horse **(b)**. The better way to help you ensure control of the shoulders and straightness on the circle is to imagine the circle line on your inside **(c)**. This will automatically bring the horse's shoulders marginally to the inside and produce the correct degree of bend.

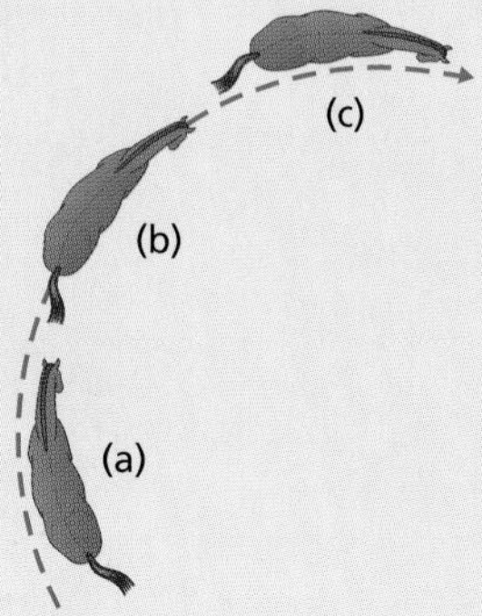

(c)

(b)

(a)

Use your inside leg to ask for impulsion and the outside rein, with the help of your voice, to control speed. These are the essential aids that are used for all school movements.

KEEPING THE CORRECT BEND

All circles should be ridden following an imaginary line on your inside (see box, bottom left). This helps to combat two common problems: unintentionally riding the horse crookedly, with the narrower forehand to the outside, and the tendency of most horses to cling to the outside of the arena. To help you develop the habit of imagining a line on the inside of your horse, place cones on the inside of a circle. With cones as guides, you will find your hands automatically move a little towards the inside at times, without pulling back, encouraging the forehand to stay on the inside line. Following an inside line will also help you to avoid using too much inside rein, which would create too much bend in the neck.

All horses find one bend easier than the other, and all riders have to work to make their horse more supple on his stiff side. Be clear with your aids, but do not force the change of bend. First, ride your horse on the rein on which he is most comfortable, and put him between the aids. Then, work on the stiffer rein.

Smaller circles can be used for short periods to develop more bend, suppleness, and the first degree of collection. However, if you try to ride too small a circle before your horse is sufficiently collected and supple, you will force him to shorten his steps, swing his quarters out, or move his whole body sideways. However, the development of collection (see pp.156–57) will allow you to ride a volte – a 6 m (20 ft) circle – with ease.

Temporarily move both hands to the inside to keep the shoulders on the inside line of the circle

Allow the horse to use his head and neck

(a) The outside leg discourages the quarters moving sideways to the outside.

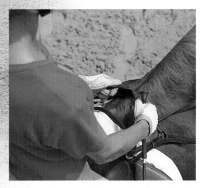

(b) Supple arms and an even rein contact produce effective rein aids.

CORNERS AND BENDS

Every corner is part of a circle. Therefore, the size of circle you can ride will dictate how well you ride corners. In turn, the size of circle you can ride depends on your ability and your horse's level of schooling. The most valuable movement is the serpentine, where parts of circles are connected to form loops, requiring you to change the bend you are riding on. It is effective in suppling and straightening the horse and your position, both of which are important for riding straight lines.

SIMPLE CHANGE OF BEND

When changing the rein – the direction you are riding in – the first thing to do is plan your route. Decide on the type of serpentine you are going to ride. Then look where you want to go, and gradually reduce the degree of bend that you already have. As you begin to do this, imagine yourself on the new bend, having changed rein. By doing this mentally first, you will find that you automatically use the aids that will bend your horse in the opposite direction: the aids are the inside rein for direction, outside leg to control the horse's quarters, inside leg for impulsion, and outside rein to control speed.

SERPENTINE BENDS

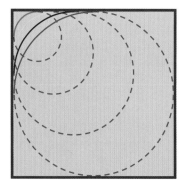

CORNERS A novice horse in canter may only be able to cope with a 20 m (65 ft) circle corner, whereas a novice horse in medium walk can easily cope with a 10 m (32 ft) circle corner. Practice corners regularly, but always maintain the quality of the steps.

Your weight should also move very slightly to the inside of your new bend, or circle. Be consciously aware of changing from riding off the inside line of the rein you are on to riding off the inside line of the rein you are joining. To begin with, you will really have to concentrate to do this, but with practice you will find it becomes natural.

SERPENTINE LOOPS

Serpentine loops (see diagrams, right) have three advantages, which make them the most valuable of all shapes for changing the rein on young horses and for novice riders.

Firstly, they encourage you to make frequent changes of bend because the shapes are comfortable for your horse and easy for you to ride. Frequent changes of bend are desirable because they encourage alternate contraction and relaxation of all the horse's main muscle groups that are used in lateral bending (see pp. 146–49). This is wonderful for suppling the horse, and it also helps to prevent the muscular tiredness and strain that can be produced by staying on one rein.

Secondly, serpentine loops have no straight lines. This is important, given that riding on a straight line is probably the most difficult thing to do. It is not until your horse is evenly developed on both sides that you can begin to ride straight lines correctly. If you use the circles and serpentine changes of rein exercises progressively, however, you will develop your horse evenly and make it possible to ride a straight line.

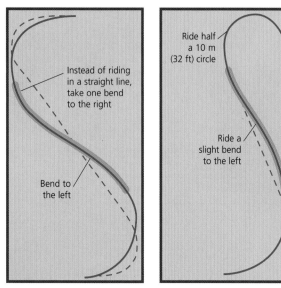

SERPENTINE CHANGE OF REIN A straight line is the most difficult shape to ride, so make the change of rein easier by gradually taking the bend away and then immediately beginning the bend in the other direction.

Instead of riding in a straight line, take one bend to the right

Bend to the left

HALF CIRCLE AND SERPENTINE Once you have a bend, it is fairly easy to make it slightly tighter. By riding half a 10 m (32 ft) circle before the change of bend, the remainder of the change of rein will be easier.

Ride half a 10 m (32 ft) circle

Ride a slight bend to the left

Thirdly, and most importantly, serpentine loops allow you to gradually reduce the bend from the rein you are on and then gradually introduce the new bend. When changing the rein on the traditional figure-of-eight shape (see diagram, below) it is necessary to make an immediate and full change of bend from one rein to the next, which is more difficult.

A gradual introduction of a change of bend makes it easier to maintain control of the horse's shoulders. If the horse's neck suddenly bends, or bends too much, it is most likely that his shoulders will move slightly to the outside, and he may then continue to fall to the outside through the shoulder. By changing the bend gradually, the risk of this happening is reduced. In addition you will have the time to focus on riding off the inside line of the bend. This will help position the horse's shoulders a small amount to the inside, which, over a period of time, will eliminate this common problem of riding crookedly with the shoulders to the outside. It also gives what is called the position to the inside, which is the introductory movement for shoulder fore (see p.145). Many master trainers talk about riders "thinking shoulder fore" all the time. Positioning to the inside and thinking shoulder fore produce the same result.

THE GOLDEN SERPENTINE

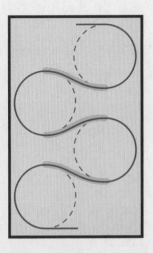

This serpentine requires the same 13.3 m (43½ ft) half circles as the standard three-loop serpentine. However, the golden serpentine is carried out in a wider, 25 m (82 ft) arena. It has an extra loop, is easier to perform, and is of more benefit. The extra arena width gives you more time to gradually reduce the bend and then gradually introduce the new bend. The forehand of a novice horse tends to slip to the outside a little on the half circle, but it will be in the right place for the new bend. You can also help to keep the forehand in the correct position by temporarily moving both your hands 5–10 cm (2–4 in) towards the inside as you go into the new bend.

SERPENTINE LOOPS

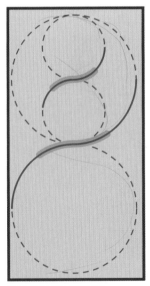

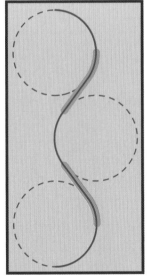

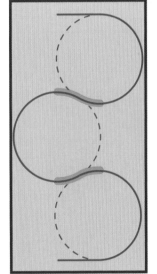

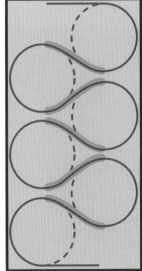

FIGURE-OF-EIGHT

A classic change of bend on a figure-of-eight shape is difficult because it requires the horse to instantly change the bend from one direction to the other. Compromise by riding one stride of the change straight.

THREE-LOOP SERPENTINE

Even with these smaller, 13.3 m (43½ ft) half circles, this is an easier change of rein than a change based on two 20 m (65 ft) circles. There is more time to reduce the bend and then introduce the new bend.

SHALLOW LOOP

This loop, done off the centre line or on the long side of the arena, is not as easy as it looks, because you have two changes of bend within a shorter period of time than you have in the previous three-loop figure.

LIGHT BULB SERPENTINE

This serpentine is invaluable as a suppling exercise and for gaining control of direction and speed. If the change of bend is too slow, complete the 10 m (32 ft) circle before rejoining the serpentine.

STRAIGHT LINES AND BENDS

One of the key indications that a novice horse and rider are well trained is that they ride straight. The judge will spot crookedness when you ride down the centre line of the arena — it is even more difficult to ride straight lines on the outside track. Straight lines and bends must be considered together because riding bends correctly will help you to achieve straightness. As you begin to put circles and straight lines together you are ready to begin riding the movements of a dressage test.

RIDING ON THE OUTSIDE TRACK

Of all the straight lines to ride, the most difficult are those on the outside track (next to the edge of the arena). The boards of the arena, or the walls of the school, seem to have a magnetic effect on horses, encouraging them to ride with their forehand slightly to the outside. This tendency is exacerbated by the fact that horses are narrower in front than they are behind. Such crookedness is also common after riding around a corner in the arena, when there is too much bend and the rider does not finish the corner properly.

To ride down the outside track with the horse straight, it is first necessary to ride in the shoulder-fore position (see box, far right). The rider must also remember to finish each corner.

So, as the forehand starts to come around along the next straight side of the arena, continue with the turn until the quarters are on the straight side and the forehand is slightly to the inside.

RIDING ON THE CENTRE LINE

As your horse becomes equally developed on both sides and you are able to position his forehand correctly, you will find it possible to ride a straight line. However, to achieve this when you are riding on the outside track, it may still be necessary to think shoulder fore or to ride position to the inside.

When you are riding down the centre line of the arena, always try to look ahead and ride towards a fixed point rather than trying to hold your horse on a line as if you were on a

STRAIGHT LINES

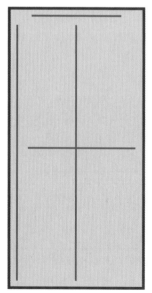

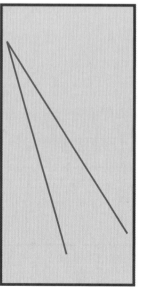

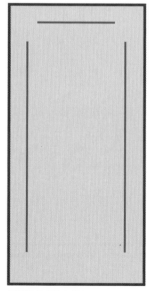

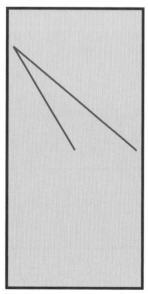

BASIC LINES Riding straight lines on the outside track is more difficult than riding ones on the centre and half-way lines.

LONG DIAGONAL LINES These lines are difficult to begin if the horse hangs to the track. You must think "shoulder fore" to finish.

INSIDE TRACK The horse will be straighter on the inside track. Riding on the inside track helps add variety to your work, so use it as often as possible.

SHORT DIAGONAL LINES These are more difficult to begin and finish because there is a greater likelihood of losing the shoulders to the outside.

tightrope. Any horse made to keep on a straight line for any length of time will move his forehand to his favourite side, so beware of this when you are out hacking. As a general rule, straighten the horse by putting his front end in front of his hind end rather than by trying to push the hind end over. This is easier and will avoid confusing the horse; trying to manipulate the hind end to achieve straightness makes it difficult to maintain a consistent aid system.

The worst thing you can do is to force straightness, because this will inevitably cramp and restrict the horse's steps. So, start off gradually with the working trot, a very symmetrical pace in which the regularity is least likely to be disrupted. Then do more in the walk, but be very careful about maintaining the natural movement of the horse's head and neck. Be particularly careful with the canter, which naturally tends to be crooked with a permanent bend. Correct it gradually and keep mixing the trot and canter paces, changes of rein, and circle and straight line exercises (see diagram, below).

STRAIGHT LINES WITH BENDS

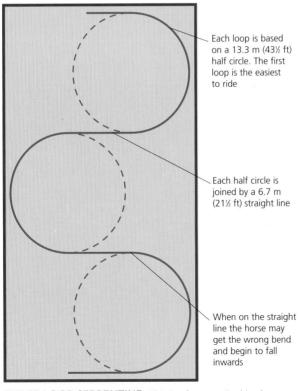

Each loop is based on a 13.3 m (43½ ft) half circle. The first loop is the easiest to ride

Each half circle is joined by a 6.7 m (21½ ft) straight line

When on the straight line the horse may get the wrong bend and begin to fall inwards

THREE-LOOP SERPENTINE This is often required in the 20 x 40 m (22 x 44 yd) arena. It is more difficult than the light bulb serpentine (see p.143) because it demands riding almost 7 m (22 ft) on a straight line between each half circle. The horse often anticipates the new rein and falls into it with the wrong bend.

SHOULDER FORE

Combined with the serpentines and circles, the exercise of shoulder fore will help you produce straightness in your horse. In shoulder fore, the horse goes forwards with the forehand slightly to the inside while the quarters remain square to the track. This cannot be achieved without sufficient bend. So, ride into this position after a corner, making the corner last a little longer than necessary. Then ride straight down the track, controlling the horse's shoulders by moving your hands a little to the inside or outside as necessary. Shoulder fore is primarily a controlling exercise for the shoulders, but it will also make the inside hind leg carry a little more weight. Here, the horse's legs are on four different tracks – outside hind, outside fore, inside hind, inside fore. This gives a guide to the angle required to ride shoulder fore.

Use your inside leg to direct the horse forwards, not sideways

Use your outside leg to stop the quarters from swinging out

LEG YIELDING

The term lateral work applies to exercises in which the front and hind legs move on different tracks, and it includes shoulder-in, travers, renvers, and half pass. The main introductory exercise for lateral work is leg yielding, where the horse yields to the rider's leg and moves sideways and forwards at the same time. Leg yielding can be done in both walk and trot, but not in canter. A related exercise is the turn about the forehand: with the horse in walk, his hindquarters move around his forehand.

INTRODUCING LATERAL WORK

Leg yielding is the most basic of all natural work exercises. It is used to introduce lateral work to novice horses and those that need retraining. It is also used in warm-up, before the horse is ready for collected work, and it is good for loosening the horse and improving acceptance.

To leg yield, the rider brings one leg back a little and keeps the horse as straight as possible. Then the horse is asked to yield sideways, moving away from the pressure of the leg at the same time as going forwards. As the horse yields, his legs on one side pass and cross in front of his legs on the other. Initially, it may be necessary to get the horse to yield to the leg by practising the turn about the forehand (see box, below), when the horse's quarters, rather than his whole

TURN ABOUT THE FOREHAND

Starting from walk, decrease your speed and then bend the horse to the right by drawing your right leg back a little. The horse will yield to the pressure of the leg, moving his hindquarters from right to left, with his forelegs moving on a 0.5 m (1½ ft) circle.

LEG YIELDING Here, the horse moves sideways from the right to the left in walk, going from the three-quarter line towards the outside track. The horse is almost straight apart from a little bend at the poll (1) as the rider asks him to yield to pressure using her right leg. She stays upright and looks where she wants to go (2, 3). If necessary, the rider's right leg can be taken a little further back (4) to move the horse's hindquarters more. Before reaching the arena boards, the rider prepares to complete the exercise and ride forwards on the inside track (5, 6).

body, move away from the pressure of the rider's leg. To reduce strain on the horse's forelegs, it is better if this is done from walk until the horse fully understands the exercise.

WHERE TO LEG YIELD

In the arena, there are a number of places to leg yield. However, because horses like going towards the side of the arena, you will probably find it easiest to practise leg yielding from the three-quarter line (see p.112) towards the arena boards. You can leg yield in the opposite direction, going away from the boards, but most horses will initially be less willing to do this. It is also normal to leg yield as you go down the length (rather than the width) of the arena, facing the horse in towards the centre of the arena at an angle of approximately 35 degrees. The horse therefore goes down the long side with his quarters on the track and his forehand just to the inside. The reverse of this is also done, with the horse's head facing the boards and his quarters on the inside, but although this helps to control the horse, it is often confusing to him, especially to begin with. These two variations of leg yielding can also be done on the diagonal line of the arena. To do this, the rider should visualize the diagonal line as though it was the long side of the arena.

A slightly different variation of this is to ride on a small circle and then leg yield on to a bigger circle. Horses are very willing to do this because large circles are easier to ride than smaller ones, but it is not classical leg yielding because the horse will maintain a little bend towards the centre of the circle. An unusual variation of leg yielding is to put the horse at an angle on a circle, with his hindquarters to the outside of the circle. This requires the hind legs to take bigger steps sideways in order to keep up with the forelegs. This is the same as making a very big turn about the forehand and emphasizes the connection between these two exercises.

REIN YIELDING

Rein yielding, like leg yielding, is a basic exercise in acceptance. Once taught, it is rarely used, unless better acceptance is required. Pressure is increased on one rein at the same time as the opposite rein is lightened (see below). The moment the horse yields to the rein pressure even slightly, the rein is given away as a reward. Then normal rein contact is resumed with both reins. It is best to do this in either walk or trot, and it should be done only occasionally, not continuously, or the horse may become rubber-necked.

The legs on the right cross in front of the legs on the left.

SHOULDER-IN

Shoulder-in means going forwards with the horse's forehand to the inside and with a uniform bend through the horse. When executed with a small angle, it is primarily a shoulder-controlling exercise. As the exercise is developed, however, it also improves collection because it makes the horse's inside hind leg carry more weight. As you practise riding shoulder-in, giving and retaking of the reins is a good exercise to carry out to ensure that your rein contact remains soft and allowing.

USING SHOULDER-IN

The majority of horses have a tendency to ride with their forehand falling to the outside. This happens on both reins, although the fault is likely to be more acute on one rein than it is on the other. The tendency is most often confirmed when riding in the arena, because horses tend to stick near the boards, and, as already mentioned, they are narrower in front than behind, which encourages crookedness.

To straighten the horse you need to be able to place the forehand directly in front of the hindquarters without sacrificing the quality of the steps. (If you force the straightness, the steps will become stilted.) Shoulder-in is invaluable for this because it enables the rider to have more control over the forehand. In addition to its value as a straightening exercise, it is a useful collecting exercise because the inside hind leg has to carry more weight as it moves forwards under the centre of the horse. These advantages mean that almost any exercise is improved if preceded and followed by shoulder-in or by shoulder fore (which is the shoulder-in position assumed to a lesser degree). Shoulder-in is usually carried out in trot, because this pace makes it easier to maintain impulsion.

ANGLE OF SHOULDER-IN

It is more important to maintain the quality of the steps than to achieve a particular angle for the shoulder-in. The angle will be dictated by the degree of bend in your horse. With the horse assuming the bend of a 20 m (65 ft) circle, you can position the forehand to the inside at an angle of around 10 degrees to the boards to achieve a small degree of shoulder fore. With the bend of a 15 m (50 ft) circle, shoulder fore can be done with an angle of around 20 degrees; with the bend of a 10 m (32 ft) circle, you can achieve shoulder-in at an angle of 25 to 30 degrees. If you get too much angle, the horse's quarters will turn to the outside. This is counter-productive because the quarters must remain square to the track, otherwise the inside hind leg will move towards the outside rather than towards the centre of the horse. In shoulder-in, the horse's forelegs will usually be just to the inside of the hind legs.

SHOULDER-IN The bird's-eye view (see inset, left) clearly shows how the bend of the horse takes his shoulder to the inside, without moving his hindquarters out. Here the bend is equivalent to that of a 10 m (32 ft) circle and the angle is approximately 25 degrees. The position of the quarters – square to the track – and the degree of bend through the horse's body is more important than the angle. Only when the correct bend is combined with the correct position does the inside hind leg come under the horse's centre of gravity.

AIDS FOR SHOULDER-IN

You can ride into shoulder-in from any corner of the arena. Maintain the bend of the corner for a little longer than is normally necessary until the forehand is slightly to the inside. This happens quickly. Then, use the outside rein to prevent the horse from continuing around the circle while moving both your hands temporarily to the outside to show that shoulder-in is required. Ride forwards from the inside leg as normal. It is important that you do not push the horse sideways from the inside leg because this will turn the exercise into leg yielding. If required, your outside leg can stop the quarters moving out, and your hands can temporarily move slightly in or out to maintain the shoulders in a consistent position. Your weight should stay central and the saddle must not slip to the outside.

GIVING AND TAKING THE REINS Giving away the rein for a stride or two, before once again taking up a normal rein contact, enables you to test the self-carriage of the horse. When the rein is given away, the horse should maintain his balance and outline. It is a useful exercise for reminding the rider as well as the horse that the rein contact is a communication point, not a support point. However, it can also be done as a reward, and not just as an exercise, in a test.

REIN-BACK

In rein-back, the horse takes three to five steps backwards with his legs moving in diagonal pairs. Introduce this exercise carefully because forcing it can cause breaking up of the diagonal pairs, shortening of the neck, and misunderstandings. From halt, gently ask the horse to walk forwards, but do not allow with your hands, preventing forwards movement, and the horse will go back. Start with one or two steps. Initially, you can supplement these aids by slightly moving your legs back. Then, ride forwards and reward.

To give away the reins, move the hands up the crest of the neck until there is no rein contact. The horse will learn to consider this as a reward

FLYING CHANGE

A flying change is a change from one canter lead to the other while remaining in canter. It is not an artificial movement, but something that horses do naturally. If flying changes are repeated after a specific number of strides, they are called sequence changes. The aid for a flying change is the same as for a strike-off to canter from trot, so if a horse is between the aids and has a good-quality canter it is a movement that any level of rider can perform.

PERFORMING SINGLE CHANGES

Do not do flying changes until your horse fully understands the canter aid and also canters straight, otherwise he will learn to leap sideways as he changes lead. He must be able to achieve a first degree of collection in the canter and be happy in counter-canter (see box, opposite). Showjumpers use the flying change to alter their direction between fences, and they often do it better than dressage riders. Following their example, it can be more effective to begin single changes with a lighter seat.

Be patient and establish the counter-canter first – tension and anticipation will work against you. If you ride across the arena in canter, going on to the new rein on the diagonal line, the horse may change easily. However, on the next occasion, he

A SINGLE FLYING CHANGE Starting with cantering to the left, the aid is given and the horse does the flying change in the period of suspension, coming back to the ground cantering to the right, with his left hind leg being the first beat of the stride.

TWO-TIME FLYING CHANGE This five-stride sequence shows two two-time flying changes – stride, change, stride, change, stride. The horse is cantering with his right leg leading (**1**). The rider uses his outside leg to give the aid for the change to the left, which occurs in (**2**). The horse is cantering with his left leg leading (**3**), and the aid is given for the change to the right, which occurs in (**4**). The horse finishes cantering on his right leg (**5**).

Give the aid for the flying change with the left leg

After the flying change, return your lower leg to its natural position

COUNTER-CANTER

Before you start teaching your horse to do a flying change, you need to be able to perform counter-canter. This is, in effect, intentionally cantering on the wrong leg, with your horse cantering with his outside foreleg leading, instead of his inside fore leg. So, for example, on the left rein, he will canter with his right leg leading. To go around corners in the arena in counter-canter, you need a degree of collection in the canter. You must ensure that the horse keeps a little bend to the outside throughout – this helps him understand that counter-canter is required. In addition, keep a little extra weight on the side of the leading leg. Being able to keep your horse in counter-canter is required if the horse is going to do the flying change on a specific stride when you ask for it, rather than when he decides it is the right time. Try some counter-canter exercises (see diagrams, right).

COUNTER CANTER Going on the left rein, the horse canters with his right leg leading.

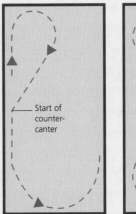

EXERCISE ONE Ride a 10 m (32 ft) half circle before returning to the track in counter-canter.

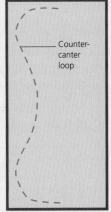

EXERCISE TWO A 5 m (16 ft) loop in counter-canter is a useful preparatory exercise.

may anticipate the movement or get excited. Go around the whole arena in counter-canter, and then ask for the change when you are ready and the horse is calm. Make the horse straight, then imagine yourself on your new rein, pretend you are in trot, and ask for canter with your outside leg. Reward immediately. The change stride should be the same length as the canter strides before and after the change.

SEQUENCE CHANGES

If you take as much time as you need to establish a good-quality single change, progressing to sequence changes will be relatively easy. A two-time sequence change (see below) is when the horse does a flying change every second stride. Since the change stride is counted as a stride, there is, in effect, just one stride between each change. With one-time changes, there is a flying change of stride every stride, so the aid for the next change has to be given every stride. Start by doing a sequence of two five-time changes (with a flying change every fifth stride), then canter on for ten strides and do another five-time change; then repeat. Start to take out strides between the pairs of flying changes until eventually you do four five-time changes. To help your concentration and to maintain the rhythm, count each change as you do it. In the case of five three-time changes, count each change, as well as the two strides that follow each change: "One, two, three; two, two, three; three, two, three; four, two, three; five".

Give the aid to change with your left leg

4

During the flying change, the horse's neck should remain straight

5

TRAVERS, RENVERS, AND HALF PASS

Travers, renvers, and half pass are all variations of the same movement in that they all involve going forwards and sideways at the same time. However, each is done in a different place in the arena. Half pass is a beautiful and impressive sight if it is done well, but it requires a good understanding of the movement because a small change of angle can have a detrimental effect on the regularity of the steps and the level of impulsion. The key to half pass is, initially, to ride it like travers.

TRAVERS AND RENVERS

Before attempting the half pass, you need to be confident in travers. Travers can be considered as the opposite of shoulder-in because it involves going forwards with the quarters to the inside (see diagram, far right). Your horse will look straight down the track so that his forehead is square to the boards. There is a bend from his head to his quarters, taking the quarters to the inside. Because the bend begins at the poll,

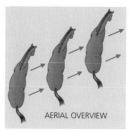

AERIAL OVERVIEW

HALF PASS RIGHT This is an advanced half pass, but the quality of the movement is more important than the acuteness of the angle. If your horse struggles at all, or goes with unlevel steps, immediately make the exercise easier by reducing the angle or come out of the exercise altogether.

Bend the horse to the right and draw your outside leg back

Use your outside leg to go sideways and your inside leg to go forwards

Continue with the movement if the strides are regular and level and impulsion is maintained

Keep your weight into the direction of the movement. Here, the saddle has slipped to the left

To finish, change the bend, think shoulder-in, and ride forwards

even the forelegs are taken marginally to the inside. The bend appropriate for this movement is that of a 10 m (32 ft) circle, which will give an angle of approximately 30 degrees. However, you should start with a smaller angle.

To begin travers, you need a degree of collection in walk on the short side of the arena. Then enter the corner, using the corner to get the bend you need. When your horse's head is facing down the arena's long side, but with his quarters still on the corner, use your outside leg to hold the quarters in that position; then, progress down the long side, continuing to keep the quarters to the inside. Once the horse understands the exercise, progress to trot. Always remember to maintain the regularity of the trot throughout the exercise.

The aids, as usual, are inside rein for the direction, outside leg to control the quarters, inside leg for impulsion, and outside rein to control the speed. In this exercise, the outside leg is the most important aid. Your weight should be slightly to the inside; you must avoid slipping to the outside, which is the most common positional fault. It is easy to get too much bend in the neck, so use the outside rein to control the degree of bend, making any necessary alteration to prevent this problem.

Renvers is essentially the same movement as travers, but it is done in a different position in the arena. So, if you imagine the horse in travers, transported in that position to the opposite long side of the arena, you have renvers. The position adopted by the horse's body is identical (see box, right). In travers, the forehand is on the outside track with quarters and bend to the inside; in renvers the forehand is on the inside track with the quarters and bend to the outside. Renvers has the great advantage of keeping the horse's shoulders away from the outside track, so it should be used regularly instead of travers.

Getting into renvers demands a little more thought than getting into travers. You can start a shallow loop after the corner and begin renvers as soon as the bend is changed, or you can go on to the inside track and start from that position. The best method is to go into shoulder-in and then just change the bend while keeping the horse at the same angle.

HALF PASS

The key to riding half pass is initially to ride it like travers. To do this, imagine the arena swivelled around to create an imaginary long side on the diagonal line (see box, right). Then as you ride around the corner before the half pass, make sure you do not start the half pass until your horse is looking straight down this diagonal line. In this way, you will never get the quarters leading (a common error), and you will find it easy to keep the bend.

To ensure your horse maintains sufficient impulsion and level steps in the half pass, use a small angle and ride only a few steps in half pass at a time before riding forwards again. As you become more advanced, the horse has to be at an angle greater than 30 degrees to the line of progression. At this point, the half pass is slightly different because, although the angle is increased, the bend is not. The effect of this is that, increasingly, the horse cannot look where he is going (see sequence, opposite). If he can look where he is going, you know there is too much bend. As the angle increases, make sure the diagonal pair of legs both move the same distance sideways, otherwise the steps will become stilted.

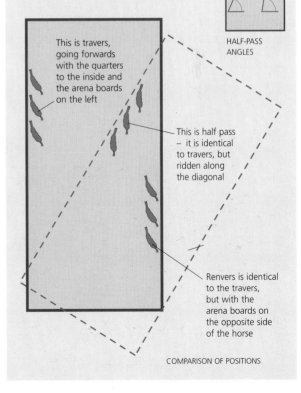

HALF PASS AND TRAVERS

Travers is one of the simplest exercises because it is relatively easy to keep a consistent bend and angle. When riding half pass, however, riders often get the quarters leading, lose the bend, and lose their position. It therefore helps to imagine you are riding travers. If the angle of travers position is increased beyond 30 degrees, the horse will no longer be able to look straight down the track. This is also the position for an advanced half pass.

HALF-PASS ANGLES

This is travers, going forwards with the quarters to the inside and the arena boards on the left

This is half pass – it is identical to travers, but ridden along the diagonal

Renvers is identical to the travers, but with the arena boards on the opposite side of the horse

COMPARISON OF POSITIONS

PIROUETTES

The canter pirouette, in which the horse moves his forehand around his quarters while his hind legs stay in almost the same spot, is one of the classical movements that epitomizes good training and it feels magnificent to ride. It requires a level of collection higher than normal so that the horse can lower his quarters a little in order to lighten the forehand. The preparation for canter pirouette starts with the walk pirouette, and with the horse accepting the basic aids.

WALK PIROUETTE

The walk pirouette requires a degree of collection. Start by riding into it as you would ride into travers, with the quarters to the inside (see pp.152–53). Start well away from the track and collect the walk a little. Have a bend to the inside, equivalent to a small circle, and your weight slightly to the inside **(1)**. Then, ride into travers position but direct the forehand to the inside by temporarily moving both hands to the inside and back again. Use the outside leg to control the quarters **(2)**. Throughout the movement, be careful not to let your body slip to the outside (as it has in **3**). After a few steps of pirouette, walk forwards again and reward the horse. As your horse becomes more advanced, the hind end will stay more in one place. You can cease thinking of travers and, instead, your outside leg can just prevent the hindquarters from moving out.

You may find it helpful to ride in a square, pirouetting at each corner so that the horse does a 90-degree turn on to each side of the square. You can then progress to riding a triangle, pirouetting through 120 degrees at each of the three corners.

CANTER PIROUETTE

Canter pirouette is a very advanced movement. It demands collection plus in canter (see pp.156–57). You ride a few canter

strides of travers on a circle, gradually reducing the circle until you are doing one or two strides of canter pirouette. Few horses maintain the period of suspension in canter as they do this, but it is possible with good training.

WALK PIROUETTE To begin with, let the hind legs walk a few steps of a 1–3 m (3–10 ft) circle, then gradually tighten the circle over a period of months. The steps must maintain the normal regularity of walk.

CANTER PIROUETTE Nicole Uphoff of Germany and her horse Rembrandt in canter pirouette. For a complete 360-degree turn the horse will take six to eight canter strides. The horse must be light through the rein otherwise he will not be in the right balance, sitting on his quarters. This requires collection plus (see pp.156–57), which can be achieved only after several years of progressive work.

COLLECTION AND EXTENSION

Shortening and lengthening the steps is called collection and extension respectively. Having established the working paces, it is possible to begin first a little shortening and then a little lengthening. As the impulsion and carrying power of the horse increases, this shortening and lengthening leads to true collected and medium paces and eventually to collection plus and extended paces. If the horse remains at ease and under control in all these paces, the training has been excellent.

SHORTENING AND LENGTHENING

In collection, the steps are shorter, and the horse will carry more weight on the hind legs, while in medium work the steps will be longer. The tempo (speed of the rhythm) should stay the same throughout, and the sequence of steps of each pace should remain correct. For this to be possible the speed has to decrease for collection and increase for medium, which cannot be done without sufficient controlled impulsion. This can only be achieved if the horse is accepting, calm, forwards, and straight.

The defining quality of good collection is lightness through the rein; the defining quality of extension is the quality, not the size, of the step. It is tempting to make the steps in the medium paces as large as you can, but this will make the medium and extended paces indistinguishable when there should be a clear difference between them. All horses are different, so it is difficult to generalize, but in walk, trot, and canter respectively there should be at least 20 cm (8 in), 30 cm (12 in), and 60 cm (24 in) clear difference between medium and extended step lengths. The

The neck is a little short but the horse is comfortable and at ease

MEDIUM TROT

With good medium or extended paces the horse will spring off the ground, making the movement appear just as effortless as in the working paces. The high level of impulsion required makes athleticism essential.

With such engagement the horse has an advanced balance

The power from behind creates a lightness in front

same applies to the difference between medium and working paces, and working and collected paces (see pp.126–27).

ADVANCED COLLECTION

As collection develops, the horse will have a shorter stance time (the time his feet are on the ground) and a longer period of suspension. This is sometimes called cadence. With cadence, the horse will spring off the ground and be lighter on his feet.

The greatest degree of collection is collection plus. It is easiest to begin developing collection plus in the trot, starting from the walk, because the horse is usually calmer in walk and there are no balance problems. Add more impulsion, but do not allow the horse to trot forwards until he naturally springs into short steps (called half steps). It is important that these steps are in diagonal pairs with a period of suspension, as in normal trot. This is the beginning of piaffe (see box, below). From piaffe, it is possible to begin moving forwards into passage, although passage can also be developed from collected trot. The vital thing is always to guard the purity of the paces and the impulsion. Never do these advanced movements as tricks but always as a logical development of the basic work.

ADVANCED EXTENSION

Advanced extension is an expression of power and lightness. It comes as a result of good collection, good impulsion, and athletic ability. Bear in mind that not all horses have the athletic ability required for an extended trot. A good-quality extended trot will not be hugely difficult to sit to because the horse will remain soft and supple through the back.

COMBINATION OF EXERCISES

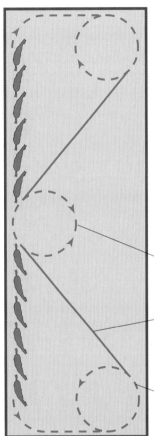

USING COLLECTION AND EXTENSION Working at collection is a prerequisite for extension, but extension will also help improve the level of impulsion and in turn help the collection. There are many exercises to develop both extension and collection but this is a classic example. By using a combination of shoulder-in and small circles in collection, medium, or extended trot on the diagonals, plus regular changes of the rein, both collection and extension can be improved.

You can ride half pass back to the outside track from this point

Here, it is better to use a good-quality medium trot than to over-extend your horse

Ride small circles in one of the shortened or lengthened paces before riding on the diagonal to the outside track

PIAFFE AND PASSAGE

These movements bring audiences to their feet. They are a combination of advanced collection and impulsion. Both involve a very elevated trot with an accentuated flexion of the knee and hocks and additional spring. In passage, however, the horse moves forwards slowly while in piaffe he trots on the spot. Piaffe requires the horse to sit on his quarters and to maintain the impulsion so that the period of suspension is not lost. Different aids are needed to help the horse distinguish between collected trot, passage, and piaffe. Using continuous pressure with both legs for passage, and alternate leg pressure in time with the steps of piaffe, is one solution to this challenge.

PASSAGE

PIAFFE

COMBINING THE EXERCISES

When preparing for dressage tests, you should practise mixing the exercises, including paces, transitions, school movements, and lateral work. This will reflect the progression of exercises used in the tests. There is a need to identify movements that lead neatly into each other, and work that is different but complementary. For example, lateral work and smaller school movements fit together, while shortening and lengthening of the paces complement each other.

WORKING WITH THE PACES

All dressage tests are done through the medium of the paces — walk, trot, and canter. As we mix and match the elements that combine to form a dressage test, it is vital to build from paces that have a natural outline and sequence of steps.

The simplest mixing and matching involves using all three paces on both reins. The horse has to be worked in both directions for even development, and all three paces should be combined and used for their advantages. For example, the walk is a good pace for providing more time for your horse's understanding of and response to the aids, as well as for rest and relaxation, but it is not useful for achieving impulsion. For this, you can use trot or canter. The trot is often preferred to canter because it is easier to maintain straightness and regularity in the trot, but some horses need the canter to get them thinking forwards. Initially, it is usually easier to go faster in canter without losing the purity of the pace, than it is in trot. If your horse needs more forwardness, go for a strong canter rather than a strong trot. If you use the paces in this way, you can view them as a team of exercises that complement each other.

A TEAM OF EXERCISES

As you train, you will discover the advantages and disadvantages of each exercise, and you can then try to fit them together so that they complement and improve each other. For example, a small circle can have the disadvantage of discouraging forwardness, although it is good for balance, whereas medium trot is good for forwardness and not so useful for balance.

Then there are small teams of exercises that are like jigsaw pieces because they lead into each other so neatly. The most

USING THE ARENA
As you train at home and design your own freestyle tests, be imaginative and use all parts of the arena. Every shape you use should, of course, be of benefit to your horse's way of going, but many horses are hindered in their development because of a lack of creativity in the training exercises

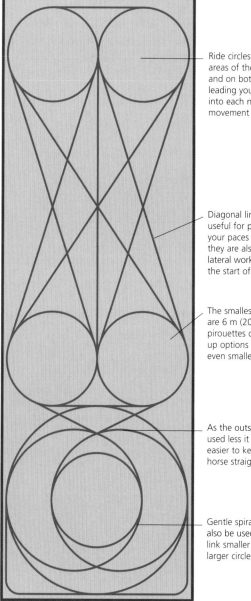

Ride circles in all areas of the arena and on both reins, leading your horse into each new movement

Diagonal lines are useful for practising your paces on, but they are also used for lateral work or for the start of a circle

The smallest circles are 6 m (20 ft), but pirouettes open up options to use even smaller steps

As the outside track is used less it becomes easier to keep your horse straight

Gentle spirals can also be used to link smaller or larger circles

COMBINATION ARENAS

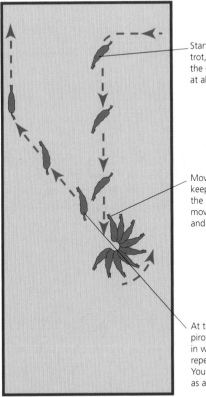

Start in travers, in walk or trot, going forwards with the quarters to the inside at about 30 degrees

Move into walk pirouette, keeping the regularity of the steps and natural movement in the head and neck

At the end of the pirouette, half pass in walk or trot, then repeat on the other rein. You can use medium trot as an alternative

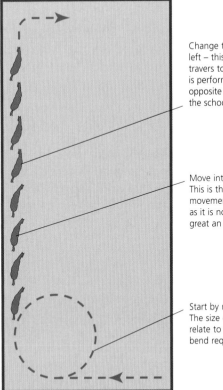

Change to renvers to the left – this is identical to travers to the left, but is performed on the opposite side of the school

Move into shoulder-in. This is the most important movement of all, as long as it is not done with too great an angle

Start by riding a circle. The size of circle should relate to the amount of bend required

TRAVERS TO PIROUETTE TO HALF PASS In all these exercises, the legs on the outside of the bend pass and cross in front of the inside legs. This makes it possible to move seamlessly from one exercise to the next. The priority must still be the horse's understanding of the exercise and the quality of the steps.

SHOULDER-IN TO RENVERS It is not possible to go seamlessly from shoulder-in to travers, half pass, or pirouette, because the legs cross in the opposite way. But it is possible to go seamlessly from shoulder-in to renvers. All that is required is a change of bend. It is one of the very best exercises.

obvious of these are the simple progressions: going from a good working trot to a little shortening and lengthening; going from 15 m (50 ft) circles to 10 m (32 ft) and 20 m (65 ft) circles, and going from shoulder fore to shoulder-in.

There are also different exercises that fit together seamlessly, such as half-circles and serpentines, travers and pirouette, and shoulder-in and renvers (see diagram, top right). In lateral work, it is easy to fit together any combination of travers, half pass, and pirouette because the legs cross in the same way (see diagram, top left). They all require a degree of collection so they also fit together well with smaller circles and half circles.

As you begin to understand the relationship between exercises, it will be possible for you to be more imaginative in your choices. This means you will be able to link teams of exercises in an educated manner and progress towards riding actual dressage tests.

THE COLLECTIVE MARKS

As you put exercises together, assess the work in relation to the constant components: acceptance, calmness, forwardness, straightness, and purity. At the end of a test, the judge will award you collective marks. There are collective marks for: paces (their purity), impulsion (the basis of which is calmness, forwardness, and straightness), and submission (acceptance). There is also a collective mark awarded for the rider's position and effectiveness. It is easy to forget the importance of these collective marks, which clearly indicate the training priorities. Do not worry too much about a little inaccuracy in a movement or delay in a transition, particularly at the lower levels. The priorities are quality and regularity of the paces, acceptance and understanding, and impulsion. These all reflect the rider's ability.

EXERCISE OVERVIEW

The paces, transitions, movements, and exercises can be blended together progressively, ranging from trotting a 20 m (65 ft) circle, to doing flying changes in canter for every stride on a circle. Knowing when to start introducing each exercise, whether a rein-back or a canter pirouette, and understanding the movement's advantages and disadvantages, and its relationship with the other exercises, is a vital part of becoming an effective rider.

THE PACES AND THEIR VARIATIONS

The description and definition of paces is based on objective analysis of a natural walk, trot, and canter. However, the description and definition of the variation of paces is a more subjective process that is still evolving. The variations refer to different stride lengths and balance within the same pace.

Many people look upon the collected, medium, and extended variations of paces as being equally spaced, with the working trot set apart as a variation that is used just for warming up and for working novice horses. This is not a true reflection of the paces as used in the dressage arena, where the medium trot is obviously closer to the extended trot than to the collected trot. It is also evident that the collection required for the piaffe or the canter pirouette is substantially greater than the collection required for the half pass.

It is therefore more logical to define five equally spaced gears within each pace – the working pace being in the middle, with two higher gears (the medium and extended paces), and two lower gears (collection and collection plus).

Although it is true that many riders offer working paces that are closer to medium paces, this is due more to the competitive nature of riders trying to outdo their rivals than to rule-book definitions. It is important to remember that you should begin with just a degree of collection and medium work, and that this can still be highly marked if the quality of the work is good.

TRANSITIONS, MOVEMENTS, AND EXERCISES

It must never be forgotten that the transitions, movements, and exercises are all done from one pace to another, or within a particular pace, which has to remain true and correct. As explained, a progressive transition is one in which no intermediate pace is excluded in a transition, such as going from walk, to trot, to canter. A direct transition is one in which a pace is left out, such as going directly from walk to canter. The same definitions apply to the variations within each pace. To begin with, you go progressively between collection, working, medium, and extended, but later on you may make transitions directly from collection to extension.

All the exercises in the chart (see opposite) are expressed as maximums at each level of riding ability. Level One relates approximately to an introductory level of competition; Level Two relates approximately to a novice level of competition; Level Three relates approximately to an intermediate or medium level of competition; and Level Four relates approximately to the introductory level of international competition. The benchmarks will help you gauge how to increase the level of difficulty of the exercises, which is the key to progress.

It should also be remembered how important a general exercise programme is to your horse. It should include jumping and riding outside over undulating ground in order to develop all-round athleticism and fitness, and to maintain the horse's interest in his work. Jumping, in particular, is uniquely placed to help the anaerobic development of your horse's muscles (see pp. 321–23), something which is vital in the dressage horse.

DEVELOPING THE HORSE

Dressage exercises are part of a bigger picture that is concerned with developing the horse's mind and body, and producing a partnership between horse and rider. An individual exercise is mechanical, but the overall training has to be based on feel, empathy, acceptance, agreement, calmness, confidence, and willingness. The marrying of these mechanical and mental elements is reflected in the opening statement of the governing body for equestrian sport, the FEI (Fédération Equestre Internationale): "The object of dressage is the harmonious development of the physique and ability of the horse ... It makes the horse calm, supple, loose, and flexible, but also confident, attentive, and keen, thus achieving perfect understanding with his rider. Thus the horse gives the impression of doing of his own accord what is required of him." This bigger picture is important because a good rider is not just a technician, and the exercises can be used successfully only if they are part of a holistic approach that respects the senses and mind of the horse.

DRESSAGE BENCHMARKS

EXERCISES	LEVEL ONE	LEVEL TWO	LEVEL THREE	LEVEL FOUR
Paces	• Free walk • Medium walk • Working trot • Lengthening strides in trot • Working canter • Halt	• Collected trot* • Medium trot* • Collected canter* • Medium canter* • Rein-back * First degree only	• Collected walk • Extended walk • Collected trot • Extended trot* • Collected canter • Extended canter* * First degree only	• Half steps in trot • Extended trot • Collection plus in canter • Extended canter
Transitions	• Halt to walk • Walk to halt • Walk to trot • Trot to walk • Trot to canter • Canter to trot	• Halt to trot • Trot to halt • Walk to canter • Canter to walk • Rein-back to collected trot	• Collected to medium, and medium to collected, in walk, trot, and canter • Rein-back to collected canter	• Collected to extended, and extended to collected, in walk, trot, and canter
Movements	• 15 m (50 ft) circles in trot and canter • 10 m (32 ft) half-circles in walk and trot • Four-loop serpentine in trot — 40 m (44 yd) arena • Giving and retaking the reins • Straight lines	• 10 m (32 ft) circles in medium walk • 8 m (26 ft) circle in collected trot • Counter-canter, half a 20 m (65ft) circle	• 20 m (65 ft) circles in medium canter • 6 m (20 ft) circle in collected trot and canter • Counter-canter, half a 15 m (50 ft) circle	• Counter-canter, half a 10 m (32 ft) circle
Lateral work	• Position to the inside • Turn about the forehand • Leg yielding	• Shoulder fore • Small travers and renvers	• Shoulder-in • Travers and renvers • Half pass at 20°	• Half pass at 30° • Counter change of hand in trot
Pirouettes		• Large half pirouette in walk	• Walk pirouette	• Half pirouette in canter
Flying changes			• Single changes	• 5 x 4 and 5 x 3 time changes
Other activities	• Showjumping level 1 (see p.231)	• Showjumping level 2 (see p.231)		

RIDING THE NOVICE TEST

The novice test is designed to encourage good basic dressage skills to be developed. It requires working trot and canter, medium walk, and progressive transitions, using movements that are flowing and straightforward. Your horse must show regular, unhurried, and natural paces, be between the aids, and be calm, forwards, and straight. As a rider, you must have a balanced seat and use your arms and legs independently, without making your aids obvious.

ANALYSING THE TEST

While you are waiting for the bell to signal the start of your test (see box, far right), ride around the warm-up arena on your horse's stiff side. This will help you get his neck straight so that you achieve a straight entry into the arena at A and a clean movement down the centre line.

Take the time to remind yourself of your strategy for riding the test. In the second half of both the two 20 m (65 ft) circles in trot, you should aim to move an extra metre down the arena, away from X. This will help you get back into the track half a horse's length early, which will look accurate from the judge's viewpoint and will help you into the 10 m (32 ft) half circle which follows. Aim to be straight on the centre line for one stride, then make the second 10 m (32 ft) half circle half a metre bigger than it should be so that you can get back into the track at the half-way marker. You should also aim to ride well into the arena corners during the trot, walk, and trot transitions. This will both help the downward transition and show that you know how to use the arena.

As you ride into canter on the last 20 m (65 ft) circle, look where you want to go so you do not lose the shape of the circle. To help the giving and retaking of the reins in canter on the diagonal line, you may need to use the previous corner to help you slow down and rebalance. (The judge will be expecting you to do this just before X, where many riders make it too obvious.) Aim to give the reins away for two whole strides, one before and one after X.

The walk in the penultimate movement is a free walk on a long rein, but keep your hands moving with the horse's mouth so that he is encouraged to use his neck freely. In training, the last halt should be practised between a pair of planks on the ground. This will help straightness.

THE JUDGES' SCALE

Every movement and the collective marks are graded out of ten. Some judges are negative and work by deducting marks from ten. It is better to start from zero and reward for what is right. A good judge will also add comments to explain their marks. Aim for minimum scores of fives and sixes. If you do not achieve these levels, do more training before competing again.

0 – NOT PERFORMED	6 – SATISFACTORY
1 – VERY BAD	7 – FAIRLY GOOD
2 – BAD	8 – GOOD
3 – FAIRLY BAD	9 – VERY GOOD
4 – INSUFFICIENT	10 – EXCELLENT
5 – SUFFICIENT	

REACHING NOVICE LEVEL When your horse is between the aids, as shown here, you are ready for the novice level. Progress will be delayed if you compete without your horse working well through his back.

A NOVICE TEST

You will be given your test sheet to study in advance (see below). Read it from left to right – each movement leads directly into the next movement. The alphabetical arena markers (see p.112) act as your guides and will help you memorize each part of the test. X refers to the centre mark, although this is not marked on the arena. In your preparation, there needs to be an emphasis on the trot,

and on the transitions from trot to walk, and walk to trot, of which there are three of each. The most difficult movement is going up the centre line at the start and finish because you need to keep your horse straight. The other testing movement is the change of rein through X using two 10 m (32 ft) half circles. All the other movements, however, are straightforward.

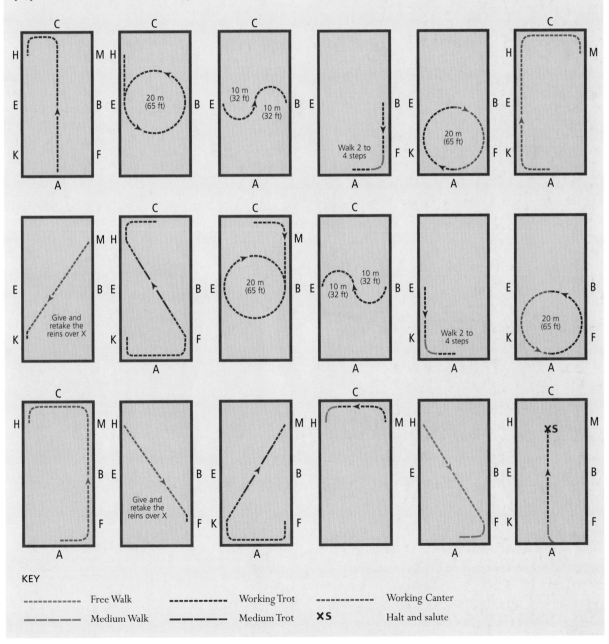

KEY

--------- Free Walk	----------- Working Trot	---------- Working Canter
———— Medium Walk	▬▬▬▬ Medium Trot	**XS** Halt and salute

RIDING THE ELEMENTARY TEST

When you reach elementary level through good quality work, you have a real sense that the level above this – medium – is well within your grasp. The collection and medium work required at elementary level is of the first degree only, but they need to be clearly shown from the start of each movement. By now, your horse will also show improved muscular development and impulsion and will easily cope with more demanding movements.

ANALYSING THE TEST

Always analyse the test (see box, right) before you ride it. Think about your main strategies. The 10 m (32 ft) circles at A are often ridden inaccurately. The judge can easily see if you go beyond the three-quarter line, so practise riding these circles with someone watching. The trick is to divide the space between the outside track and the centre line as you look around from A, and then as you cross the centre line. When returning to the track after the two medium trots, and when going into the counter-canter, plan to come back into the track a little early. This is the danger period in the counter-canter, when a horse might be tempted to do a flying change, so the key is to keep a secure contact with your outside leg drawn back. Do not be tempted to straighten the horse's neck.

There are two separate marks for the halt and rein-back, so make sure you do halt before performing the rein-back. There are also separate marks for the short periods of canter from A to the start of the 20 m (65 ft) circles. Aim to complete your corners so that the horse's quarters reach the outside track on the long side, rather than staying to the inside as you go down the long side of the arena to P or V.

ELEMENTARY LEVEL This horse has a good natural outline for this level and shows good impulsion in working trot. The rider is well-balanced and, together, they form a good partnership.

AN ELEMENTARY TEST

This test is an example of an official FEI (Fédération Equestrian Internationale) dressage test used in a one-star level three-day event. There is a good balance of movements, and approximately the same marks available for trot and canter. The medium trot is made easier for the less experienced horse and rider as it may be ridden in sitting or rising trot. The transitions to and from medium canter may be done gradually, and all transitions can be progressive. The test is also made easier by having the canter work in consecutive movements. You need to score 75–80 per cent to be competitive. If you can produce this quality of work, progress to the next level will be relatively easy.

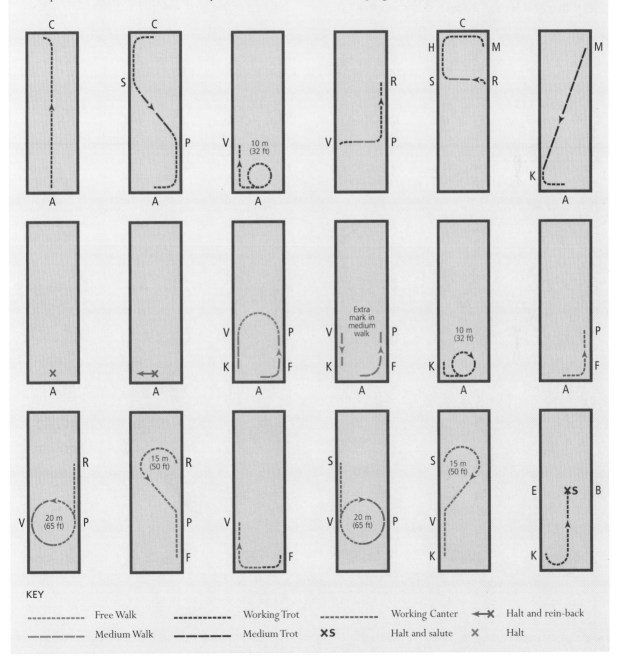

KEY

----------- Free Walk	--------- Working Trot	----------- Working Canter	◄━✗ Halt and rein-back
——— Medium Walk	▬▬▬ Medium Trot	✗S Halt and salute	✗ Halt

RIDING THE MEDIUM TEST

The medium test, which follows elementary level, is the first time you will be expected to show true collected and medium paces and first-degree extended paces. You will have to do single flying changes in canter and a full pirouette in walk. A further improvement in impulsion will need to be shown, with lighter steps and a continued demonstration of ease throughout. If you can reach medium level with good quality work, given time, you will achieve Prix St George.

ANALYSING THE TEST

Before your test (see box, right), make sure you are prepared. In your training, avoid always doing single flying changes on the centre line. Linking serpentines with circles (see p.143) will help prevent your horse anticipating a flying change.

Entering the arena in canter and showing straightness is not easy, but you can choose either rein. You will need to show direct transitions from canter to halt, and halt to trot. The shoulder-in on the centre line is a good test of your training – make sure you do not push the quarters out to achieve the position. The shoulder-in should then flow seamlessly into the 8 m (26 ft) circle, which in turn leads to the half pass. Wait until your horse's head is pointing to the quarter marker before starting the half pass. If you are losing the regularity in the lateral work, do easier work at home and aim to improve the level of impulsion.

You also need to be able to do good transitions within each pace. If it helps the quality of your transition, you may score more highly by only going for 80–90 per cent of your maximum in the extension.

MEDIUM LEVEL This horse shows the muscular development and strength required for medium level, and a good balance in collected trot. As more weight is carried on his quarters, his neck shortens and his head lifts. The rein contact is light.

A MEDIUM TEST

In this test, there is an extra emphasis on the canter, and just one mark for the walk. However, the quality of the walk will also be reflected in the collective mark for the paces. This is a flowing test, and the movements all complement each other well. The separation of the trot and canter work make the test easier. However, you will only be competitive if you can produce good quality single flying changes.

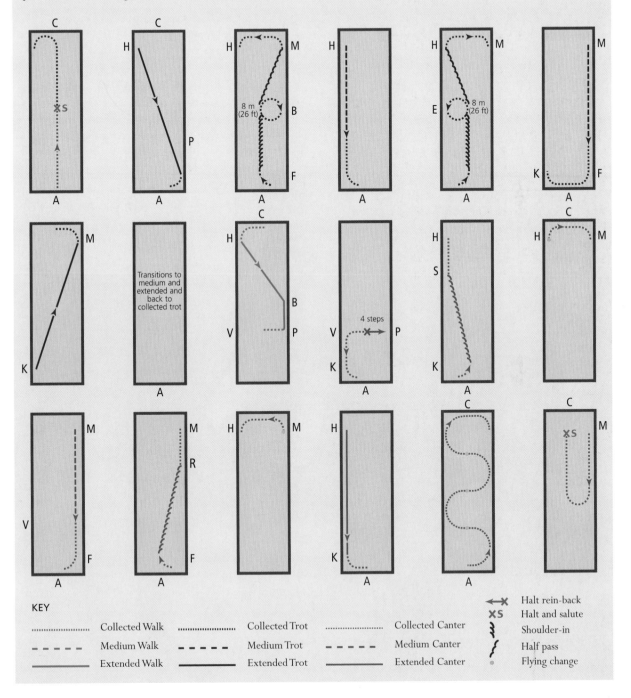

KEY

············· Collected Walk	············· Collected Trot	············· Collected Canter
- - - - - Medium Walk	- - - - Medium Trot	- - - - - Medium Canter
—— Extended Walk	—— Extended Trot	—— Extended Canter

Halt rein-back
Halt and salute
Shoulder-in
Half pass
Flying change

RIDING THE ADVANCED TEST

When you reach the advanced level, you are not just riding a test, but producing a display, showing your horse to the best of his ability. The sequence flying changes and half-pirouettes in canter are the two audience-pleasing additions at this level. The judges will expect your horse to have the ability to change instantly from collected to extended paces and back again, and be able to spring off the ground with ease and elegance.

ANALYSING THE TEST

For this test (see box, right), make sure you are well prepared. In canter, you are asked to produce a counter change of hand, going from the quarter marker towards X in half pass, with a flying change at X and then back to the quarter marker. To make this easier, aim to finish the first half pass just before X, and have just a small bend. Then push the quarters slightly out at the end to ensure that your horse is straight, before asking for the flying change and going back in half pass. Moving the quarters will also stop an early flying change. In your preparation for the canter half-pirouette, keep your horse straight, rather than moving the quarters over early. Do a slightly big half pirouette rather than lose the canter.

With the sequence changes, you can prepare for the higher level tests by learning to count the number of each change. If your single changes are good, with an obedient response to the aids and a straight change, you will find the sequence changes happen quite easily, as long as you and your horse stay calm.

ADVANCED HORSE Further collection enables the horse to lower his quarters and sit on his hocks, which gives the impression of his forehand being raised. There is a lightness, ease, and joy about this partnership.

AN ADVANCED TEST

This is an FEI Prix St George test, the entry level test for international competition. There are four marks for the walk, an extra mark being given for the collected walk before and after the half-pirouette. There are two sets of sequence flying changes, but only one mark for each set, so a mistake here will not have a huge effect on your score.

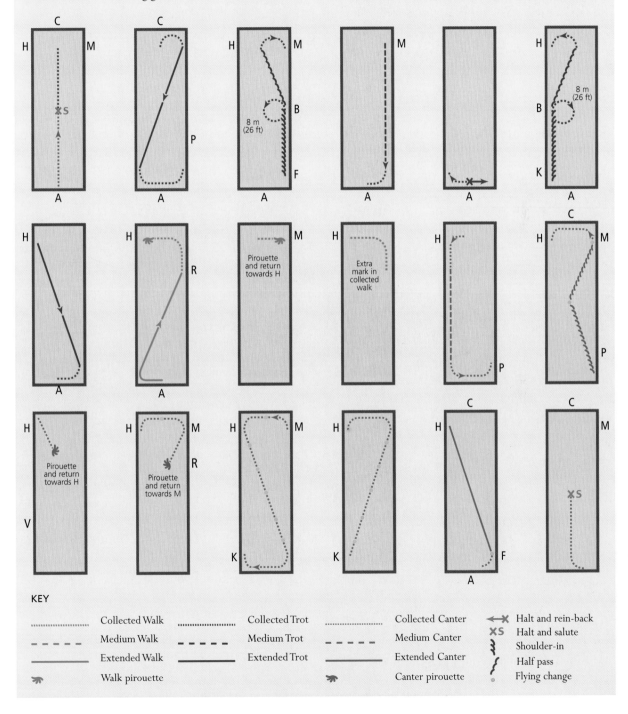

KEY

⋯⋯ Collected Walk	⋯⋯ Collected Trot	⋯⋯ Collected Canter
– – – Medium Walk	– – – Medium Trot	– – – Medium Canter
⸺ Extended Walk	⸺ Extended Trot	⸺ Extended Canter
🐾 Walk pirouette		🐾 Canter pirouette

⟵✗ Halt and rein-back
✗S Halt and salute
〰 Shoulder-in
〰 Half pass
• Flying change

AT THE COMPETITION

Everyone needs a little luck in competition, but in reality, success comes through good preparation and opportunity. It is the competition that provides the opportunity, and making the most of it depends on how you handle yourself on the day.

This includes knowing how best to warm up your horse, remembering the test, and understanding how to use the experience positively. You also need to know how to show yourself and your horse to best advantage from the judge's perspective.

PREPARING FOR A COMPETITION

Before arriving at the competition, you need to have set yourself performance goals. In order to achieve these goals, you need to plan the most appropriate warm-up. Analyse the dressage test required for the competition to see if there is anything in it that might affect your preparation. A well-designed test should have a balance between trot and canter work, but it is not unusual to find an imbalance. Your preparation and warm-up need to be directed specifically at making the most of the situation, bearing in mind both the test and your goals.

WARMING UP

Every horse will be different, but at home try to get your horse used to coming out of the stable and working immediately, after which he has a period of relaxation. If you get in the habit of having to spend 2 hours preparing for a test, then neither of you is going to be in the best condition for it. The horse will have gone off the boil and neither of you will be fresh. If your horse does have a tendency towards being unsettled, it can help to travel to competitions where you are not competing, just to get him used to such surroundings.

In the warm-up, allow sufficient time for just walking around, so that your horse can relax and get used to the atmosphere. Half an hour spent standing still, watching everything that is going on, is better than spending half an hour fighting for his attention in the warm-up arena.

When starting work, concentrate initially on achieving acceptance and calmness; use big easy movements, rising trot, and possibly a light seat in canter. As you start working more intensely, start on a positive note by doing the things that you do well together. Next, put a few movements together.

Many horses dislike the warm-up arena, associating it with a bad experience, so remember that the training should be done at home, rather than left to the day of the competition. Most horses benefit from being ridden actively for the last 10 minutes of the warm-up. This means that you can ride straight into the competition arena knowing you are in gear.

Finally, it is important afterwards to analyse how you have warmed up and how the test went. Keep a diary and be prepared to make small changes for next time. In your analysis, try to ask why things went right, as well as wrong. Then you can repeat situations that produced good results.

PUTTING ON A PERFORMANCE When you get in to the arena you need to be prepared to perform and to sell yourself. You may also have to improvise and plans may have to be adapted; your horse is not a machine and no two performances will be the same. Pictured left is Jennie Loriston-Clarke, the first British dressage rider to gain international recognition and one of the first exponents of dressage to music.

DRESSAGE TO MUSIC

Dressage to music has become an increasingly popular element of the sport and, at top level, is called the kur. It produces some spectacular performances. When you prepare for a competition, the first step is to design a test. There will be a list of mandatory paces and movements. Having assessed those that you and your horse do well, design a draft test that suits your strengths and is in a sensible order. Then look for small, unique elements to provide added value. An extra little movement of your head or a smile in time with the music, can make all the difference. Spiral and curl movements can all increase the element of surprise without sacrificing quality. Allow for flexibility with circles, which can be made bigger or smaller to help you get back in time with the music. Horses have narrow bands of rhythm and tempo so it is not easy to find suitable music. Get into the habit of having music playing as you train. It will become obvious what pieces of music suit your horse and make him respond well.

Notice the speed of the rhythm of each pace. The tempo should stay the same, even when the stride length changes, and this will be emphasized when you ride in time to music. Remember that, as you train, your horse's period of suspension in trot and canter may improve, causing the tempo to slow.

TIMED TO PERFECTION Dressage to music in pairs, or quadrilles of four horses, opens up new avenues for creativity. Whether individual or team, the test needs to be timed accurately before the music is collated.

RINGCRAFT

In the arena there are two major optical illusions of which you need to be aware. Firstly, when going away from the judge, horses tend to look crooked, with the forehand to the outside (see picture, below), although the same horse can look straight when coming back. This is due to the width of the horse's quarters and the perspective the judge is viewing from. Therefore, when going away from the judge, make it a habit to bring the forehand in a little. Practise this in training.

Secondly, when you are going away from the judge across the arena, and returning to the track, it always looks as

though you are joining the track later than you actually are (see inset picture, far right). This is exaggerated if the judge is looking at the letters ½–1 m (1½ ft–3 ft) outside the arena, and not at the red stick marking the position of the letter on the boards. Therefore, aim to come back to the track about half a length early at the end of a diagonal line or circle. The further you are from the judge, the more you have to do this, so aim to reach the top quarter marker a length early.

Ringcraft is the ability to show you and your horse in the best possible light, by promoting your strengths and hiding your weaknesses. It is a major contribution to success because

RIDING AWAY FROM THE JUDGE These pictures are taken at the same time, but from different angles. The main picture below shows the judge's view, in which it looks as if the horse's forehand is to the outside, instead of straight. When seen from behind, however, it is obvious the horse is straight **(a)**. Therefore, when going away from the judge, it helps to ride shoulder-in.

Move the forehand more to the inside so the horse looks straight to the judge

(a) The horse is riding straight along the outside track.

The horse is wider behind, and, from this view, his hindquarters are accentuated

it helps you gain the marks that can give you the winning edge. Ringcraft is not something that can be left to the competition, it has to become a habit that is established in training, otherwise thinking about it too much at the competition may make your performance deteriorate.

RIDING FOR THE JUDGE

The first and most important rule to remember is that a dressage test is a performance, not a training session. Even when riding a test at home, you must see it through to the end and make the most of the situation. At the competition, a judge may not always see something that goes wrong, so do not emphasize the fault by making an over-obvious correction or by pulling a face. If you need to make a correction, then do it facing away from the judge, towards the A end of the arena. If there is just one judge, they will also find it difficult to see exactly where you are when you turn across the arena on a circle and are parallel to them. This is where you can sneak an extra ½–1 m (1½ –3 ft) into the size of a circle, which may help you show better work.

It will also make a big difference to the overall impression if you and your horse look at peace with the world and as if you are enjoying the experience. The judges will like this. The opposite impression may suggest there is something wrong with the training and may lose you marks.

When riding around the arena before entering for your test, avoid showing the judge something you do not do well. Instead, show something at which you can impress them. For example, if your horse has one rein on which he tries to bend too much, ride him on the opposite rein.

The performance starts from the moment you begin circling around the arena prior to entering it, and it does not end until the judge has finished giving you the collective marks, which may not be until after you have left the arena at C. Therefore, after you have saluted, smarten up your position in the walk and reward your horse. If walk is not your horse's best pace, when you have left the arena, take up the rein and go into trot.

It must be remembered that even the cleverest ringcraft is no substitute for good-quality work, so your main efforts should always be directed into getting the horse going properly, with ringcraft being used to add the finishing touch.

RETURNING TO THE OUTSIDE TRACK

When returning to the track at the A end of the arena, away from the judge, it always looks as if the forehand is to the outside and the horse is late getting to the track (a). It is an optical illusion, which you can counteract by coming to the track half a length to one length early, and then riding position to the inside. This will also help you prepare for the next movement.

REMEMBERING THE TEST

When learning a test, mark out a miniature arena on the ground or draw the movements on paper so you can visualize them. Learn the test in pairs of overlapping movements, for example, movements one and two together, then two and three together, then three and four. This method will ensure that you remember what comes next after each movement.

Remembering a test is largely down to confidence. If you think positively, your brain will cope better. Practise positive thinking and develop a strategy to cope with stress. Repeating words to yourself, such as "calm" and "forwards" may be effective. Try doing abdominal breathing and saying "stop" as you breathe out. If you feel stressed, keep things simple and just concentrate on your direction and speed. Above all, be proud of yourself for reaching the competition and enjoy the moment.

Finish every diagonal line by positioning the forehand to the inside

Returns to the outside track correctly

(a) From the judge's view, the rider is late at the corner

RIDER CHALLENGES

CHALLENGE	POSSIBLE CAUSES	SOLUTIONS
BUMPING IN SITTING TROT	• Lack of suppleness	• Being supple enough to go with the horse's movements demands good posture and control of the lower back, and this takes time and effort to achieve. Exercises off the horse's back (see pp.332–51) can really help in this area.
	• Horse not using his back	• The better your horse uses his back, the easier it is for him to cope with a rider sitting to the trot. If the horse's back is stiff, the rider will bump more, and this in turn makes the horse's back even stiffer. Sit to the trot only a little to begin with – spend time in the walk and canter with your seat in the saddle to give you plenty of opportunity to practise your sitting position.
	• Unsuitable saddle	• A dressage saddle that makes you ride too long will tend to put you on your fork (see p.114) and stiffen the lower back, making the sitting trot difficult. A saddle that makes you ride too short will put your seat further back, which makes a harmonious sitting trot almost impossible.
LOOSE LEG CONTACT	• Riding too long	• For the lower leg to be in contact there must be sufficient bend in the knee joint. The most typical reason for a loose leg contact is riding with stirrups that are too long. The wider the horse, the shorter a rider's stirrups will have to be.
	• Unsuitable saddle	• If a saddle is too straight in the front, it will force the rider to ride too long. As a result, good leg contact will be difficult. Use a saddle appropriate for the activity you are doing.
	• Lack of suppleness	• With some riders, poor leg contact is simply a question of being too tight in their seat and hips. Specific suppling exercises off the horse's back will make an immediate difference (see pp.342–45).
NON-ALLOWING REIN CONTACT	• Lack of understanding	• The rein contact is a communication point and not a support point. As soon as riders understand this, they tend to improve the quality of the rein contact they have with the horse.
	• Poor balance	• If you feel that you need the rein contact to support yourself, try improving your balance by removing the rein contact altogether for short periods of time.
	• Poor suppleness	• Some riders are simply stiff through the shoulders or find it difficult to carry the weight of their lower arm. This can be easily corrected with regular exercise (see pp.346–47).

CHALLENGE	POSSIBLE CAUSES	SOLUTIONS
ONE-SIDED USE OF THE BODY	• A one-sided rider	• Most people find turning in one direction more difficult than turning in the other. By deliberately turning on your bad side, whether you are on your feet or on a horse, you can make significant progress. If you jog on a running track, for example, run both ways around the track. Use your weaker hand to hold a mug, open doors, and hold the telephone; you will quickly become more ambidextrous. This is vital for effective riding.
	• A one-sided horse	• Like humans, horses are one-sided to a greater or lesser degree. As a result, this pushes the saddle and the rider's seat to one side and encourages increased use of the hand and the leg on the horse's stiff side. Being aware of this and working at the equal development of both sides of the horse will help make your riding less one-sided. It helps both to ride better-schooled horses and horses that are crooked in the opposite way from your own horse.
SITTING CROOKEDLY 	• Lack of suppleness	• This is primarily a result of being one-sided. We all tend to put the seat slightly to the outside on the rein we find easiest, with extra weight in the less co-ordinated leg. At the same time, we tend to keep one shoulder back. Work at the even development of the horse and rider, as described above.
	• Horse leaning on the rein	• Crookedness is exaggerated if the horse tends to lean on the rein or pull against the rider, but the remedy is the same as for lack of suppleness. Remember that a horse can only lean against you if you give him something to lean against. Try to develop a more allowing rein contact and remember to keep it allowing as you give your rein aids.
POOR FEEL	• Lack of balance	• This makes you grip inwards and hold on with the reins, which makes it difficult to feel what is happening underneath you. Improve your balance with exercises (see pp. 340–41) and lunge lessons.
	• Lack of harmony	• Let your seat go with the movement of the horse's back, your legs with the horse's sides, and your hands with the horse's mouth.
	• Lack of understanding	• It helps to have a clear understanding of the sequence of steps and the way of going required for each pace. With the help of your coach, continually assess and reassess what is happening during a lesson. The key question to ask yourself is how did it feel? As you compare and contrast different feelings, you will develop a sense of feel.

RIDER CHALLENGES

CHALLENGE	POSSIBLE CAUSES	SOLUTIONS
MISUSE OF DRESSAGE WHIP	• Poor positioning of the hands	• The dressage whip – or stick – should lie across your knee and thigh so that a twist from the wrist will put it in contact with the horse's side just behind your leg. Give a light tap, not a strong slap. After the right response, immediately reward the horse. Next time, use a leg aid alone and make sure your rein contact is allowing.
	• Stick held between the wrong fingers	• Some riders find the stick difficult to use because it hangs too far forwards. This is normally because they are putting all four fingers around it instead of holding it between the thumb and first finger. This also stiffens the hand and largely prevents the use of finger aids. Carry the stick so that it goes over the bottom of your thigh with your hands in the normal position.
	• A bad attitude	• Riders with a bad attitude may use the stick too strongly, which is inexcusable. Use a more solid, less whip-like, stick.
INEFFECTIVE WARM-UP AT COMPETITION	• Lack of time	• The amount of time needed to dress, tack up the horse, and ride to the warm-up area is often underestimated. Most horses and riders benefit from walking for 20 minutes before starting serious work. Then, leave time for a 10- or 15-minute break during the warm-up so you can do any last-minute grooming.
	• Unsure of strengths and weaknesses	• If you concentrate on exercises you find hard, both you and your horse will become tense and everything will deteriorate. Aim to do good-quality work in a small number of areas. Establish the constants (see pp.122–23), and everything else will fall into place.
	• Neglecting to analyse the test	• Analyse the test beforehand and let this influence your warm-up. Concentrate on matching your horse's strengths to the test.
UNDER RIDING IN TEST	• Frozen by stress	• Try to keep a positive attitude (see pp.364–65) and stay calm. Analyse what is causing the stress, such as unrealistic expectations. Long-term planning and goal setting will help (see pp.362–63).
	• Over-concentration on appearance	• Some riders are ineffectual because they are concentrating on the way they appear. Remember that position and effectiveness go hand in hand – a static position is not a beautiful position.
	• A sensitive horse	• Some riders are passive because they are worried about their horse reacting. Some horses have to be ridden carefully, but many perform better if their energy can be directed into an exercise.

CHALLENGE	POSSIBLE CAUSES	SOLUTIONS
OVER RIDING IN TEST	• Trying too hard • Lack of preparation • Lack of feel	• Many novice riders over ride simply because they are trying too hard. This is not a bad fault, as long as you learn from your mistake. Here, the value of having a coach to watch your tests will become apparent. Look carefully at the remarks of the dressage judge. • In your preparation and training, you need to do work of a slightly higher level than you will be asked to do in competition. • In competition, you will have to make your own decisions, so having a good sense of feel is essential. It is possible to improve your feel by working at your harmony, by riding as many different horses as possible in as many activities as possible, and by occasionally riding higher level horses. Most riders will lose some of their feel through stress, so work on your ability to stay calm.
FORGETTING THE TEST	• Mental block • Lack of preparation • Lack of concentration	• This is usually down to nerves; keep a positive frame of mind. • As well as practising the test a few days before the competition, draw the movements out. On the ground, draw out a miniature arena so you can practise the test on your feet. • Some riders are so involved in the way their horse is going or in wondering what the judges are thinking, that they lose concentration. As ever, the variables (see pp.128–29) must take priority in the competition, and the first two variables are direction and speed. As you enter the arena, prioritize correct direction and speed.
UNDER-PERFORMING IN THE COMPETITION	• Not prioritizing • Negative state of mind • Unrealistic expectations	• If you do not analyse the test and work from your strengths, it will be impossible to prioritize. For example, you need to work out how you should warm up and decide how demanding you can be of your horse in individual parts of the test. • Seeking a personal best rather than trying to win every competition will make you more positive. • Recognize and value your strengths. Focus your attention on the percentage you receive for the test, rather than on the final result of the competition. Then compare this with the percentage you had set as your goal before the competition. It is normal to do practice work of a slightly higher quality than in competition because most horses are distracted to a greater or lesser degree when they are at a competition venue.

HORSE CHALLENGES

CHALLENGE	POSSIBLE CAUSES	SOLUTIONS
LACKING ACCEPTANCE	• Poor understanding	• Lungeing your horse without a rider is the key to establishing understanding, and getting the horse to use his back (see pp. 72–73). Make sure you are not asking more of your horse than his training has prepared him for.
	• Rider stiffness	• Work on your suppleness off the horse. If you are stiff through nerves, learn to relax by doing some of the mental preparation exercises (see pp. 352–71).
	• Discomfort	• Discomfort is often a result of the horse not being able to use his back, which in turn is often because the rider is too stiff to be in harmony with the horse. Horses may also be uncomfortable because of sharp teeth, or badly fitting bits, nosebands, and saddles. Always check tack before looking for other causes.
LACKING CALMNESS	• Poor preparation	• Calmness needs to be established as a habit from an early stage in a horse's training. Lungeing is once again effective, combined with as natural a stable-management routine as possible (see pp. 50–51). Many horses are unsettled because they spend too much time in the stable and are given too much hard feed. You have to have sufficient patience to progress slowly to begin with so the horse is always given the chance to settle.
	• Over riding or discomfort	• Some riders are too ambitious or macho in their attitude. As a result, they over ride and make their horses tense. Some horses are tense because of discomfort caused by hollow backs, resulting from lack of training, or badly fitting equipment.
LACKING FORWARDNESS	• Lack of confidence	• Many horses are labelled unwilling when in fact they are just lacking in the confidence that progressive training would give them. Break training exercises down into simple steps.
	• Restricting rein contact	• Many horses lose their willingness to go forwards because they are not being ridden forwards from the rider's leg. Instead, they are being manipulated through the rein contact, with the rider trying to shorten the neck unnaturally. This is confusing and uncomfortable.
	• Discomfort	• Other major causes of discomfort are pain in the front feet and restricted use of the back. Have a vet check your horse. If it is back pain, your horse may require both a new saddle and a new way of going. Work on the lunge is very effective.

CHALLENGE	POSSIBLE CAUSES	SOLUTIONS
LACKING STRAIGHTNESS	• Riding off the outside line of a circle	• A one-sided rider will tend to make the horse crooked, as will riding off the outside line of a circle. Imagine and follow a line on the inside of a circle (see p.140), not on the outside. Your horse will automatically be straighter, and you will ride straighter. It will help if you think shoulder-in (see pp.148–49).
	• Too much use of one rein contact	• Always think shoulder-in, and work on both reins regularly. The serpentine is a terrific exercise to develop straightness (see pp.142–43) and will emphasize the need to have neither too much nor too little bend in the neck. It will also get your horse to bend laterally. Equal use of both sides of the horse, plus the ability to position the forehand in front of the quarters, will produce straightness.
LACKING PURITY	• Restriction of the head and neck	• A lack of use of the head and neck restricts purity in the walk. This is primarily caused by a restrictive rein contact. For this reason, the dressage rules allow a slight lightening of the rein in extended walk.
	• Restriction in the back	• In trot, lack of purity is most often seen in a shortened period of suspension caused by a lack of impulsion. This is often caused by riders doing too much sitting trot before they are able to go with the movement of the horse's back. In canter, the period of suspension is often lost completely because of both a lack of impulsion and the rider asking for collection too early in training. The purity of the paces is at the heart of all dressage training (see pp.124–25) and no movement can be done well without it. Progressive training will establish and protect the natural paces so that these types of problem do not arise.
LACKING IMPULSION	• Lacking calmness and forwardness	• Controlled impulsion is achieved through having all the constants in place – acceptance, calmness, forwardness, straightness, and purity (see pp.122–23). However, lack of calmness and lack of forwardness are the most frequent reasons for the absence of impulsion.
	• Lacking assertive riding	• A horse may also lack impulsion because the rider is too passive. It is important to be clear with your aids and ride assertively, particularly if your horse is bored or lethargic. To find out how much your horse can give, you have to occasionally ask slightly too much. Often, you will be surprised about how much impulsion your horse can produce.

HORSE CHALLENGES

CHALLENGE	POSSIBLE CAUSES	SOLUTIONS
MOUTH RESISTANCE	• Restriction by the rider	• It is true that horses can show resistance in the mouth because of discomfort through a badly fitting noseband or sharp teeth. However, a more common reason is restriction through the rein or excessive use of running reins or a martingale. Always remember that the rein belongs to the horse not to you, and that an unnatural position of the head and neck will adversely affect his way of going. Having his head in a fixed position may also make the horse angry, which in turn instinctively makes him want to open his mouth.
	• Lack of impulsion	• If a horse has sufficient impulsion, this will have a direct and positive effect on the way he accepts the bit and rein contact. Developing all five constants (see pp.122–23) will help achieve better impulsion and better acceptance of the bit. This is why good riders use few types of bit.
	• Habit	• Unfortunately, once a horse has developed a habit of resisting in the mouth it will tend to stay with him. Once again, the emphasis is on good basic training so that this problem never arises. Riding in a bitless bridle for 6 months may break the habit.
NOT BETWEEN THE AIDS – HOLLOW OUTLINE	• Discomfort	• If a horse is uncomfortable with the tack or the weight of the rider it will be difficult to put him between the aids. Lungeing in comfortable tack and without a rider will help overcome both of these problems.
	• Lack of impulsion	• Concentrate on developing all five constants (see pp.122–23). If necessary, take a step back in your training.
	• Habit	• In some cases, especially with older horses, going in this way becomes a habit that can be difficult to change. In these circumstances, the temporary use of a chambon (see p.386) may be helpful. A chambon should only be used on the lunge. It is a gadget that runs from between the forelegs to the poll and down to the bit. It puts pressure on the poll to encourage the lowering of the head and lengthening of the neck. From this stage, you can ask the horse to go more forwards and use his back. As with all these gadgets, its use should only be temporary or the advantages will be outweighed by the disadvantages, the main one being an unnatural way of going.

CHALLENGE	POSSIBLE CAUSES	SOLUTIONS
NOT BETWEEN THE AIDS – A SHORT NECK	• Inappropriate use of gadgets or a restrictive rein contact	• The horse's neck is flexible, and it is easy for the horse to learn to shorten his neck in isolation from the use of his back. The horse may drop the bit when he is doing this, making it difficult for you to take up a rein contact. This reaction is typical after there has been excessive use of running reins and a restrictive rein contact. Dropping the bit is a serious problem because it makes it virtually impossible to develop real impulsion. Work on the lunge with a chambon (see p.386) may help. In addition, working the horse up- and downhills and over jumps, when he will naturally use his head and neck a great deal, will also be useful. The horse has to learn that it is a good thing to use his head and neck and take his head forwards so you must be very quick to reward the right reaction.
	• Pain	• Organize a veterinary check to ensure that your horse is not in pain.
SHYING IN THE TEST	• Poor impulsion	• If the horse is genuinely between the aids you will find that most shying behaviour will stop. He will focus on where he is going, accept the rider, and tend not to be distracted.
	• Past experiences or restricted vision	• Horses that have been frightened by something in the arena, such as plastic walls getting caught by the wind and blowing away, will tend to remember this. In addition, restricted vision when the neck is in a rounded shape (see p.46), leaves the horse more susceptible to fright, and therefore to shying, because he is less likely to see objects before they move suddenly into his line of vision. If a horse begins to shy, avoid punishing him. Instead, put him in the shoulder-in position (see pp.148–49) away from the distraction and ride forwards quietly.
RUNNING STEPS	• Rider lacking harmony	• When the horse gives short, running steps, this shows a lack of purity in the pace. Often this is caused by the rider not being in harmony with the horse – in particular, not allowing the seat to move with the horse's back in sitting trot.
	• Lack of impulsion	• This is caused by a lack of one of the constants (see pp.122–23).
	• Habit	• If a rider is unbalanced when changing the diagonal, the horse gets used to shortening his steps over point X in the arena. Put more weight through your legs in rising trot and vary changing the diagonal from the X point.

HORSE CHALLENGES

CHALLENGE	POSSIBLE CAUSES	SOLUTIONS
BREAKING IN TROT AND WALK	• Lack of calmness	• If a horse lacks calmness, he will tend to break his pace. Increase the work programme, create a more natural routine, and reduce his hard feed.
	• Lack of impulsion	• With sufficient impulsion, it is usually easier for the horse not to break his pace, and he will normally take the easiest option.
	• Over riding	• A horse may also break his pace because the rider asks too much. This is often combined with a stiffening of the seat. This is where good feel, softness, and harmony will supply a long-lasting solution.
NOT SQUARE IN HALT	• Lacking straightness	• If a horse is not developed evenly on both sides he will be crooked and he will also halt crookedly. Lungeing work and training to help him become more even will be necessary.
	• Being tapped up in halt	• If a horse has more weight on his forehand than his quarters as he comes to halt, he will tend to have his hind legs apart. If you then tap up the leg that is left behind with the dressage stick, you may find that this leg then goes too far forwards. If you tap up the other leg, the horse ends up like a circus elephant on a drum with his hind legs too far underneath him. It is natural for a novice horse to have the hind legs a little apart in halt. This is not a major problem as long as he is still and has weight solidly on each leg. As the training progresses and he carries more weight on his hind legs, it is natural for him to take the extra half step with one hind leg and finish square in halt from the walk. In trot and canter, it will be necessary to do at least one stride of collection for the horse to go straight into a square halt, not stopping on the forehand.
INACCURATE MOVEMENTS	• Lack of preparation	• Inaccuracies are often caused by the rider not thinking ahead. Draw the movements out on paper and know exactly where you should go. A typical example of inaccuracy is to make a 20 m (65 ft) circle at E or B too big when you are in a 60 m (65 yd) arena. The tendency is to touch the RS and VP lines (see arena diagrams, p.112). However, for a 20 m (65 ft) circle you should be 2 m (6½ ft) to the X side of these lines. Try to prepare for transitions and return to the track a little early rather than late.
	• Unaware of optical illusions	• Make sure you compensate for the effect of optical illusions in the arena (see pp.172–73).

CHALLENGE	POSSIBLE CAUSES	SOLUTIONS
CHANGING LEGS IN THE COUNTER-CANTER	• Lacking calmness	• If a horse is tense, he is likely to change the canter lead to the inside. Do not punish him for this, but work to achieve greater calmness.
	• Not understanding the aid to canter	• If he understands the aid, he is much more likely to change legs only when he is asked. Work on improving his response to the canter aid, which is also the aid for a flying change (see pp.150–51).
	• Discomfort	• Counter-canter (see p.151) requires the balance of a first degree of collection. If the counter-canter is started too soon, the horse will be uncomfortable and will find it easier to change legs without being asked.
QUARTERS LEADING IN THE HALF PASS	• Beginning a movement too early	• Some riders find this a continual problem in half pass but it is easy to correct. Make sure you do not begin the movement too early; wait until the horse's head is facing in the direction you wish to go. Then, think travers rather than half pass (see pp.152–53).
LOSS OF IMPULSION IN LATERAL WORK	• Restricting rein contact or a lack of harmony	• A loss of impulsion is sometimes caused by the rider trying too hard and being restrictive with the rein contact, or by not staying in harmony with the horse's movement. Do this work little and often, and ensure you have some impulsion before you begin.
	• Progressing too quickly	• A good-quality trot should not deteriorate in lateral work. However, some horses are asked to do too much lateral work too quickly, with the result that they cannot cope and the trot deteriorates. In particular, there is a loss of the period of suspension caused by a lack of impulsion. When you introduce any of the lateral work exercises, reduce the degree of difficulty by going only a little sideways and for just a few steps at a time.

CHAPTER SIX

SHOWJUMPING TRAINING AND COMPETITION

There is a real feeling of flight when riding, and never more so than when showjumping. To a spectator, a course of fences may appear simple, but to a rider, it is a mind game that is won not by strength, but by knowledge. This chapter will take you through the equipment used in showjumping, the right position for jumping different kinds of fences, and how to judge and adjust to the distances between them. It will show you how to plan your training schedule, progressing from simple novice exercises to advanced courses that require jumping on an angle or a circle. You will also see how to work out the best route around a course to gain the winning edge in a competition. Finally, a troubleshooting section provides solutions to any challenges that you may come up against.

INSPIRATIONAL SHOWJUMPING

Showjumping brings together as diverse a gathering of participants as you will find in any sport. The common ground is not only a love of horses, but a passion for precision riding and an appetite for a challenging, exciting activity that is as demanding as it is exhilarating. Whether you are new to the sport or already an accomplished competition showjumper, watching top horses and riders jumping the big, technical courses will inspire you to achieve more.

THE CHALLENGE OF SHOWJUMPING

Showjumping is both a science and an art. The science lies in understanding centres of gravity and angles of ascent, and in the ability to judge stride lengths and take-off points. The art is in the style and flair that you bring to the challenge, as well as in developing a partnership with your horse that will enable you to reach the top of the sport.

Finding the right take-off point for a fence requires not only precise control of your horse but also an ability to judge a distance. Top riders are consistently within 30 cm (1 ft) of the desired take-off point, while novice riders may struggle to be within 1 m (3 ft) of this point. Many consider this ability a genetic gift, but it is in fact something that can be learned, particularly if training is correct from the start. If you are consistently presented with exercises in which you automatically have an even stride length and the right take-off point, you will develop the ability to judge a distance.

Rounds are often against the clock, so finding the most efficient route around the course in order to finish in the fastest time is a key skill that showjumpers must develop.

A SPORT FOR ALL

It was not until the 1950s that women were allowed to compete at the highest level, and showjumping is still seen by many as a man's game (this used to be the general view about dressage as well). The first female winner of an international medal in showjumping was British rider, Marion Coakes, on the pony Stroller, who won a silver at the Mexico Olympic Games in 1968. The gold-medal winner in these games was the massive and magnificent Snowbound, ridden by William Steinkraus from the USA. This famous David and Goliath contest is a superb example of the wide range of horses and riders that take part in the sport.

It used to be said that the big European warmbloods (such as the Hanoverian) were a must for showjumping because of their sheer size and power. The emphasis is now on horses being quick to react and careful to clear fences even at the gallop, and many European riders are now riding horses with more Thoroughbred blood.

TECHNICAL SKILL

Thorough training is essential, particularly as showjumping courses now demand more precision than they did in the past. In the 1968 Mexico Olympic Games, for example, not a single rider in the team event managed a clear round; this was despite the use of heavy 4.9 m (16 ft) poles in deep cups, designed to make the jumps quite difficult to knock down. In those days, the fences were massive and a horse's courage was at a premium — many successful horses consistently rattled

INSPIRATIONAL JUMPING New Zealand-born Samantha McIntosh, who is one of relatively few women to reach top level, competed for Bulgaria on Royal Discovery at the 2002 Olympics.

poles without bringing them down. Today, shorter 3.7 m (12 ft) poles are used in shallower cups. Horses have to take greater care in order to achieve a clear round.

ALL-ROUND EXCELLENCE

You cannot showjump without doing dressage. During a 1½-minute showjumping round at the highest level, a horse may spend only 15 seconds in the air. It is during the rest of the time, on the flat, that the competition is won or lost. Horses that can reach the highest levels in both dressage and showjumping are rare, but sometimes we see superb dressage in a showjumping round. Britain's John Whitaker and his magical horse, Milton, inspired many. Milton jumped beautifully, but his paces, his flat work, and the standard of his schooling were exceptional. He was able to shorten and lengthen strides better than many dressage horses, and he never looked anything less than elegant. Another such combination was Ireland's John Ledingham and Kilbaha, who won three Hickstead Derbys, delighting onlookers during every step of every round.

SMALL JUMPER Only 15.3hh and all quality: the diminutive mare Touch of Class, ridden by Joe Fargis from the USA, won the gold medal at the 1984 Los Angeles Olympic Games.

WORLD LEADER Britain's John Whitaker and the 16.2hh grey Milton won the World Cup in 1990 and 1991. When showjumping is good, it is also beautiful.

EQUIPMENT AND FACILITIES

As showjumpers perform many hours of dressage in their training, much of the equipment required for showjumping is the same as that used in dressage. The main difference is in the shape of the saddle and in the safety equipment worn by the horse to prevent injury while jumping. In addition, you need access to a suitable arena for training and the necessary fence equipment.

THE RIDER'S EQUIPMENT

Your clothes must be comfortable, and they must allow you to move freely. Boots should have a non-slip sole and be flexible around the ankle joint to allow movement. They should also be fairly thin on the inside to allow close leg contact with the horse. Spurs can be worn to reinforce the leg aids, but they should never be sharp or capable of causing injury to a horse's sides, and they should not be worn by a beginner. A whip can be carried to reinforce your aids.

The showjumper's movement in the saddle is greater than that of a dressage rider. A short jacket should be worn so that it does not get caught between your seat and the saddle. It must have sufficient freedom in the shoulder area to allow you to move your arms without restriction, especially when jumping quite large fences. An approved hat is essential.

THE HORSE'S EQUIPMENT

The flat shape of the jumping saddle allows you to ride with shorter stirrups (see p.94) and lets your seat rise and return to the saddle unimpeded. Since this type of saddle provides less security than one with a deeper seat, it is important that you are able to maintain a secure, well-balanced position.

A saddle pad may be placed under the saddle to ensure that the front and back are kept level. The pad should not go all the way down the saddle flap – if it does, it is harder for the

A running martingale stops the reins going over the horse's head.

Running martingale

Mexican grakle

Hat with chinstrap

D-ring snaffle

Stoppers

Gloves

Showjumping jacket

Whip

BELLY GUARD

A belly guard helps prevent injuries that can be caused if the horse injures his belly with a front stud. This can happen when a horse folds his forelegs to clear a jump, particularly if he has not been trained to use his shoulders properly.

COMPETITION GEAR

For a showjumping competition, a rider must wear a jacket, shirt, tie, breeches, boots, gloves, and hat. The horse's equipment includes a specialized saddle, bridle, and protective boots.

rider's legs to stay close to the horse's sides. An elasticated insert in the girth gives the horse more freedom. With this type of girth, a breastplate is worn to prevent the saddle from slipping back.

A Mexican grakle noseband should be used instead of a cavesson to avoid squashing the sensitive tissue inside the horse's mouth against the outside edge of his top molar teeth. A running martingale prevents the reins flying about or going over

The seat on a jumping saddle is flat, to allow the rider to stay close to the horse over the top of the fence and on descent.

Saddle pad

Elasticated girth

Fetlock boots

Foreleg boots

Overreach boots

the horse's head if the rider drops them. It should not be used to pull the horse's head down, nor should it be so tight that it restricts him. Stoppers on the reins prevent the martingale rings getting caught up on the bit. The plain-jointed, D-ring snaffle is used in training and competition: the D-shaped rings prevent the bit from slipping through the mouth, helping the rider to steer the horse more accurately. A slightly stronger snaffle, such as a twisted snaffle, may also be used in competition (see p.384), as may stronger bits, such as gags and pelhams. Your coach can advise you. However, you should always try to train your horse in a plain snaffle.

Foreleg boots should be worn to protect the tendons at the back of the forelegs in case the horse treads on himself when landing over a fence. Likewise, overreach boots are worn to protect the heels of the forelegs. Fetlock boots on the hind legs prevent injury if a hind foot brushes against a hind fetlock.

SUITABLE ARENAS

Indoor arenas are useful in bad weather, but few are big enough for many of the jumping exercises. An outdoor school that is approximately 60 x 30 m (200 x 100 ft), with rounded sides and no square corners, is ideal. It is important that the arena surface is consistent. It must be firm enough to support the horse at the moment of take-off and landing, and it should spring back quickly, leaving only a slight imprint of the horse's hoof. If the surface is too soft, the horse can lose confidence.

USING STUDS

Studs can be inserted into the horse's shoes to provide more grip. The size used varies according to the ground. They may need to be changed during a competition, for example, if the ground becomes slippery after rain. Knowing which studs to use comes with experience but, generally, bigger studs are used in the hind feet. On firmer surfaces, which can be the most slippery, sharper studs are used (c, d, e), while in muddy conditions, fatter studs are required (f, g, h). Four studs may be needed per hoof for jumping at speed in slippery conditions. Road studs (a, b) may be used on the road or as an alternative to fillers to keep the stud holes protected.

TYPES OF FENCE

Different types of fence present different challenges to the horse and rider. For training purposes, you will use other varieties of fence to achieve particular results from your horse (see box, below). In showjumping competitions, a course will include verticals, triple bars, and oxers (see box, below right).

A full course with all the different fences is not required for schooling, but to carry out the principal training exercises you will need around 30 poles, measuring 3.7 m (12 ft), and a set of 16 uprights to hold them off the ground. These can be either simple pencil uprights or wider, more substantial-looking wingstands. The advantage of wingstands is that they help guide the horse to the middle of the fence. They discourage him from being disobedient and avoiding the fence by going around it, which is known as running out. With oxers you need only use wingstands for the front fence; the back poles can be supported on pencil uprights.

If you use plastic poles, fill them with sand so that they cannot be blown off in the wind. If you are jumping a big fence on a young horse, however, use light, wooden poles because these will break easily if the horse hits them. Poles should be placed in safety cups (see box, opposite).

A SHOWJUMP
When putting a fence together, ensure that the poles are heavy enough so that they cannot blow down easily, and that fillers are anchored to the ground so that they are secure.

Poles are available in wood or plastic and in a variety of colours

Wingstands give a fence extra width and discourage running out

This filler is painted to resemble a brick wall to make it appear substantial

TRAINING FENCES

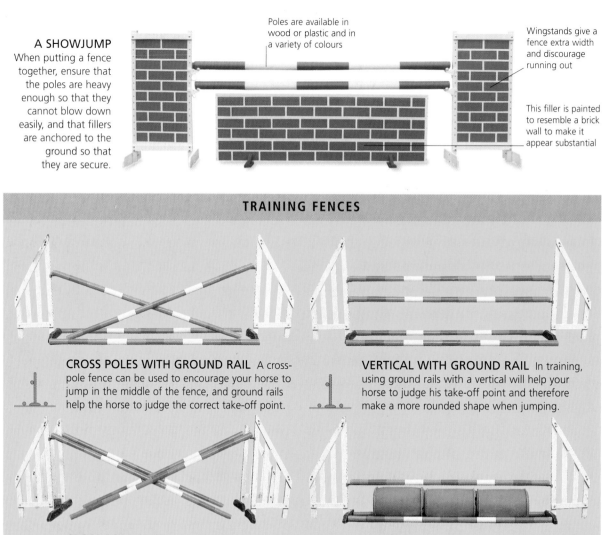

CROSS POLES WITH GROUND RAIL A cross-pole fence can be used to encourage your horse to jump in the middle of the fence, and ground rails help the horse to judge the correct take-off point.

VERTICAL WITH GROUND RAIL In training, using ground rails with a vertical will help your horse to judge his take-off point and therefore make a more rounded shape when jumping.

CROSS-POLE OXER The cross poles encourage the horse to jump in the middle of the fence while the width encourages him to keep straight over the jump rather than veering to one side in the air.

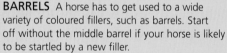

BARRELS A horse has to get used to a wide variety of coloured fillers, such as barrels. Start off without the middle barrel if your horse is likely to be startled by a new filler.

FENCE FILLERS

Fillers are used in the area beneath fence poles to give a fence definition and to provide a baseline to help the horse judge its height and spread. They come in all shapes and colours and are usually made of wood or plastic.

Fillers should be solid enough so that they cannot be blown over in the wind, and they must not have sharp edges. Small gates can be dangerous because a horse could trap his feet in them. Plastic barrels are safe and very useful, but they must always be used with poles alongside them to ensure that they do not roll away; roll-top fillers have a semi-circular profile and do not roll. Half-walls (wooden blocks painted to resemble brick walling) are particularly useful because they give the fence a very solid appearance, which will encourage the horse to treat it with respect. Half-walls that are 1.8 m (6 ft) long and approximately 60 cm (2 ft) high and 45 cm (1 ft 6 in) wide are ideal, but a little heavy to manoeuvre.

GROUND PLANKS

For training, approximately six planks will be needed for use on the ground. Planks are safer than ground poles because they will not roll if the horse treads on them, which could

SAFETY CUPS

Safety cups should be used under the back poles of all oxers and wide fences. These collapse easily on impact, allowing the pole to drop so that the horse does not straddle the fence and get injured. In addition, cups should have rounded edges to reduce risk of injury to riders in case they fall on to them.

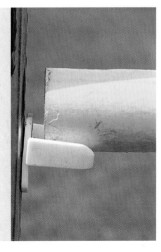

cause serious injury. They should not have metal attachments. Poles are acceptable if they are heavy enough or if they have a flat side to stop them rolling. When buying any jump equipment, make sure that neither horse nor rider could hurt themselves if they fell on it. Metal drums and protruding pieces of timber, for example, are dangerous.

COMPETITION FENCES

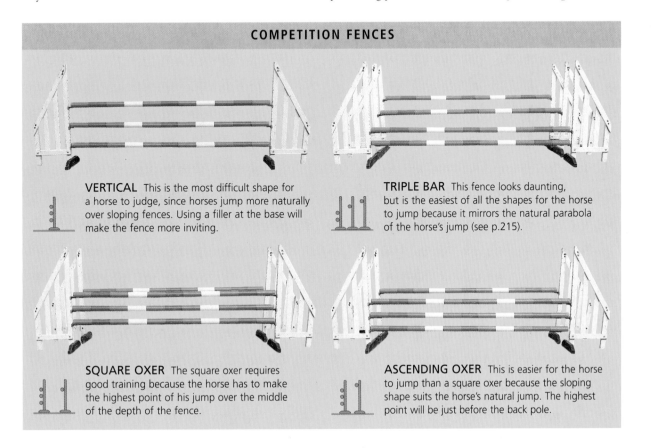

VERTICAL This is the most difficult shape for a horse to judge, since horses jump more naturally over sloping fences. Using a filler at the base will make the fence more inviting.

TRIPLE BAR This fence looks daunting, but is the easiest of all the shapes for the horse to jump because it mirrors the natural parabola of the horse's jump (see p.215).

SQUARE OXER The square oxer requires good training because the horse has to make the highest point of his jump over the middle of the depth of the fence.

ASCENDING OXER This is easier for the horse to jump than a square oxer because the sloping shape suits the horse's natural jump. The highest point will be just before the back pole.

THE RIDER'S POSITION

As with all equestrian activities, the rider's position and effectiveness are inextricably linked. The main influences that affect the showjumping rider's jumping position are the ability to maintain a good balance; being able to move in harmony with the horse; achieving a good form (or shape) during a jump; and maintaining security in the saddle. The more you can develop and improve these qualities, the more capable, comfortable, and effective a rider you will become.

ACHIEVING A CONSISTENT BALANCE

A horse will perform most easily under a rider who can maintain a consistent balance – a still load is a light load. The horse will be aware of, and affected by, changes in the rider's weight distribution, which are caused by a loss of balance. As a showjumping rider, your main priority is to find a way to stop your weight moving around and disturbing your horse's natural movement.

It is not efficient for the horse, nor is it easy for the rider, to jump when the rider's weight is in the saddle. This is because, if your seat stays in the saddle, you will not be able to stay in harmony with the horse's movement. As the horse jumps, you have to keep your centre of gravity in line with his. Therefore, jumping riders should keep a light seat that only gently touches the saddle when it is in contact.

The rider's weight is taken through the legs, with some of the weight dispersed inwardly through the contact of the leg, and the remainder on the stirrup irons. In turn, this weight is taken on the bars of the saddle. So, as far as the horse can feel, the rider's weight is just behind his withers and acts in the same vertical line as his centre of gravity (see pp.92–93).

STAYING BALANCED

You could simply stand up in your stirrups, with a straight leg, to achieve balance. Certainly the horse would not feel any difference. However, this would leave your own centre of gravity very high and your position unstable.

Imagine erecting an extendable ladder to its full length. In this state, it would be difficult to balance. If you collapsed the ladder down into its connected sections, however, it would become more compact and stable, even though its weight would not have changed. Similarly, a rider becomes more stable as the angles of the knee and hip joints close, bringing their centre of gravity lower.

In order to achieve this lowered centre of gravity and stable balance, you must adjust your stirrups to around three to five holes shorter than you would for dressage. Experiment to find the right length of stirrups to suit you. Bear in mind that if

A GOOD JUMPING BALANCE
Riding with shorter stirrups and her seat out of the saddle allows this rider to lower her centre of gravity and keep her weight consistently above the horse's centre of gravity.

ON THE FLAT Even when working on the flat, the jumping rider's balance stays the same, with the seat lightly touching the saddle, but still moving with the horse's back.

you ride too short it will be difficult to balance when you ride on a turn and it will be difficult to apply leg aids. Riding with shorter stirrups allows you to use your knee and hip joints easily – and, to a lesser extent, the ankle joints – to act like a spring and absorb the movement and forces of a jumping horse. Opening and closing these joints also minimizes the movement of your head. Your sense of balance comes from the signals received by the brain from the eyes and ears, so it is best to keep your head as still as possible.

HARMONY WITH THE HORSE

By keeping a consistent balance, remaining in harmony with the horse's movement (going with the horse) becomes possible. Even if your seat is just touching the saddle, it must still go with the movement of the horse's back or there will be bumping. The main priority is to keep your hands in harmony with the movement of the horse's mouth. Few things cause bigger problems for a jumping horse than the reins being pulled during the jump. At worst, this will stop the horse jumping and, at best, this will cause a restricted jump. As in dressage, the rein contact should be allowing. This is achieved by opening your shoulder and elbow joints rather than opening your fingers to let the reins slip through. If your fingers are opened, the rein contact tends to be lost on landing from a fence and it takes time to regain control of the horse. Some riders move their hands along the crest of the neck as they go with the horse but the most direct line is to move your hands along each side of the horse's neck (see box, below).

Initially, it is better for novice riders to fully release the reins when they jump, while perhaps holding on to the mane or breastplate for security. Later on you should be able to give away the reins without holding on to anything. When you are truly balanced, you will be able to allow with your hands while retaining a light contact. However, even an advanced rider needs to be able to jump without a rein contact at times (for example, when jumping a big fence), so this is always a useful skill to practise.

REIN CONTACT OVER THE FENCE

Most horses immediately jump better if their heads are not restricted by the rider's rein contact. When you have rein contact, your hands must go with the natural movement of the horse's mouth, and therefore of his head and neck. Only more advanced riders should maintain rein contact over a fence. However, all riders need to be able to learn how to do this eventually for when they jump against the clock at a competition. To keep a contact, you can either keep the hands closer to the mane **(a)**, so that you have more support more readily if you need it, or you can maintain a more direct line to the mouth, while keeping the hands lower **(b)**. The latter position is more suited to specialist showjumpers. Novice riders need to be able to release the rein totally while holding on to the mane for support **(c)**. More advanced riders will release the rein over a bigger fence while keeping their hands lower **(d)**.

(a) HANDS HIGHER – WITH CONTACT   **(b)** HANDS LOWER – WITH CONTACT

(c) HANDS HIGHER – WITHOUT CONTACT   **(d)** HANDS LOWER – WITHOUT CONTACT

THE RIDER'S FORM

During a jump, the rider's lower leg must remain perpendicular to the ground. However, the form, or shape, of the rider changes through the phases of the jump. In particular, the hip and knee joints need to open on both the ascent and descent, and this opening and closing of the joints alters the angle of your body. If you do not do this, you will not be able to keep in line with the horse's centre of gravity on ascent, and the back of the saddle will hit your seat on the descent. In both cases, your balance will probably be lost. As the jumps become bigger, this opening of the joints is more important because the angles of ascent and descent increase (see box, right).

As you approach a fence, keep your weight through your legs **(1)**. On the ascent, open the hip and knee joints a little **(2)**, letting the horse rotate around your knees **(3)**. (Here, the rider has moved her knee a little far back.) Then, close the hip and knee joints over the top of the fence **(4)**, before opening them again on the descent **(5)**.

JUMPING LARGER FENCES

As you progress to jumping bigger fences, you will have to open your knee and hip joints more to compensate for the steeper angle of ascent and descent. In order to keep their centre of gravity almost perfectly over the horse's centre of gravity, the rider on the right has had to adopt an almost vertical standing position over the horse.

JUMPING A MEDIUM FENCE

JUMPING A HIGH FENCE

JUMPING POSITION OVER A SMALL FENCE For an ideal position, your centre of gravity should stay directly over your base of support – your legs. Ideally, the two red lines shown here should always roughly align. Your lower leg should stay perpendicular as the horse rotates around your knee, and your hip and knee joints should open and close according to the stage of the jump.

Try to keep your weight through your legs, rather than in the saddle

Keep your weight through the leg

Begin to open your knee and hip joints for the ascent

Keep your upper body over the horse's centre of gravity

It is also necessary to maintain a good, neutral alignment of the spine (see p.336). In the sequence below, the rider's back is good in **(4)** but is slightly rounded in **(5)**, which restricts her ability to go with the horse.

KEEPING A SECURE SEAT

The security of the rider comes largely from having a good balance and keeping in harmony with the horse, but it is also dependent on maintaining the weight through the lower leg, and keeping the lower leg perpendicular to the ground. If a jumping rider rides with the stirrups too long, security is lost in the second half of the jump. This is because the lower leg has to swing back initially in order for the rider to keep the upper body balanced over the fence, and then it does not come forwards on descent. Security is also increased if the rider is sufficiently fit and strong – riding with shorter stirrups demands more strength in both leg and back muscles. Tiredness will create a loss of control and, therefore, a loss of security.

The rider's spine should align with the horse's spine

JUMPING STRAIGHT Riders tend to put more weight on their stronger leg and this unbalances the horse. When you jump a fence, make sure your weight is evenly placed through both legs.

4

Close your knee and hip joints over the top of the fence

5

Open the hip joints on descent

6

Start to readjust your balance – here, the upper body is too far forwards

FEELING A STRIDE

To be effective, a showjumper must develop their knowledge of the jumping exercises and their use of the aids. The most important skill, however, is the ability to feel a stride so that your horse is provided with the right take-off spot for a fence.

These progressive exercises will help you understand the way your horse moves and help you develop your ability to feel and count canter strides over correct distances. Then, finding the right take-off point will become automatic.

JUDGING STRIDE LENGTHS

A human long jumper will aim to take a certain number of regular strides in order to reach the take-off board, rather than suddenly adjusting speed and stride length at the last moment — this would be inefficient and would restrict the jump. Similarly, a showjumper must be aware of the horse's stride in relation to a fence and make the minimum alterations necessary to find a take-off point that will suit the horse. When approaching a fence, a rider has to be aware of the horse's stride length even from some distance: an advanced rider can judge six or more strides ahead.

The take-off point for a jump starts at the end of a canter stride. For a vertical fence, the perfect take-off point out of canter is approximately 1.8 m (6 ft) from the fence. Therefore, the rider must ensure that the horse's canter stride ends at this point. As mentioned, an advanced rider will take his horse consistently to within 30 cm (1 ft) of the right take-off spot, but it is important to remember that if the canter is good and the horse experienced and jumping within his

ability, it is possible to be 80 cm (2⅓ ft) away from the ideal spot and still have a comfortable jump. It is more important to keep a consistent canter than to make sudden or large changes in front of a fence in order to achieve the perfect take-off spot.

A good coach will do three main things to help a rider develop a feel for a stride. Firstly, the rider will be helped to develop harmony and feel on the flat. The more a rider can go with the movement of the canter, the easier it will be to have a sense of what is happening with the horse's strides.

Secondly, the coach will introduce you to grids. A grid is a series of fences set up over specific distances to help you develop your position and the horse's jumping technique progressively. Initially, your coach will ensure that the distances between the fences are easy for your horse and designed to give him ideal take-off points. Even if you are concentrating on keeping a good position, you will subconsciously become aware of the canter strides and take-off points, and this awareness will increase as you progress.

Thirdly, your coach will teach you how to count strides by using progressive exercises (see below), in trot and then canter. By counting canter strides, it is possible to feel the end of each stride and start to maintain a consistent showjumping canter.

COUNTING STRIDES

Your coach will set up a progressive exercise in which you first jump a placing plank and fence in trot. A canter plank will then be placed on the ground to simulate a second fence (see sequence, above right). Poles laid out in a funnel-shape at the beginning, middle, and end of the grid will act as guides to keep your horse on a straight line. The coach will set up the exercise to ensure your horse is keeping to a 3.7 m (12 ft) canter stride — this is the standard stride length for showjumping. Initially, the canter plank will be placed just two strides away from the first fence.

Regular repetition of this exercise will develop your feel for a stride but the secret to getting the most out of it is to count the strides out loud. Approach the grid with your horse

---

TAKE-OFF POINTS

Practise finding the right take-off points for a fence by using a canter plank instead of a fence. A canter plank allows you to repeat the exercise many times without exhausting your horse. As you develop the correct canter and your feel for a stride, your take-off points will become more accurate.

TAKE-OFF POINT TOO CLOSE   TAKE-OFF POINT TOO FAR AWAY

in trot. Land after the first fence in canter. On landing, say, "land" to yourself. Then, count each stride out loud. This will help you to focus your mind. As you regularly achieve the right take-off point over the canter plank, the distance between the fence and the canter plank can be lengthened progressively to add extra strides, until you are able to count up to six strides.

The reason this exercise works so well is because the 3.7 m (12 ft) canter stride is also the distance between the take-off point and landing point when a horse jumps a vertical fence.

Therefore, even though you are not jumping a second fence, cantering to a plank on the ground gives you the same take-off and landing points as if you were jumping a real fence.

The next stage is to substitute the placing plank and cross poles for one canter plank and canter over them. Start with a distance of 7.3 m (24 ft) between the two planks – allowing for landing and take-off points, this gives you one non-jumping stride between the planks. Then, follow the same progression, adding one 3.7 m (12 ft) stride at a time.

STRIDE LENGTHS This grid has been set up so that the horse, after landing from the first fence, must take two strides to the take-off point for the canter plank. A funnel of poles helps keep him straight. This is a useful exercise to help you develop your ability to judge a stride.

AERIAL OVERVIEW OF THE GRID

Trot plank   Cross pole   Canter plank

Land in canter, keeping a soft rein contact

Count the first stride out loud

Count the second stride

PROGRESSIVE EXERCISES FOR COUNTING STRIDES

With a placing plank set at 2.7 m (9 ft) away from a cross pole, approach in trot. Land from the cross pole in canter and do one non-jumping stride before going over a canter plank set 6.1 m (20 ft) away.

Then, move the canter plank progressively further away, one canter stride at a time, to give two, three, four, five, and then six non-jumping strides.

Throughout each exercise, count each stride, and keep the canter constant so that you consistently meet the canter plank at the right take-off point.

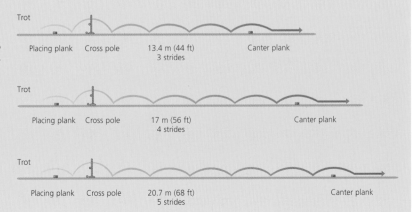

Trot — Placing plank   Cross pole   13.4 m (44 ft) 3 strides   Canter plank

Trot — Placing plank   Cross pole   17 m (56 ft) 4 strides   Canter plank

Trot — Placing plank   Cross pole   20.7 m (68 ft) 5 strides   Canter plank

ANALYSING THE HORSE'S JUMP

As in dressage, there are factors that must constantly be in place for the successful showjumping horse. The horse must accept his rider at all times; he must remain calm while thinking forwards; and he must use both sides of his body evenly so that he can remain straight. The perfect jump may prove to be an elusive achievement, but gaining an understanding of the biomechanics of the jump can help to improve your performance.

ACHIEVING THE CONSTANTS

A jumping round can be compared to a dressage test with jumps between movements, so the constants required for showjumping are the same as for dressage: acceptance, calmness, forwardness, straightness, and purity (see pp.122–23). These produce the controlled impulsion – or power – necessary for a horse to jump, while jumping also requires a natural, pure technique.

ACCEPTANCE AND CALMNESS

The horse must accept his rider and the aids throughout the round. Without acceptance, it is not possible to have precise control of the horse. Tension can reduce a horse's potential as a jumper, so the aim is to have the horse able to gallop calmly to a big fence and to stay calm both over and after the fence. In training, we must ensure that acceptance and calmness are in place before progressing further.

FORWARDNESS AND STRAIGHTNESS

It is essential that the horse rides and jumps willingly – that he has forwardness. This willingness can be quickly destroyed by an over-demanding rider who asks the horse to perform tasks that are beyond his ability. Most horses enjoy jumping, but loss of forwardness, and therefore loss of confidence, will result in loss of enjoyment, for the rider as well as the horse.

It is not possible for the horse to harness his full power unless he uses his hind legs together on take-off and keeps himself straight – using both sides of his body evenly – both on approach to a fence and during the jump itself.

This is where dressage work is so important, because it helps develop the two sides of the horse equally and trains the horse to use his back, which is a vital part of the process of achieving straightness. A horse who jumps in a one-sided manner will find everything difficult.

POLE-VAULT EFFECT Before take-off, the horse's front legs stretch out in front of his withers. This lowers his forehand (his front weight). As his forehand passes over his forelegs, a pole-vaulting effect pushes the horse upwards.

PURITY OF THE JUMP

Many horses are prevented from producing a natural, efficient jump (a pure jump without unnecessary movements) due to restriction in the rider's rein contact and a changing balance.

Yet it is important to recognize that the perfect jump rarely exists. All horses have strengths and weaknesses in their technique, but horses that really try to jump safely and cleanly will overcome many faults, especially if they are happy and comfortable in their work. Good training is the key.

Although the centre of gravity of a horse moves only a little during various exercises, the more a horse is able to bend around a fence, the lower his centre of gravity will be and the more efficient the jump will be. As the horse's centre of gravity is lowered over the top of the fence, he will remain in the same vertical alignment as before.

UNDERSTANDING BIOMECHANICS

The act of jumping comprises several variable factors, including direction, speed, impulsion, and stride length, as well as various horizontal and vertical forces applied at different times. The horse and rider together act as a projectile, subject to the forces of gravity in the same way as a stone that is thrown.

When jumping with a rider on his back, the horse's centre of gravity will be raised by approximately ten per cent (see p.92), which is why a horse with a rider is inherently more unstable. As a unit, the centre of gravity of the horse and rider must stay in vertical alignment, or the natural jump, movement, and equilibrium of the horse will be adversely affected. To look at this in more detail, it is helpful to analyse the phases of a jump (see pp.200–203).

TAKE-OFF, ASCENT, AND DESCENT

When a horse jumps a fence, the angle of ascent equals the angle of descent – both halves of the jump are the same. Ideally, the centre of the jumping parabola (see p.215) will be over the highest part of the fence. However, poor training often leads to the horse achieving the highest point of his jump beyond the highest point of the fence. This makes the effort inefficient and produces problems with related distances between fences because the horse lands too far forwards.

The same take-off point, about 1.8 m (6 ft) away, is used for both a 1.2 m (4 ft) and a 1.8 m (6 ft) vertical. As the fence gets higher, however, the horse must leave the ground at a steeper angle. This requires strength and good preparation. A novice horse may start

with an angle of ascent of about 20 degrees and increase it to 30 degrees for the 1.2 m (4 ft) fence and to 50 degrees for 1.8 m (6 ft). As the fence gets higher than this, the horse can no longer increase his angle of ascent, so he will take off further away. Here, the horse is taking off too far away from the puissance wall (see below), so the angle of ascent is slightly smaller.

Studies show that the horizontal distance between the take-off point and the middle of a puissance wall is almost exactly the height of the wall. When jumping a 2.1 m (7 ft) wall, most horses will take off about 2.1 m (7 ft) from the middle of the wall. It follows, therefore, that when it is smaller, they will take off closer.

PHASES OF THE JUMP

The action of a jump can be divided into several phases: approach, take-off and ascent, flight, descent and landing, and riding away. Throughout all these phases, the rider must keep their centre of gravity over the horse's centre of gravity, so as not to hinder the jumping action.

APPROACHING THE FENCE

The key to the approach is maintaining a canter that is calm, forwards, and straight, with the horse accepting the rider and the aids. The rider must not restrict the movement of the horse's head and neck, so the approach must be made with a light rein contact. The approach should be timed so that the horse can take a full-length stride (1) before take-off. At the end of this stride, the horse uses his forelegs like a vaulting pole (2), starting to lift his forehand off the ground and creating a momentary period of suspension before the hind legs touch the ground.

AT A GLANCE

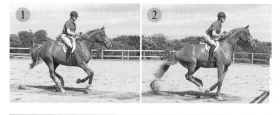

TAKE-OFF AND ASCENT

This is the most important part of the jump. In the approaching canter, the hind legs land separately (1), but they come together for take-off (3) in order to provide enough power for the jump. The horse puts his hind feet in front of the imprint his fore feet have just made. He needs to be able to bend his body and back in order to do so – a horse that is

FROM APPROACH TO ASCENT
The horse completes the last stride before gathering his hind legs underneath his hindquarters to provide power for the jump.

The horse naturally raises his head on the approach

The horse begins his final stride

stiff or that has a rider who sits too heavily will have difficulty. The joints of the hind legs begin to open (see circle inset, below) as the horse pushes off the ground. On the ascent, the horse stretches his neck forwards, and begins to tuck his hind legs underneath him **(4)**, ready to clear the fence.

3

The horse begins to lengthen his neck and tuck his legs up

4

The horse's head is gradually lowered over the top of the jump

The hind legs land and the joints then open, propelling the horse into the air.

THE FLIGHT

As the horse curves over the top of the fence, he stretches his neck out and keeps his legs tucked up underneath him. The shoulders are brought forwards, which also has the effect of bringing the elbows and knees forwards **(5)**. The forelegs and hind legs work as identical pairs, so neither knee is in front of the other, and neither hock is in front of the other.

Ideally, if the horse is using his shoulders well, his knees will be higher than the line of his belly and then the studs in his shoes are not in danger of hitting his belly (see p.188).

DESCENT AND LANDING

As the descent begins, the horse starts to release his hind legs, stretching them out behind him so that they follow the line of his belly – this is especially necessary to clear the back pole of an oxer – and to raise his head ready for landing. Initially, the weight of the horse comes down on just one foreleg, with what will be the leading leg of the canter coming down fractionally afterwards, in front of the first foreleg **(6)**. Then all the horse's weight goes on to this leading leg. The fetlock joint presses low to the ground because of the forces involved

FROM FLIGHT TO RIDING AWAY The landing is important because the first stride is the start of the approach to the next fence and the rider should already be thinking ahead.

The horse keeps his hind legs tucked underneath him to clear the fence

5

As the descent begins, the hind leg joints start to open.

(see picture, right). If the forelegs reached the ground at the same time, the horse would probably fall over because of the automatic locking system of the front legs – the same system that allows a horse to sleep while standing up.

RIDING AWAY

After the forelegs have landed, there is a brief period of suspension again when the forelegs leave the ground just before the hind legs return to the ground – first the outside hind and then the inside.

Both horse and rider should return to a horizontal equilibrium in the first stride. Here, they are slightly out of balance and take a longer stride than normal (7). The horse regains his equilibrium by using his back to get his hind legs underneath him.

ABSORBING SHOCK As the horse's forelegs reach the ground, his withers sink down and the fetlock joints act like shock absorbers. Over big fences or when jumping at speed, the fetlocks may even touch the ground.

6

The horse begins to raise his neck on landing so that he keeps his balance

7

The horse lowers his neck in the first stride as he slightly loses his balance and falls forwards

The leading leg lands a little in front of the other foreleg and then takes the whole weight of the horse

JUMPING VARIABLES

The variables are the factors that alter from one exercise to another. In showjumping these are: direction, speed, impulsion, balance, and timing, and the rider needs precise control of all five. In addition, consistency lies at the heart of a good performance, especially the ability to maintain a constant 3.7 m (12 ft) stride, because this is what all the distances are based on. It is possible to achieve this stride by maintaining the right speed and direction, so these are the two key variables.

CONTROLLING DIRECTION

The variables for a showjumping round change less than for a dressage test, mainly because it is carried out at the same pace and at the same speed. Showjumping, in which fences are set apart by so many strides, is effectively a dressage test in a big arena, consisting of a mixture of straight lines and parts of circles with fences in between. Therefore, the right direction is the most important variable to achieve because the angle of approach will affect the number of strides your horse needs to take between fences.

You need to approach every fence at the correct angle and follow a precise track between fences. Getting the right direction is even more important in a competition jump-off round (where you are jumping against the clock) because saving time is the key. Many riders work on their direction by practising riding around a course made up of planks on the ground, aiming to achieve a precise line from start to finish.

MAINTAINING SPEED

In showjumping, speeds are given in metres per minute, but for ease of accessibility, they are also shown in miles per hour throughout this book. The right speed is vital because speed and stride lengths are inextricably linked. A horse will naturally increase and decrease his stride lengths as he goes faster and slower. When cantering at a speed of approximately 375 m/min (13.8 mph), an ideal showjumping horse does a 3.7 m (12 ft) canter stride, so this is the correct speed to be established.

If your horse has naturally short strides, you will have to ask him to go faster in order to produce a 3.7 m (12 ft) stride length. If he has naturally long strides, he will have to go slower. Unfortunately, the quality of the jump can be affected in both cases. Going faster will mean that more of the horse's momentum will be going forwards, at the expense of the vertical uplift needed for take-off. Conversely, going slower may mean that not enough of the horse's momentum will be going forwards to carry him over the top of the fence to the other side. Going slower may also mean that you incur time penalties when competing against the clock; some competition classes are judged purely on speed in the first round, so long strides can be a distinct disadvantage.

DEVELOPING IMPULSION

Impulsion is a combination of suppleness, strength, and spring. It originates from the engagement of the hindquarters and the proper use of the horse's back, to create power and energy. The higher the level of competition, the greater the impulsion required. It is important to give your horse time to develop impulsion, rather than making him jump big fences before he has sufficient strength and core stability. Controlled impulsion can only exist if the constants (see pp.198–99) are established. Also, the horse must be worked anaerobically to develop his strength and spring (see pp.320–23).

KEEPING A GOOD BALANCE

When you achieve consistent speed and impulsion during a showjumping round, you rarely need to adjust the balance. A horse that is able to use his back and put more weight on his hindquarters will be naturally well balanced and able to make an effective, strong take-off. If the rider tries to improve the horse's balance by forcing him to adopt a shorter outline, movement through the back will be blocked and the horse will be physically restricted.

TIMING STRIDES

The horse's stride has to be timed so that he can get the right take-off point for each fence. Horses will gain confidence and fulfil their potential if they can be brought consistently to the right take-off point without the rider making any major changes to their speed. Although timing is important, it will count for little if you do not get the other variables right, and it will count for nothing if the constants are not in place.

If the right direction, speed, impulsion, and balance are in place, then timing the stride is less important, as long as the horse is not jumping at his height limit. If you are under pressure, concentrate on keeping things simple, and on getting the right direction and speed.

JUMPING A ROUND Having approached this massive 2.1 m (7 ft) fence in canter at the correct speed and with impulsion, the rider simply has to stay in harmony with the horse and enjoy the moment.

A TRAINING PROGRAMME

It is important to have a carefully designed progressive training plan that ensures the physical and mental development of both you and your horse. Start by deciding what your long-term aims are as a showjumper – whether you want to work towards introductory classes or to jump on the international circuit. Work backwards to create a timetable for the intermediate goals you need to achieve to get there, and then form a week-by-week schedule of progressive exercises.

LONG-TERM PLANNING

In the long term, extraordinary things are possible. Jumping in the World Cup finals or the Olympic Games is attainable if you start with this aim, but much less likely if you do not set yourself a goal to work towards. Not everyone may aspire to the highest level, but if you harbour these ambitions you need to familiarize yourself with the international scene.

There is a thriving tier of introductory shows for which you can aim. Each class has a maximum height of fence, ranging from 80 cm (2 ft 7 in) to 1.5 m (5 ft). Beyond this, the Nations Cups (an international series of team competitions) and major championships have a limit of 1.6 m (5 ft 3 in). Of course, in these competitions the challenge is not just the height of the fences – the course builder will create more challenges to test the technical skills of the horses and riders, such as placing fences on angles or placing them so that you have to adjust your horse's stride length.

NOVICE LEVEL You do not need an Olympic-standard horse to learn the basic techniques. A sound position, good basic dressage, and expertise in simple jumping exercises can all be gained on normal horses without exceptional ability.

MEDIUM-TERM PLANNING

When you have decided your long-term aims, you can form a training programme that will help you make steady progress each year. Obviously, not all horses have the ability to jump a 1.6 m (5 ft 3 in) fence, but the majority can cope with 1.2 m (4 ft) fences and, having achieved this level, can go further, aiming to progress 10 cm (4 in) a year. At each stage, your aim should be to jump with quality and ease, before moving on to the next stage. In this way, you will carefully build the foundations of future success.

Watch the best riders at each level and make it your business to ask questions. Try to put yourself under the wing of an experienced coach or rider who is travelling to shows on a regular basis.

SHORT-TERM PLANNING

In order for you and your horse to develop, a weekly programme of varied work is required. Most horses are willing to work hard, as long as the rider is sensitive and they finish their work sessions feeling calm and comfortable. Four or five flat-work sessions a week are enough, mixed with jumping two or three times a week. However, you should only jump when your horse is settled and not tired. If you are jumping regularly at shows, you will probably not need to do extra jumping work at home.

In order to develop the horse's spring, jump for short periods at a time. Spend your sessions working both on improving your own position and the quality of your horse's jump – working with grids is very effective. The idea should be to give your horse a challenge, but not frighten him with excessive demands, such as fences that are too high. Finish sessions with the horse willing to give a little more, rather than having been asked to do too much.

It is important to vary the horse's environment and routine by taking him on hacks. In terms of intensive work, 40 minutes at a time is usually enough. If you need to do more, taking a break will yield better results. It also works well if the arena you train in is a 20- to 30-minute ride away

INTERMEDIATE LEVEL
A gradually widening range of skills, including good stable management and a developed feel for a stride, will take your partnership to an intermediate level. You will be jumping higher fences on different related distances and achieving more accurate take-off points.

from the stable, because this gives the horse time to ease into work mentally as well as physically, and allows him the chance to cool down at the end of a session. You will still be improving your jumping skills when you are out hacking, because it is of considerable benefit to your balance to regularly trot and canter slowly up gradual inclines.

Every horse and rider partnership has individual needs, but a typical weekly programme should be based around good-quality dressage training. In the week before a show, you should concentrate more on flat work, so that your horse becomes obedient. A few days before, you might do a fairly demanding jumping session, working on related distances and small groups of fences.

A good coach will help you create the right balance, and you will find your weekly successes slowly taking you closer to the fulfilment of your dreams.

ADVANCED LEVEL
The Brazilian showjumper Rodrigo Pessoa, the 1998 world champion, is a prime example of an advanced rider with excellent harmony and feel – here, he is riding Baloubet du Rouet. If good long-term preparation has been in place, such success is possible.

UNDERSTANDING DISTANCES

When you are a novice rider, you must rely on the knowledge and expertise of your coach, who will set up exercises for you with suitable distances between fences. However, as you become more experienced, you will learn to do this yourself.

This will give you more insight into the responses of your horse and improve your own skills as a rider and trainer. At a competition, it will mean you will be able to walk the distances between fences and decide how to ride the course.

WALKING THE COURSE

Fences can be arranged in various ways. A double consists of two fences with only one or two strides between them. A combination (or treble) is the same, but with an additional fence. A related distance is where two fences are separated by a fixed distance of between three and ten strides. The majority of doubles, combinations, and related distances are based on a 3.7 m (12 ft) horse stride. This is true of both national and international competitions.

At a competition, showjumpers walk the course before the jumping begins to find out what distances the course designer has set between fences. To do this, they take 90 cm (3 ft) steps between fences – this is often slightly longer than a natural human stride. Four of these strides is equal to the equivalent of one of your horse's strides.

When you are walking distances, remember that a horse will land approximately two of your steps away from a fence and will take off two of your steps away from the next fence.

So, for example, if you walk 16 steps between two fences, two of these steps will be for landing and two for take-off, leaving 12 steps in between. Divided by four, this gives three horse strides. So a standard three-horse-stride related distance is equal to 16 of your steps. Likewise, four strides is equal to 20 steps, and five strides is 24 steps.

The reason for measuring distances is not simply to find out the number of strides but to assess whether the distance is short or long – this is part of the test. If your steps do not divide exactly by four, it will mean that the distance is either short or long. If you have one step extra, for example, you will have to encourage your horse to lengthen his stride in order

WALKING DISTANCES Practise measuring out and marking a distance on the ground equal to two horse strides – 7.3 m (24 ft). Walk the distance every day until you regularly do exactly four of your steps for each of your horse's strides.

IMPERIAL AND METRIC STRIDE LENGTHS

At working canter, most horses produce a stride of approximately 12 ft. This equals exactly 3.66 m, a rather unwieldy figure (which in this book has been rounded to 3.7 m). Many course builders working in metric use 3.5 m instead, which equals 11 ft 6 in. Therefore, when reading books with metric dimensions or when riding courses, find out whether the distances are based on a 12 ft/3.66 m or on a 11 ft 6 in/3.5 m stride.

COMMONLY USED STRIDE LENGTHS	SUITABLE FOR
Imperial 12 ft (3.66 m) Metric 3.5 m (11 ft 6 in)	Competition showjumping – novice to international level.
Imperial 11 ft (3.35 m) Metric 3.25 m (10 ft 8 in)	Riding club and training competitions with both horses and large ponies; gymnastic grids.
Imperial 10 ft (3.05 m) Metric 3 m (9 ft 10 in)	Training – riding school cobs and smaller ponies; gymnastic grids.

JUMPING DIFFERENT FENCES

VERTICAL

OXER

TRIPLE BAR

COMPARING THE JUMP The fences used here are a 1.3 m (4 ft 3 in) vertical fence, a 1.1 x 1.3 m (3 ft 6 in x 4 ft 3 in) square oxer, and a 1.3 x 1.5 m (4 ft 3 in x 5 ft) triple bar. It can be seen that almost identical jumping efforts were needed to clear all three fences. These photographs show that a horse should have the highest point of his trajectory over the middle of the fence and that he needs to jump higher to clear an oxer than he does to clear a vertical of identical height. The oxer here requires the same effort and flight as a vertical 23 cm (9 in) higher.

to make the correct take-off point. If you are one step short of a unit of four, you will have to encourage your horse to shorten his stride. If you have two left over, this is a half stride. In this case, you can either shorten for the extra stride or lengthen and take out a stride (see p.224). This does not apply to doubles and combinations where half strides will not be used.

WALKING DOUBLES AND COMBINATIONS

You can use the method to find out the distances between double and combination fences. This can be further refined by understanding the different take-off and landing points for the three main types of fence – verticals, oxers, and triple bars. Comparing the horse's jump over each of these fences helps us understand why different distances are used between different types of fences in doubles and combinations. The distance from the take-off point to the fence is longest with a vertical and shortest with a triple bar.

If you look at the vertical and the oxer (see pictures, left), you can see that the distance between the take-off point and the oxer is 60 cm (2 ft) shorter than with the vertical. This suggests that the distance between the vertical and an oxer should be 60 cm (2ft) less than the distance between two verticals in order for the horse to achieve the right take-off point. In practice, course builders often only make the distance 30 cm (1 ft) shorter, because the oxers will be of a similar height to the verticals when they really should be at least 25 cm (10 in) smaller. Therefore, the horse takes off a little further away in order to make the height, and uses the same angle of ascent as he does for the vertical.

As you become experienced, you will be able to judge more accurately where your horse will take off and land in each case. For example, if a triple bar is wide, your horse will land further away from the fence than normal, even though the take-off point for a triple bar will be fairly close to the fence.

VARYING TAKE-OFFS AND LANDINGS

The horse's distance away from the vertical on take-off (see picture, above left) will surprise riders who like to put their horses closer than this. It is useful to train a horse to cope with a steeper angle of ascent by getting between 30 to 60 cm (1 to 2 ft) closer to the fence than normal. However, if you do this in competition, taking off a little closer and slowing down slightly, this increases not only the angle of ascent but also that of descent, which in turn creates extra distance to the next fence. This can cause difficulties in doubles and other related distances. In addition, if the horse does not complete the final stride, it will significantly reduce his ability to jump. Try to ride verticals more positively and keep the canter and speed more consistent.

WORKING WITH DIFFERENT DISTANCES

The distance charts shown here are intended to give a starting point for your work and to indicate a possible progression, but there are no rigid rules. Both you and your coach must be aware of the individual strengths and weaknesses of your horse and choose and adjust the exercises accordingly. Each horse will also have to be ridden in a slightly different way to take account of his temperament and ability.

The jumping technique and attitude of the horse must be observed at all times. If these begin to deteriorate, then it is probable that the heights or distances have been changed too much and you should return to an easier exercise. Always be fair to your horse, and use distances which will accelerate his progress, rather than over-extend him, either mentally or physically (see box, right).

Standard exercises are usually based on a 3.7 m (12 ft) stride length, but in the case of novice or smaller horses and in some types of competition, different stride lengths are used (see p.208). If you are working with a smaller stride length, adjustments must be made to the distances shown here. If necessary, get advice from your coach. As you gain experience, it will become obvious what type of distance is appropriate.

PRACTISING WITH PLANKS

Initially, your task is to learn about basic distances rather than worrying about difficult ones. Over time, you will easily work out whether a distance is a little short or long by walking the

BASIC GRID DISTANCES

It takes experience to build a grid. Start with small fences and progress a step at a time. The height of the cross poles should be 50–70 cm (20–27 in) and they should have a ground line approximately 50 cm (20 in) away. The height of the other fences should be 0.7–1.2 m (2 ft 3 in–4 ft).

EXERCISE	DISTANCES
WALK PLANKS	80 cm–1 m (2 ft 9 in–3 ft 3 in)
TROT PLANKS	1.25–1.45 m (4 ft–4 ft 9 in)
TROT PLANKS TO CROSS POLES	2.5–2.9 m (8 ft–9 ft 6 in)
SINGLE TROT PLACING PLANK TO CROSS POLES	2.5–2.9 m (8 ft–9 ft 6 in)
CROSS POLES FROM TROT TO A VERTICAL IN ONE STRIDE	5.8–6.4 m (19–21 ft)
VERTICAL TO OXER IN TWO STRIDES	9.8–10.4 m (32–34 ft)
VERTICAL TO OXER IN ONE STRIDE	6.1–6.7 m (20–22 ft)
CROSS POLES FROM TROT TO A BOUNCE	3–3.3 m (10–11 ft)
CANTER PLANKS	3–4.25 m (10–14 ft)

distance on your feet. The same applies to related distances. Cantering over ground planks at a fixed distance is an invaluable exercise to help to develop both the canter required and your feel for a stride (see pp.196–97).

Bear in mind that the middle of the canter stride should be over the plank. The importance of this becomes apparent when the plank is followed by another plank at a fixed distance. If you get too close to the first plank, it will have the effect of shortening the distance to the next plank; if you are too far away, the distance will be

JUMPING WITH A PONY Where ponies and horses are jumping at the same competition, course builders usually use distances based on a 3.3 m (11 ft) stride, rather than a 3.7 m (12 ft) stride. Your coach will advise you on the distances being used.

COMPETITION DISTANCES

The chart below shows the distances used between particular fences in normal conditions. All distances can be plus or minus 15 cm (6 in). Horses tend to stand off (take-off early) to oxers and run deep (take-off close) to verticals, which is why the difference in distances is not greater. Young horses and novice riders should not attempt doubles or combinations with two consecutive oxers or an oxer at the end because, for safety's sake, there should be room for error. For the same reason, triple bars should be used only as the first fence in a double or combination.

FIRST FENCE	SECOND FENCE	DISTANCE IN BETWEEN
VERTICAL	VERTICAL	7.9 m (26 ft)
VERTICAL	OXER	7.6 m (25 ft)
VERTICAL	ASCENDING OXER	7.45 m (24 ft 6 in)
OXER	VERTICAL	7.75 m (25 ft 6 in)
OXER	OXER	7.45 m (24 ft 6 in)
OXER	ASCENDING OXER	7.3 m (24 ft)
ASCENDING OXER	VERTICAL	7.9 m (26 ft)
ASCENDING OXER	OXER	7.6 m (25 ft)
ASCENDING OXER	ASCENDING OXER	7.45 m (24 ft 6 in)
TRIPLE BAR	VERTICAL	8.05 m (26 ft 6 in)
TRIPLE BAR	OXER	7.75 m (25 ft 6 in)
TRIPLE BAR	ASCENDING OXER	7.6 m (25 ft)

lengthened. However, the opposite is true when jumping fences. When the take-off is close, the landing will be close (the angle of ascent and descent will be steeper), and vice versa, unless the horse is jumping unnecessarily high.

VARYING STRIDE LENGTHS

It is also necessary to take into account the different factors that affect your horse's stride length. Strides tend to lengthen when your horse is going faster; down an incline; around a large arena; or towards home. They lengthen if the horse is fresh or supple; the ground is good; fences are flimsy; and the rider is allowing. Conversely, stride lengths tend to shorten when the horse is going slower; up or down a steep incline; around a small arena; approaching a daunting fence; or away from home. They shorten when the horse is tired or stiff; the ground is soft or very hard; or when the rider is stiff and restrictive.

USING GRIDS

The aim of grid work is to improve the horse's jumping ability, not to cause him stress. Adjustments to the size of fences and the distances must be gradual, and the approach should be totally consistent or the exercises can harm your horse's training. Changes should be made 10 cm (4 in) at a time.

When jumping a basic grid, it is normal to trot to a small cross pole, land in canter, and take one stride to a small vertical and one or two strides to an oxer. The distances will be slightly shorter than in a competition because the approach is in trot, not canter, which shortens the first canter stride after the fence by about 60 cm (2 ft), and because the fences are relatively small, which reduces the take-off and landing distances. Gymnastic grids are those that encourage a more athletic jump – shorter distances are used. Before gymnastic exercises can be attempted, the horse must have grounding in basic dressage and jumping exercises. He will need a degree of collection in the canter (see p.126) and he will have to achieve closer take-off points. This necessitates a steeper angle of ascent, which is achieved by increasing the horse's strength and agility.

DISTANCES FOR TRAINING EXERCISES

The following distances can be used for training purposes. Always start an exercise with distances that your horse finds easy. When jumping a fence from trot, the first canter stride after the fence will be a little shorter than when the approach to the fence is in canter, hence the different distances. When using canter planks, place them the same distance apart as if they were two verticals.

NUMBER OF NON-JUMPING STRIDES	APPROACHING FIRST FENCE IN TROT			APPROACHING FIRST FENCE IN CANTER		
	CROSS POLES TO CANTER PLANK	CROSS POLES TO SINGLE OXER	CROSS POLES TO OXER IN GYMNASTIC GRID	OXER TO OXER IN GYMNASTIC GRID	CANTER PLANK TO CANTER PLANK	VERTICAL TO VERTICAL
1 STRIDE	6.1 m (20 ft)	5.5 m (18 ft)	5.45 m (17 ft 9 in)	5.5 m (18 ft)	7.3 m (24 ft)	7.3 m (24 ft)
2 STRIDES	9.75 m (32 ft)	9.15 m (30 ft)	8.8 m (28 ft 9 in)	9 m (29 ft 6 in)	11 m (36 ft)	11 m (36 ft)
3 STRIDES	13.4 m (44 ft)	12.8 m (42 ft)	12.2 m (39 ft 9 in)	12.5 m (41 ft)	14.6 m (48 ft)	14.6 m (48 ft)

JUMPING A NOVICE GRID

By introducing different combinations of fences set at specific distances, you can tailor an exercise to match your abilities and develop particular areas of your horse's jumping. Start with warm-up exercises, introducing your horse to each element of a simple grid before jumping it as a whole. When you have mastered this exercise, you can try bigger fences and more demanding grids to develop your own and your horse's skills further.

WARMING UP

Be realistic about the demands you set for yourself and your horse. Too many horses have been frightened by difficult grids, so aim to increase the level of difficulty gradually.

For example, novice horses will benefit from being introduced to different fence fillers, but you should never suddenly introduce a new filler at the end of a training session, and especially not at the end of a grid. This is because your horse's attention will be drawn to the filler, and he may make mistakes as he jumps the fences before it. Instead, introduce a filler under a single fence at the beginning of the exercise, and use it as part of your warm-up so that the horse has the chance to become used to it.

In the grid below, the last fence incorporates two roll-top fillers (4). For your warm-up, use a placing plank 2.7 m (9 ft) away from a small fence and use the roll-tops as wings. Jump the fence a few times, approaching in trot, until the horse is settled. Then move the roll-tops under the fence to become fillers. Then you can build up the grid fence by fence, and practise each phase until you are ready to jump it as a whole.

JUMPING THE GRID Once your horse is jumping each individual fence with confidence, you are ready to jump the complete grid. Concentrate on maintaining an even canter stride and adjust your horse's speed and direction when necessary.

BUILDING UP THE GRID

The aim is to keep a good balance and an even rein contact throughout. Start by riding over placing planks in walk and then trot, to help achieve an even stride. Add a cross pole fence (1) to the exercise and land in canter. Next add a vertical (2) at a distance of one stride. Finally, set up an oxer two strides away from the vertical. This distance allows you time to adjust your horse's speed and direction (3) in order to achieve the right take-off point for jumping the oxer (4). Two strides after the oxer, lay out two poles in a funnel shape and a canter plank (5). These will help keep your horse focused and maintaining an even pace, even after the last fence. Once your horse can jump the grid with ease, and you can ride without rein contact and with a consistent balance, try raising the height of the fences.

HORSE AND RIDER'S VIEW OF THE GRID

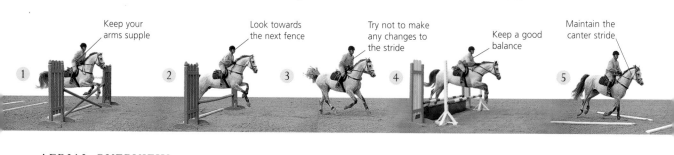

Keep your arms supple — 1

Look towards the next fence — 2

Try not to make any changes to the stride — 3

Keep a good balance — 4

Maintain the canter stride — 5

AERIAL OVERVIEW

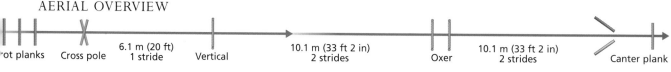

Trot planks   Cross pole   6.1 m (20 ft) 1 stride   Vertical   10.1 m (33 ft 2 in) 2 strides   Oxer   10.1 m (33 ft 2 in) 2 strides   Canter plank

JUMPING THE OXER If you have started the grid well and maintained a good, even canter stride, you will take off at the right point over the oxer. Land in canter and keep your horse focused on the end of the grid. Only add the back pole to the oxer when you feel that your horse is jumping confidently.

GRIDS FOR ALL LEVELS

Oxers are useful because they encourage a horse to make the highest point of his jump over the middle of the fence, which produces good technique. Variations on the two-oxer grid (see below) will help any level of horse. Start with small fences and easy distances. Take note of your horse's take-off and landing points and analyse his technique. Your first aim is to achieve a symmetrical jump. Then you can develop athleticism with shorter distances and bigger fences. The width of each oxer can be increased by 10 cm (4 in) at a time to a maximum of 1.5 m (5 ft).

TWO-OXER GRID This grid has a vertical, followed by two oxers, which are set up with two strides between them. Once your horse is jumping this well, a more advanced grid can be created by lengthening the distance between the two oxers by 30–90 cm (1–3 ft).

	2.7 m (9 ft)	2 strides 8.5–9.4 m (28–31 ft)	2 strides 8.8–9.7 m (29–32 ft)
Trot			

| Placing plank | Vertical: 35 cm (2ft 6in) | Oxer: Height 80 cm–1 m (2 ft 6 in–3 ft 3 in) Width 1.1 m (3 ft 6 in) | Oxer: Height 90 cm–1 m (2 ft 9 in–3 ft 6 in) Width 1.1 m (3 ft 6 in) |

REDUCING THE DISTANCE Reduce the distance to the first oxer to one stride and gradually increase the size of the oxers. Do this by moving the front pole back and the back pole forwards so that the mid-point stays the same. This will increase the angle of ascent on take-off and develop your horse's athleticism.

	2.7 m (9ft)	1 stride 5.5–6.25 m (18–20 ft)	1 stride 5.8–6.55 m (19–21 ft)
Trot			

| Placing plank | Vertical: 35 cm (2 ft 6 in) | Oxer: Height 90 cm–1.1 m (3 ft–3ft 6 in) Width 1.1 m (3 ft 6 in) | Oxer: Height 1–1.2 m (3 ft 3 in–3 ft 9 in) Width 1.1 m (3 ft 6 in) |

IMPROVING YOUR HORSE'S JUMP

When you are familiar with your horse's strengths and weaknesses, you can improve the quality of his jump. Use placing planks and trotting planks to achieve a consistent approach and the correct take-off points. Work with different fences and grids to improve specific aspects of your horse's technique, such as the angle of ascent, the use of the forelegs, and the shape of the jump. In particular, having the hind legs together on take-off is crucial for efficient jumping.

ACHIEVING CONSISTENCY

The key to grid work is to start with a consistent approach at the right speed. To help you achieve this, you can use trotting or placing planks on the ground before the first fence in a grid (which should ideally be a cross pole). This will help your horse achieve even strides and the right take-off point. The hind legs should take off exactly half-way between the last plank and the fence. The landing point should be the same distance away from the cross poles.

An effective method of ensuring a settled approach to a grid is to ride in a figure-of-eight before the placing plank or trotting planks, using 10–15 m (32–50 ft) circles (see box, below). Turning circles before a grid gives horse and rider the chance to establish balance, which can then be maintained during the exercise. Approaching a jump in rising trot will keep you from stiffening and encourage the horse to stay in trot rather than falling back into walk or breaking into canter. Trotting will also help you keep a light seat, which is useful for riders who tend to get out of balance at the moment of take-off.

USING DIFFERENT FENCES

Once you have achieved a consistent approach to – and departure from – the cross pole, try putting another fence two or three strides away. (Leaving only one stride between fences allows you less time to adjust the horse's speed and direction; with more than three strides, it is more difficult to keep the strides sufficiently consistent to achieve the right take-off point.)

Using an oxer as the second fence will encourage the horse to make a symmetrical trajectory – with the highest part of his jump over the middle of the fence. The ascending oxer (see p.191) will build the horse's confidence because it fits the natural shape of his jump, but it will tend to make him jump with the highest point close to the back pole. The square oxer (see p.191) improves almost every part of a horse's jump, especially when the horse is asked to take off closer to the fence. Verticals with ground lines are good at the beginning and end of a grid because they are easier for the horse. When your horse consistently jumps oxers with good quality, he is ready to jump verticals without ground lines.

A placing plank helps the horse find the right take-off point

FIGURE-OF-EIGHT

It can help to trot in circles in front of a fence until the horse is facing the fence in a calm manner. This technique enables you to delay jumping until the horse is settled. Try circling a few times in one direction, and then once in the other.

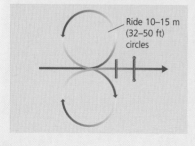

Ride 10–15 m (32–50 ft) circles

AIMING FOR A SYMMETRICAL JUMP

The most efficient jump is one with the highest point over the centre of a fence. To achieve this, the horse must adjust his take-off and landing points accordingly.

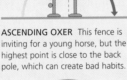

ASCENDING OXER This fence is inviting for a young horse, but the highest point is close to the back pole, which can create bad habits.

SQUARE OXER Using a square oxer will encourage the horse to achieve his highest point over the middle of the fence.

VERTICAL This is how a vertical should be jumped, but some horses take-off too close, with the highest point of the jump beyond the fence.

GETTING THE HIND LEGS TOGETHER

The quality and height of the jump is largely dictated by how the two hind legs push off the ground. Getting them well underneath the horse is important, but having them together as a pair, pushing off the ground equally, is the first requisite for good jumping. If a horse consistently leaves one hind leg behind the other, flat work will help resolve the problem. Practise cantering in circles – keep the hind leg that tends to trail on the inside. This will help the horse develop both sides of his body equally, because the inside hind leg stays a little forwards of the outside leg in the canter and has to work harder. Jumping small fences on the same rein on a circle can also help because the weaker hind leg will stay forwards on take-off.

A bounce grid, where there is no non-jumping stride between two fences, is a useful exercise as the horse has to take off for the second fence as soon as he has landed from the first. This gymnastic exercise will improve agility and suppleness in your horse and encourage quick-thinking; it will also encourage him to take off with both hind legs together. However, care must be taken to ensure the horse still jumps over the fences, rather than using a stepping motion, with the hind leg staying on the ground for slightly too long. If you use bounces, bear in mind that it is difficult for the hind legs to come as far forwards under the horse at the moment of the second take-off, so bounces should be at least 30 cm (1 ft) lower than the other fences in a grid. It is important to remember that bounces are demanding: they should not be overused, especially by inexperienced horses or riders.

MORE ADVANCED GRID EXERCISES

The following exercises are aimed at improving particular aspects of your horse's jumping ability, including agility, suppleness, and using his body to make the jump. During these exercises, maintain a consistent balance and either a light rein contact or no contact. This will ensure that the horse keeps his own balance, is allowed to complete the last stride with his forelegs well in front of his shoulders, and is able to use his head and neck. It will be helpful if you have these exercises videoed and then study the jump a frame at a time.

BOUNCE GRID This exercise helps improve agility and suppleness and gets the horse's hind legs together. As the horse lands in a bounce, first one foreleg and then the other touches the ground and then leaves the ground before the hind legs land. The hind legs must then immediately push off the ground together. Start with one bounce and then add up to a maximum of four.

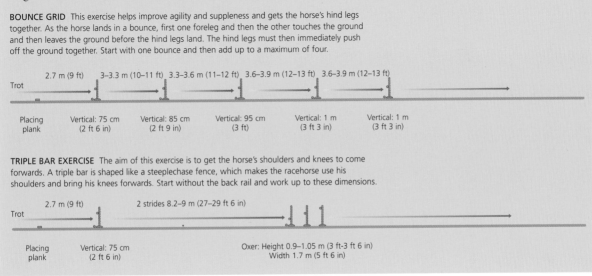

| | 2.7 m (9 ft) | 3–3.3 m (10–11 ft) | 3.3–3.6 m (11–12 ft) | 3.6–3.9 m (12–13 ft) | 3.6–3.9 m (12–13 ft) |

Trot

| Placing plank | Vertical: 75 cm (2 ft 6 in) | Vertical: 85 cm (2 ft 9 in) | Vertical: 95 cm (3 ft) | Vertical: 1 m (3 ft 3 in) | Vertical: 1 m (3 ft 3 in) |

TRIPLE BAR EXERCISE The aim of this exercise is to get the horse's shoulders and knees to come forwards. A triple bar is shaped like a steeplechase fence, which makes the racehorse use his shoulders and bring his knees forwards. Start without the back rail and work up to these dimensions.

| | 2.7 m (9 ft) | 2 strides 8.2–9 m (27–29 ft 6 in) |

Trot

| Placing plank | Vertical: 75 cm (2 ft 6 in) | Oxer: Height 0.9–1.05 m (3 ft–3 ft 6 in) Width 1.7 m (5 ft 6 in) |

JUMPING A MORE ADVANCED GRID

Placing two fences at a shorter distance than usual will encourage your horse to put his hind legs together on take-off, while using wide oxers will train your horse to release and lengthen his hind legs in the second half of the jump. In order to achieve the maximum benefit from this exercise, the rider must maintain a good balance throughout, so as not to interfere with the jump. Introduce your horse to each element of the grid before attempting to jump the full sequence.

JUMPING THE GRID

Start the grid by approaching the poles laid out in a funnel shape in trot (1) and jumping the cross poles (2) – this set-up guides your horse so that he jumps in the middle of the fence. The following bounce distance (where your horse must take-off again immediately after landing) encourages your horse to be well balanced (3), and ready to take one complete stride to the first oxer (4). Check that your approach to this fence is straight, and adjust your direction if necessary. The slightly short distance to the fence means that your horse will be encouraged to put his two hind legs together on take-off. Then, the two strides to the second oxer will allow time for you to make any necessary minor alterations of speed and direction before reaching the next close take-off point at the second oxer. If you maintain a light rein contact, the horse's forelegs will be able to finish the final stride to this fence without being restricted (5). Focus on keeping a consistent stride length, even to the last canter plank (6).

After this exercise, jump three or four different fences on a course to see if you can maintain the improved technique, with your horse using his hind legs effectively.

Hind legs are together

THE GRID

Keep your weight down through your leg to your heel

Look towards the end of the grid

Ensure that the horse is straight

1   2   3   4

AERIAL OVERVIEW

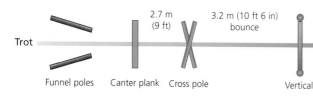

2.7 m (9 ft)

3.2 m (10 ft 6 in) bounce

6.1 m (20 ft) 1 stride

1 m (3 ft 3 in) high
1.8 m (6 ft) wide

Trot

Funnel poles   Canter plank   Cross pole   Vertical   Oxer

ENGAGING THE HIND LEGS
The shorter distance to the second oxer encourages the horse to use his hind legs together, creating more power and a slightly steeper angle of ascent.

The shoulders and forelegs start to lift

The knees come up and forwards

Hind legs move forwards ready to push off the ground

Keep the rein contact light

Be aware of the horse's speed, and make small adjustments if necessary

Continue to encourage the horse to maintain a regular stride, even up to the last ground plank

5

6

9.3 m (30 ft 6 in) 2 strides

1.1 m (3 ft 6 in) high
1.2 m (3 ft 9 in) wide

10 m (33 ft) 2 strides

Oxer

Funnel poles   Canter plank

RELATED DISTANCES AND TURNS

If your aim is to compete, your training sessions should be specifically directed to the demands of showjumping courses. Start by cantering on straight-line related distances using planks on the ground, instead of fences. Build up to jumping on turns and riding simple courses that are based on straight lines. Then, when you can easily land on the correct canter lead after a fence, you will be ready to jump your first proper course of fences.

STRAIGHT-LINE RELATED DISTANCES

The simplest exercise using a straight-line distance is to trot to a cross pole, land in canter, and take a specific number of strides to a canter plank (see pp.196–97). You can then replace the cross pole with another canter plank and canter over both planks. The distances should be based on a 3.7 m (12 ft) standard showjumping stride, with each plank being in the middle of a stride. Practise distances from between one to ten strides. You should do this regularly, in the same way a golfer practises his swing. Once you can do this consistently, begin to put different straight-line related distances together to form a course (see box, below). As you progress, you can begin to replace the planks with fences. Initially, just replace the second plank in each line and then replace the whole course.

TURNS ON RELATED DISTANCES

When two fences are related, but with a turn in the middle, this is called a dog-leg turn. You will find that the quality of your flat work and your horse's ability to turn easily in both directions will prove invaluable when you jump on a dog leg.

If you ride the turn as if it is part of a 20 m (65 ft) circle, it should be possible to keep the same canter stride throughout. In this case, a dog leg will ride just like a straight-line related distance (see box, below). If you ride the turn as if it was part of a smaller circle, your horse will have to shorten his stride on the turn and this will prevent you from riding the whole line in even strides. Place two planks at a 20-degree angle to each other and approach in canter. The turn itself should take one stride. You may find it useful to lay out poles on the ground

WORKING TOWARDS JUMPING A COURSE

Once you are able to jump a cross pole from trot and take six strides to a canter plank on a straight line **(finish 1)**, you can add a turn to the exercise (see right). If you base the turn on a 20 m (65 ft) circle, you will not need to shorten your stride for the turn. Whatever the angle of the turn, you will take six non-jumping strides between the two planks, with the turn starting at the end of the second stride. The number of strides you take on the turn will increase as the angle increases. So, for **finish 3**, two of your six strides will be on the turn.

For course work, you will jump straight-line related distances based on a 3.7 m (12 ft) stride. Once you have practised cantering to planks on the ground, ride a course of planks (see far right), with different numbers of strides required between sets of fences. Soon, you will be able to replace the planks with fences.

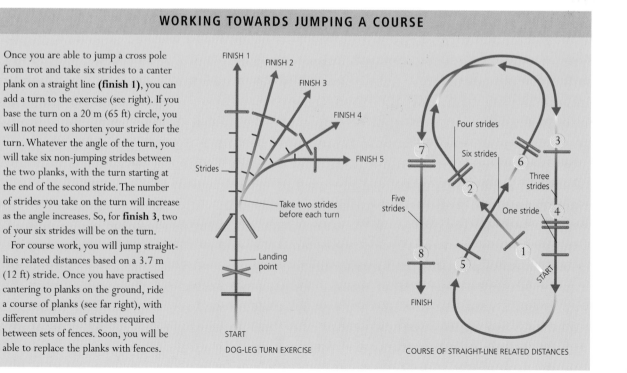

DOG-LEG TURN EXERCISE

COURSE OF STRAIGHT-LINE RELATED DISTANCES

to help guide you through the turn. Then, try riding a 45-degree turn – the turn will take two strides (see sequence, below). The key is to maintain a consistent stride length. As you progress, you can replace the second plank on the ground with a small fence. Then replace the first plank with a small fence, too.

CORRECT CANTER LEAD

The difficulty with dog-leg turns comes when you land over the first fence on the wrong canter lead, making the turn less easy to ride. If necessary, you need to improve your horse's ability to land on either canter lead after a fence (see pp.82–83). This will also come through improving your flat work so that your horse uses both sides of his body equally well and rides straight.

All horses have a favourite rein. If their less preferred canter lead is required after a fence, try slightly changing the direction of approach to the fence (see box, right). If you want to stay on the same rein after a fence, come in at a slight angle towards the side you want to go. To change the rein, do the opposite, slightly over-shooting your normal line.

CHANGING THE CANTER LEAD

Achieving the right canter lead after a fence helps you make a smoother turn. Here, following the dotted line will achieve a deeper approach to fence 1 and help you change canter lead as you jump. Take a shallower line to fence 2 so you can maintain the same canter lead and stay on the right line after the fence.

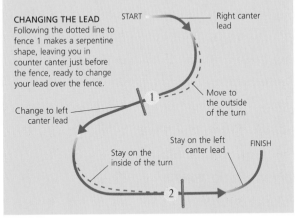

CHANGING THE LEAD
Following the dotted line to fence 1 makes a serpentine shape, leaving you in counter canter just before the fence, ready to change your lead over the fence.

START

Right canter lead

Move to the outside of the turn

Change to left canter lead

Stay on the inside of the turn

Stay on the left canter lead

FINISH

RIDING A DOG-LEG TURN
Approach the first plank in canter. After two straight strides, take two strides on the turn to the right, before taking two straight strides to the second plank.

Look in the direction you want to go

Count each of the six strides between the two planks

Put a little extra weight in the right stirrup to help the turn

Use your leg aids to keep moving the horse forwards

Be aware of the take-off point to the first plank

AERIAL OVERVIEW

JUMPING AGAINST THE CLOCK

If more than one competitor jumps a clear round in a competition, those riders will enter a jump-off round. This is usually against the clock, which means that the competitor who completes the course in the fastest time wins.

The rider who can find the most efficient routes around a course will therefore have the edge at the competition. Jumping fences on an angle, turning back to fences, and taking out strides, are strategies that will help you save time.

SAVING TIME

Simply going faster in an effort to beat the clock can be counterproductive. A young horse will jump fewer clear rounds and his style will deteriorate if you encourage him to jump too fast too soon. Instead, it is better to reduce the distances between fences by jumping the course with as few strides as possible but without increasing the speed of the canter signifcantly. The most important techniques required in order to accomplish this is being able to jump fences on an angle, and to turn back to a fence.

JUMPING ANGLED FENCES

In training, as soon as your horse is jumping straight, start practising jumping angled fences, as well as going a little faster, but always finish with your horse being in a calm state. Some horses have a tendency to veer to one corner of an angled fence as they approach, but then veer to the opposite corner as they jump. Here (see sequence below), the planks on the ground discourage this in a safe way, helping to guide the horse so that he holds exactly the same line before, over, and after the fence.

STAYING FOCUSED The take-off point for an angled fence must be far enough away to give the foreleg closest to the fence time to fold under the horse's chest. Keep the horse in gear.

JUMPING AN ANGLED FENCE
The key to jumping on an angle is to stay on the same line throughout by maintaining consistent leg and rein contacts.

AERIAL OVERVIEW

Start by approaching and jumping a fence set up at a small angle of around 20 degrees. It is vital that you maintain a consistent rein contact without restricting the horse. This, along with the leg contacts, will help to create a directional guide for your horse, making sure that he does not veer to either side. With young horses, it may be useful to increase the weight of these contacts a little, but your hands and arms must remain supple and allowing, not restricting.

When you have successfully jumped a small angle, gradually build up to an angle of 45 degrees. An advanced horse can jump at an even sharper angle over a vertical. However, even an advanced horse and rider should be careful about how acute an angle they jump an oxer, because this can dramatically increase the width of the fence. For example, an oxer that is 1.2 m (3 ft 9 in) wide becomes 1.7 m (5 ft 6 in) wide when jumped at an angle of 45 degrees, and is therefore much more difficult to clear.

NARROW FENCES

Jumping to the right or left of the centre of a fence will help you make a shorter line or improve the line to a subsequent fence. When you do this, however, there is a risk that the horse will run out and avoid the fence altogether. Practising jumping narrow fences, initially with the use of wingstands, is a useful way to train your horse. Try to maintain the rein contact.

Look where you want to go

Maintain an even rein contact and keep the horse's neck straight

If the horse is trying hard, reward him instantly

Use your leg contact to help the horse stay straight

JUMPING ON A TURN

A turnback is a development of a dog leg (see pp.218–19), taking the angle of the turn further. Like a dog leg, it can initially be based on a 20 m (65 ft) circle. The reason for this is not just that this will provide the required stride length of 3.7 m (12 ft), but that it is the smallest circle on which the inexperienced horse can maintain the necessary impulsion from which to jump.

A neat turn back will allow you to save time in a jump-off and still jump the fence safely. To enable this to happen, you must jump the fence straight, rather than at an angle. Therefore, in training, place an extra canter plank or fence directly ahead of the turnback fence (see box, below) so that you and your horse will ride straight ahead after the fence.

The turnback is essentially a half circle followed by a fence. As this is the case, the foundation for the exercise is being able to ride a circle properly. This goes back to correct flat-work training. If you bend your horse too much in his neck, for example, he will fall to the outside of the circle and you will not be able to control the turn. Some horses and riders do the opposite, coming around the turn with the bend in the neck to the outside, and with the horse falling to the inside. (Horses often do this when galloping loose in the field.) In both cases, the horse will not be able to make full use of the power of his hindquarters for the jump. The key to riding a circle is to imagine the circle shape being on the inside of your horse, not the outside (see pp.140–41). This will automatically help you keep the horse on a circle, enabling a good jump.

To help keep the forehand in the correct line of the circle, move both your reins temporarily towards the inside a little, without pulling backwards. Use your outside leg to stop the horse's body moving sideways. Avoid slipping to the outside by keeping a little extra weight in the inside stirrup. You will need to do this even more when you are riding a turnback on a 15 m (50 ft) half circle (see box, below). This requires a degree of collection in the canter (see pp.126–27), with the horse taking more weight on his hindquarters, and is therefore not possible for a novice horse.

SETTING UP A TURNBACK

Initially, practise riding a 20 m (65 ft) half circle over two planks, before turning the second plank into a small fence. To begin with, the introduction of the fence may cause you and your horse to lose the line of the circle. Put guide planks on the ground to act as indicators of the shape of the half

PROGRESSING FROM A DOG LEG TO A TURNBACK

Introduce a turn back by using canter planks on the ground. This will make the exercise easier and allow you to practise it without tiring your horse. Try to maintain an even jumping canter throughout the turn. If you find this difficult on a 20 m (65 ft) half circle, make it bigger. On a 20 m (65 ft)

half circle, most horses will do seven or eight strides between the planks. See what suits your horse and get a feel for repeating the turn consistently, but always ensure that your horse is not stressed. More advanced riders can reduce the size of the half circle to 15 m (50 ft), and then 10 m (32 ft).

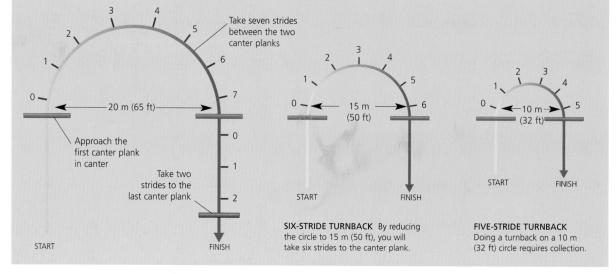

SIX-STRIDE TURNBACK By reducing the circle to 15 m (50 ft), you will take six strides to the canter plank.

FIVE-STRIDE TURNBACK Doing a turnback on a 10 m (32 ft) circle requires collection.

circle (see picture, below). If the previous exercises have been done well, your horse will quickly begin to understand what is required, and you should not have to use strong aids. Practise this exercise until it comes easily, because strong aids will restrict your horse's impulsion. With a trained horse, all you will have to do is look in the direction you want to go, and put a little weight to the inside. As the exercise becomes easier, and you can do it equally well on both reins, take all the guide planks away and do the turn back and the fence by itself. You will by now have a good feel for where the turn should start and you will be surprised at how easy it is. Most riders can judge a stride better off a turn, because it is easier to get perspective. You will also be able to find a good take-off point.

A related exercise is to do the turnback a little later. This means you will do your 20-m (65-ft) half circle and then one, two, or three strides in a straight line, before jumping the fence. If you and your horse are getting close to your maximum height of fence, you will need this extra space to make the necessary adjustments before the jump.

When you jump against the clock, there is a greater risk of error, but if your horse has had good fifth-leg training (see box, right) you should expect him to try to help you out of trouble. Sit as still as you can, but maintain the correct direction, speed, and impulsion, and allow your horse to respond positively in difficult situations.

FIFTH-LEG TRAINING

A horse that has the ability to get himself out of trouble and save himself from a fall is described as having a fifth leg. Fifth-leg training is a major part of preparation for jump-off, as well as for cross country (see pp.270–71). It encourages your horse not only to work for you, but to think for you.

Encourage the horse to respect fences by making sure all small fences are fairly solid. However, as the fences get bigger, the poles should be lighter to avoid frightening him. With small fences, do not worry about taking off slightly close or slightly far away, and try to avoid supporting the horse through the rein. He needs to learn to have self-carriage, to look at what he is jumping, to make decisions, and to know how to react to different situations. Too many riders control things to such an extent that the horse stops thinking, so that when the rider makes a mistake the horse is unable to respond, even for his own self preservation. A horse needs to be mentally engaged in his jumping. Through exercises and a reward system, he can learn that jumping cleanly is what is required.

SMALL FENCE WITH FILLERS
A solid-looking fence encourages the horse to respect fences and look after himself.

BIG FENCE WITH LIGHT POLES
Using light poles and safety cups on the back pole (pp.190–91) will help maintain the horse's confidence.

TURNBACK WITH A FENCE
Cantering over a plank on the ground before turning to a fence makes a related-distance exercise. The planks laid out on the ground help guide the rider on an accurate half circle as she turns towards the fence.

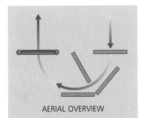

AERIAL OVERVIEW

Look in the direction you want to go

Prevent movement to the right with the use of the outside leg

Move both hands temporarily to the inside to help make the turn

ADJUSTING STRIDE LENGTHS

The foundation of your weekly work is to maintain the 3.7 m (12 ft) stride and consistently find exact take-off points. Every week, you can also begin work on shortening and lengthening your horse's strides so that you can cope with more difficult distances. Eventually, you need to be able to easily do either four short strides or three long ones in a three-and-a-half-stride distance. The level of difficulty can be further increased by adding another related distance before or after this. For example, at an advanced level you might be asked to lengthen your stride after a combination fence followed by three-and-a-half strides to a tall vertical.

Everything goes back to flat work. Initially, practise little decreases and increases of speed, which will lead to a little shortening and lengthening, and in turn to proper collected and medium paces (see pp.156–57). Start by putting two canter planks 24 m (78 ft) apart (this equals five-and-a-half normal strides). Then, alternate coming down in either six short or five long strides. If you are not meeting the first plank fairly accurately, you need to go back to trotting to a fence and cantering to a distance with an even stride (see pp.214–15).

If you can shorten and lengthen strides on demand and do either a 3.4 m (11ft) or 4 m (13ft) stride as well as the normal 3.7 m (12ft), you will be able to cope with slightly long or slightly short distances in a showjumping course.

With two connected related distances it is usually easier to go from the slower canter and the shorter distance to the faster canter and the longer distance. For instance, in a combination, which is also a type of related distance, it is much easier to go from a normal stride to a long stride than it is to go from a long stride to a normal stride. In training, however, it is better to put the emphasis on a little shortening. The improved balance used when shortening will help you as you learn to lengthen, so in training the two must go hand in hand. If you cannot immediately re-establish a normal canter after lengthening, you are asking too much of your horse.

JUMP-OFF STRATEGY

Before preparing for a jump-off round, you must decide on your strategy. Are you ready to go fast or is your horse best suited to going slowly at this stage? If you choose to go fast, is it going to be a risk or will you be riding within your horse's capabilities? If you choose to go slowly, will you do the least number of strides possible or take a longer route?

The answer to most of these questions lies in what you have been doing at home. It may be better to think in the long term and use the jump-off as a means of improving your future performance. This could mean either going faster to gain experience or slower to keep your horse calm for another day. Even some leading speed horses can take a

SHORTENING AND LENGTHENING STRIDES

You need to be able to lengthen to such an extent that you can leave out a stride, and to shorten enough to add a stride. This is more difficult than it appears. The distances below make it easy for you to see what degree of shortening and lengthening is possible. To carry out the exercise, set canter planks with a normal distance between them and then gradually shorten or lengthen the distances. As you progress, you will soon be able to take out or add strides where necessary. The key is to make sure you establish the right speed and stride length before the first plank. Always finish the exercise by re-establishing the normal stride length.

PROGRESSING TO ADDING STRIDES			PROGRESSING TO TAKING OUT STRIDES		
DISTANCE BETWEEN CANTER PLANKS	NUMBER OF STRIDES TO TAKE	STRIDE LENGTH	DISTANCE BETWEEN CANTER PLANKS	NUMBER OF STRIDES TO TAKE	STRIDE LENGTH
5 normal strides: 22 m (72 ft)	5	Normal – 3.7 m (12 ft)	5 normal strides: 22 m (72 ft)	5	Normal – 3.7 m (12 ft)
5½ normal strides: 24 m (78 ft)	6	Slightly short – 3.4 m (11 ft)	5½ normal strides: 24 m (78 ft)	5	Slightly long – 4 m (13 ft)
4 normal strides: 18 m (60 ft)	5	Short – 3 m (10 ft)	6 normal strides: 25.5 m (84 ft)	5	Long – 4.3 m (14 ft)
2 normal strides: 11 m (36 ft)	3	Very short – 2.7 m (9 ft)	4 normal strides: 18 m (60 ft)	3	Very long – 4.6 m (15 ft)

month after a major competition before they are mentally ready to gallop again. It is reasonable to aim for a personal best, but it is better to work from something you know you can do rather than trying something totally new for the first time. A good rider of speed classes is not wild and risky, but controlled and aware of what their horse is capable of. It is all about knowing where the limits are.

CHOOSING A ROUTE

Having decided on your strategy, you need to choose your route. In a small arena, reducing the number of strides around a course by taking a shorter track can often be more effective than simply going faster. Even leaving out a stride on a related distance before a turn will not always be beneficial if you are going fast: your speed will make it difficult to take the turn sharply and, as a result, you will need to take more, not fewer, strides. This will mean taking an extra two strides on the following turn because of the speed you are going.

However, if the course is in a big arena, then going fast may be

necessary if you are to be competitive. If you are one of the first of many in a jump-off round, taking the more difficult options may be best as this will then set a standard.

Whatever route and speed you choose, build on your result for next time. Going fast but safely is one of the most skilful and exciting things any rider can do, and you should have it in mind in every weekly training programme.

THINKING AHEAD As you begin the descent from one fence, you should already be turning, as this rider is, and looking to the next fence.

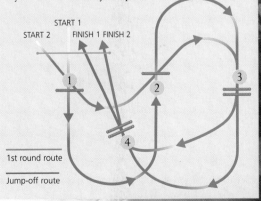

JUMP-OFF COURSE

In the first-round (red route), approach fences in a straight line, using flowing turns. For the jump-off round (blue route), reduce the number of strides by a third by jumping the verticals on angles. You will then be competitive even if you do not increase your speed.

START 1
START 2 FINISH 1 FINISH 2

1

2

3

4

1st round route

Jump-off route

COMBINING THE EXERCISES

A balanced training schedule will contain elements of grids, as well as preparation for jumping courses and going against the clock. It will also be founded on a programme of quality flat work. The jump set-ups used here are derived from two base grids (see Base Grid One, right), and are just two examples of designs that you can set up for training to mix many different exercises. If you are short of space for Base Grid One, reduce the distance between the two oxers to three strides and take away the bounce.

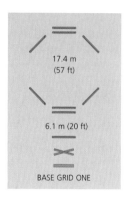

17.4 m
(57 ft)

6.1 m (20 ft)

BASE GRID ONE

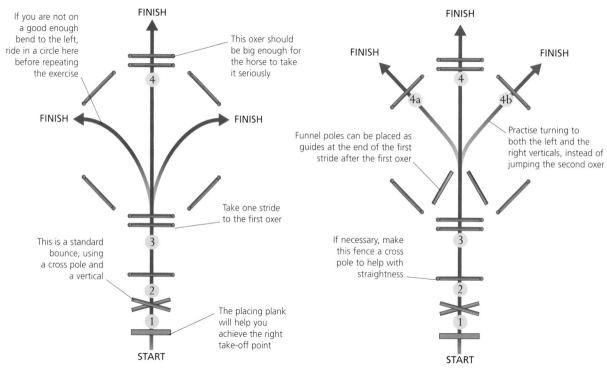

If you are not on a good enough bend to the left, ride in a circle here before repeating the exercise

FINISH

This oxer should be big enough for the horse to take it seriously

FINISH

FINISH

This is a standard bounce, using a cross pole and a vertical

Take one stride to the first oxer

The placing plank will help you achieve the right take-off point

START

FINISH

FINISH

FINISH

Funnel poles can be placed as guides at the end of the first stride after the first oxer

Practise turning to both the left and the right verticals, instead of jumping the second oxer

If necessary, make this fence a cross pole to help with straightness

START

EXERCISE ONE

The standard grid bounce over a cross pole (**1**) and a vertical (**2**) is followed by one stride to an oxer (**3**). By now, you should find this fairly easy. However, if your horse jumps this efficiently and well, he will improve just by repeating it. The first real test is to land cantering on the left or right lead on demand, without moving the horse to the right or left on landing (see p.219). This requires good straightness and you may have to return to flat work in order to achieve this. Then, as a progression, you can vary between going right or left or straight on to jump the final oxer (**4**) – this is on a four-stride related distance. You will find this exercise makes your horse listen to you, and it is a real test of your foundation exercises.

EXERCISE TWO

As a progression from Exercise One, jump either of the two verticals to the left and right of the oxer (**4**) – these are set-up as four-stride dog-leg related distances on a 45-degree angle. With the optional routes after the first oxer (**3**), your horse has to listen to you rather than anticipating his next move. If you choose to make a turn to a vertical, take one stride straight, then two on the turn, and one straight before the vertical (**4a** or **4b**). If necessary, use planks on the ground in the shape of a funnel to help guide your horse. It is tempting to land over the final fence and think you have finished the exercise, but the landing is the start of the approach to the next fence. You need to land on either the left or right canter lead.

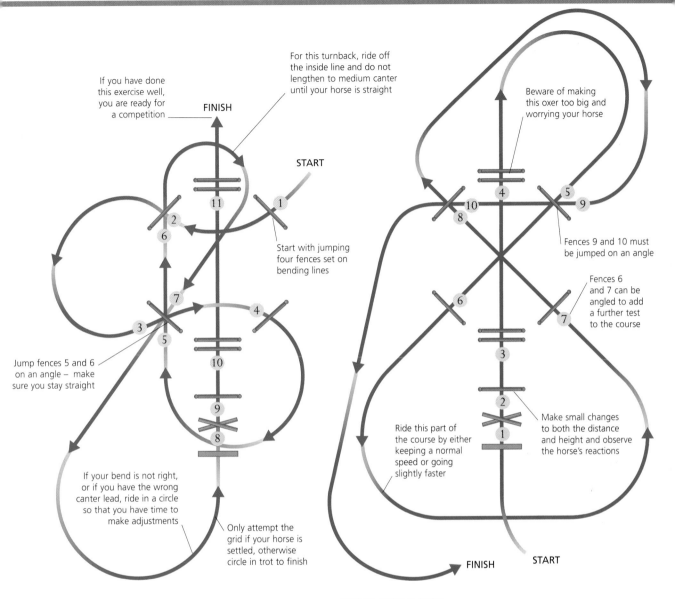

For this turnback, ride off the inside line and do not lengthen to medium canter until your horse is straight

If you have done this exercise well, you are ready for a competition

FINISH

START

Start with jumping four fences set on bending lines

Jump fences 5 and 6 on an angle – make sure you stay straight

If your bend is not right, or if you have the wrong canter lead, ride in a circle so that you have time to make adjustments

Only attempt the grid if your horse is settled, otherwise circle in trot to finish

Beware of making this oxer too big and worrying your horse

Fences 9 and 10 must be jumped on an angle

Fences 6 and 7 can be angled to add a further test to the course

Make small changes to both the distance and height and observe the horse's reactions

Ride this part of the course by either keeping a normal speed or going slightly faster

FINISH   **START**

EXERCISE THREE

This is an example of how you might bring together a grid and normal fences from a course to produce a very effective schooling track. The first four fences are set on bending lines (**1, 2, 3, 4**), with three normal strides between each. Flying changes (see pp.150–51) are necessary over two of these fences (**2, 3**), in order to achieve the correct canter lead. There are two angled fences (**5, 6**) with three normal strides between them. Then there is a 10 m (32 ft) half circle turnback, which requires a lengthening to medium canter to the next fence (**7**), before going forwards in trot and finishing with the grid (**8-11**). If the horse does not finish this exercise calmly, then you must take a few steps back in your training.

EXERCISE FOUR

There is an enormous number of possible variations, but this exercise is designed purely to encourage consistency of stride length and fluency through the turns. Three pairs of fences are separated by four normal strides (**3–4, 5–6, 7–8**). One set of fences is separated by two normal strides (**9–10**). Once you and your horse are proficient at this exercise, it is easy to change the distances to make things a little more difficult. For instance, it would be useful to have slightly longer distances across the diagonals; then make the distance slightly short between two of the angled fences (**9,10**), and the grid slightly short. In training, you may have to spend at least three sessions practising shortening for every one session you spend lengthening.

USING BASE GRID TWO

This set-up (see right) of vertical fences based on two 20 m (65 ft) circles, gives you an endless variety of exercises. You need to allow room for the horse to turn towards the outside at times, so quite a large area is required. Therefore, it is more suitable for large outdoor schools or the field. To ensure your flat work is good, use planks or poles on the ground to begin with, instead of fences. Then you can put the shapes together like movements in a dressage test. As you work on specific elements, you may want to change the distances slightly, so that you are always working within your horse's capabilities.

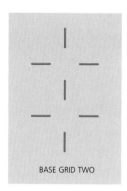

BASE GRID TWO

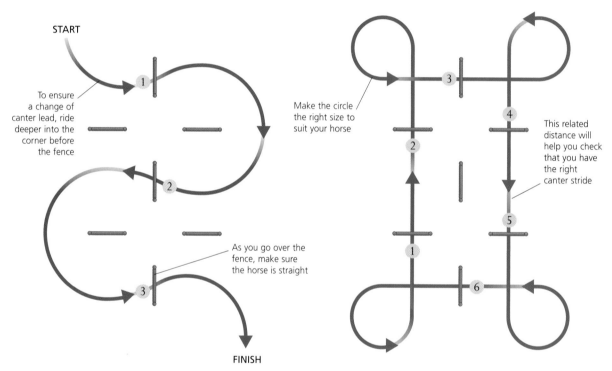

START

To ensure a change of canter lead, ride deeper into the corner before the fence

Make the circle the right size to suit your horse

As you go over the fence, make sure the horse is straight

This related distance will help you check that you have the right canter stride

FINISH

EXERCISE ONE

This type of exercise is the foundation of your preparation for jumping a course because it is so important to be able to change canter leads over a fence (see p.219). It is true that good flying changes (see p.150–51) will get you out of trouble if you are on the wrong lead, but if you cannot easily land on either canter lead then it is probable that your horse is not straight enough. If so, you must return to flat work. Riding serpentines (see pp.142–43) will help to get both you and your horse straighter, because they make you work equally on both reins. If you did this exercise by riding straight at each fence, it would be more difficult both to achieve the desired canter lead and to stop the horse falling to the inside after each fence. If you have the right bend, your horse will not fall in.

EXERCISE TWO

This is a very effective exercise, particularly for a horse that lacks acceptance of the rider and consistency in the canter. With the fences in the position shown here, the two related distances (1–2, 4–5) are both set at 20 m (65 ft), which is ideal for five slightly short strides. However, it is easy to put them at any appropriate distance. By using a 10 m (32 ft) circle to the outside at each corner, it is possible to make adjustments to the canter and train your horse not to run to the inside – horses will often do this if they are continually jumped in small arenas. If necessary, you can do an additional two or three 10 m (32 ft) circles at each corner. As with all the exercises, practise it on both reins. The entry to the 10 m (32 ft) circle is a good place to ask for the flying change, if required.

CHOOSING YOUR EXERCISES

The great advantage of a set-up that offers various routes is that you get to know it very well and it gives you a focus for your training. Before choosing your exercise, you must decide what your goals are. If you want to focus primarily on flat work, just use planks on the ground, rather than fences. Perhaps you want to improve the consistency of your canter, or practise going against the clock. Here (see picture, right), this horse and rider are practising holding their line over an angled fence, which is part of a course. Whatever work you do, make sure you do it well. If necessary, you can always break down each exercise into smaller parts. Then, gradually put together the various parts to form a course.

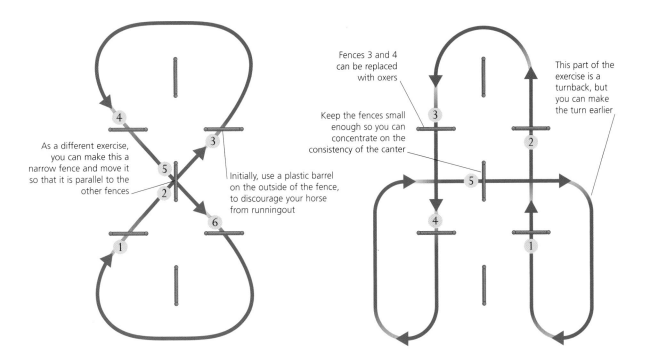

As a different exercise, you can make this a narrow fence and move it so that it is parallel to the other fences

Initially, use a plastic barrel on the outside of the fence, to discourage your horse from running out

Fences 3 and 4 can be replaced with oxers

Keep the fences small enough so you can concentrate on the consistency of the canter

This part of the exercise is a turnback, but you can make the turn earlier

EXERCISE THREE

This exercise tests your ability to jump fences at an angle. Start off by having all the fences 13.7 m (45 ft) from the centre fence. This will give you three slightly short strides, which works well because it is always easier to be a little more under control with angled fences. You may wish to place some planks on the ground in a funnel-shape in front of each fence to act as guides for your horse.

If you can do this exercise well, a useful progression is to shorten the distance between the first set of fences (1–2, 2–3) to 12.8 m (42 ft) and lengthen the distance between the next set (4–5, 5–6) to 14.6 m (48 ft) or slightly longer. The constant shortening and lengthening prepares you and your horse for going against the clock.

EXERCISE FOUR

This is an example of just one course that you can jump with this set-up. To begin with, concentrate on getting the direction and canter right, possibly by using just poles or planks on the ground before replacing them with fences. Initially, use standard four-stride distances between the first two pairs of fences (1–2, 3–4). Then shorten the distances between the first two fences (1–2) by 90 cm (3 ft) and lengthen them between the next related distance (3–4) by 90 cm (3 ft). As a progression, you can replace two verticals with two oxers (3, 4). Then, practise going a little faster and longer to the verticals and going a little slower and shorter to the oxers. With the verticals, use ground lines to make it easier for your horse to judge his take-off points.

EXERCISE OVERVIEW

Each horse will need his own exercise programme for every stage of his training. It is important to be progressive and systematic so that you give yourself and your horse the best possible chance of achieving your aims. It is also important not to overdo it — always be ready to make any necessary adjustments to a programme. Effective exercises are based on feel, empathy, and good communication, all of which are essential if the work is to be enjoyable for both horse and rider.

LEVELS OF ACHIEVEMENT

The chart opposite can be used to assess your current level of ability and to identify areas of your strengths and weaknesses. The levels in the chart do not necessarily relate precisely to existing competition levels, although there is a broad connection. They are primarily to show the normal progression of exercises: Level One relates approximately to a training or introductory level of competition; Level Two relates approximately to a novice level of competition; Level Three relates approximately to an intermediate or medium level of competition; and Level Four relates approximately to the introductory level of international competition. These showjumping benchmarks can be looked at in conjunction with the benchmarks for dressage (see pp.160–61) and cross-country (see pp.296–97) exercises.

It is vital that good-quality work is achieved on a regular basis. The main advantage of devising a system of progressive, varied exercises is that it should always be possible to find something to do well. The aim is to move forwards one step at a time. It may even be that a horse has to go back to the young horse training exercises to find a good-quality base from which to move forwards (see pp.60–89). For example, lungeing is good for horses that have problems in their basic way of going.

When you are doing preparatory exercises for jumping courses, there are particular factors to bear in mind. For example, verticals will tend to be 10 cm (4 in) higher than oxers in the same round, while oxers will tend to be 10 cm (4 in) wider than their height. The length of a course will depend on the size of the arena being used. When you are practising turnbacks, only do so on a half circle that is an appropriate size for the level and confidence of your horse.

THE IMPORTANCE OF VARIED WORK

It is impossible to separate the showjumping exercises from the dressage exercises. The dressage exercises have to be done before the jumping exercises because every showjumping round comprises flat work as well as jumping. In addition, a horse needs to do a variety of work — he needs to be able to hack out, play, and do cross-country work. He also needs good stable management, and to be given suitable rest periods.

GOOD FLAT WORK
You must do dressage exercises, as well as jumping exercises. It is not possible to fulfil your potential as a showjumper without doing good work on the flat.

SHOWJUMPING BENCHMARKS

COURSE ELEMENTS	LEVEL ONE	LEVEL TWO	LEVEL THREE	LEVEL FOUR
Fence height and width	0.9–1.1 x 1–1.2 m (2¾ –3½ ft x 3–3¾ ft)	1.1–1.2 x 1.2–1.4 m (3½–3¾ ft x 3¾–4½ ft)	1.2–1.3 x 1.3–1.5 m (3¾–4 ft x 4–4¾ ft)	1.3–1.4 x 1.4–1.6 m (4–4½ ft x 4½–5 ft)
Speed	350 m/min (12.9 mph)	350 m/min (12.9 mph)	350 m/min (12.9 mph)	375 m/min (13.8 mph)
Length of course	300–400 m (330–440 yd))	350–500 m (400–550 yd)	400–550m (450–600 yd)	400–650 m (450–700 yd)
Number of jumping efforts	First round: 9–10; no second round	First round: 10–12; second round: 6–8	First round: 12–14; second round: 6–8	First round: 12–16; second round: 6–8
Doubles and combinations	1 double	1 double and/or combination	2 doubles or 1 double and 1 combination	2 doubles or 1 double and 1 combination
Types of fences	Verticals, ascending oxers, fillers	Oxers, triple bars, tables, water trays	Water ditches and poles over water	Open water, banks, devil's dyke
Related distances	3 and 4 strides – normal stride length	5 and 6 strides	7 and 8 strides	9 and 10 strides
Maximum dog-leg angle	Quarter turn (22.5°)	Half turn (45°)	Three-quarter turn (66.5°)	Right angle (90°)
Maximum shortening and lengthening		5½ strides in 6 short or 5 long strides	4½ strides in 5 short or 4 long strides	3½ strides in 4 short or 3 long strides
Related distances and combinations		Normal to long and vice versa	Short to normal and vice versa	Short to long and vice versa
Taking out strides		5 long strides in 6 normal distance	4 long strides in 5 normal distance	3 long strides in 4 normal distance
Fences at an angle		Vertical – 22.5°	Vertical – 45°; oxer – 22.5°	Vertical – 67.5°; oxer – 22.5°
Turnback		8 strides on a 20 m (65 ft) half circle	7 strides on a 15 m (50 ft) half circle	6 strides on a 10 m (32 ft) half circle
Maximum speed		Around 450 m/min (16.7 mph)	Around 550 m/min (20.4 mph)	Around 600 m/min (22.2 mph)

NOVICE COURSE

If your preparation has been done well, this novice course should be easy to ride. All the distances are normal and all the turns are wide, so the emphasis is simply on putting your horse in gear, and then maintaining the right direction and the right speed. If you are performing at this level with ease, the progression to the next stage is relatively easy. However, if you or your horse are finding anything difficult, analyse the problem and go back to the relevant, basic exercises.

THE NOVICE PARTNERSHIP

There is a huge range of horses that may be suitable for showjumping, but whatever the type, they need two main attributes: they have to canter calmly down to a fence on a 3.7 m (12 ft) stride, and they need to jump confidently and economically. Attributes such as a good trot are not mandatory.

When you are riding a novice course, you must concentrate on getting the right direction and speed, and keeping a consistently balanced position. Maintain a light rein contact and let your horse do the rest. Remember that a course of showjumps is nothing but a series of basic exercises put together, which you have already practised at home.

As you become more confident, your feel will improve, and you will become more aware of your horse's stride lengths. Then, a quality performance is possible.

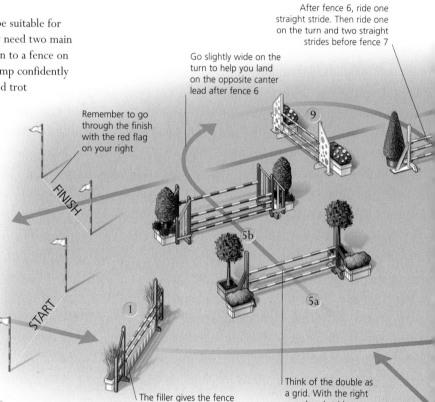

After fence 6, ride one straight stride. Then ride one on the turn and two straight strides before fence 7

Go slightly wide on the turn to help you land on the opposite canter lead after fence 6

Remember to go through the finish with the red flag on your right

The filler gives the fence a sloping profile, which makes it easier and more inviting for the horse

Think of the double as a grid. With the right speed and stride length, the distance will ride perfectly

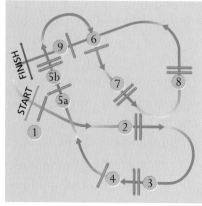

AERIAL OVERVIEW The height of the fences is 1.1 m (3 ft 6 in) and the width of each oxer is 1.2 m (3 ft 9 in). The length of the course is 400 m (440 yd) and it should be ridden at a speed of 350 m/min (12.9 mph). The time allowed for the round is 69 seconds. Before you jump your round, look at the course plan as a matter of habit. You will have to do this at the higher levels.

Even if you do get slightly too close or too far off on take-off to this vertical, it will not be a problem

A CONFIDENT PARTNERSHIP

Here, the rider has a good rein contact and a supple position that has the potential to be excellent. He must take more weight through the leg and firm up his lower leg so that he remains secure when he jumps bigger fences. The horse is trying to jump cleanly, and is calm and athletic, although he should not be asked to jump bigger fences until he can get a little closer to the fence.

Fence 9 is difficult because it is a vertical and it is facing the exit, which tends to make horses careless. Check your horse is not over-excited here.

Use this turn to adjust your balance because 8 is the biggest fence and your horse may be getting tired

7

8

If you are on the wrong canter lead, move out to the left and then do a flying change

2

Do not worry about the distance between fence 1 and 2: just maintain a good canter

Jump the ascending oxer from right to left slightly to help your horse land on the right canter lead

After fence 3, you need to be on the right canter lead, so slightly undershoot this turn. If you go too wide you will go from fence 3 to fence 4 diagonally on a difficult distance

3

4

Then do one stride on the turn and one straight stride before fence 4

Ride straight for the first two strides of this four-stride dog-leg quarter turn

ELEMENTARY COURSE

This level of course requires the rider to maintain a consistent length of canter stride over longer distances – the related distances have increased to six strides. In addition, slightly long and short distances have been introduced, requiring either 4 or 3.4 m (13 or 11 ft) strides. If you do well in the first round, the jump-off presents an exciting challenge. Many riders are content to stay at this level, especially as the next stage requires a horse with more athletic ability.

THE JUMP-OFF

If you make it into the jump-off round, set your own goals and avoid being led by others. You may wish to jump a smooth round without going faster, or you may decide to go fast. If you have chosen the latter, concentrate on finding a shorter route with fewer strides, and look to see where you can increase the speed. If you increase your speed, it will lengthen the horse's stride, which may cause problems between related distances. Leaving out a stride between fences 9 and 10 is an option, but only if you maintain sufficient control for the turn after fence 10. You could also take out a stride between 6 and 7 if you are able to ride positively to fence 6.

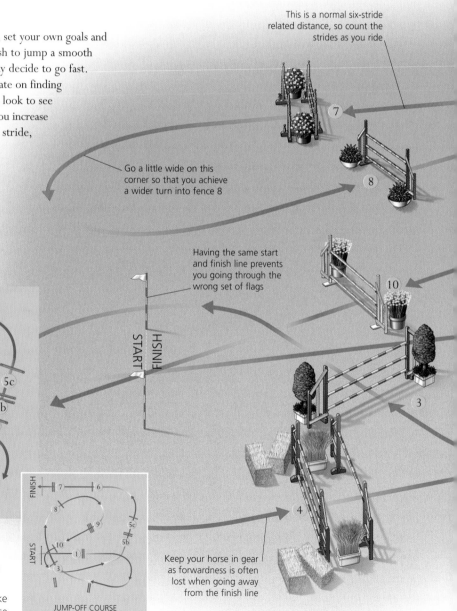

This is a normal six-stride related distance, so count the strides as you ride

Go a little wide on this corner so that you achieve a wider turn into fence 8

Having the same start and finish line prevents you going through the wrong set of flags

Keep your horse in gear as forwardness is often lost when going away from the finish line

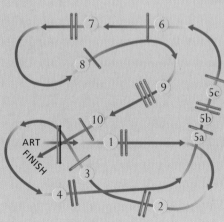

AERIAL OVERVIEW The fences are 1.2 m (3 ft 9 in) high, with spreads of up to 1.4 m (4½ ft). The course is 525 m (575 yd) long, to be ridden at a speed of 350 m/min (12.9 mph) in a time of 90 seconds. When you walk the course, make sure you take note of the jump-off course.

JUMP-OFF COURSE

READY TO PROGRESS

This rider has her weight through the leg, and an easy balance that will enable her to jump even bigger fences. She is focused on the line to the next fence and is under control. Her horse is making good use of his shoulders and knees, although he is dangling his lower forelegs a little.

With the slightly long distances after the combination, do not be tempted to go too fast to the vertical – slow down

In this combination, there is one normal stride between the first two fences, and two slightly long strides between the last two

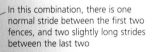

This six-stride related distance is slightly short – avoid over riding the triple bar and then having to take five long strides to the vertical

Ride the first fence as if was a single fence. Then jump the oxer and ride a little more forwards to the third fence to cope with the slightly longer distance

Make sure your horse is in gear before you jump this square oxer

Trust your preparation and maintain a steady canter. There are two straight strides, followed by two on the 45-degree turn, and two straight strides before fence 3

The next fence leads into a six-stride related dog leg. Landing on the right canter lead is important, so slightly undershoot this corner

MEDIUM COURSE

As you progress, the relationship between fences becomes more important. For example, here the course designer is encouraging riders to go longer and faster between fences 6 to 10 because the distances are long between several of the fences. However, a wise rider will be a little careful before the vertical at fence 8 and will consider adding an extra stride between fences 9 and 10. This will help at fence 11, the combination, which includes a slightly short distance.

THE JUMP-OFF

The jump-off track (see inset, below right) for this course is relatively straightforward, but it offers the opportunity to use different stride patterns than the ones used in the first round. Some of the fences are omitted from this round, too, so you must take careful note of the course plan.

Leaving out a stride between fence 2 and 3 is easy to do by just taking a straighter line. Leaving out a stride between fences 9 and 10 is more difficult and seven strides may be the solution, particularly because the next fence is a vertical. A good turn after fence 3 and back to fence 9 could win the class for you.

Jump this oxer like a single fence out of your best canter

This is seven slightly long strides. Shorten to fence 8 to help your horse take care at the next vertical

9

8

Make sure you know where you will make the turn to fence 9 – do not leave it to luck

2

Achieve a good approach to fence 2, which is followed by a six-stride dog-leg turn on a correct distance

6

The distance from 6 to 7 is long, but only increase your speed as you land over fence 6

1

After the first oxer, maintain an even stride to fence 2

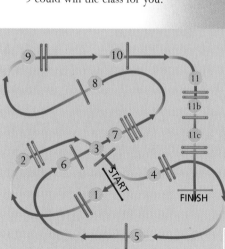

AERIAL OVERVIEW Fences are 1.3 m (4 ft 3 in) high with spreads of up to 1.5 m (4 ft 9 in). The course length is 525 m (575 yd), to be ridden at a speed of 350 m/min (12.9 mph) in a time of 90 seconds. Check the jump-off plan to see what fences are being taken out.

JUMP-OFF COURSE

TOP-LEVEL TECHNIQUE

This horse is showing the sort of technique that is necessary for a real international showjumper. He is bending himself around the fence and making great use of his head and neck. His shoulders, elbows, and knees are well forwards and the knee joints are closing to take the lower leg away from the fence. The rider is maintaining a straight line from his elbow, to his hand, to the horse's mouth, and has a totally secure balance.

The treble is one slightly long stride followed by two normal strides. Maintain an allowing rein contact

If the triple bar has made your horse excited, use the corner to regain composure after fence 7

Having successfully negotiated the previous fence, keep focused on the next small vertical

A flying change is required over this fence and the next

The turn from fences 3 to 4 is a seven-stride dog leg. Keep your horse even on both reins

Maintain your canter stride over the finish line

It would be easy to turn to fence 2 by mistake here, instead of fence 6, so maintain your concentration

11a

11b

11c

4

7

START

FINISH

5

ADVANCED COURSE

As you are asked to go a little faster at advanced level, you have to think ahead and be quicker to react. In addition, there are more technical problems offered by the course designer at this level. For example, on this course there are eight long strides between fences 4 and 5. There is also a difficult line between the combination and vertical – a slightly long distance followed by three and a half strides – forcing you to make a decision about using either three long or four short strides.

THE JUMP-OFF

Leaving out a stride or two between fences 8 and 9 in the jump-off (see inset, below right) is not difficult, but beware of trying to turn in the air over any oxer: this is difficult for a horse and may cause him to hit the fence. Three long strides here should be relatively easy for an advanced horse. The route you take to fence 11 will depend on your horse, but turning to the left will be the quickest. You can also approach fence 11 at a slight angle to create a little extra room.

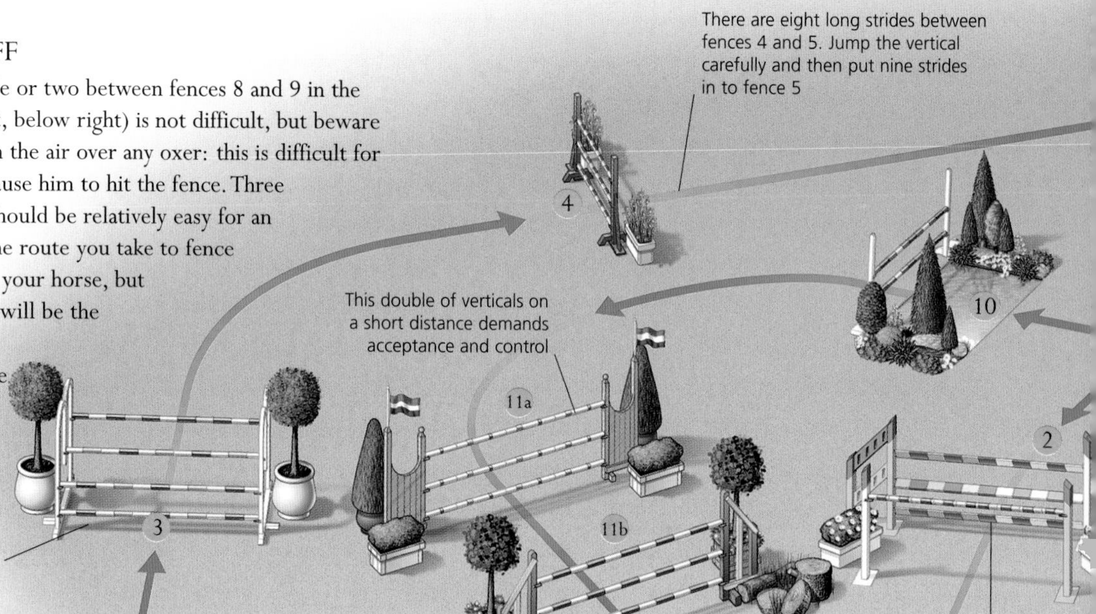

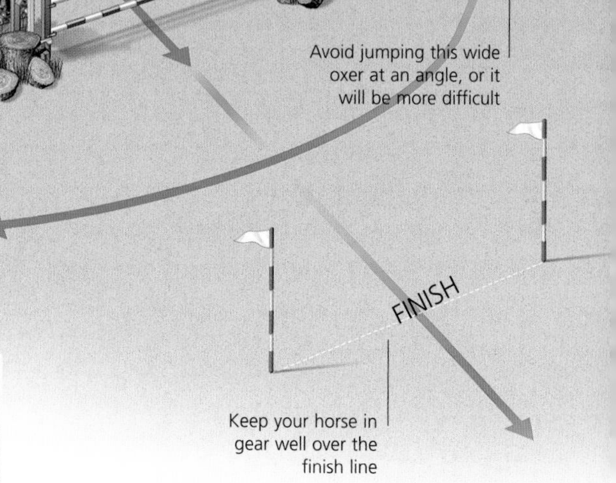

There are eight long strides between fences 4 and 5. Jump the vertical carefully and then put nine strides in to fence 5
4
10
This double of verticals on a short distance demands acceptance and control
11a
2
The triple bar is easy to jump
3
11b

Avoid jumping this wide oxer at an angle, or it will be more difficult
FINISH
Keep your horse in gear well over the finish line

5
4
START
1
10
6a
6b
6c
11a
2
9
3
11b
7
FINISH
8

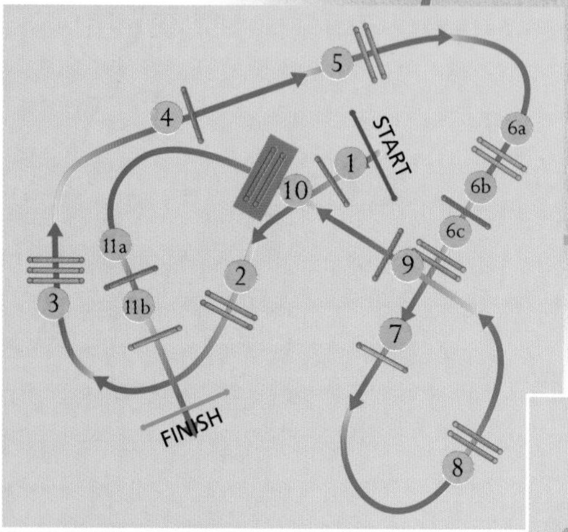

AERIAL OVERVIEW Fences are 1.4 m (4½ ft) high with spreads of up to 1.6 m (5 ft 2 in). The distance of 450 m (490 yd) requires a speed of 375 m/min (13.8 mph) for a time of 72 seconds. Plan your strategy for the jump-off.

5
6c
11a
9
11b
7
FINISH
8
START

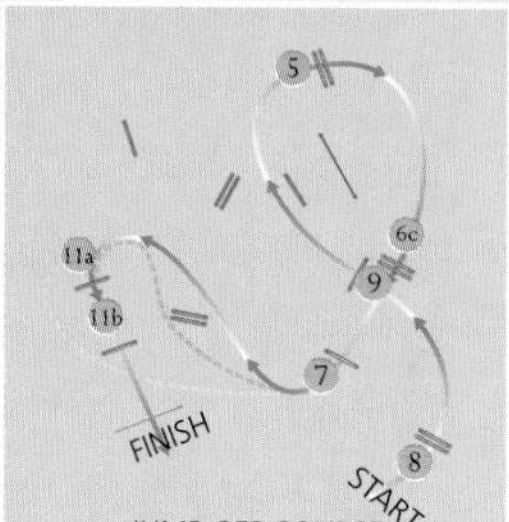

JUMP-OFF COURSE

TECHNIQUE LIMITATIONS

Top showjumping horses all need to jump cleanly and have plenty of spring. This horse has yet to develop these qualities – he is having to jump 25 cm (9½ in) higher than the fence because he does not use his shoulders, elbows, and knees well enough.

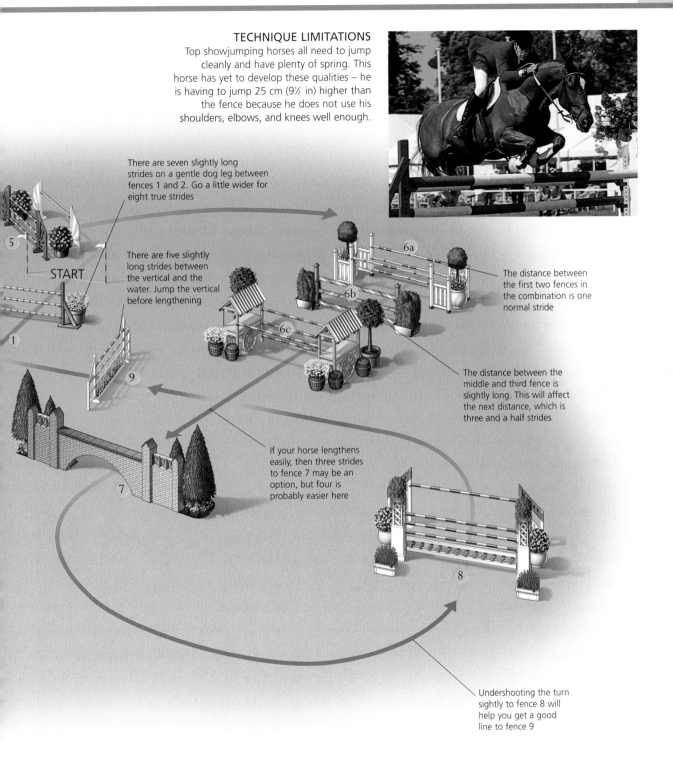

There are seven slightly long strides on a gentle dog leg between fences 1 and 2. Go a little wider for eight true strides

There are five slightly long strides between the vertical and the water. Jump the vertical before lengthening

START

The distance between the first two fences in the combination is one normal stride

The distance between the middle and third fence is slightly long. This will affect the next distance, which is three and a half strides

If your horse lengthens easily, then three strides to fence 7 may be an option, but four is probably easier here

Undershooting the turn sightly to fence 8 will help you get a good line to fence 9

AT THE COMPETITION

For many riders, the competition is the highlight and the main goal of their training. However, some people let their inner fears breed negative thoughts and, for them, the prospect of competing can seem a nightmare. Having a set of procedures for warming up and for walking and remembering the course will help you approach competitions with confidence. After your round, review your performance objectively so that you can build on your achievements.

WARMING UP

When you arrive at the competition, find out exactly where and at what time you will be jumping, so that you can complete your warm-up 5 to 10 minutes before your round starts.

Warm up on the flat. Then, start your 10–15 minute jumping warm-up approximately 20 minutes before your round. There will normally be two or three practice fences in the warm-up arena, which will be flagged – red on one side, white on the other – so that everyone jumps the fences in the same direction. Always keep the red flag on your right. This should mean that everyone will stay on one rein, which makes it easier to keep things moving smoothly. If the fences do not suit you, your coach or helper can put up appropriate fences for you. Always be aware of other riders and keep out of their path. When you are not using the fences, lead your horse to a quiet area in the arena.

PRACTICE FENCES

Start your practice fences by trotting or cantering to a cross pole or a small vertical with a ground line. Jump it five or six times, raising it slightly on each occasion until it matches the height of the fences in the arena.

WALKING THE COURSE If there are any distances you are unsure about, it is perfectly acceptable to go back and walk them again, until you are satisfied with your measurements.

Concentrate on the simple things: getting the right canter and keeping things calm and consistent. If your horse is sleepy and unresponsive, do not be afraid to do a few medium canters to get his adrenaline pumping. After the vertical, jump a small ascending oxer, once again increasing the height – and the width – quite quickly until it is the same as those in the arena. Only start with a normal width oxer if you and your horse are full of confidence. You might then finish with one or two square oxers.

An older horse can become bored with lower level practice fences. In this case, it may be of benefit to use a vertical fence without a ground line to make it harder for him. However, this should only be done under the guidance of your coach.

Work in the warm-up arena is not a substitute for schooling at home, so this type of warm-up should be quite sufficient. As you progress to a higher level, it will be easier to determine the type of warm-up your horse requires. For important classes, a warm-up session 4 hours in advance of the class (in addition to your usual warm-up just before you jump) will usually be of great benefit.

WALKING THE COURSE

When you walk the course, remind yourself that it is just a collection of exercises joined together: turns, related distances, and types of fence that you have already practised at home. Look at the course through your horse's eyes, too. For example, make a note of a flapping flag that could distract his attention.

Look at the course plan and check it against what you see in the arena. Carry a small pen and pad so that you can note down the designated jump-off fences as you go around – the jump-off course will omit some fences from the first round.

With any double, combination, or related distance fences, walk your chosen line between the fences, counting your steps. Four of your steps equals one horse's stride. If you have practised making accurate and consistent steps (see p.208), you will be able to work out how many strides your horse needs to take between fences and whether the distances are short or long. For vertical fences, do not forget to allow two of your steps for take-off and two for landing in addition to the horse strides between fences. At oxers, you can expect to take off 30 cm (1 ft) closer to the fence and, at triple bars, it will be nearer again (see p.209).

Having walked the course once, walk it again to fix the route in your mind. Then walk the jump-off course: you will not be given an opportunity to look at the jump-off later on. Some people think that it shows over-confidence to walk the jump-off in advance of getting a clear round, but omitting to do so is unprofessional, and you may come to regret it if you do manage to reach the jump-off stage.

TYPES OF CLASSES

There are four main types of showjumping class: equitation, hunter and working hunter, speed, and jumper classes. Within these classes is a range of heights and levels of difficulty. There are special classes restricted to either novice or more advanced, riders. In addition, there are novelty classes. For instance, a mirror track is where two riders race against each other over identical courses. Another interesting class is a six-bar competition, in which you jump a line of six fences, each two strides apart, with the fences getting progressively bigger.

EQUITATION CLASSES Originally designed for young riders, there are now an increasing number of these classes for adults. They are designed to judge the rider, not the horse, but it is a mistake to think that what is required is just a beautiful rider. Every rule about a rider's position has a reason, and effectiveness is made possible by a good position. Courses are designed to test the ability of the rider, with different options regarding lines and stride lengths. Equitation classes are an excellent grounding for those who wish to compete later on over bigger fences in the jumper classes. At some competitions, an outline of the course is sent to riders in advance. This gives a focus to training and encourages quality work.

HUNTER AND WORKING HUNTER CLASSES In these classes the horse is judged. Courses tend to be straightforward and are designed to show the jumping ability of the horse rather than the rider. In practice, though, the horses that are ridden by the best riders tend to perform the best, which once again emphasizes the value of good riding.

SPEED CLASSES These classes seem to be the opposite of hunter classes. Judged on speed in the first round, they often require dramatic changes of direction and pace, as well as inventiveness from the rider in finding the shortest routes. However, the basic requirements for success are the same as in hunter classes: correct flat work and a horse that really tries hard to jump cleanly. Unlike a hunter, a speed horse tends to be short striding. This allows him to go faster in related distances without exceeding the 3.7 m (12 ft) stride lengths. It also enables quicker turning.

JUMPER CLASSES In these classes, clear rounds are the priority. The height of fences ranges from 90 cm (2 ft 9 in) to 1.6 m (5 ft 3 in) at Grand Prix level. The novice classes tend to have either no jump-off or an immediate jump-off round, which is not against the clock. In the latter, you actually jump two courses one after the other, so it is a memory test for the rider. After novice level, classes tend to have one jump-off round against the clock, although some do have two rounds, with only the second one against the clock.

REMEMBERING THE COURSE

Some riders find it difficult to remember a course, but it is easy if you stay calm and focused. It can also help to practise when you are not in competition circumstances. For example, it can be helpful to walk a course at a competition that you are not competing in.

At the competition, walk three or four fences of the course, stop for a moment, and repeat the fences to yourself or look back at them. Do the same thing after another three or four fences, but look right back to fence one. Then, at the end, recall all the fences to yourself with your eyes closed. Later on, after your warm-up, you will find it of immense benefit to close your eyes and visualize jumping the course.

Do not be embarrassed to write down the number of strides between the various related distances. You may not look at your notes again but, having written them down, you will rarely forget this information. It is also worthwhile to watch other riders jumping the course. However, try to choose those with horses similar to your own so that you are not confused about stride patterns.

IN THE COMPETITION ARENA

Competition arenas can feel enormous to a novice rider, and the presence of a crowd can be especially daunting. As a result, the temptation will be to go too fast. It can help if you remind yourself that the related distances in a big arena are the same as those you have practised at home.

If you feel overawed by the situation, just remember the key variables – speed, timing, balance, impulsion, and direction (see p.204). By simply concentrating on getting the right direction and speed, you will find that the rest will begin to fall into place by itself. The two most common reasons for losing your way on a course are tension and distraction. Keeping focused and thinking positive thoughts will help release the tension. Concentrating on the feel of your horse will help you avoid distraction. Riders rarely lose their way in a jump-off course because the higher demands of this exercise concentrate the mind wonderfully.

If your horse is young and new to big arenas, try to give him his initial competition experience over a smaller height of course than you have been jumping in your training. You should also give him plenty of time before the round to take in the new sights and sounds.

DEALING WITH INNER FEARS

Admitting to nerves and negative feelings is not easy for many riders, but it is the first step towards overcoming fears. Nerves should not be considered a problem, but a challenge. For example, you may be intimidated by riding in front of a crowd. The negative voice in your mind will say, "I have a problem." But see how different it feels when you say, "I have a challenge." One of the most useful devices to keep a rider positive is role play and visualization (see p.357 and p.369). In addition, it is beneficial to surround yourself with a supportive team. The golden rule is to make it a habit to focus on what you have to do, rather than on what you should not be doing.

ASSESSING YOUR ROUND

It is rarely beneficial to assess your performance when you are tired or fed up after a round. It is much better to wait for a day, or possibly 2 days, but no longer than this because memories fade quite quickly. Even advanced riders benefit from making an unemotional assessment of a round. No one wants paralysis by analysis, but a little positive refining of techniques is useful.

There is also value in assessing the good rounds as well as the less successful rounds. We all tend to ask why things have gone wrong, but we rarely ask why things have gone right. Doing this regularly will highlight your strengths and encourage a positive outlook.

While you must acknowledge the causes of an unsuccessful performance, it is equally productive to recognize personal bests and minor triumphs. We all look for that winning edge.

Failure can often be measured by fractions: just brushing a fence, or being beaten by hundredths of a second in a round against the clock. Therefore, if you can make progress by fractions or hundredths of a second on a daily basis, then the winning edge will be there.

It may help to ask your coach to video your round so that you can review it after the competition. It is also useful to film some of the best riders in the same class to compare and contrast your performance.

THE BIG OCCASION It is an extraordinary achievement to canter into a huge international arena like this, knowing you are both fully prepared and the course is well within your ability. For the rider, it is simply a matter of concentrating on each fence with a view to the next, while the horse should prick his ears, enjoy the big fences, and relish his moment in the limelight.

RIDER CHALLENGES

CHALLENGE	POSSIBLE CAUSES	SOLUTIONS
SLIPPING SADDLE	• A loose girth	• A breastplate should be standard jumping equipment at all times, and tightening the girth should be a habitual part of your preparation before and after mounting. The girth should not be too tight, but it is normal to tighten it a hole when you first get on the horse. Tighten it a little more after another 10 or 15 minutes, when your horse is more relaxed and the leather of the saddle and girth has become warmer and more supple.
	• Shape of the horse	• The saddle may slip back because of the horse's shape or if he has lost weight. A non-slip racehorse pad and an overgirth (a strap that goes over the top of the saddle) will help. Be quick to move the saddle forwards if necessary. Ask an expert saddle fitter for advice.
	• A badly fitting saddle	• The more equal the distribution of weight over the saddle is, the less likely it is to slip. Ensure the underneath of the saddle mirrors the shape of the horse's back by having it professionally stuffed.
GETTING JUMPED OUT OF THE SADDLE	• Horse jumping too big and stiffly	• This may be due to your horse lacking in confidence, or progressing too quickly. Take him back a few steps in his training.
	• A stiff riding position	• If you are stiff, it is difficult to absorb the movement of the jump. Do exercises to help you become more supple so that you can stay in harmony with the horse's movements (see pp. 342–45). One cause of stiffness is fear: make sure you are working at the right level for you.
	• Weight in the saddle, rather than through the legs	• Putting too much weight in the saddle can throw you off balance, so sit lightly and with good bend in your joints. Skiing is a good sport to help you develop this ability.
LOSING THE STIRRUPS	• Being jumped out of the saddle	• See above.
	• Slippery soles and stirrups	• Try to keep the soles of your riding boots mud-free. Rubber or metal grips are available for stirrups, and it is easy to slightly roughen the surface on the sole of your boots. Jockeys wrap their stirrups with a non-slip material. If you do this, make sure you remove any old wrapping before adding a new layer or it will build up too much.
	• Keeping too much weight in the stirrups	• If you press down too much on your stirrups, closing your ankle joint to the limit, there is a greater risk of slipping out of them. Allow some of your weight to go inwards to the girth.

CHALLENGE	POSSIBLE CAUSES	SOLUTIONS
THROWING THE BODY FORWARDS IN MID AIR	• Gripping with lower legs	• If you grip with the lower leg during take-off, you will have to throw your upper body forwards in order to keep your balance. Correct this by jumping small fences without a rein contact and deliberately lightening your leg contact.
	• Jumping for the horse	• Riders can be prone to push upwards as though they, rather than the horse, were physically jumping the fence. Instead, keep your weight distribution as consistent as possible.
	• Riding young horses	• If you have been riding young or inexperienced horses, you may have got in the habit of sitting back in the saddle on approach to a fence so that you can use your legs more easily. This will affect your balance. Get out of this habit by practising on a trained horse.
GETTING LEFT BEHIND	• Lack of confidence	• If you lack confidence, go back a few steps in your training and make the exercise easier. If you are unhappy with the horse, seek advice from your coach. If you are still feeling unsure, try doing some mental preparation exercises (see pp. 352–71).
	• Inadequate use of shoulders and elbows	• As your horse jumps, your hands should move forwards to go with the movement of his mouth. Focus on the feeling in your rein contact and deliberately try to push the mouth forwards as though the reins were solid. As you do this, let your elbows hang down.
	• Loss of balance	• Most horses can cope with your weight being a little far back, but few can cope with a rider consistently being left behind and pulling on the mouth. Many young horses will start refusing or become restricted if this continues. Practise keeping your balance by jumping small fences in a grid with no rein contact, initially holding on to the mane and then with your hands in the normal riding position or with your arms held out.

RIDER CHALLENGES

CHALLENGE	POSSIBLE CAUSES	SOLUTIONS
OVER RIDING	• Riding young or difficult horses	• Riders who have difficult or spoilt horses, or who mostly ride young horses, tend to become over-assertive. You need to have the opportunity of riding easier horses if you want to develop your abilities, as well as do progressive training exercises.
	• Anxiety	• Many novice riders tend to over-react to situations because they are trying too hard to put the techniques they have learnt into practice. This will be exacerbated if you have a bad coach who over-reacts when you make a mistake. As a novice rider, you should initially have to do very little, until your feel develops and it is reasonable to expect you to have quicker reactions to situations. You must also have the opportunity to develop good feel before you can expect to ride assertively.
UNDER RIDING	• Negative thinking	• Many people do not ride assertively enough because they are afraid, stressed, or not breathing properly. Role play and relaxation techniques can help (see p. 357 and pp. 358–59).
	• Trying to look beautiful	• Some people under ride because they are conscious of how they look and they fear that giving effective signals will adversely affect their appearance on horseback. Remember that every aspect of the correct position has an effect on your effectiveness. A good position allows good feel and communication.
	• Riding highly strung, assertive horses	• Some riders get used to sitting quietly, not daring to move for fear of upsetting the horse. This is very common if you ride highly strung and assertive horses. Then, when you ride a quiet horse, you are likely to find it difficult to react and be assertive. Riding a variety of horses soon provides the necessary expertise and cures this problem.

CHALLENGE	POSSIBLE CAUSES	SOLUTIONS
NOT FEELING STRIDES	• Lacking the constants	• Check the constants are in place (see pp.198–99). If your horse lacks acceptance, calmness, forwardness, straightness, or purity it is more difficult to feel a stride. The better the canter, the more leeway you have to make small errors in feeling a stride.
	• Lack of consistency	• Check the variables (see p.204) and, in particular, work on keeping a consistent speed – this is the backbone for feeling a stride. If you are not performing as well in competition as you do at home, practise mental preparation techniques (see pp.352–71).
	• A negative attitude	• Tension, anxiety, and stress will dull your reactions and make it difficult to feel a stride. Use mental preparation and build on your strengths. Remember that thoughts are often self-fulfilling, so develop a positive attitude and believe in your methods.
GETTING NERVOUS IN FRONT OF CROWDS	• Lack of self-esteem	• Be proud of being at the competition and having a go. What people think is unimportant as long as you aim for a personal best.
	• Lack of support	• Surround yourself with positive people. Make the crowd your friend and be delighted that people have come to watch you.
	• Lack of preparation	• Make sure you are always well prepared for a competition, so that there are no surprises on the day. Good mental preparation can be of enormous help. The more you can concentrate on the exercises, the feel of the horse, and the next fence, the less you will be disturbed by those watching you.
FORGETTING THE COURSE	• Nerves and lack of concentration	• Remembering the course is all about concentration and confidence. You need to be disciplined and meticulous in your course-walking method. After walking three fences, stop, close your eyes, and repeat the first three fences to yourself. After six fences do the same thing, but repeat all six fences. If necessary, look back to refresh your memory, and do not continue until you can picture the fences clearly in your mind. Walk the rest of the course in the same manner (see pp.240–42).
	• Poor preparation	• Even when you are not competing, it is useful to go to competitions to practise learning courses (see pp.240–42). If you still have problems at the competition, then it is clearly down to the pressure of the event. Work on your mental preparation to help you resolve this (see pp.352–71). Role playing, for example, can help you become more confident and positive.

HORSE CHALLENGES

CHALLENGE	POSSIBLE CAUSES	SOLUTIONS
EXCITED AND STRONG	• Fear in the horse	• In some cases the horse can be frightened of his rider. In these situations the horse's instinct is to flee, which in turn makes him hit fences; this can develop into a vicious circle. Try lungeing the horse without a rider so that trust and communication can be re-established (see pp.72–73). Then, gradually reintroduce jumping exercises.
	• Lack of calmness	• Lack of calmness can be either because the horse is fresh or because of insufficient training. Horses are creatures of habit, so if calmness is not established when they are young it may require considerable time and patience to achieve. The exercise of trotting to a fence with a placing plank and doing figures-of-eight in front of the fence is excellent for producing a calmer approach (see p.214). Many horses respond quickly to being turned out more, having a reduction in feed, and more regular exercise. Try not to be too controlling. Go for long, slow hacks and canters regularly.
	• Pain	• Horses that are in pain tend to be wooden and to become quicker in their reactions, as if they are trying to run away from the discomfort. This causes them to hit fences, which then starts the vicious cycle in which they become upset, tense, and resistant. Arrange a thorough veterinary check to make sure that your horse is not in any pain.
LACK OF CONFIDENCE	• Lack of progression in training	• Make sure your training is progressive to help breed confidence in both the horse and rider. By taking one small step at a time, you will achieve quality, high-level work.
	• Slippery or soft surfaces	• Sometimes a lack of confidence results from unfamiliar ground conditions, often exacerbated by the lack of appropriate studs in the shoes. A horse cannot respond normally on take-off if he is slipping or if the ground gives way at the moment of take-off. Studs are part of the solution (see p.189). Sometimes four studs are required in each foot, particularly when you are riding against the clock. However, the horse needs to become familiar with different types of going. If a horse is always ridden in an arena with a perfect all-weather surface, then grass, mud, and undulating ground will all come as a shock.
	• Rider restriction	• Make sure you are not restricting your horse's movements. Some horses are sensitive to any restriction by a rider, particularly through rein contact, so do not be afraid to hold on to the mane instead if necessary.

CHALLENGE	POSSIBLE CAUSES	SOLUTIONS
DISLIKE OF DOUBLES AND COMBINATIONS	• Jumping canter not established	• With good preparation a horse learns to look upon doubles and combinations with great confidence. The key to preparation is establishing the 3.7 m (12 ft) canter stride, because all distances in novice competitions are based on this. If you approach a double or combination with the correct canter and jump the first fence successfully, then the remainder becomes a simple grid that many horses find easier than a single fence.
	• Grids too demanding	• Some horses are frightened in training because the rider progresses to advanced grids before the basics have been established. For example, do not make the mistake of making the last fence of the grid bigger and bigger until the horse lands on the back pole. Always err on the side of caution and take great care when using grids. This where your coach's knowledge is invaluable.
DISLIKE OF NEW FILLERS AND DITCHES	• Bad early experiences	• If small fillers and ditches are introduced to a young horse at an early stage of his training, they will rarely cause a problem. It is important that they are introduced before the horse gets into the habit of jumping fences without them. Once this habit has been established, it will take time and patience to introduce fillers. Gradually build his confidence until he accepts them.
	• Lack of preparation	• Many horses are conditioned to react badly to new fillers. For example, if a filler is introduced that is bigger than normal, the horse will do a bigger jump, which the rider may not be prepared for, resulting in them pulling on the horse's mouth. The horse then associates this pull in the mouth with new fillers. A horse must be prepared at home for what he may face in competition.
REFUSING A FENCE	• Being overstretched	• Every horse has a limit to the height and spread he can jump. Recognize when a horse is struggling because of a lack of athletic ability. With good training, such horses can still be very successful in competitions with smaller fences.
	• Pain	• The main reason for a horse persistently refusing at even small fences is pain, most commonly in the front feet. The forces involved in jumping mean that horses with foot problems will increasingly find things difficult. A veterinary examination is vital.
	• Rider restriction	• Rider restriction and lack of confidence are common causes of refusals. Practise jumping without rein contact and work on improving your balance.

HORSE CHALLENGES

CHALLENGE	POSSIBLE CAUSES	SOLUTIONS
DISTANCES BETWEEN FENCES RIDING SHORT	• Canter stride too long	• Sometimes a normal distance between fences seems short. A common reason for this is that you are going too fast, and thus producing a canter stride that is too long.
	• Overjumping	• Even at the right speed, the distances sometimes ride short. This can be because the horse is jumping extravagantly, which means that he lands further away from a fence, and therefore the distance to the next one is short. This is often a problem in horse trials when the showjumps can be relatively small for talented horses.
	• Over fresh	• Ensure your horse has sufficient work on the days leading up to a competition and jumps enough fences before he goes into the ring so that he is calm and jumps consistently and efficiently.
DISTANCES RIDING LONG	• Canter stride too short	• This occurs when the correct length of canter stride has not been established. Even small horses can develop the right length of stride if they are sufficiently supple, although they may have to go faster than big horses with a naturally long stride. Going faster may slightly restrict the vertical force of take-off and their ability to jump their maximum height but, in a normal round of showjumping, the right length of stride is more important.
	• Overcautious	• A horse may be cautious if the exercise is a little difficult. This quickly becomes a vicious circle unless he is ridden more assertively and the severity of the exercise is reduced.
	• Pain	• A veterinary check should be carried out.

CHALLENGE	POSSIBLE CAUSES	SOLUTIONS
JUMPING CROOKEDLY	• Uneven development on the flat	• If the horse's movement or ability is not the same on both reins, aim to improve him on his stiffer side with good flat work so that he becomes symmetrical. It is easy for a horse to get into a habit of jumping crookedly. This is compounded if he jumps fences that are too big early on in his life, which forces him to rely on his stronger side and hind leg.
	• Rider is unbalanced	• We all tend to put more weight in one leg and to use the other leg more strongly. Do exercises off the horse to help improve your balance (see pp. 332–51).
	• Restricted vision	• Make sure you do not restrict the movement of your horse's head and neck, so that he does not have to tilt his head or bend his neck in order to see.
NOT TRYING TO JUMP CLEANLY	• Rider over riding	• Over riding tends to put the horse's concentration on the rider, not the fence. A horse must be able to look at what he is jumping and be encouraged to take responsibility for small decisions.
	• Lack of fifth-leg training	• Horses can become adept at shortening or lengthening a stride to achieve a good take-off without the rider doing anything. If they respect the fences most horses will try to be careful. Spend time doing fifth-leg training (see p. 223).
	• Pain	• Horses that are in pain tend to try to land over a fence as soon as possible and not jump too high or wide. Always check your horse's general health regularly.
HITTING FENCES WITH THE FRONT LEGS	• Take-off out of balance	• If the hind legs are not together on take-off, or if stiffness prevents the hind legs getting far enough forwards under the horse to provide sufficient power for the jump, then the highest point of the jump will probably be too near the rear of the fence. Further flat work and progressive use of grids is required.
	• Take-off too close	• The horse may be getting too close to the fence on take-off. You need to work on your feel for a stride and use ground lines with verticals to achieve a better take-off point. The horse must be allowed to stretch his head and neck forwards as the jump begins. This allows the use of his shoulders and elbows, which in turn enables his knees to come up out of the way of the fence. In addition, using triple bars can be effective in improving the use of his shoulders, elbows, and knees.

HORSE CHALLENGES

CHALLENGE	POSSIBLE CAUSES	SOLUTIONS
HITTING FENCES WITH THE HIND LEGS	• Not opening the hind leg joints	• If the horse uses his head and neck well over the second half of the fence, stretching it down and forwards, he has a chance to open up and release his hind legs as they reach the highest point of the jump. You can also encourage your horse to open his hind legs over a jump up by using oxers rather than verticals in jumping grid exercises.
	• Rider restriction	• Help your horse by not restricting the movement of his head and neck with your rein contact.
	• Turning in the air	• When going against the clock, it is tempting to try to make a change to your direction when you are actually jumping a fence. This should be avoided with young horses because it tends to stiffen their backs and make it difficult for them to finish a jump properly.
CARELESS TOWARDS THE END OF A ROUND	• Lack of consistency in the canter	• As a round progresses, many horses tend to go a little faster and become a little less settled, which affects both the length of the canter stride and the balance of the canter. In training, it is important to link fences together gradually – first two or three fences and then, progressively, building up to a full course – so that it becomes a habit to maintain a consistent canter. To help in this, it is useful to use planks on the ground instead of fences.
	• Tiredness	• With long courses or in muddy conditions, carelessness may be caused by tiredness. The physical preparation of your horse must match the demands you place on him: if you are entering two classes a day in a three-day show then your horse needs to be very fit. It is usually better to jump in fewer classes and ensure good-quality work.
	• Lack of fifth-leg training	• Good training will encourage the horse to take responsibility for himself and his rider. Fifth-leg training is particularly important (see p.223). Many rounds against the clock finish with a vertical on a long, related distance, and, if you want to win, it is important that your horse keeps trying for you. Even when you are going faster, the horse needs to maintain a good balance and understand that you want him to jump cleanly. The horse's balance and understanding will be developed if, from the earliest stages of training, you reward him for respecting fences and jumping cleanly.

CHALLENGE	POSSIBLE CAUSES	SOLUTIONS
LOSING THE LINE IN THE JUMP-OFF	• Lack of control	• If a rider becomes over-excited in a jump-off, control of the canter can be lost. It is then difficult to keep an accurate line over fences. In your preparation, practise different jump-off lines and only go faster if the constants remain in place.
	• Giving away the rein contact	• Giving away the rein contact as you jump can also be a cause of losing the line, because you will also tend to land without a rein contact and to take a stride or two before getting it back. This wastes valuable seconds in a jump-off because it makes it difficult to maintain control on landing. Your aim should be to always ride with a rein contact so that steering aids can be given at any time.
	• Not thinking ahead	• Successful jump-off riders must focus their eyes on where they want to go. You must always think ahead.
PERFORMANCE DETERIORATING TOWARDS THE END OF A SEASON	• Discomfort and tiredness	• If the horse's performance begins to deteriorate, check that he his healthy and not in pain. Particularly with hard ground, many horses develop little points of soreness that will affect their performance. Similarly, he may be physically or mentally exhausted by travelling and competing.
	• Lack of mental maturity in the horse	• A sensitive rider will notice when there is a small problem with their horse and take action, rather than wait until he has a bad experience that affects his future work. Be prepared to change a competition programme and to allow additional rest periods.
	• Gaps in the range of the rider's technique	• Make sure you have a regular check-up with your coach so that you can work on any weaknesses in your riding technique.
TOO MUCH BEND IN THE NECK	• Overuse of the inside rein	• If your horse does not respond to small rein aids and a small change of weight to turn, you must avoid pulling with the inside rein. Doing this will cause too much bend in the neck and make your horse fall sideways to the outside. If turning is difficult, neck rein by using both reins together towards the inside (see p.25) and avoid pulling backwards.
	• Not paying attention to the priorities	• You will rarely have major training problems if you pay attention to the key priorities – maintaining the constants (see pp.198–99). If your horse accepts you and is calm, forwards, and straight in his work from the beginning, you will be able to spend the majority of your time making progress rather than troubleshooting.

CHAPTER SEVEN

CROSS-COUNTRY TRAINING AND COMPETITION

Of all equestrian sports, cross country requires an entirely trusting partnership between horse and rider, for this discipline demands courage as well as skill.

In this chapter you will learn about the equipment and training facilities used, the safety precautions you should take, and the ways to improve your position and effectiveness. You will learn how to devise a training programme and how to tackle different kinds of obstacle, from fences to water-filled ditches. The exercises in this chapter are designed to build confidence in both the horse and the rider, and to allow your horse to develop his own decision-making skills. A troubleshooting section is included to help you overcome any challenges you may encounter.

INSPIRATIONAL EVENTING

Cross country is the main discipline on which the increasingly technical sport of eventing is based. Dressage, showjumping, and cross country combine to make one competition, with scores added together from each phase. Horse and rider need a high level of training to excel in dressage; they have to be fearless, fit, and athletic to meet the challenge of jumping a variety of fences at speed across country; and they need to be accurate and disciplined in the showjumping arena.

THE COMPLETE TRAINING TEST

"Riding across country is not just a test, it is the ultimate goal of all training, including dressage", wrote Wilhelm Museler in his classic dressage book *Riding Logic* (1937). This statement sums up the view of many dressage and showjumping trainers who have the greatest respect for those in eventing who are able to master three major riding disciplines.

Eventing requires a high level of physical fitness as well as efficient training, two aspects that have led to the sport contributing significantly to raised standards of coaching and stable management worldwide. The event horse has to be prepared like an athlete: feeding and fitness play a vital role. In training, each section has to be worked on with the other two phases in mind and, thus, the end result provides the best framework for all riders.

The high rate of female success is due to the fact that eventing is based on efficiency, not strength. The British stars Lucinda Green, Mary King, Ginny Elliot, and Pippa Funnell have won Badminton, the world's leading three-day event, an impressive 12 times between them. King, Elliot, and Funnell excelled in dressage, in which an increasingly high standard is

WORLD CLASS Jimmy Wofford, both a successful rider and now a respected coach, and Carawich, completing the final phase at the 1978 World Championships at Lexington, USA.

now required to be truly competitive, for the advanced level test requires the quality of work of a pure dressage horse.

TOP ACHIEVERS

The achievements of horses like Charisma, Murphy Himself, Supreme Rock, Biko, Custom Made, and Gilt Edge bear comparison with top horses from any sport. Most were bred in Ireland, the leading country for producing eventers, a factor which proves that, in this sport, Thoroughbreds or traditional cross-breds (Thoroughbreds with one-quarter Irish Draught) are still the most successful types.

As the sport has evolved, there has been less emphasis on endurance and more on skill. Gone are the days when sheer courage and physical strength topped the list of requirements. A real partnership with the horse, who tends to become just as famous as the rider, is crucial.

RECORD BREAKER
Lucinda Green, pictured left on Village Gossip, is the best-known female eventer ever. She won a record six Badmintons on six horses, and inspired generations of riders.

THE ULTIMATE HORSEMAN
New Zealander Mark Todd, right, who is considered the greatest all-round rider of all time, and the diminutive Charisma, winning an Olympic gold medal, their second, at Seoul in 1988.

CROSS-COUNTRY EQUIPMENT

Safety and comfort are the priorities for both rider and horse, with all clothes and equipment needing to remain functional, even in wet and muddy conditions. The rider wears the same head and body protection as that worn by jockeys in racing and uses a saddle that provides secure support for the leg. The horse should wear protection on all four legs, and tack must be soft and properly fitted to prevent rubbing, even when the horse is sweating.

THE RIDER

The most obvious addition to the rider's normal clothes is a body protector, which is compulsory for competing. It must be of an appropriate standard and should fit snugly, while not restricting your movement. A standard skull cap and harness is mandatory at all times. Although the skull cap and body protector should never be considered a substitute for good preparation and accident prevention, there is no doubt that their use has contributed to a reduction in injury. On your upper arm, you should also wear a special holder for your personal medical details, as this will facilitate appropriate treatment in the event of an accident.

At the higher levels of competition, and for speed practice at home, you will need a stopwatch. This should have recessed controls so that you do not accidentally turn it on or off.

You will need to wear a top with sleeves to protect you against injury in a fall and it is always advisable to put on gloves, which will make it easier to slip the reins over a drop fence or to grip if the reins become slippery in the rain or with sweat. Choose a snug-fitting pair of breeches that do not hold water or become slippery when wet. This can make all the difference to your safety if it is raining.

Boots should be comfortable and allow maximum flexibility of the ankles, as this will help you in dropping your heel and feeling more solidly connected with your horse. The stirrups should have non-slip grips so that your feet do not slip as you push your heels down.

THE HORSE

The bit shown here is a snaffle. Some horses may need something stronger, such as a pelham, which works by exerting pressure on the tongue and lower jaw through a curb chain that fits around the chin. A horse that tends to lift his tongue or get it over the bit is better suited to a gag. Pressure on the gag raises the bit in the mouth, which puts pressure on

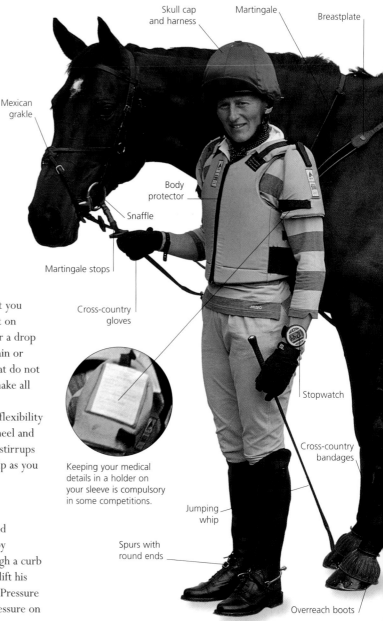

Skull cap and harness

Martingale

Breastplate

Mexican grakle

Body protector

Snaffle

Martingale stops

Cross-country gloves

Keeping your medical details in a holder on your sleeve is compulsory in some competitions.

Stopwatch

Cross-country bandages

Jumping whip

Spurs with round ends

Overreach boots

CROSS-COUNTRY BANDAGING

Cut lightweight, plastic sleeves to fit around the cannon bone, allowing for the bend of the knee **(1, 2)**. There should be the same width around the whole leg, so there are no pressure points **(3)**.

Using an elasticated, sticky bandage and starting at the top, create an even support by winding the bandage down and back up with regular turns **(4, 5, 6)**. Tape the bandage for security **(7, 8)**.

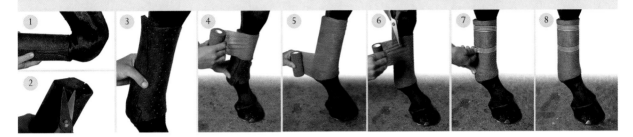

Cross-country saddle

Numnah

Non-slip stirrup

Surcingle

Brushing boots

HORSE AND RIDER READY FOR CROSS COUNTRY

Every piece of clothing and equipment has a purpose and is essential. With the addition of colour co-ordinated shirt and silk on the skull cap, and possibly co-ordinated bandages, horse and rider can also look superb. Everything should be cleaned and checked after a competition and before the next. Leather is a safe and comfortable material for riding, but it can become worn or lose its strength if it is not oiled and kept in a warm tack room.

the corners of the mouth and the poll. The noseband used here is a Mexican grakle, which is ideal, as it is comfortable and does not interfere with the action of the bit. A running martingale or Irish martingale should also be used so that the reins do not go over the horse's head if they are accidentally dropped.

The saddle should be fairly flat to enable freedom of movement and it should not feel slippery or hard. The rider's leg should fit comfortably into the saddle, which may be fitted with raised padding or blocks just above the thigh to give a greater feeling of security. Always use a numnah (a shaped saddle pad) underneath to prevent rubbing. The saddle should be secured both by the girth and by a surcingle (an overgirth – a strap that goes over the top of the saddle). These should have elasticated inserts so that they are more comfortable for the horse. A breastplate will prevent the saddle sliding back.

Common types of leg protection are synthetic or leather boots or elasticated sticky bandages, which are wrapped over a lightweight, waterproof sleeve (see box, above). Apply grease to the front of each leg to help prevent cuts. Overreach boots protect the bulb of the heel but must not be loose and cause the horse to trip. As in showjumping, studs may be used according to conditions (see p.189), usually with bigger ones in the hind shoes. The more studs you use, the greater the risk of pulling a shoe off, so use the minimum necessary. Avoid using studs on only one side of the shoe: this creates a twisting force that can take the shoe off.

A CROSS-COUNTRY FACILITY

A cross-country schooling course is invaluable for introducing horses and riders to the different types of fences encountered on a real course, including banks, ditches, drops, and water fences. It also allows more experienced riders to practise their skills and introduce young horses to new challenges. The correct progression of fences, from miniature to more advanced, all sited inside a relatively small fenced area, will make a safe and effective schooling ground to train within.

AN IDEAL TRAINING FACILITY

Cross-country training is often neglected simply because of the lack of a suitable practice area and, as a result, some riders take the opportunity to do their schooling during competitions, which can create more risks. Those who have the use of, or can hire or borrow, a well-designed schooling course know how valuable it is for all types of horses and riders, including those who wish to specialize in showjumping or dressage.

The progression of the fences is vital. A schooling facility should feature every type of cross-country obstacle in miniature, with two or three progressively bigger versions of the same fence. Then it is always possible to build from success and not frighten horses or riders by over-facing them.

Apart from the standard shapes of verticals, oxers, and triple bars used in showjumping (see pp.190–91), there are five main types of cross-country fence: banks, ditches, drop fences, water, and bullfinches (upright brush fences). All of these can be used in various combinations at different distances and angles. There should be options in distance in order to suit all types of horses going at different speeds.

PROGRESSIVE TRAINING

With novice horses and riders, it is important to allow some time to relax and get used to the area before jumping. It is also vital to have done sufficient work on the flat to get in gear. Start by jumping out of trot up and down small banks and over small logs. Follow this by walking around in the water or jumping a tiny ditch. When you and your horse are confident with jumping miniature fences out of a showjumping canter, you can go a little faster, but only if your horse stays controlled and settled. Remember that cross-country fences do not have to be jumped at speed.

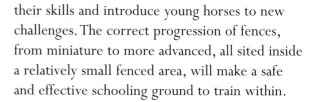

A CROSS-COUNTRY PLAYGROUND Apart from a large variety of fences, it is important that the surfaces on a cross-country facility are suitable. They must be secure around take-off and landing points, so that the horse does not slip and lose confidence. If you are to compete on softer ground, it is important that your horse also gets used to coping with muddy conditions. Do this by hacking out in woods or similar areas when the ground is soft.

The merry-go-round consists of seven small fences requiring a short, normal, or long three strides between them. It is invaluable as a basic exercise to improve control before or after going faster.

FOLLOWING A LEAD HORSE Do your cross-country schooling in company, if possible with a more experienced horse and rider. This will give you and your horse more confidence and it will satisfy the horse's naturally gregarious nature.

GETTING THE NOVICE HORSE USED TO WATER Before jumping into water, the novice horse should walk in alongside a more experienced horse. Do this several times to reassure him that both the water and the surface under the water are safe.

INTRODUCING DITCHES Ditches can be frightening for horses because they are difficult to see. Start in trot with small ditches that have wings at the side, and follow a lead horse. Hold on to the mane in case your horse takes a big jump.

This water complex provides more than 30 variations of route and approach, including a fence situated in the water, under the roof.

Starting with a 50 cm (1 ft 8 in) water ditch, it is possible to develop the confidence of both horses and riders. The bigger ditches all have poles over them.

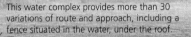

AN INTRODUCTION TO BANKS Small banks are the best type of fence to start your cross-country schooling. Begin by walking up the slope and letting the horse drop down the other side. Then reverse this exercise and gradually trot into slightly bigger banks. On the up banks, hold on to the mane to help keep your balance. On the down banks allow the reins to slip through your hands.

A bank complex like this can be used by novice horses and riders from the walk or trot, or by more advanced horses at a slow gallop. The edges of the banks provide different depths of drop fences.

TAKING SAFETY PRECAUTIONS

Cross-country riding is not a high-risk sport in the category of mountain climbing or motorcycle racing and, statistically, it is safer than swimming or sailing. At competitions, rules and regulations are there to safeguard the rider, but during training you still need to be vigilant about maintaining safety standards. It is important for a rider to identify the key elements of safe practice and to be methodical in their approach to safety.

A SAFE SPORT

Cross-country riding is safe if a horse is working well within his physical limits and if he and the rider are training progressively, under the guidance of a coach.

The sport of eventing is often associated with steeplechasing, where horses are raced over fences at high speed, but there are basic differences. Firstly, you go across country by yourself rather than in the company of other horses, which should encourage a more level-headed approach. Secondly, you do not ask your horse to go at maximum speed across country. At an international level, a horse should have a maximum speed of approximately 800 m/min (29.8 mph) – compared to a steeplechaser with a top speed of about 1000 m/min (37 mph). In competition, however, you will rarely go above 600 m/min (22.2 mph) or 650 m/min (24.1 mph) in the steeplechase phase. This means that the event horse will be working well within his capabilities, a factor which substantially reduces risk. (In cross-country and showjumping, speeds are usually given in metres per minute. However, for ease of accessibility, speeds are also shown in miles per hour throughout this book.)

As a horse goes faster, this has an exponential effect on the energy required to produce the increased speed. Thus a horse that has worked close to his maximum will tire more quickly in comparison to one working within his capabilities. In racing, a horse is taken close to his limit of available energy and invariably finishes tired. But if the preparation is right, a cross-country horse should never finish tired. If your horse is anything more than a little fatigued, you should retire because a tired horse is a danger to both you and himself. Your horse should always finish ready and willing to do a little more.

TRAINING SAFEGUARDS

When taking part in a competition, safety procedures are stipulated and enforced by the rules of the sport. The rule book is constantly evolving, and is backed up by official scientific research. Judges, stewards, and others in authority will put these rules into practice to ensure that you ride in an acceptable manner at an appropriate level and on an appropriate horse.

However, accidents can also happen in training, where the same rules and supervision do not always apply. This means that you have to take a more pro-active responsibility for your own safety. Always check the various risk factors as a first step to safe practice. If you are vigilant and sensible, you can reduce the risks and be free to enjoy your training (see box, below). When you are at a training facility, you should check

ACCIDENT PREVENTION

Accidents can be minimized by using well-qualified coaches, safe facilities, and progressive exercises. General fitness and muscle tone will also help. If you are fit enough to vault on to a horse, for example, then riding will be a safer activity. Standard safety equipment will reduce the risk of injury (see pp.258–59). The skull cap is the same as that worn by jockeys, but standards change and you should check that yours is a currently approved model. A hunting tie, or stock, fastened without a tie pin, is recommended to support the neck. The body protector with shoulder pads is effective in reducing injury and should be worn. Make sure it fits and that your movement is not restricted.

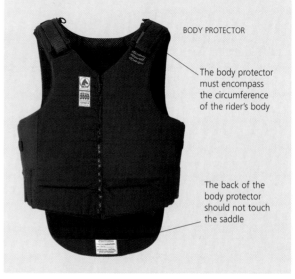

BODY PROTECTOR

The body protector must encompass the circumference of the rider's body

The back of the body protector should not touch the saddle

that normal safety procedures are in place and that a risk assessment exercise has been completed (see box, below), either by you or your coach.

A SAFE HORSE

A cross-country training philosophy in which the horse learns to take responsibility for himself and his rider is an important factor in safety. An experienced horse will be more familiar than you with most situations. You must trust him to take decisions on your behalf. Learn when to leave him alone, because if he is distracted by the rider or ridden in a mechanical way, he will not jump as safely. A horse who looks carefully at what he is jumping and can make automatic alterations is said to have a fifth leg. Developing this fifth leg should be an integral part of your training programme (see pp.270–71).

WALKING THE COURSE

Walking the course beforehand with an experienced coach or rider is arguably one of the best investments in safety a rider can make. It is important that your advisor has seen you ride, so that they know your strengths and weaknesses, and those of your horse. This will enable them to give you advice that is both sensible and relevant.

It is more difficult for a cross-country rider than a showjumper to evaluate distances because of the variable factors involved. This is an important area in which to seek advice. There is no substitute for experience on the subjects of stride lengths, and take-off and landing points at different types of fences and in different circumstances. Awareness that a distance is going to ride long or short can make the difference between riding safely and taking a risk. The philosophy of your

SAFE ADVICE FROM A TRAINER Even top riders walk high-level courses with coaches and other riders. Novice riders must not set out on a cross-country course without having taken advice about the routes to take and the pitfalls to watch out for.

cross-country riding should always be to leave room for error, so a small inaccuracy does not create a dangerous situation.

The experienced coach will get you into the habit of treating a course walk as a positive experience. They will concentrate on what you should do, rather than what you should not, and will only ask you to attempt things of which you are capable. They will also help you understand why certain routes and fences are easy if ridden in a particular way. Doubt and lack of confidence will reduce your ability to react, and this leads to unsafe riding. As you reduce the element of doubt, and increase your confidence in how to ride the fences, you are more likely to achieve the desired result and ride safely.

RISK ASSESSMENT

Before visiting a cross-country facility, be sure to have the appropriate insurance arranged for yourself. You should also have your competitor's medical card (see p.258) with details such as your blood group, allergies, and medical history. Check out the facility's own insurance arrangements. If you are with a coach, they should have carried out an assessment of the facility and its suitability for you and your horse. However, you should get into the habit of looking at this for yourself.

Take note of the following factors:
- Suitability of fences in relation to your ability – do they ask too much of you or your horse?
- Provision of warm-up fences – there should be a selection of small fences over which to build confidence and get in gear before you tackle combinations.

- The progression of fences – is it logical?
- The condition of the ground – hard ground can cause tendon strain, especially if it is rough, as can deep, boggy mud. Check the preparation of take-offs and landings.
- Fence construction – is there anywhere the horse could get trapped? Are there nails or sawn-off ends of wood sticking out? How deep is the water? What is the surface below the water like?
- Security of the training arena – for example, if your horse gets loose, can he gallop on to a road, across a cattle grid, or into a wire fence. Shut any gates that lead on to slippery concrete.
- Ease of access to the training area – is the approach safe?
- Availability of a first aid kit for the rider.
- Availability of a first aid kit for the horse.
- Availability of a contact number for a vet.
- Availability of a telephone in case of an emergency.

THE RIDER'S POSITION

When going across country, the rider's position must be secure. This is achieved by maintaining a strong, steady lower leg, with the weight dropped down into the heel, and through the rider's ability to slip the reins. This will eliminate the risk of the rider getting in front of the horse's movement, which is when problems occur. You must ride with slightly shorter stirrups than for showjumping so that you have a more stable balance over the top of each fence and when riding drop fences.

SHORTENING THE STIRRUPS

The priorities for achieving the correct rider position are the same in cross country as for showjumping. The rider's weight acts in exactly the same place, with the seat out of or just touching the saddle, so the horse will feel that the rider's balance is identical to that for showjumping.

For cross country, however, the stirrups should be approximately 2.5 cm (1 in) shorter — two holes — which will bring the knee slightly higher and encourage the heel to be a little lower. This position will give the rider a more secure feeling, which can be further improved by dropping the weight on to the heel, rather than the ball, of the foot.

There are two main reasons for shortening the stirrups. Firstly, it allows a more stable balance over the top of a fence, with the knee and hip joints closing to a tighter angle and the rider's centre of gravity becoming lower in relationship to the lower leg. This gives the rider greater security in the event of a horse hitting a fence. (Steeplechase jockeys ride with even shorter stirrups, which allows them to have their seat on the same horizontal level as their knees.)

A GOOD CROSS-COUNTRY POSITION It is important to maintain a consistently balanced position, so that your weight always feels the same to the horse. Here, the rider is soft and supple, and in harmony with the movement of the horse as they go up the hill and over the jump.

Close the angle of the knee and hip joints over the jump

Keep the upper body close to the horse's neck as he goes uphill

Secondly, it allows a rider to maintain stability when jumping big drop fences. With these, it is necessary to open up your knee and hip joints in order to keep your weight through the leg and avoid your seat being pushed forwards by the back of the saddle. By riding with shorter stirrups, the seat is kept marginally further away from the saddle and the rider is able to achieve a straight line from shoulder to hip to heel on descent (see box, right).

SLIPPING THE REINS

In the safety position, your hands move further away from the horse's mouth. It is necessary, therefore, to slip the reins through the fingers to avoid being pulled forwards and to prevent restriction of the horse's head and neck. Then, on landing, keep the rein contact as you hold both reins in one hand and slide one hand at a time up the rein to a normal length. At big drops or when jumping downhill, you can move your heel forwards 5 to 10 cm (2 to 4 in) to provide additional support. This makes the lower leg firmer and more secure, but it is important that the rest of your position stays supple to help you go with the movement of the horse.

SAFETY POSITION

At any fence across country and in particular at drops, it is important to open up the knee and hip joints on the descent. This is so that your centre of gravity can stay over both the horse's centre of gravity and your lower leg, which is your base of support. This is known as the safety position.

Maintain a soft and allowing rein contact

Drop weight to the heels

Give clear aids to control direction

BEING EFFECTIVE

The elements that create an effective cross-country rider are the same as those for showjumping and for dressage: a good knowledge of the exercises, empathy with the horse, and the ability to communicate with and control the horse with clear language. But the key requirement is good feel: the ability to sense whether you need more or less impulsion, whether or not your horse is tired, and whether or not you have the right speed for each type of fence.

WORKING WITH YOUR HORSE'S STRIDE

The large variety of fences seen in cross country means that the rider has to cope with several lengths of stride. This is a significant difference between showjumping and cross country and is why the cross-country horse needs to learn to think for himself so that he can negotiate the fence safely, even when his rider is unable to feel a stride before take-off.

Rather than leaving it all to the horse, however, a rider still needs to learn how to adjust the stride subtly without interrupting the horse's concentration or restricting his freedom. Be aware of your horse's stride, and work with it, not against it, so that he can feel comfortable taking off either slightly further away or slightly closer to the fence, as he deems appropriate. Riders who have not learnt this skill tend to try to dictate their horse's every stride. Then, when they make a mistake, they find that the horse is still concentrating on them and not the fence: because he has not been allowed to think for himself, he does not know how to avoid problems.

If the horse needs to take off further away, he must be allowed sufficient impulsion and freedom by the rider. If he needs to take off closer, the rider must sit still and maintain a consistent speed. Put these two practices together and you have the basis for riding down to a fence on any stride. A rider's feel for a stride can be developed over time (see pp. 196–97), and it will become increasingly possible to make minor alterations that will facilitate an easier take-off.

JUDGING YOUR SPEED

Develop a precise feel for the various speeds and stride lengths required from the beginning. Even within the confines of an arena, you can put up wingstands or markers 100 m (330 ft) apart and, wearing a stopwatch, learn what speeds of 200, 300, and 400 m/min (7.4, 11.1, and 14.8 mph) feel like. Then, using a larger area, you can do the same to get the feel of 500 m/min (18.5 mph) and practise adjusting your speed. This process has the added advantage of getting you used to

USING A STOPWATCH

Using a stopwatch in training will teach you to develop a feel for specific speeds. Stopwatches are forbidden at lower levels of competition so, at these events, you can test your feel without being distracted by the watch or being tempted to ride too fast.

Divide a course into 2- or 3-minute sections and work out specific points at which to look at your watch and check your speed. Make allowances for slower or faster sections, for fences where you are taking a long route, and for your own performance goal for the day. Never look at your watch on approach to a fence or push your horse to exceed his capabilities.

It is important to use a watch during the steeplechase at a three-day event to avoid wasting energy or taking risks by going too fast. Divide the course into minute-points and aim to finish no more than 5 seconds inside the time. One second outside shows good judgment, but 15 seconds inside may cause the horse to suffer cramps or tiredness the next day.

SPEED AND STRIDE LENGTHS

Different activities and fences require different speeds. As you cannot look at a speedometer on horseback, the ability to feel the different speeds and change from one to another is of vital importance. You can practise this in training by timing yourself over short measured distances, as long as your horse remains calm and is fit enough for the work. Speed has a direct effect on stride length, so this chart will help you choose the right stride length for related distances.

SPEED	STRIDE LENGTH	TYPES OF ACTIVITY OR FENCE
300 m/min (11.1 mph)	3 m (10 ft)	Coffins and drops
365 m/min (13.5 mph)	3.7 m (12 ft)	Showjumping
400 m/min (14.8 mph)	4 m (13 ft)	Combinations; difficult, single fences
450 m/min (16.7 mph)	4.5 m (14½ ft)	Basic canter for conditioning and stamina
500 m/min (18.5 mph)	5 m (16 ft)	Easier, single fences; between fences for novice riders
550 m/min (20.4 mph)	5.5 m (18 ft)	Conditioning canter for building stamina and speed
600 m/min (22.2 mph)	6 m (20 ft)	Between fences; steeplechase-type fences
650 m/min (24.1 mph)	6.5 m (21 ft)	Steeplechase speed for novice three-day event
700 m/min (25.9 mph)	6.5 m (21 ft) (frequency increased)	Maximum speed in training

using your stopwatch away from a competition. With practice, you will find that it is possible to start feeling the difference between 350, 450, and 550 m/min (12.9, 16.7, and 20.4 mph), and you will be able to choose exactly the right speed for each type of activity or fence and the correct stride length required in a combination. Bear in mind that a supple horse's stride length will vary with his speed (see chart, above). The slower the horse goes, the shorter his stride, while the faster he goes, the longer his stride. As he nears the limit of his speed capacity, it is the frequency of the stride that will increase, rather than the length. Every horse will be slightly different, but the chart above is a good guide.

A TIRED HORSE

If your horse starts to feel a little unresponsive, slow him down between fences to allow him to recover before getting him back in gear to jump. If he feels more than just a little tired, you should retire – there is always another day.

Whatever the circumstances, you must always analyse what happened. Work out whether the tiredness was due to your horse being ill, caused by your going too fast, or the result of an inadequate fittening programme. Analysis will turn a negative into a positive and you will learn from the experience. Examination of the situation will also substantially reduce risk of further problems and help to keep your horse happy in his work.

A JOB WELL DONE Your horse should always finish ready and able to do more than was required. If you have prepared well, he will feel that he has had a pleasant experience and you will have had a wonderful time.

KICKING ON

It is easier and safer to start out on a cross-country course if both you and your horse are in gear mentally and physically. Being in gear does not mean that the horse is running away, which is dangerous; being in gear is about being properly warmed up, with the rider thinking forwards and the horse responding promptly to both the forwards aids from the leg and the slowing-down aids from the rein. Therefore, when warming-up, work on lengthening and shortening the canter to establish your horse's responsiveness to the aids.

When out on the course, you must be prepared to kick at times and, if necessary, back up the leg aid with the spurs or stick in order to maintain the horse's forwards attitude. The whip and spurs should not be used as substitutes for good preparation or because the task is too difficult, but when the horse has forgotten the urgency of staying in gear and the situation demands it. Using the whip and/or spurs is preferable to jumping a fence half-heartedly or awkwardly, which may frighten the horse and possibly dislodge the rider. It is always safer to be in gear across country.

The stick should never be used in anger. It should mainly be used on the horse's bottom and in one single stroke. Do not use the stick on the delicate flesh around the horse's flank. You can also use it down the horse's shoulder, but this may make him move sideways and lose his jumping line.

Unless your horse is over-sensitive to the leg, spurs with big, round, soft ends should be used if required. If you have to use spurs continually, however, it means that there is something wrong with your preparation. In this case, you should assess the situation to decide whether your horse needs more flat work, or to gain confidence by riding over smaller fences, or to be checked for pain and discomfort. (Many horses become unwilling across country because they are suffering from foot pain or a pinching saddle).

GETTING IN GEAR You can send the horse forwards and make your legs more effective by sitting into the saddle with your heel close to the girth. Reward the horse when he responds.

STICKING ON

The two main factors which help you to stay on when riding across country are a secure lower leg, with the weight dropping down through your heels and the heels lower than the toes, combined with a relaxed, harmonious position. A rider is more likely to be secure and stick on if their position remains supple and soft. A rigid rider can get bounced off like a ball off a tennis racket. Mental tension and a negative attitude are the most common causes of rigidity, so it is essential that you progress slowly, maintaining confidence and feeling in control. Riders often lose softness through fright. In this case, the only remedy is to take a few steps back in your training to some easier exercises until you regain your confidence.

Many people say that they ride best when the adrenaline is flowing, but it is important to distinguish between motivation

TURNING THE WHIP OVER

When you are riding across country, it may occasionally be necessary to use the jumping whip – or stick – once on the horse's bottom to help put him in gear.

As you ride, hold the stick between your thumb and first finger (1). To use the stick, you will have to turn it upside down in order to reach the horse's bottom and to use it firmly. Take

both reins in one hand by bringing the stick hand behind the other hand (2, 3). Holding the stick without the rein (4), let it drop down between your first two fingers (5) and turn it to grasp it, just as you would a tennis racket (6). After using the stick, reverse these steps to finish back in the normal position (1) – otherwise, you risk poking yourself in the eye.

and fright. If you are motivated, you can concentrate and have quick reactions, but if you are frightened you may become tense and lose suppleness, and your reactions will be slower.

Problems can also occur at drop fences, because riders instinctively feel they should be leaning back. As a result, they sit in the saddle and bring the lower leg back in an effort to balance. The combination of this weak lower leg and the rider's direct contact with the saddle results in them being knocked forwards by the back of the saddle. Then, on landing, they end up either clinging around the horse's neck or simply falling off. To prevent this, you should think "up" instead of "back". This will open up the knee and hip joints until you are in the equivalent of the dressage position with the weight through the leg and a vertical line from shoulder to hip to heel (see box, p.265). As you do this, slip the reins and look ahead, not down. It is also vital that you maintain a vertical line from the middle of the knee to the ball of the foot and, if in trouble, push the heel slightly forwards.

GETTING ON NEXT DAY

If your horse is ready and willing to work the day after doing a cross-country course, then you will continue to make good progress in the sport. Correct preparation will allow you to ride the next day, rather than you or your horse being unable to work due to stiffness, wounds, or a loss of confidence. A horse is not a machine, so ensure that his training is truly progressive and enjoyable. A well-planned fittening programme is a non-negotiable part of your overall plan (see pp.324–29). Any other approach is not humane.

FORWARDS GOING
New Zealander, Andrew Nicholson, demonstrates a secure, supple seat. Though the horse has twisted in the air, the rider's lower leg is secure. Horse and rider are maintaining a positive attitude and looking ahead.

A horse should not be just fit enough, he should be more than fit enough if he is to avoid tiredness and injury. In addition, you, the rider, must be fit enough to ride for 15 minutes with your seat out of the saddle before you tackle a cross-country course of 5 minutes' duration.

An efficient training programme will ensure longevity in the event horse's career. This means always aiming to conserve the horse's energy, avoiding strain by jumping fewer fences, and generally putting less stress on the horse. The key is to fit dressage, showjumping, and cross-country work into an integrated programme so that every exercise helps the horse in several areas simultaneously. This is why it is important to work with a coach who understands the overall demands of the sport of eventing.

CONSTANTS AND VARIABLES

As in showjumping, the cross-country horse needs to constantly show acceptance, calmness, forwardness, and straightness, as well as a good jumping technique. However, the ever-changing nature of cross-country terrain and types of obstacle mean there are more variables in terms of direction, speed, impulsion, and balance. The constants are the foundation of success and safety, but it is essential to achieve the right variables as you face the challenges of riding across country.

THE IMPORTANCE OF IMPULSION

The constants of acceptance, calmness, forwardness, straightness, and purity (see pp. 122–23) together produce controlled impulsion, which is the most vital requirement for a good cross-country round and for safety.

If any of the constant components are missing, controlled impulsion will be adversely affected. This can lead to an erratic and therefore unsafe performance. Some riders go across country without their horses listening to them or behaving calmly, and this makes it impossible to cope with the precise demands of a modern course.

The horse needs to ride forwards willingly in order to remain in gear. If he is using both sides of his body evenly so that he is straight, and achieving a natural, pure jump, this will produce an efficient performance. This is important in an activity such as cross country, which requires great stamina and where it is necessary to conserve energy. In addition, forwardness will make it easier for the rider to maintain a balanced position.

BEING FLEXIBLE

The more advanced the competition, the more advanced the partnership between the horse and rider needs to be in terms of communication, awareness, and speed of reaction. If, in times of difficulty, you can maintain the correct direction and speed, this will solve most challenges, because these variables (see pp. 128–29) form the basis of effective cross-country riding. As you become more advanced, it will be possible to feel how much impulsion you have and whether you need more or less. Although in dressage and showjumping the rider tends to be looking for more impulsion, in cross country there is often a need to have less, so that energy can be conserved and the horse has time to look at fences and make decisions.

Different balances are required for different fences so you must always be ready to adapt. For example, the balance for approaching a coffin (a combination fence of a rail, a ditch, and a rail) or drop fence needs to be weighted more on the hind end of the horse. For a steeplechase fence, your horse will need a more horizontal balance.

The timing of, or feel for, a stride is not easy to learn for a cross-country rider who has to work with many different stride lengths (see pp. 270–71), but it can be developed.

UNDERSTANDING THE FIFTH LEG

A horse that consistently gets himself out of trouble across country is said to have a fifth leg. This is an attribute that can be cultivated and is an essential factor in safety because it means that the horse is able to adjust his stride and save himself, even if he has met the fence on the wrong stride.

The fundamental aim of your cross-country training should be to develop the horse's ability to look after himself – to use his brain and to take both mental and physical responsibility for actually getting over a jump. Training in this way, by allowing the horse to think for himself, will allow room for error and encourage him to always find a fifth leg.

Some people say that it is impossible for the horse to find a fifth leg when you are galloping down to a fence at speed, but the top-class steeplechase riders provide the best example of how it works. If you watch good jockeys, you will see that they do not make major changes to the horse's stride on approach to a fence and, as a result, the horse learns to be clever and adjust his stride independently.

TIPS FOR FIFTH-LEG TRAINING

There are several ways to train your horse to think for himself:
• Allow the horse to be in self-carriage. Do not try to support him through rein contact because this only restricts the use of the head and neck and encourages him to take more weight forwards as he tries to lean on the contact. The reins must always be a communication point, not a support point. Both on the flat and when jumping, the emphasis should be on the horse gradually taking a little more weight on his hind legs to produce an improved balance and self-carriage and to be lighter at his front end.
• As far as possible, turn your horse out on hillsides and in fields with varied terrain so that he gets used to going up and down hills. This is especially important for a young horse.

Watching horses gallop freely and nimbly over undulating fields should also encourage riders to trust their horses to look after themselves.

• When hacking, deliberately walk, trot, and canter up and down banks and over undulating ground. You may not live in the country or in an area suitable for hacking, but this is of such benefit to your horse that you should consider transporting him to somewhere with good hacking on a regular basis so that he learns to become more agile.

• With the help of a coach, practise loose schooling your horse – without a rider or tack – over fences. This will teach the horse to make decisions about how to respond to the exercises without relying on his rider to guide him.

• During jumping training, make sure you interfere with the horse's jump as little as possible. It is difficult to sit still and make only the smallest of changes as you ride but, if you can do this, it will greatly benefit your horse's fifth-leg training.

• Put logs or sleepers in front of every stable door, between fields, and along riding tracks. In this way, your horse will have to continually practise looking after himself and watching where he puts his feet.

• Try doing your dressage training on varied ground occasionally. It is useful if part of your schooling area has a small incline so that you can practise maintaining controlled impulsion as you go up and down a slope. As well as the benefits for fifth-leg training, this has considerable advantages for the physical development of your horse.

• During a jumping training session, start with standard jumping distances, but then both slightly shorten and slightly lengthen them. A standard showjumping stride length is 3.7 m (12 ft), but you can gradually train your horse until he automatically copes with a 3 m (10 ft) or a 4.2 m (14 ft) stride length. This process may take many months to achieve.

CANTERING DOWNHILL In training, cantering uphill will develop your horse's strength while reducing impact on the forelegs. In competition, however, you should avoid going uphill too fast, because it is tiring. Instead, you should go as fast as you can during downhill phases of the course. Avoid going across the hill, and keep your horse as straight as you can with the weight on his hindquarters. Do this by going a little slower than your horse wants to.

• Make all your small, 50–60 cm (20–24 in) schooling fences as solid as possible so that your horse treats them with respect. Do not worry if he hits a fence, because this will help him develop a safe jumping technique. Do not school over big, solid fences at home for reasons of safety and maintaining the horse's confidence.

DEVELOPING A PARTNERSHIP

Safe cross-country riding requires a division of responsibilities – a true partnership between a horse and rider. The rider's job is to provide the right approach to each fence by putting the horse in gear, and indicating the right direction and speed. The horse's job is to respond positively to the rider's controls and to physically jump the fences. He must assess the size and type of each fence carefully, and be able to judge the take-off points accordingly.

A HORSE AND RIDER PARTNERSHIP

From the start, the rider should visualize the division of responsibilities in cross country as a contract between them and their horse. The rider must sign up to an agreement in which physical responsibility for actually jumping the fence is awarded to the horse. It may seem obvious, but many riders mistakenly assume complete control, as though the legs on the ground were their own and the horse was partially blind.

On the contrary, the rider must both encourage and allow the horse to make decisions about the most appropriate take-off points, and the size of effort required to get over each fence. If you remove these responsibilities from your horse, you will substantially reduce his potential. A horse that cannot think for himself can become unsafe because he will not have developed the instincts that get him out of trouble.

The rider's primary responsibility, having ensured the horse is in gear, is simply to indicate the right direction and the correct speed. Again, this may sound simplistic, but it is a crucial point.

THE RIDER'S RESPONSIBILITIES

Having the horse in gear is the same as achieving controlled impulsion – the horse going forwards with energy and balance. For this, the five constants – acceptance, calmness, forwardness, straightness, and purity – are required and must always be in place (see pp.270–71). Correct dressage training develops the constants and is therefore at the heart of effective cross-country training. The variables of direction and speed are as important in cross-country riding as they are in dressage and showjumping. Therefore, working to one structure in your training for all three of these activities will bring consistency to your riding. Timing of the stride is the last variable a cross-country rider needs to consider. Helping your horse to a good take-off point is important, but you must be careful not to distract him close to the fence by making last-minute changes.

HORSE LOCKED ON TO A FENCE The rider must allow the horse his responsibility to assess the fence. This horse has been given that opportunity; he has locked on to the fence, and is therefore concentrating.

THE HORSE'S RESPONSIBILITIES

It is remarkable how much a horse will do for you if allowed, but many riders find it difficult to leave him alone to find his own balance. You cannot balance a horse by rein contact alone. Pulling on the rein will only develop into a battle of strength between you and the horse, which the horse will win because he is stronger. All you will achieve by fighting him through the reins is the increased likelihood that he will put his head up and pay even less attention to the fence.

Instead, you can balance him by sitting still, without leaning back, and by keeping the rein contact constant. In this way it is possible to make even a horse who has become too strong look and think a little more. The horse must learn that it is better to look at what he is jumping without panicking, and to treat the fences with respect. Avoid any alterations to his stride unless he is just going faster and faster.

Schooling over small, solid fences with ground lines to help give the fence a more defined shape, should give both you and your horse the confidence to divide your responsibilities. However, if your horse does not respond, return to basic exercises with showjumping fences and grids. Set aside a month for nothing but cantering over planks on the ground, trotting into small fences, and jumping small grids. In addition, check your horse's physical health, because his lack of co-operation may be a response to pain he is experiencing while jumping.

HORSE AND RIDER RESPONSIBILITIES

The rider's responsibilities include:
• Ensuring the horse is in gear.
• Providing the right direction and speed.
• Sitting still and keeping a consistent balance.
• Working with the horse's stride, not against it.
• Going with the horse and being in harmony with him.
• Setting realistic goals that never overstretch the rider or horse.

The horse's responsibilities include:
• Going forwards in self-carriage.
• Paying attention to the rider's directional and speed controls.
• Looking at the fence and judging its size and type.
• Looking at the fence and deciding on a take-off spot.
• Physically jumping the fence.
• Coping with emergencies by providing a fifth leg – using his proprioceptive sense, co-ordination, and natural instinct.

HORSE AND RIDER IN GEAR The legendary partnership of Ian Stark and Murphy Himself was never anything less than in gear.

A TRAINING PROGRAMME

The key to an effective training programme is to decide on your medium- and long-term goals. Then you can create a weekly programme that allows you to progress through small, daily action steps towards these goals. Every horse is different so you cannot be too prescriptive, but as you get to know your horse you can become more precise. When you are preparing for an event, the key is to be efficient: training for dressage, cross-country, and showjumping phases must be complementary.

LONG-TERM PLANNING

Extraordinary achievements are possible if you have a plan. Competing in a world championship or at the Olympic games can be a real possibility, but only if a rider starts out with that specific goal, rather than just taking it a day at a time. Not everyone aspires to reach the highest level, but those who do need to be familiar with the international scene.

There is a thriving international calendar of three-day events, from one-star (novice) to four-star (championship) level. Competing in a one-star event is in itself a worthy long-term goal, while the four-star calendar includes world championships plus major three-day events such as Badminton and Burghley in England, Lexington and Atlanta in the USA, and Adelaide in Australia. In between are two- and three-star competitions, which complete a logical progression.

Cross-country requirements at one- and two-star level are shown in the exercise overview (see pp.296–97) under levels 3 and 4. There are also international one-day events at these levels, which are increasingly popular.

MEDIUM-TERM PLANNING

If your aim is to progress through the competition levels, both you and your horse need to complete qualifications, via both one-day and three-day events. Horses rarely do an international event before the age of seven, but after that it is possible to plan out a programme based on progressing by approximately one-star level per year. Obviously, not all horses have the scope to reach three- or four-star level and it is important to remain realistic in your goals, but the majority of sensible, quality horses can achieve one-star with the correct training.

Your year-round programme might include a period of just doing dressage or showjumping work, especially in the winter, to improve your skills in those areas. Your schedule should also include three or four short breaks for the horse rather than one long holiday. At competitions, spend time observing the methods of the best riders and make it your business to ask them questions. It is important to be under the wing of an experienced coach who travels to competitions regularly and is conversant with the standards required.

SHORT-TERM PLANNING

The paradox of an event horse's fitness is that he has to be conditioned to gallop and jump for several miles at a three-day event yet be calm and obedient for the dressage and showjumping phases. The calmer he is, the easier he will adapt to travelling and strange places and the less likely he will be to lose energy in fretting.

Make sure your stable-management routine is built around keeping your horse calm. The more he can live outside in a natural environment, the better. He does not need to be stabled full time until you start preparing for a three-day event. Even then there should be an opportunity for him to be turned out each day and perhaps be given the freedom of a small yard attached to the stable. Maintain a meticulous programme of health checks, worming, and blood tests to establish both what is normal for your horse and what is abnormal, so that a small problem can be treated before it becomes a major issue.

NOVICE COMPETITION For this level, this horse and rider look happy and confident, although the rider needs to establish a firmer lower leg position to be more secure.

INTERMEDIATE LEVEL There is quite a difference between novice and intermediate level. This rider's lower leg is a little loose for comfort. However, use of the snaffle bridle, and the rider's calmness and focus, suggests an educated approach.

ADVANCED HORSE AND RIDER This is a typical big corner at Badminton. It demands great accuracy, and anything less than total commitment from the horse will result in him running out. This pair is confident and committed; the rider is secure and has allowed the horse the freedom to jump.

WEEKLY PROGRAMME

In eventing, there is a greater need to plan ahead with training than in other sports because there is so much to fit in. Just as a human athlete does when training for a decathlon, you have to balance conflicting demands while simultaneously trying to make training as complementary as possible.

For instance, it is possible to improve your dressage as you hack or jump, and you can improve your showjumping during cross-country training. The more you can use the same aids and approach for all three activities, the more efficient your training will be.

A weekly canter programme (see pp. 328–29) is essential, but the remainder of your schedule needs to be sufficiently flexible to suit the needs of your horse. For example, a typical weekly programme might be: Monday – rest, light work, or lungeing; Tuesday – jumping and a hack; Wednesday – cantering or stamina work; Thursday – dressage work and a hack; Friday – lungeing and jumping; Saturday – cantering or stamina work; Sunday – dressage work and a hack. Again, it is important not to be too prescriptive. You might have individual weekly periods when you concentrate on just one area of training and you should always be prepared to be flexible. Be alert for boredom, fatigue, and loss of confidence.

NARROW FENCES

Competitions are often lost by a frustrating run-out or disobedience at a narrow fence, also known as a skinny. A horse should become accustomed to the idea of jumping narrow fences from his early training through a progression of exercises that enable him to understand what is required. It should become a habit for the horse to jump even when things go wrong on the approach, while it is the rider's job to focus the horse so that it does not occur to him to run out.

A BASIC UNDERSTANDING

The key to jumping narrow fences is to teach a horse to understand what is required. As soon as they realize that the purpose is to go over the narrow fence, and not around it, most horses remain obedient. However, if a horse learns that it is an option to run out, or if he is just held on the line to the fence by the rider's physical strength alone, then there will always be a risk of disobedience.

Begin by aiming your horse deliberately at different parts of small fences. Make him jump to the left or right to check he is not jumping the middle of the fence through habit. A horse must learn to jump the part of the fence the rider wants. Then create your first narrow fence of 1.8 m (6 ft), a half-length such as a small wall or two barrels end to end, perhaps using wingstands as guides. Always use poles on the

(a) The reversed wings guide the horse to the centre. Poles on either side stop the barrel rolling.

(b) Without wings, the rider's even rein and leg contact form a passage to guide the horse.

NARROW FENCES ON A DOG LEG Practise jumping over a barrel with wingstands at each end **(a)**. Then jump the barrel without the wingstands **(b)**. Gradually build up to jumping two narrow fences on a dog leg (below). The second fence can be introduced as two barrels on their side at first and then increased to a spread of this size.

Use your leg aids to control the turn through the blocks

Close your seat to the saddle to increase feel and security

1

2

3

4

5

ground to stop the barrels from rolling. Gradually reduce the width of the fence and increase its spread. This is easily done with additional barrels. The ones used here are 95 cm (3 ft) high and 60 cm (1 ft 10 in) wide. For less experienced riders there are smaller standard barrels of 70 by 40 cm (2 ft 4 in by 1 ft 4 in). When your horse is jumping two barrels on their side easily, add two more behind them to double the spread.

When you are confident with this, stand up the two barrels on the far side of the spread and add one more so that you have the same width (see sequence below). Practise jumping this fence. Then, add a single barrel fence four strides before it, on a turn – this set-up encourages the rider to control direction precisely. Approach this first narrow fence in trot **(1)**. On landing, take one stride straight on **(2)** – markers on the ground will help guide you and the horse. Use your rein and leg aids to turn during the second stride **(3)**. Then, take two straight strides **(4, 5)** to the next narrow fence **(6)**. Keep the horse straight and focused through consistent hand and leg contacts. Maintain these on landing **(7)** and during riding away **(8)**.

USING A PLACING FENCE

If the take-off point is a long way from the narrow fence, the horse is more likely to run out. To prevent this, use a placing fence two or three strides away to create a take-off point slightly closer to the fence. This should instill the habit in your horse to jump the narrow fence and cope with any take-off point.

PRACTISE NARROW FENCES Jump narrow fences as a regular part of your training, approaching first from trot and then canter. Never let your horse run to the side of a fence – always make him start the exercise again, or he will learn that he can avoid doing work. Reward him instantly for jumping well.

Try to maintain a forwards lower leg position

Keep a consistent rein contact, sit up and look ahead

Be ready to focus on the next fence, both physically and mentally

ANGLED FENCES

Angled fences are important because, together with narrow fences, they form the preparation for jumping corners. Also, if you and your horse can become confident jumping at an angle, it will give you more flexibility when choosing a line through a combination fence and can save you valuable time. The preparation begins on the flat, when the horse is taught to be straight, and learns how to maintain a line at a gradually increasing angle without relying on the rider's strength.

JUMPING AN ANGLED FENCE

Warm up by getting your horse cantering and jumping on a straight line. Then jump one fence at an angle, canter in a circle, and return over the fence going in the other direction, thus performing a figure-of-eight, with the centre of the fence as the crossover point. This exercise is good practice for jumping at an angle. It teaches the rider to control the direction over an angled fence and it prepares the horse for jumping a corner.

Set up a vertical at an angle of approximately 20 degrees and use ground planks to help guide the horse over the fence at an angle. You can gradually increase the angle to 45 degrees. As you progress, replace the vertical with an oxer, building up

BARRELS AT AN ANGLE This horse is jumping from right to left at an angle of approximately 20 degrees. This brings the right-hand side of the fence closer to the horse on take off than the left, so he is finding it difficult to lift his right shoulder, elbow, and knee up and forwards in time to clear it. The control of the direction, however, is good.

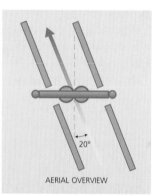

AERIAL OVERVIEW

to a 1.2 m (4 ft) spread at a maximum angle of 30 degrees. If you have also completed the narrow fence exercises successfully (see pp.276–77), you are now ready to tackle a 60-degree corner, although you should start by jumping a corner fence with a lesser angle at first.

RELATED ANGLED FENCES

In order to save time against the clock, showjumpers need to clear fences on an angle. Cross-country horses are required to do this when the design of the fence is angled and it is the only route available, or when jumping at an angle achieves the correct distance between two fences.

With the jump illustrated below, it is not possible to aim straight at both fences. Jumping from the middle of the first fence to the middle of the second is least likely to cause the horse to run out, but the distance is difficult because the

combination is set on three short strides. The rider could opt to jump to the left of the two fences, which would provide a longer and easier distance, but this increases the risk of the horse running out at the second fence. If the horse remains bent in the neck to the right, the rider is more likely to fall to the left and the horse run out, so the rider should straighten the horse's neck. The final option of going faster and aiming for two long strides will reduce the control the rider has over the horse and make the jump over a possible third fence more difficult.

JUMPING TO THE LEFT AND THE RIGHT

Many horses are naturally stronger on one side than they are on the other. This means that your horse is likely to find one angle easier to jump than the other. This needs working at in training to avoid a weakness developing. Most horses run out to the right more frequently because they tend to bend their necks and bodies to the left.

The key is to improve your horse's flat work because this is the real basis for effective jumping. In the short term, if there is too much bend in the neck to the left, try cantering to the fence on the right (as opposed to left) canter lead. This tends to bend the horse the other way.

ANGLED COMBINATION The distance between these two fences is 12.8 m (42 ft) – 2½ jumping strides. It is possible to make the distance ride well by slowing down and shortening from a 3.7 m (12 ft) showjumping stride to a 3.4 m (11 ft) stride.

CORNER FENCES

A corner is a significant test for a horse and should be treated with respect. On a competition course, corners start at angles of about 40 degrees in novice classes and reach 90 degrees at the highest level. They are generally built filled in.

A corner combines the skills required for jumping both a narrow and an angled fence, and is a logical training progression. The secret is to train your horse to understand what is required so that he actually wants to jump the fence and not run out.

PROGRESSION TO THE CORNER

As with all jumping, successful negotiation of the corner begins with dressage training, when your horse is taught to canter straight. It continues in showjumping, when he learns to hold a straight line in front of a fence. When he has reached this stage, you can simultaneously start training him over narrow and angled fences (see pp.276–79). If you then bring these techniques together, you will find that your horse will immediately understand what is required at a corner.

The first stage is to jump a corner made of poles (see picture, below). To begin with, it is helpful to use a placing fence three strides – 13.7 m (44½ ft) – away from the corner in order to facilitate the right take-off point. You could also

place a wing on the corner so there is little risk of running out, and a large shrub inside the corner so the horse is not tempted to jump a part of the fence that is too wide. Here, the horse is guided by the poles on the ground and by having three barrels at which to aim. The barrels used here have rounded edges and are therefore safe. Do not use metal barrels, sawn-off wooden stands, or pointed plastic stands because if your horse landed on any of these he could injure himself.

At first, jump the corner with no back pole. Then add

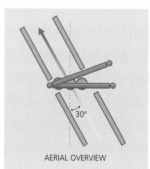

30°

AERIAL OVERVIEW

JUMPING A CORNER OF POLES
Here, the angle of the corner has been gradually increased to 60 degrees. The horse is jumping the corner with confidence and both horse and rider are looking ahead to the next test. All the rider has to do is sit still and control the horse's direction.

A line of three barrels under the corner will guide the horse to the jumping point

Widen the second pole to an angle of 60 degrees

Place poles on the ground to guide the horse

it at an angle of 20 degrees. Gradually increase the angle to 60 degrees. Start with a small corner that you will be able to jump confidently, and this will accelerate your progress.

JUMPING FILLED-IN CORNERS

The majority of corners encountered in real competition are solid and filled in (see picture, below). This makes them safer and more forgiving; if your approach is wrong, a horse will be able to balance himself on the solid top of the obstacle. However, accuracy is still needed when planning the point at which you are going to jump the fence.

Success at corners depends on the rider being focused and looking ahead. If you know where to jump, you will have no problems. To find a precise route, line up two points. For example, you could line up an obvious point on the fence with a tree in the distance behind it.

Unless you use two points like this, you cannot guarantee you will find exactly the right line. If you do not plan a precise line your horse may run out or jump a wider part than you intended. Beware of corners on a downhill slope as these tempt the horse to run out.

JUMPING A 60-DEGREE CORNER

Start with six barrels in two rows of three and jump diagonally across them. Progress to four barrels in a star/diamond shape **(set-up 1)**. Remove a barrel and create a 60-degree corner **(set-up 2)**, using poles as guides. Jump this at the narrower point **(line 1)**, and then the wider point **(line 2)**. Finally, jump three barrels on their own on a diagonal line **(set-up 3)**. In this way, a horse will learn what is required at a corner.

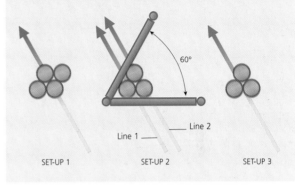

Line 1 ____   ____ Line 2
60°

SET-UP 1   SET-UP 2   SET-UP 3

(a) A barrel is placed at the point of the corner to help keep the horse on a good line.

JUMPING A FILLED-IN CORNER
Practise jumping a filled-in corner by using a barrel as a guide (a). Then remove the barrel. Here, the rider is leaning slightly to the left, but this has not affected the horse's willingness to jump the fence.

DITCHES

A wide ditch can look frightening but, as you and your horse build confidence, it will probably become the easiest of all obstacles. A horse normally jumps twice the height of a fence in length from take-off to landing, so even a ditch 3 m (10 ft) wide is physically easy for him. This group of schooling ditches provides a perfect introduction, both through the progression of fences and the use of placing fences to provide exactly the right take-off points.

JUMPING DITCHES

Over riding is a common fault in jumping ditches because they can look frightening – a fence with a ditch underneath it always looks bigger. Consequently, the horse associates ditches with the rider becoming anxious and pushing too much. This can create a vicious circle in which the horse no longer trusts the rider in front of a big ditch.

You can instill confidence in your horse by schooling over a set of ditches like those here (pictured below, right). Begin by jumping a small water ditch with a rail at the side to stop the horse running out (1). Ride this in trot and canter before tackling the small ditch and rail (2). It helps to use a small placing fence (see aerial overview, above right) to achieve a consistent take-off point, which in turn helps horse and rider to relax. Here, the placing fence is 22 m (72 ft) away from the ditch – this is exactly five showjumping strides.

When your horse has settled to this line, jump the same placing fence, but aim for the wider ditch (3), knowing that you can now reproduce the correct take-off point. The distance from the placing fence to the biggest ditch (4) is set at 25.6 m (84 ft) which is six normal

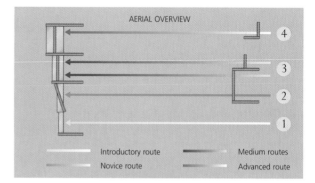

AERIAL OVERVIEW

Introductory route	Medium routes
Novice route	Advanced route

A SMALL DRY DITCH This horse is jumping confidently, but a horse can surprise you by jumping higher than necessary over a ditch. Be ready to hold on to the mane for added security.

WATER DITCHES This progression of water ditches and placing fences will help you and your horse develop confidence by demanding different stride lengths and speeds in a controlled way. You will learn how to produce exactly the right stride lengths to suit the distances being used in a competition.

A WIDE DITCH Horse and rider are making the 3 m (10 ft) ditch look easy, despite taking off almost 1 m (3 ft) from the water. This is because their progression has been made simple. The shape of fence used, with a good ground line, is the easiest for a horse to jump; it is simply a matter of developing his confidence. The rider's position would be more secure if her lower leg was a little firmer and her heel 5 cm (2 in) further forwards, but she shows good balance and a lovely softness in her position. She has an excellent, allowing rein contact, which is needed as the horse stretches his neck for the jump.

strides. Once you have established a consistent way of going at the smaller ditches, you will be surprised how quickly you can progress to this width of water.

Remember that a horse has to put his head down quite low to see a ditch (see pp.46–7). Often he will concentrate on the top pole over it and the ground in front and will not see the ditch. Therefore, to help guide the horse, make sure you look where you want to go, which is over, not into, the ditch.

ACHIEVING DIFFERENT STRIDE LENGTHS

This type of ditch complex will teach you how to produce different stride lengths on demand. The 3.4 m (11 ft) stride is used when jumping into most water fences; the 3.7 m (12 ft) stride is mainly used in showjumping and many cross-country combinations; and 4 m (13 ft) is the basis for cross-country work before you learn to go faster.

We have already discovered that using ditches with the placing fence 22 m (72 ft) away in five strides equals a 3.7 m (12 ft) stride. Ditch 3, preceded by the narrow placing fence, 23.8 m (78 ft) away in six strides, produces a 3.4 m (11 ft) stride. The same line in five strides produces a 4 m (13 ft) stride. Eventually you can work at a longer stride by using ditch 4 with a placing fence. This 25.6 m (84 ft) distance in five strides equals 4.3 m (14 ft) strides. Make sure you are travelling at the right speed before the placing fence. Practise until it becomes automatic.

SUNKEN ROADS

A sunken road, which comprises a drop down followed by a jump up again after one or two strides, is like a bank in reverse. It is a key preparation for water fences and emphasizes the importance of the horse not jumping too extravagantly, and maintaining the right speed and stride length. In this example, the horse and rider must also make a small turn in the sunken road and the horse must not be distracted by the water and drop to his right.

BUILDING TRUST

After you have introduced a novice horse to a small bank (see pp.260–61) you can progress to a sunken road obstacle. This is a wonderful exercise for building trust between you and your horse, because although sunken roads initially look strange to the horse, they are generally easy to negotiate. They are also a good introduction to water, because the majority of water obstacles are just sunken roads filled with water.

There are two additional factors in the sunken road shown below that make it more difficult. Firstly, after jumping down into the sunken road, it is necessary to steer a dog-leg turn of approximately 25 degrees. This type of exercise is excellent because it teaches the horse to pay attention to the rider's steering, stopping, and forwards aids as he jumps. Secondly, this sunken road is on the edge of the water jump, which may worry some horses. It is an important part of training for the horse to jump without being distracted by other factors, so jumping an obstacle such as this is good practice. It helps reinforce the trust that the horse has in the rider's ability to act as herd leader and protect him from harm.

NEGOTIATING A SUNKEN ROAD

The priority for the rider is to maintain the right direction and speed. In this sequence, the sunken road contains a slightly short distance of 9.5 m (31 ft), which means that riders should approach by trotting into it slowly. The normal take-off point for jumping down a bank is less than 1 m (3 ft)

SUNKEN ROAD ON A DOG LEG The width of this sunken road is 9.5 m (31 ft), which is designed to give two strides in the bottom when approached in trot. Here, the horse jumps a little extravagantly and therefore gets close to the bank going out. To create extra distance, he jumps to the left.

1

Slip the reins to allow you to open the angle between knee and hip

Turn the horse without pulling back on the rein

2

LANDING EFFECTIVELY It is a vital part of a horse's technique for going down banks or drops that he gets in the habit of landing with his front legs apart. Horses that are worried or frightened tend to put their two forelegs together, which causes the legs to lock and can result in a stumble or fall.

horse has jumped in a little too big **(1)**, which has the effect of making the distance within the sunken road shorter. This is a common problem and emphasizes the importance of the rider working out the correct approach beforehand.

Because of the big jump in, the horse has to take two fairly short strides in the sunken road. The dog-leg shape of the complex requires the second stride to be a turning stride. Do this by moving both your hands towards the inside by about 10 cm (4 in) without pulling backwards **(2)**. Complete the second stride **(3)** before jumping out **(4)**.

MAKING PROGRESS

Most horses do not find sunken roads daunting. Your horse should end the exercise having had a pleasant experience and one which he found simple. Here, the whole exercise is a happy one. The horse's ears are constantly pricked; he looks confident and is ready to perform the same route in reverse.

As progress is made, with different-looking fences being introduced successfully, your horse will begin to trust you more and more until he is prepared to take on almost every fence you point him at. It is therefore important not to betray this trust by asking him to jump something that is beyond his ability and stage of training. At top-level competition, the sunken road is likely to have only a bounce distance and will include fences before and after. However, if the horse's confidence has been maintained, he will view this as no more than a simple exercise.

from the lip of the bank, instead of approximately 1.8 m (6 ft), which is the usual take-off point in front of a fence. This is an important factor to take into account. The landing point in this instance should be 2 m (6½ ft) from the bank. Here, the

Stay close to the horse before take-off, maintaining a good balance

Allow the horse the freedom to stretch his neck up

Try to stay further forwards with your weight over the lower leg

BANKS AND DROPS

Nothing symbolizes the naturalness of a cross-country course more than a bank. It is a wonderful fence at which to encourage the horse to look after himself and show respect for what he is jumping. For the rider, it divides a jump into two parts, providing an opportunity to practise both maintaining balance and the safety position. You can never guarantee what is going to happen at a bank, so it is also useful for the horse's fifth-leg training.

A BANK COMPLEX

Apart from water, a bank complex is the most valuable part of a cross-country facility. The one shown here provides a large variety of routes for all standards of rider, building up to jumping the most advanced bank, which is known as a Normandy bank. This involves bouncing – jumping on and off the bank without taking a stride in between. Although it is possible to ride slowly onto the Normandy bank and put a stride in, this creates a steeper angle of descent and then makes it impossible to jump a fence on the ditch-side of the bank.

When you walk a course to work out the expected landing and take-off points, remember that banks usually have shorter distances because horses will tend to both land and take off fairly close to the edges. Therefore, although a standard one-stride distance with two fences is approximately 7.3 m (24 ft), it will be closer to 5.9 m (19 ft) with a one-stride bank. Of course, by choosing the right speed and stride length it is possible to cope with almost any distance. You must never gallop at banks, however, because this could be dangerous.

MEDIUM ROUTE OVER BANK COMBINATION The medium-level route is a double-bounce combination and is good preparation for jumping the most advanced route. The horse has to bounce from the first bank onto the second bank and off again without putting in any non-jumping strides. The addition of a ditch placed in front of the first bank means that this complex demands real confidence.

AERIAL OVERVIEW

Novice route
Medium route
Advanced route

As you jump the ditch, slap the left shoulder with your stick to stay straight

1

On the bounce to the second bank, let your hands go with the horse's mouth

2

3

JUMPING THE BANK

In the medium-level route across this complex (see sequence, below), the width of each bank is 4 m (13 ft), which is fairly long. You must approach at a speed of 450 m/min (16.7 mph). This ensures that the horse has the right stride length to match this long double-bounce bank. (It is also the same speed and stride length as that required for the Normandy bank.)

The novice rider in the sequence below has made a strong jump over the ditch and onto the bank **(1)**, and does well to stop her horse drifting further to the left. The horse bounces straight from the first bank **(2)** to the second **(3)**. At this stage, the rider's heel needs to be further back to give better security. She also has her weight too far forwards and the reins too tight as the horse bounces off the bank **(4)**. The horse lands with his front legs too close together and stumbles slightly as he canters away **(5)**. The rider has tipped forwards in the upper body but has done well to stay with the horse.

IMPROVING YOUR POSITION

Banks like this are excellent for teaching riders how to keep a safe balance both down drops and for the second half of fences. This is because it is possible to trot slowly onto the bank and give yourself time to make alterations. The rider in this sequence should come off the bank with a similar position to the rider dropping into the water (see picture, above right), getting the weight to the heel and opening up the knee and hip joints. It is helpful to practise this movement in halt. Close your eyes and visualize it before actually doing it, slowly, as you jump

DROP INTO WATER   This is an excellent drop on the part of both rider and horse. The rider has opened the knee and hip joints to give a straight line from shoulder to hip to back of heel, which is ideal for a big drop. The horse's forelegs are apart and the next stride is going to be easy for them both.

off the bank. This same action is required in the second half of jumping a normal fence, so this training will also help your basic jumping position (see p.194–95). Bank jumping is never an exact science so you must allow your horse to make decisions, and keep your lower leg in a secure position at all times.

Try to keep your knee back, in line with the ball of your foot

4

Let the reins slip through the fingers and bring the heels forwards

5

Allow the horse freedom of the head and neck to balance

JUMPING IN AND OUT OF WATER

At a competition, the water jump tends to be the place where the crowds gather, and riders feel under pressure to perform well. Although they can appear daunting, most water jumps are nothing more than a simple drop followed, after at least two strides, by an up bank – in other words, a sunken road with water in it. If horse and rider are confident and have a solid technique for both jumping on and off banks, and for drop fences, there is little to fear from water fences.

TRAINING FOR WATER JUMPS

In your training, practise jumping banks, tables, and sunken roads to establish both the rider's safety position and the horse's technique for going down drops and up banks. Getting used to these types of obstacles without water can be of enormous psychological value to both rider and horse before attempting a water jump. Then walk your horse through water that has a good secure base so that the horse learns that there is nothing frightening under the surface.

In the water, the rider should ensure that the horse is calm and responsive. This removes the need to have a strong contact on the reins, which would restrict the horse's ability to see what he is doing and therefore balance himself. A minor trip in water can be off-putting. This is where proper fifth-leg training will pay dividends, with the horse reacting quickly and safely to any situation, and the rider remaining calm and concentrating on re-establishing the right direction and speed.

JUMPING INTO WATER

In the sequence below, there is a fence before the drop into water. Make sure that you approach the jump from a straight angle and achieve a good take off **(1)**. As you approach the drop, be prepared to adopt the safety position **(2)** – landing in water is less predictable than landing on dry land and the

INTRODUCING YOUR HORSE TO WATER The first stage is to walk the horse quietly into water and allow him to move about in it. This will get him used to the feel of the water and the splashing, and reassure him that the surface underneath is safe.

horse may be surprised. Remember when jumping into water to ensure that the horse lands with his forelegs apart **(3)** – in the same position as they would be after jumping a normal fence. If the horse is not properly prepared and his forelegs remain straight and as a pair on landing, then the automatic locking system of the forelegs comes into effect. This will be a dangerous situation for you and your horse, as it could cause him to stumble or fall.

AT A GLANCE

1 Keep the horse's neck straight over the narrow fence

2 Ride forwards for one long stride

3 Keep the weight in your heel to maintain balance

4 Slow down for the first and second strides

5

6 On the third stride, allow the horse freedom to jump

JUMPING INTO WATER The fence before the water lines the horse up for the drop. There is then a 45-degree turn in the water, which requires the rider to be thinking ahead on landing.

Keep a normal rein contact during the forwards stride

Slip the reins a little

Start to open the knee and hip joints

Wait for the next stride before making the turn, but begin to look ahead in the right direction

JUMPING FROM WATER

Take your time when in the water **(4)** so that the horse remains calm and splashing is kept to a minimum. This will make it easier for him to see where he is going **(5)**. Less experienced horses can underestimate the power needed to jump a fence situated in water **(6, 7)** so they need plenty of encouragement in order to jump it cleanly.

When jumping from water onto land, again allow time for the horse to look at what he is about to jump **(8)** so that he can find a suitable take-off point, get his hind legs together, and jump out of the water **(9)**. This horse has struggled out slightly, but the rider is secure and able to help him forwards **(10)**.

CHECKING THE VARIABLES

For success in water, the variables of direction, speed, impulsion, balance, and timing need to work together. Approaching at an angle can result in lack of normal support from the horse's legs on take-off, but a slow speed allows him to have a little more impulsion and a collected balance. This produces the slightly shorter, rounder stride that helps get through the slowing effect of the water, and also reduces splashing. Here, having the right direction and speed will make the fences ride like a grid and there will be no need to think about your timing to get the right take-off points. This greatly simplifies your task.

7

Maintain the safety position as you jump back into the water

8

Keep your eyes on the next fence and maintain a controlled speed

Maintain the weight through your leg up the bounce bank

9

Hold the mane in case of loss of balance

10

BOUNCES AND COMBINATIONS

The bounce – a combination of two fences where you land and take off again immediately – is a challenge for a horse. It requires quick reactions and an athletic jumping technique. Like all combinations, bounces can have different distances in between fences, which require different stride lengths on approach. It is important to know which factors lengthen and shorten a horse's stride so that the right ingredients can be found to create any stride length.

JUMPING A BOUNCE COMBINATION

This combination begins with a vertical that has a good ground line in front of it. It is followed by one fairly long non-jumping stride before a bounce with a distance set long (pictured below), then three slightly shorter strides to a final vertical. The distances between the first two fences and in the bounce are approximately 1 m (3 ft) longer than normal showjumping distances, at 8.2 m (27 ft) and 4.2 m (13½ ft). The final three strides are set at 14.3 m (47 ft), which is a little shorter than normal.

Approach slightly faster than showjumping speed to the first fence, as this will make the first distance and the bounce ride perfectly. A bounce requires particular agility on the part of the horse. The key to your approach (1) is for the horse to have the confidence to jump the first part of the bounce (2) in a fluent and supple manner. Without this confidence, the jump becomes tight and the horse will lose his athleticism. The right speed will ensure you land at the right spot (3), half-way between the two fences.

As the forelegs land, they have to take off again before the hind legs come to the ground (see inset, below right). This is known as a period of suspension. Because of this, many horses

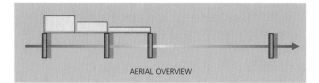

AERIAL OVERVIEW

BOUNCE COMBINATION This is an excellent example of a rider showing a safe position on each landing. There is no risk of her falling forwards and no restriction of the horse on take off.

Encourage the horse to move forwards with your leg aids

Keep a steady, non-restricting rein contact

Maintain a secure lower leg while giving the horse freedom

tend to bring their hind legs more quickly than normal over the first part of a bounce, which is why they sometimes hit it with their hind legs. In this sequence, the horse is leaving one foreleg on the ground for slightly too long **(4)**, which may cause him to hit the second part of the bounce with this leg when coming out, so this is not desirable. Start to slow down slightly **(5)** for the final vertical in order to make three complete strides.

TAKING SHORT AND LONG STRIDES

Distances will appear short when the horse is jumping extravagantly, and will appear long if he is just creeping over the fences. Always bear in mind that the horse's stride will lengthen when he   going faster or riding down a slight incline, when he is enjoying good ground, when he feels fresh and supple, when he is jumping flimsy fences that he does not respect, or when he is heading for home.

A horse's stride will shorten when he is going slower or up an incline, when he is struggling with soft ground or if he is feeling reluctant about leaving home, if he is tired, if the rider is restricting him, or if he is stiff and lacking a period of suspension. These factors emphasize the need to know your horse well and to use the experience of your coach to find the right speed and stride lengths. A horse with a good fifth leg (see pp.270–71) will be able to do much of the work for you.

TWO FENCES AT AN ANGLE A slow canter is needed to fit in three short strides between this angled-fence combination. This horse's neck is not straight, which means he could easily run to the left. Jumping left is another option, but risks the horse running out.

4

Maintain a perfect balance for take-off

The horse's front legs take off before the hind legs meet the ground

5

Slow the horse for three slightly short strides to the next fence

JUMPING UP- AND DOWNHILL

The horse's stride length and his take-off and landing points change as he jumps up and downhill. When going uphill, the stride tends to shorten; when going downhill, it will lengthen. Uphill the horse will land closer to the fence; downhill, he will land further away. In turn, the rider must stay sufficiently forwards with the horse when going uphill, and not get too far forwards and, therefore, out of balance when going downhill.

JUMPING DOWNHILL

A downhill fence is a drop fence in which the landing slopes away. This makes the landing point a little further away than normal because the horse will have spent a longer time in the air than with the same fence on the flat.

When a person runs down a hill, they tend to go faster and faster until they either fall over or they slow down to stay on their feet. A horse also has to slow down to maintain his balance, but some horses forget this natural reaction if they are only used to listening to a dominant rider.

In this sequence, the distance between the two logs is 13.7 m (45 ft), approximately 1 m (3 ft) short of three normal showjumping strides. However, it rides 2 m (6½ ft) short because, when going downhill, horses tend to use a longer stride. If you ride it as three short strides, the distance will work smoothly and it will be easier to balance the horse.

DOWNHILL COMBINATION These two logs are set on a curve. The effect of the hill makes the distance ride like three short strides when going downhill, but three long strides when going up. Going up involves considerably more energy.

Keep your upper body back, not forwards, and maintain contact

Control speed from the moment of landing

Regain balance and start to slow down for the next log

A GOOD POSITION The rider is in a good position with her heel in line with her shoulder. She is opening her fingers to slip the reins and allow the horse to stretch his neck without pulling her body forwards. She must be careful not to drop the reins.

Make sure you keep a strong lower leg position, maintaining a vertical line running from the knee to the ball of the foot by opening up the knee and hip joints. After take-off over the first log **(1)**, be ready to control the horse's speed on landing **(2)**. Maintain the correct balance **(3, 4)** and sit close in the saddle before taking off over the second log **(5,6)**. Again, be ready to have your weight back and be balanced **(7, 8)** so that you can look ahead to the next challenge.

JUMPING UPHILL

Horses do not find jumping uphill as difficult as downhill because it is easier for them to keep their balance. Therefore, all the rider has to do when going uphill is to concentrate on maintaining sufficient energy and riding faster, as though there were three long strides.

Jumping the logs uphill will obviously involve a considerable amount of extra energy on the horse's part, so it is important that the rider helps him. You can do this by not sitting on the back of the saddle, but pushing your weight down into your heel so that you can come forwards into a lighter position with your own centre of gravity over the horse's centre of gravity.

JUMPING UPHILL If you measure the height of this fence from the point of take off, it is very big. Here, the horse has taken off too early and has lost energy. As a result, he has to make a huge effort to jump the log through sheer strength, and his hind fetlock joints are almost touching the ground. Despite this, the rider is showing a good balance and position.

Sit into the saddle and maintain forwards impulsion

When there is a raised take-off, the horse's jump is minimal, but still try to keep the weight into the heel

5

6

7

Press down through your heel. Otherwise, your weight will be too heavily in the knee, making the balance insecure

Look ahead and keep your weight in your heel

8

JUMPING AT SPEED

The ability to ride at speed over fences is an essential skill for a cross-country rider and it is the ultimate thrill. For safety's sake, however, it requires preparatory work and consolidation at novice level through steady, progressive training.

As you learn to go faster over steeplechase fences at three-day events, you will find that your horse can cope safely and ably with taking off at any point and that the whole experience will be totally exhilarating.

GOING FASTER

As with driving a car, nothing uses up energy more than acceleration. If you learn to jump at speed, you will avoid wasting energy by having to slow down in front of a fence and then accelerating afterwards. The prerequisites for going faster are for the preparatory dressage and showjumping work to have been completed and for the horse to be fit enough. As the horizontal forces of the gallop reduce the height that a horse can achieve, the fences have to be smaller than for showjumping.

The major difference to showjumping is take-off and landing points. As you go faster, the ideal take-off and landing points will be a little further away from the fence. When jumping at 500 m/min (18.5 mph) it is normal to take off approximately 2.5 m (8 ft) away from the highest point of the fence rather than at the standard showjumping take-off point of 1.8 m (6 ft). In the steeplechase, this will increase to approximately 3 m (10 ft). Many riders are worried about finding the

right take-off point for a steeplechase fence so it is helpful to consider the possible options (see box, below). The key is to sit still and not interfere with your horse's jump. You will find that he will either find an acceptable take-off point without changing his stride or he will chip in – add – a short stride.

In practice, horses will not have to cope with a very short stride before take-off because they will have realized what they have to do two or three strides earlier and will make some of the adjustment before the final stride. So, if you are unsure of the stride, just sit still and be confident that your horse will be able to cope. This strategy is the key to jumping all cross-country fences. Once you understand the logic of this and put it into practice you will gain confidence. You will become more aware of the stride that you are on and be able to work with it to the horse's benefit by only making the smallest of changes. Avoid over riding in front of a fence; suddenly lengthening the stride must be avoided for this strategy to work.

TAKE-OFF POINTS

These diagrams illustrate different approaches to a steeplechase fence. Without altering his stride or the parabola of the jump, a galloping horse can cope easily, whether he takes off a little close or a little far away (standing off) from the fence. If the final stride is too far away, however, the horse will have to chip in an extra, shorter stride before take-off. This will shorten the length of the jump and slow the speed, but it will be safe.

GREY AREA INDICATES
TAKE-OFF / LANDING AREA

SHORT STRIDE ZONE

THE IDEAL TAKE-OFF POINT
take-off point
final stride
landing point

STANDING OFF THE FENCE
take-off point
final stride
landing point

A LITTLE CLOSE
take-off point
final stride
landing point

CHIPPING IN A SMALL STRIDE
take-off point
final stride
landing point

JUMPING A BULLFINCH FENCE

A bullfinch is a solid brush fence with twigs or small branches extending out of the top. It is vital to approach it straight so that the horse can see daylight through the branches and understands that he can jump through them.

Unlike a steeplechase fence, which has a sloping profile, a bullfinch is vertical. As the bullfinch is so tall, getting close to it on take-off is not an option — your horse is likely to refuse. You only have two options: either you can find the ideal take-off zone, or you can stand off a little — take off a little early. So, it is best to approach a bullfinch at a speed of 400–450 m/min (14.8–16.7 mph), and to jump out of a canter that has a little extra impulsion. This will help you if you have to stand off. In more advanced courses, bullfinches may be placed after a turn or on a related distance to make you go slower. This makes them more difficult.

BULLFINCH This bullfinch has 50 cm (20 in) of light brush above the solid part of the fence. For a successful jump, it is necessary to slow down and aim straight at the fence, so that your horse has time to assess it and not lose his confidence.

STEEPLECHASE FENCE Mary King of Great Britain, pictured jumping a steeplechase fence, is completely safe at speed because she and her horses are always so well balanced and at ease.

EXERCISE OVERVIEW

An ordered progression of exercises will help you to set goals and will encourage safe and steady training. It is important to be aware of the dimensions and types of fences, as well as the speeds and distances required at different levels of competition. For instance, when you can fulfil the demands of level 3 (see chart, right), you are ready for your first one-star (novice) international three-day event, while level 4 shows the requirements of a two-star three-day event.

CHALLENGES FOR AN EVENT HORSE

After you have begun to feel comfortable with both dressage and showjumping at level 1 (see p.161 and p.231), you are ready to start the progression of exercises for cross country. In the chart opposite, Level One relates approximately to an introductory level of competition; Level Two relates approximately to a novice level of competition; Level Three relates approximately to an intermediate or medium level of competition; and Level Four relates approximately to the introductory level of international competition.

For a rider used to showjumping, the maximum heights and spreads met in cross country seem reassuring, although the spreads are slightly wider. In practice, however, there is a huge difference between the two sports. A 1.15 m (3 ft 8 in) vertical showjump placed on level ground half-way around a 550 m (600 yd) showjumping course is quite different to a 1.15 m (3 ft 8 in) corner placed on a blind turn on a hill half-way around a cross-country course that is ten times longer. If your horse is trained to react quickly, and if he is fit, then the corner will not pose a problem.

While horses need exceptional scope and athletic ability for top-level showjumping, there is a wider range of horses that can do the job in horse trials, provided they have the correct training and level of fitness. Fitness is required not only for the distances, but also for the increased number of jumping efforts. Too much jumping when a horse is still maturing physically can leave him in difficulties, as he simply loses the power to jump. Foresight is needed if the event horse's competing lifespan is to be preserved and extended. A fittening programme must be tailored to meet the needs of your horse (see pp.324–29).

ADAPTING YOUR SPEED

The event rider has to cope with a wide range of speeds, which should be worked up to gradually. The novice rider must be content to get time faults at a competition — it is always better to jump slowly and safely than to take risks. Establish a method for jumping at showjumping speed before going slower, as required for drop fences, and faster for single fences with a sloping profile. The speeds required at each level are averages. There will be parts of the cross country where you will have to ride faster to make up for the slower parts of the course.

WHEN TO GO FASTER

A cross-country fence with a sloping profile requires a faster speed on approach so that the horse can get a bigger and more fluent jump over it. Here the rider has approached with sufficient energy and given the horse freedom of his neck so that he can stretch and enjoy jumping at speed.

CROSS-COUNTRY BENCHMARKS

COURSE ELEMENTS	LEVEL ONE	LEVEL TWO	LEVEL THREE	LEVEL FOUR
Maximum height of fence	90 cm (2 ft 9 in)	1 m (3 ft 3 in)	1.1 m (3 ft 6 in)	1.15 m (3 ft 8 in)
Height of fence with brush	1.1 m (3 ft 6 in)	1.2 m (3 ft 9 in)	1.3 m (4 ft 3 in)	1.35 m (4 ft 4 in)
Spread at highest point	1.2 m (3 ft 9 in)	1.3 m (4 ft 3 in)	1.4 m (4 ft 6 in)	1.6 m (5 ft 2 in)
Spread at base	1.8 m (5 ft 9 in)	1.9 m (6 ft 2 in)	2.1 m (6 ft 9 in)	2.4 m (7 ft 9 in)
Spread without height	2.3 m (7 ft 5 in)	2.5 m (8 ft 2 in)	2.8 m (9 ft 2 in)	3.2 m (10 ft)
Drops	1.2 m (3 ft 9 in)	1.4 m (4 ft 6 in)	1.6 m (5 ft 2 in)	1.8 m (5 ft 9 in)
Steeplechase height			1.4 m (4 ft 6 in)	1.4 m (4 ft 6 in)
Speed for cross country	480 m/min (17.7 mph)	500 m/min (18.5 mph)	520 m/min (19.2 mph)	550 m/min (20.4 mph)
Speed for steeplechase			640 m/min (23.7 mph)	660 m/min (24.4 mph)
Speed for roads and tracks			Phase A: 220 m/min (8.1 mph) Phase C: 160 m/min (5.9 mph)	Phase A: 220 m/min (8.1 mph) Phase C: 160 m/min (5.9 mph)
Maximum jumping efforts	20	25	30	35
Angled fences	15°	25°	35°	45°
Narrow fences	1.8 m (5 ft 9 in)	1.5 m (4 ft 9 in)	1.2 m (3 ft 9 in)	90 cm (2 ft 9 in)
Corners		40 degrees	60° and two 40° corners on a turn	75° and two 60° corners on a turn
Introduction of fences and combinations	Logs, tables, banks, dry ditches, water ditches, going into water without jump, narrow fences	Drops, corners, steps, bounces, drop or jump into water, simple combinations, bullfinches	Jump into water with drop, four-stride combinations with a turn	Directional or speed changes in three-stride combinations
Shortening and lengthening on flat	3.3 m (10 ft 9 in)– 5 m (16 ft 4 in)	3 m (9 ft 8 in)– 5.2 m (17 ft)	3 m (9 ft 8 in)– 6.5 m (21 ft 3 in)	2.7 m (8 ft 9 in)– 6.7 m (21 ft 9 in)
Required dressage and showjumping levels	Dressage level 1; showjumping level 1	Dressage level 1; showjumping level 1	Dressage level 2; showjumping level 2	Dressage level 3; showjumping level 3
Distance 1-day event	2,000 m (2,188 yd)	2,500 m (2,730 yd)	3,500 m (3,830 yd)	4,500 m (4,920 yd)
Distance 3-day event			4,680 m (5,120 yd)	5,500 m (6,000 yd)
Distance roads and tracks A			4,400 m (4,810 yd)	4,400 m (4,810 yd)
Distance steeplechase			2,240 m (2,450 yd)	2,310 m (2,530 yd)
Distance roads and tracks C			6,400 m (7,000 yd)	6,400 m (7,000 yd)

DIAMOND BANK AND COFFIN

As you progress in your training, you can begin to mix different fences and exercises to create different lines of approach and new challenges. This bank and coffin complex is like a mini cross-country course, and includes two banks, a narrow fence, a sunken road (or a coffin), two ditches, and a drop. It also includes related distances. As you practise new cross-country exercises, you will find that good dressage and showjumping training will prove invaluable to you.

ANALYSING THE SET-UP

The diamond-shaped bank is a useful schooling fence to have access to, particularly if it is sited so that one of the smaller angles is on the edge of a slope. This will provide a drop off on one side of the bank, which will allow riders to practise moving into their safety position, without having to go fast or jumping a frightening fence.

This bank has space for one comfortable non-jumping stride on the top. This means it can also be used as an easy fence for a novice to practise on, because it is possible to stay on the same level on approach and departure. In addition, the diamond bank offers a small corner with an angle of 45 degrees and a bigger corner at 70 degrees. The corners are safe because they are filled in, so if you get the line wrong your horse can balance by putting his feet down.

A coffin is a combination of a rail, ditch, and rail – the ditch is usually situated in a hollow. The complex pictured here and on pp. 300–301 has two alternative coffins – a deep ditch 1.8 m (5 ft 9 in) wide with a log over it, or a shallow ditch only 60 cm (1 ft 10 in) wide. The Irish bank at the end (see pp. 300–301) also offers options to just go straight up and down without jumping any ditches or logs. When taking the route to the bigger of the logs, it presents the psychological challenge of feeling as though you are jumping into space, but as soon as the horse has taken off, the landing point is obvious.

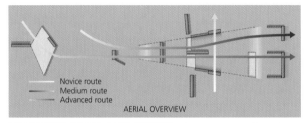

Novice route
Medium route
Advanced route

AERIAL OVERVIEW

DIAMOND BANK AND COFFIN There are a number of routes, but it is important not to jump too many fences. Choose the exercises that are appropriate for the goals of your training session and your horse's level. Bear in mind that it is more difficult jumping into a coffin than out.

ADVANCED ROUTE AT A GLANCE

1 · Look in the direction in which you want to go

2 · Maintain an even rein contact

3 · Land from the diamond bank, ready to jump again

4 · Keep the horse's neck straight on approach to the narrow fence

Banks like this are great exercises for encouraging your horse to look after himself and look at what he is jumping. Avoid being too dominant in your riding – this exercise should give the horse real freedom to react as appropriate and find the right balance.

This set-up provides other routes, including sunken roads on different distances, across the complex from side to side. These routes allow the rider to experiment with the effect of varying speeds and distances. The horse enjoys all the challenges because none of the fences are too big. His confidence soars as he works out how to react to all the different fences and lines.

THE ROUTE

In the sequence below, start by riding up the steep hill to the diamond bank (1) at a showjumping speed. There is one stride on the top of the bank (2). Look to the left to see the line to the narrow log. This distance measures a short three strides, but it rides perfectly because the turn shortens the stride a little (3). Beware of over riding to the log, even though your horse cannot see what is on the other side, or under riding to compensate for the short distance.

After jumping over the log (5), there are four fairly short strides to the ditch in the coffin. Ignore the logs that are dug into the ground at the top and bottom of the slope (7) – they are misleading in relationship to the beginning and ending of each stride.

Do not allow your horse to trot down the slope or take an extra short stride on the slope itself (8). If he does this, he will jump off the bottom of the slope without leaving enough room to fit in a full stride before the ditch.

INTO THE COFFIN After jumping the narrow log on level ground, stay in canter and bounce down the slope to get the right striding for the big ditch. Here, the horse is trotting down the slope, which will produce an awkward stride to the ditch from the bottom of the slope.

Over the narrow log, encourage the horse to keep moving forwards

Keep your weight in your heels and retain a supple position

Encourage the horse to ride forwards into the coffin, using your leg aids

Encourage your horse to bounce down the slope

Slow the horse for one short stride

The width of the ditch **(9)** makes it tempting to over ride, which will lengthen the stride and result in a bad take-off point over the log, making the rest of the line difficult.

After the ditch, there are three normal showjumping strides to the ditch at the base of the Irish bank **(10)**. Then there is 6 m (20 ft) from the ditch to the log on the top of the hill, which will ride perfectly on one stride **(11)**.

The log requires the horse to jump into space **(12)** down a drop (see also picture, right), so remember to keep the weight down in your heels and open up your knee and hip joints. If you are to control your strides, you have to land in balance **(13, 14)** and not spend one or two strides getting back into balance.

COMPLEMENTARY TRAINING

Everything you do in dressage and showjumping should complement and back-up your cross-county work. Therefore the type of dressage or showjumping training that forcefully dominates the horse is unhelpful, and even dangerous, because it removes the horse's ability to think for himself.

What is required is an obedient horse who accepts the rider, but not a submissive horse who waits for the rider to make every decision and does not use his brain.

The most essential dressage preparation for cross-country work are the exercises that teach shortening and lengthening of the stride, which lead to true collection (see pp. 156–57). A genuine ability to shorten strides, as opposed to shortening them by tightening the steps but having no impulsion, is of the greatest importance.

Most short-striding combinations and approaches to drops and coffins – including the exercise pictured here – suddenly become easy if your horse can shorten his strides with supple, athletic steps. This will also help

JUMPING INTO SPACE Having practised your safety position going slowly off the banks, this is an opportunity to put it into practice at speed. The jump is easy for the horse as long as he has confidence – it will almost feel as if there is no fence.

ADVANCED ROUTE AT A GLANCE (CONTINUED)

9

Keep a soft, allowing rein contact over the log

him take off with greater sharpness and spring and will therefore lead to a cleaner, more athletic, jump.

Showjumping training is of equal value as the basis for cross country. If the horse learns to come to a showjump on an even stride, he will have a chance of learning to do so at a faster speed in front of a cross-country fence. Work on your basic jumping technique is also vital. There is little point in going faster over fences until a horse has learnt to take off with his hind legs together (see box, right), to use his shoulders and elbows by bringing them forwards, and to stay straight.

The combination of good dressage and showjumping training will produce a responsive, athletic horse who has the physical and mental strength to go across country. Dressage and showjumping training should not only form the basis of your preparatory work for cross country. You should also continue revising your jumping and flat work when you are working on your cross-country exercises

Using this type of exercise with the diamond bank and coffin allows you to bring all your skills together. A brave young horse and assertive rider could jump every fence in the complex in one session, but this would be of little value if the standard of flat work between fences and the quality of the jump were poor. Walk every line before riding it and imagine the fences at maximum height. This will remind you why every detail of the approach to and departure from a fence is important.

GAINING IN EXPERTISE

Progressive training over the right fences can produce an immediate improvement in your jumping technique. This horse began a schooling session with his hind legs apart and with his body flat and long, instead of compact, in the last stride before take-off. However, after some training, his hind legs start to come forwards together while the front legs are still on the ground. With his hind legs together, the horse becomes like a coiled spring before take-off, creating the power that makes jumping easy for him.

Keep your weight central over the horse's centre of gravity as you jump the ditch

10

Keep your weight slightly back for the Irish bank

11

Maintain a perfect balance in flight

12

13

Open up the knee and hip joints

14

ADVANCED WATER COMBINATION

As you compete in higher level competitions, you will find that the water complexes tend to include a variety of fences and routes. Here there is a log pile, followed by one long stride to a big drop into water, then three short strides to a fence in the water, and three fairly long strides to a bounce bank. Individually, all the fences are relatively easy; it is their relationship, plus the additional element of water, that makes this a more advanced exercise.

TAKING THE ADVANCED ROUTE

Before you school your horse for an advanced route through a water complex, decide what you are trying to achieve. The aim for this horse and rider is to jump more positively into water and then to practise controlling and changing the speed. Always walk the fences beforehand, as though you were in a competition, and think about your tactics.

Here, the first test is a distance problem – it is 6.8 m (22 ft) between the log pile and the drop into water (**1**) instead of the easier distance of 6.2 m (20 ft). Therefore, you need to come in a little faster than showjumping speed, at 400 m/min (14.8 mph), landing about 3.5 m (11 ft 5 in) into the water. This reduces the available distance to the middle fence (**2**), which is three fairly short strides. It is tempting to ride this on two long strides, but the extra splashing and longer, flatter stride will increase the element of risk.

Having landed over the middle fence, there are then three slightly long strides to a bounce bank, which is 3.5 m (11 ft 5 in) wide (**3**). The horse shown here was too far away from the bank on take-off and short of impulsion. As a result, he put a short stride on top of the bank; if there had been a fence after the bounce bank, he would not have been ready for it.

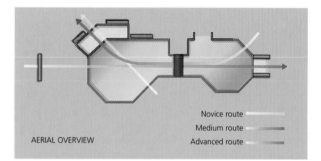

AERIAL OVERVIEW

Novice route
Medium route
Advanced route

A CONFIDENCE BUILDER Practising over a training complex like this, which provides over 18 routes and 30 exercises, will ensure you have a sound and comprehensive preparation before a competition. You will be reassured, knowing that your horse will not be frightened by water.

Jump the logs and the drop into the water

Jump the fence in the middle of the water complex

DROP INTO WATER The rider is showing the ideal position for going down a steep drop. Her centre of gravity is over the horse's centre of gravity, and her lower leg remains vertical, with weight into the heel. Because she has taken a fast approach into the water, she has achieved a reduced angle of descent, but she must then slow down to shorten the strides for the next fence.

ASSESSING THE VARIABLES

This exercise shows, again, that if you concentrate on the right variables of speed and direction, most combinations will be relatively easy to ride. Bear in mind, however, that striding in water is never a completely exact science because of the dragging or slowing effect of the water on a horse's legs.

Here, the direction is a straight line. The speed at which to enter is 400 m/min (14.8 mph). The rider must reduce the pace to a slightly slow showjumping speed before the fence in

the water, and increase to a slightly fast showjumping speed for the jump out. It is important to maintain a level of impulsion because the horse needs power to jump the fence in water.

An easier option would be to put in two short strides before the drop into the water. Although this means the horse would drop down more steeply, it makes the two three-stride distances in the water ride more easily because no shortening is required. In turn, this makes it easier to maintain impulsion for jumping out onto the bounce bank.

JUMPING A FENCE IN WATER Horses will jump fences situated in water easily, provided they are on a comfortable stride. The rider is showing a safe leg position.

JUMPING OUT OF WATER The horse has lost impulsion because he did not go forwards enough after the previous fence. He will have to chip in – add – a short stride on the bank.

Stay on a straight line
to the bounce bank
out of the water

AT THE COMPETITION

Competing in horse trials requires not only riding skills but organizational ability and a cool head. Walking and learning the cross-country course should be a top priority. Your equipment must be organized, your timetable exact, and your helpers briefed. You need to be disciplined and keep to a precise schedule to make the most of each competition. With experience, this will become automatic, but initially you need to be methodical so you can relax and enjoy the event.

THE ONE-DAY EVENT

At a well-organized one-day event, dressage comes first, the showjumping phase is normally one hour later, and the cross country is one hour after that. This means that you have to finish walking the cross-country course before the dressage phase begins. When you have found out your times for each of the three phases, you can plan backwards to make sure you have enough time.

Arrive in plenty of time to park, collect your competitor's number, which has to be worn whenever you are on the horse, and orientate yourself. As you warm up for dressage, remember that you have two more phases to come – make it as brief as possible. A well-prepared horse will not need a long warm-up. Many people find their horses showjump better because they worked earlier and, similarly, you will not need more than approximately 15 minutes to warm up before the cross country, because your horse will already be loosened up. Ensure you and your horse are in gear for cross country by doing some of your warm-up at cross-country speed.

Walking the Course

Walking the cross-country course requires great concentration. Big gaps between fences can cause the mind to wander. The first walk is important because this is the impression the horse will get. Think about what may be surprising to him and be aware of possible distractions. For instance, knowing where spectators will stand may influence your choice of route at a water fence; or the changing position of the sun may make a fence more difficult to see later in the day. Two course walks are advisable.

Novice courses will be deliberately designed to be simple and inviting, but you should get into the habit of being aware of more than just the order of fences. Practise remembering points between fences, so that your route is more precise, and deliberately line up a point on a fence with something behind it (see p.281) to ensure a precise line. These are things you will have to do at the higher levels. When fences are close to each other, work out how many strides to expect. Work out where the horse is going to land and take off and walk between these points. There will be different possibilities, so have a flexible approach and be ready to take a different route. Four of your steps equal one stride for your horse at showjumping speed. For every 50 m/min (1.8 mph) faster that you go most horses will increase their stride length by approximately 50 cm (20 in). They will also take off and land approximately 25 cm (10 in) further away than normal. Spend time watching where horses take off and land, and you will soon get a good feel for what is normal.

Numbering of combination fences and the routes available through them are important. It is crucial that you understand all possibilities so that you can make a quick decision if something goes wrong. A combination may either be numbered separately or as one fence, with the individual parts labelled A, B, and C. If it is the latter, the fences must be jumped in an obvious line. If you do stop at the second or third part, you may be able to start again from where you stopped, depending on the layout of the complex, or you may have to start again from A or switch to a longer, alternative route. Do whatever is easiest. When fences are numbered separately, you can circle in between them to get the right line. You will not be penalized as long as you are not judged to have deliberately presented your horse at a fence and run out.

Keeping a Performance Record

Stopwatches are generally banned at novice level – and you will learn more about judging pace without one – but it is important to note your cross-country time. Record this in a training diary, together with the recovery time of your horse, the length of the track, and the conditions, such as hot weather, and hard or soft ground. This information will be invaluable in assessing your performance, setting new goals, and increasing the efficiency of your fittening programme.

PERFECT HARMONY
Australia's Olympic gold medallist Andrew Hoy on Darien Powers, one of the world's greatest cross-country combinations. Always in balance and harmony together, they are pictured making it look easy at Badminton.

THE THREE-DAY EVENT

At a three-day event the order of competition is dressage, cross country, and then showjumping, all of which take place on separate days. The fitness requirements for the increased mileage, the international rules to be grasped, and the bigger crowds all present a much greater technical challenge.

Cross country is much tougher due to the addition of three three preceding phases – two roads and tracks and the steeplechase. Phase A, roads and tracks, is a timed hack that is completed either in trot or in a combination of walk and canter, and acts as a warm-up for Phase B, the steeplechase, a jumping and galloping course of brush fences. Phase B should ride well because the fences are generally straightforward, slope away from the horse, and have a ground line in front of them. (In parts of Europe, especially France, Phase B takes place on a real racecourse where the layout is different, with varied fences that can include walls and ditches).

Phase C, like the first phase, is a set of roads and tracks. There is enough time to walk for 5 minutes to let your horse recover after the steeplechase. There is then a vets' inspection before Phase D, the cross country.

Briefing of Competitors

The official briefing of competitors, usually by the event director and judges, takes place on the day before the dressage. A rider representative, who acts as a link between competitors and officials, will be introduced, and you will be told where you can warm up and at what times you can do jumping practice. This is for safety reasons and because riders may only jump in the presence of an official steward. Anyone found jumping unsupervised is likely to be eliminated. Your rider number must also be worn at all times, as must a hard hat. Listen carefully for any special information about how the cross country has been flagged.

Assessing the Cross-country Course

You will either be allowed to ride the route of the roads and tracks, in which case you need to build this into your schedule, or you will be taken on a drive around the route. This will also be your first sight of the steeplechase, Phase B, which will need to be measured before the cross-country day.

On the initial cross-country walk, look at all the options and keep an open mind. Assess the course as a whole before you select routes. You will walk the cross-country course at least three times before riding it, twice with your trainer. Do not be afraid to ask an experienced rider to accompany you, but remember that you know your horse best, so do not be persuaded to do something you instinctively feel will not work. Aim to have a final walk the night before

THREE-DAY EVENT TIMETABLE

Two days are usually needed for the dressage test. This is followed by a day of cross country, which always draws the biggest audience, and then the showjumping finale. The draw (order of competing) will have been set by the organizer and, once times have been set, there is no leeway at all for riders to be late. For example:

Wednesday a.m.	Briefing of competitors
	Assessment of the course
Wednesday p.m.	First horse inspection
Thursday	Dressage
Friday	Dressage
Saturday	Cross Country Phases A–D
Sunday a.m.	Second horse inspection
Sunday p.m.	Showjumping

the cross country. On the actual morning, there may be time for you to watch a few riders tackle certain fences.

The second walk should be done with a measuring wheel. Having formulated a strategy after your first walk, take your time and think about your routes. Make contingency plans in case of a run out, or in case your horse loses confidence and needs a reassuring route. Study the terrain and work out where you will need to go slower and where you can gallop and make up time. Aim to take the shortest line between fences.

MEASURING THE COURSE Use a measuring wheel to calculate where you should be on the course at certain times. Look for a marker such as a flag or tree at these points. This will help you achieve your own performance goals.

First Horse Inspection

The purpose of the first horse inspection is for the judges (known as the ground jury) to check that your horse looks fit and sound enough to start. They will first inspect the horse, who must be wearing a bridle, standing still, and then you will be required to lead him at the trot up and down an area that has a hard surface. The horse should be well turned out, with a plaited mane, and you should be smartly dressed because presentation will help to make a good impression. Take care when your horse is surrounded by other horses – you do not want him to sustain an injury through shying or being kicked.

The judges will take advice from the official vets and, if they are in any doubt about your horse's fitness, they may ask to see him again after the dressage phase. Some horses do not naturally trot up well. Practise at home so that he trots obediently and loosely beside you. As you turn him around, stay on his outside so that he does not move sideways through excitement and hit one of his legs with another. Do not hold the reins tightly near his mouth because, if the judges feel you are supporting his head, and therefore concealing his true action, they will make you run up again.

Dressage Day

The aim before dressage at a three-day event is to have your horse as settled as possible, especially if this is likely to be the first time he has seen an arena with seating around it. There are generally more distractions than at a one-day event, including flags, flowers, loudspeakers, and more people.

Acclimatize your horse by riding around the site the day before and working him until he is going well. Most horses also benefit by being worked on the day in advance of the dressage test until they are settled and obedient. This may also be the time to ride through your whole test. If the ground is quite firm and slippery, you will need to have studs in.

Your horse should have a break of 1 to 2 hours before being warmed up for the actual test. Do not be tempted to over-work him before his test; 30–45 minutes' exercise should be the maximum. Riders often complain that their horse has worked much better outside the arena and this can be due to his being stale by the time he enters the arena. Other horses, however, are lifted by the atmosphere in the arena. It is a question of knowing your horse. Enter the arena with purpose, aiming to produce a performance in which you show your horse at his best and make the most of every movement.

After the dressage you should jump a few fences to show your horse that he has to move into another gear for the cross-country day. Psychologically, it is good for both horse and rider to go a little faster, but avoid turning it into a training session.

Cross-country Day

This speed and endurance test is seen by many riders as the most challenging part of the whole three-day event. The atmosphere and crowds can be nerve-racking for a novice, and even highly experienced riders will feel tense. This is why it is important for all your equipment to be well-organized (see pp. 310–11) and for your helpers to be properly briefed.

Prepare a card to tape to your arm with timings for each phase. This must be clear enough for you to assess at a glance. The information you need to put on it is the time you should start and stop each phase and the various positions of your mental markers on the steeplechase and cross-country phases. You will also need two watches: one that you set at zero from the start of Phase A and another on standard time, as a back-up.

As the 10-second countdown to Phase A starts, all you have to remember is to start your stopwatch. There is no better feeling than being on a fit and enthusiastic horse at this stage. Set out positively, with a sense of enjoyment and anticipation.

Canter where you can during phase A and finish 2 minutes ahead of time. This allows time for a girth check before you get your 1-minute warning to start the steeplechase, Phase B. At 10 seconds before, you should be near the start box, then enter on 5 seconds and you will get a smooth start. Get into steeplechase speed (see p. 297) and remind yourself to sit still as you approach the first fence.

COUNTDOWN TO PHASE A

An organized lead-up to the first cross-country phase, roads and tracks, is vital. It is important to have spare time in case the unexpected happens and in order to visualize the day ahead. The horse should have at least 4 hours free after finishing his feed. A typical countdown could be:

5 hrs	Give your horse a small quantity of hay followed by a little feed if possible.
4 hrs	No more hay or feed – keep water available.
2 hrs	Lead your horse in-hand for 15 minutes.
1 hr 45 min	Groom your horse.
1 hr 30 mins	Put in studs.
1 hr 15 mins	Put on bandages and boots. Make sure they are not too tight.
1 hr	Check your horse's soundness.
45 mins	Saddle and bridle your horse.
30 mins	Be ready and dressed in competition clothes.
15 mins	Go to the start, mount, and walk around. (If Phase A is short, or with an older horse, you may need longer at this stage).

The time-markers should pass by exactly as planned and you will finish 5 seconds under the time required. Slow down gradually, keeping your horse on a straight line. Do not worry if his steps are a little uneven. This is a common occurrence.

Your helper will check your horse's shoes; it is not unusual for a horse to have a shoe replaced at this stage. Phase C, another road and track session, is largely designed as a recovery period. Aim to arrive in the preparation area – known as the 10-minute or D-box – 3 minutes early prior to the cross country, Phase D. Keep the presence of your supporters in the 10-minute box to a minimum, because you will need peace in which to concentrate. Make sure that the only person briefing you about the condition of the course is your coach, otherwise you may receive conflicting and off-putting advice. You will be given a 5-minute warning to start the cross country and you should aim to be totally ready 3 minutes before (see box, below). Perform a short circle of canter to warm your horse up and get him in gear, and then make your way to the start box.

In the start box, you will be counted down from 5 seconds. Think ahead to the first fence, and about getting the right direction and speed. Concentrate and keep thinking ahead to the next fence, throughout the course. Do not get over-excited when completing a fence you may have been worried about, as it is over-relaxation that can lead to problems. Even if most of your round goes as planned, there are always a few surprises where your horse will help you out of trouble. You should remain aware of his confidence level and opt for a less demanding route if you feel he needs a mental breather. Pay attention also to his energy levels, too, and try to conserve his strength where possible during your round.

Remain calm as you approach the last fence, where your horse should still be full of energy and jumping well. Slow down gradually in a straight line because an abrupt turn or halt from speed can cause injury.

At the End of the Cross country Day

Care of the horse is top priority after Phase D, the cross-country phase; any analysis of your round should be saved until your horse is comfortable.

As you arrive back at the finish, vets will check your horse's temperature, pulse, and respiration. Ask for the results and make a note of them for future reference. Meanwhile, loosen the horse's girth and walk him around. Get the saddle off, wash him quickly, and keep him walking. After 10 minutes, wash him again, offer him water and keep him walking. When washing, water should not be allowed to warm up on the body – it should be scraped off to aid the cooling process.

After 15 minutes, your horse should be totally recovered. Make a note of temperature, pulse, and respiration again; remove boots and bandages; offer him more water, and keep him walking. After 30 minutes the horse can have unlimited water and can be grazed in-hand if the weather is good. This is the time to inspect him for cuts, grazes, and swellings. When treating minor injuries, make sure you do not use any medication containing substances that are against the rules. If in doubt, always seek veterinary advice.

About an hour after the cross country, you can use a cooling agent on the legs and take the horse back to the stable, where he can have a small amount of hay. Give him a small feed and then leave him alone to rest for a couple of hours. If your cross country ended in the middle of the day, the horse should be walked and/or massaged for 15 minutes every 2–3 hours, but do try to leave him alone overnight.

Before settling the horse for the night, he should be trotted up to alleviate stiffness and to check for lameness. If he is lame, you must consult a vet and take their advice about the extent of the problem and the right treatment. Never get carried away by wanting to complete the competition; always look to the horse's comfort now and in the future.

COUNTDOWN TO THE CROSS-COUNTRY PHASE (PHASE D)

You will need a team of at least two helpers in the 10-minute box, one to hold and lead the horse and one to help with equipment. They need to know exactly what the procedure is and not ask questions, so that you can concentrate on the challenge ahead.

12 mins	Have someone watch your horse as you come in from Phase C. Everything should be checked, especially shoes and studs.
11 mins	Vet will check temperature, pulse, and heart rate.
10 mins	Warm or cool your horse as appropriate. Wash his mouth. Double-check shoes, boots, and bandages.
9 mins	Walk the horse around in-hand. Your helpers will brief you on the course while you stay warm and quiet. If you are thirsty, drink still water.
8 mins	Continue cooling your horse. Keep him moving and make any necessary equipment changes.
5 mins	Grease your horse's legs and dry the reins.
4 mins	Mount and check the girth.
3 mins	Take a short trot or canter to settle back into the saddle and get the horse moving.
2 mins	Visualize your chosen routes.
0 mins	Set your stopwatch 5 seconds before the start.

HORSE INSPECTION Keep to the side of your horse and run in time with him. Do not pull on the reins, but allow him the freedom of his head. Try to ensure that he is alert.

Second Horse Inspection

The purpose of the second, final horse inspection is for the judges to check that your horse has come through the cross-country day in good health and is fit for the showjumping day. Get your horse out of the stable about 3 hours before the inspection and walk him for 15 minutes to check he is sound. Return to the stable and prepare his turnout, including plaiting his mane, before walking him again and feeding. If your horse is not sound, seek veterinary advice. Otherwise, ensure that you are ready for the inspection 30 minutes before and keep the horse moving in walk and trot.

Showjumping Day

The time of your showjumping round will depend on your placing at this stage of the three-day event, because this phase is run in reverse order of merit. If you are jumping early on, you may have to start your warm-up before walking the course. As a general rule you need to be ready, near the showjumping ring, half an hour before you are due to jump.

As you walk the course, shut out any distractions. After every three or four fences, revise the course in your mind from the first fence. This will make it easier to remember. Walk the course twice, but do not start your second walk until you can close your eyes and visualize the whole route.

The length of the warm-up needs to be precise. Too short, and the horse may still be stiff after the previous day's efforts; too long, and he may become tired. The more efficient your fittening and conditioning programme has

been (see pp. 324–31), the more normal and easy this warm-up will be, but most horses will not be able to perform at their maximum because of the previous day's exertion.

Keep things simple. Initially, just concentrate on loosening the horse and getting a good response from the leg and rein aids. Ride in big circles and be aware of how your horse is feeling. Rest a little, close your eyes, and play the course back in your mind.

When there are about seven to nine horses before you jump, then trot or canter quietly over two or three small fences. Practise jumping a vertical with a ground-line and jump this three to five times at an increasing height. Many horses are jumped too much outside the ring, so at this stage you have to make a plan based on how your horse feels. If he is stiff, you may need to do a little more flat work to loosen him up before jumping again. If all is well, concentrate on ensuring he is going forwards with a 3.7 m (12 ft) stride, and jump an oxer at increasing heights four to eight times to get into your jumping mindset. At this stage there should be two or three horses left to jump before you. Keep your horse walking and stay away from distractions while you again imagine the course. Depending on how your horse feels, you may wish to jump a vertical just before going into the ring.

As you canter into the ring, remember to salute the judges and, most importantly, wait for the bell – starting before the bell results in elimination. Then just concentrate on riding in the right direction and at the right speed.

Whatever happens, as you leave the ring remind yourself what a fantastic achievement it is to complete a three-day event. You can feel justifiably proud.

SHOWJUMPING WARM-UP AREA Use dressage work to warm up your horse and establish a showjumping canter. Concentrate on achieving a consistent canter and a fluent jump before tackling a couple of bigger obstacles. Allow sufficient time before going into the arena to close your eyes and visualize the showjumping course.

COMPETITION EQUIPMENT

There are fewer competitions for the horse trials rider than for dressage and showjumping. Therefore you cannot afford to waste your opportunities through bad organization, or missing or faulty equipment. Errors such as using the wrong bit, a chinstrap that comes undone, or a forgotten medical card, can result in elimination, while broken tack can force you to retire. Categorize your equipment and pack it into separate containers or bags, as this will avoid confusion and save time at the competition. Good organization and equipment will allow you to concentrate on the event and your riding, which will help your performance.

Part of the key to success is to have a support team who knows what to do. You can make their lives easier by being organized and your own life simpler by not having to answer basic questions about equipment while you are trying to prepare for the competition. A professional approach will immediately make you feel more confident.

RIDER EQUIPMENT CHECKLIST

Constantly evolving rules in rider equipment mean it is important to be conversant with standards on such items as headgear and body protectors. A well-turned out appearance is courteous to sponsors, organizers, and owners. Remember to take smart clothes for the horse inspection and for any official hospitality at which you need to make a good impression.

CLOTHING FOR DRESSAGE AND SHOWJUMPING

Two pairs of breeches
Boots
Dressage tails
Riding jacket
Top hat
Hard hat (including pins and
    hairnet if necessary)
Socks and underwear
Two shirts (collarless, with back
    stud hole or button)
Hunting tie (stock), plain pin,
    and safety pins
Two pairs of gloves
Wrist watch
Dressage whip
Jumping whip
Spurs
Clothes brush

PERSONAL ITEMS

Clothes
Passport
Itinerary
Foreign money (if needed)
Phrase book (for foreign travel)
Medical card
Insurance

CLOTHING FOR CROSS COUNTRY

Breeches – water permeable
Boots
Skull cap and silk
Socks and underwear
Shirt (cross-country colours)
Hunting tie (stock) and
    small safety pins
Gloves
Two stopwatches
Jumping whip
Spurs
Cards and tape (for cross-country times)
Body protector

GENERAL EQUIPMENT

Waterproof jacket
Waterproof leggings
Coat
Hat
Gloves
Waterproof boots
Waterproof notebook and pen
Alarm clock
First aid kit
Running footwear, such as trainers
Rule book
Coloured breeches and chaps
Measuring wheel

HORSE FIRST AID

This list covers basic first aid items for the horse. Only vets are allowed to carry bute, tranquillizers, stimulants, syringes, drugs, or needles.

External use:
Calamine lotion
Antiseptic cream
Antibiotic powder
Lanolin
Petroleum jelly
Eye drops

Legs:
Alcohol for leg wash
Witch hazel
Kaolin poultice or cooling gel
Medicated poultices
Ice packs (a minimum of four)
Linament/deep heat rub

Aids to recovery:
Glucose
Electrolytes
Arnica cream

Digestion:
Epsom salts (digestive aid)
Nitre (diuretic)
Sodium bicarbonate
    (for wind and tying up)
Milk of magnesia/linseed oil/bran
    (for constipation)

Equipment:
Cotton wool, padded dressing
Sterile dressings and sticky plaster
Assorted bandages, pins, and tapes
Scissors, tweezers, and thermometer

HORSE EQUIPMENT CHECKLIST

There may be an element of nervousness at a three-day event, but if all your helpers know where everything is, the situation will be eased considerably. Therefore, pack horse equipment logically, labelling containers if necessary, and make sure before you leave home that your helpers understand your system.

TACK

Dressage:
Bridle – complete
Saddle – complete
Saddlecloth
Bandages
Boots

Cross Country:
Bridle – complete (with rubber reins)
Saddle – complete
Saddlecloth
Boots
Bandages
Plastic sleeves
Bootlace (to tie on bridle)
Martingale
Breastplate
Surcingle/overgirth

Showjumping:
Bridle – complete
Saddle – complete
Saddlecloth
Boots
Bandages

Schooling (as required):
Double bridle
Side reins
Lunge whip and rope
Cavesson
Assortment of bits
Numnah

TRAVEL EQUIPMENT

Headcollar and rope
Travel boots, tail guard, and surcingle
Rugs (see right)
Haynet
Bucket
Muzzle (if required)

STUDS AND REPAIRS

Farrier tools
Wrench/spanner
Nail and tap
Packing (cotton wool)
Set of studs – all types
Spare shoes and pads
Hole punch
Thread and leather needle
Tape and knife

RUGS (as appropriate)

Night rug
Blankets
Anti-sweat sheet
Cotton sheet/coolers
Smart rug/day rug
Waterproof sheet
Appropriate rollers/pads
Stable bandages and gamgee

STABLE EQUIPMENT

Feed and water buckets
Feed chart
Scoop
Feed
Hay
Haynet
Additives/salt
Succulents/apples/carrots
Hose pipe
Muck skip
Mucking out tools
Water container
Clippers
Extension lead
Clipper oil/blades
Twitch
Stall guard
Padlock and key
Bin to soak hay if required

GROOMING

Horse passport and documentation
Timetables
Horse feed list
Grooming kit, including fly spray
Plaiting kit
Tack-cleaning kit
General cleaning kit, including
    clothes pegs
Tack boxes
Padlocks and keys

CROSS-COUNTRY SPECIAL EQUIPMENT

For steeplechase and D box:
Emergency bag – small, waterproof
    hold-all
Emergency first aid kit
Spare shoes/studs
Knife, hole punch, tape, lace
Overreach boots
Brushing boots
Hoof pick, spanner

For D box only:
Waterproof hold-all
Rope and towels
Bucket, sponge, and scraper
Ice and alcohol as appropriate
Thermometer
Waterproof sheet
Seat rug
Light rug
Event grease and plastic gloves

Spares:
Reins and rein stops
Leather and iron
Breastplate
Martingale
Girth, overgirth
Numnah
Bridle and bit

RIDER CHALLENGES

CHALLENGE	POSSIBLE CAUSES	SOLUTIONS
LOSING SECURITY IN SECOND HALF OF JUMP	• Loss of lower leg position	• Concentrate on the position of your lower leg (see pp. 264–65), and put your weight in your heel rather than the ball of the foot. A good leg position is the key to maintaining security.
	• Not opening knee and hip joints	• A loss of security can occur when the saddle and the rider's seat collide on descent over a jump. This is particularly true over bigger fences and drops, and is primarily caused by the rider not opening up the knee and hip joints or riding too long (see pp. 264–65).
	• Throwing body forwards	• If you throw your body too far forwards on take-off you will lack security. Aim to achieve a better balance over fences.
LOSING SECURITY OVER DROP FENCES	• Leaning back	• Many riders are told to lean back over drop fences, but as a result their seat collides with the saddle and their lower leg is drawn back in an effort to maintain their balance. This gives a very insecure position. In this situation, open your knee and hip joints, and slip the reins through your fingers as necessary (see p. 265).
LOSING LINES IN COMBINATIONS	• Lacking directional points	• Looking in the direction that you want to go will help you react quickly to situations. However, in order to do this, you need to know the precise line you wish to take. It is not sufficient just to know which part of the fence you are jumping: you must be able to line up two points to help guide you (see p. 281).
	• Horse not jumping straight	• If your horse is jumping to the left or right, then combinations will be difficult or dangerous. Take a few steps back in your training – go back to flat work and early jumping exercises (see p. 83).
DIFFICULTY IN ACHIEVING THE CORRECT SPEED	• Lack of preparation	• When you ride across country, it is vital that you know what speed you are going. Some fences are designed for a speed slower than showjumping and others for a faster speed; for your own safety, you have to be able to feel the difference between these speeds. In your preparation, aim to feel the difference between 300 m/min (11.1 mph), 400 m/min (14.8 mph), and 500 m/min (18.5 mph) using markers at set intervals (see pp. 266–67).
	• Insufficient timing points	• In a competition, you need to monitor your speed and avoid going too fast. Work out the approximate half-way point on the course as a time-marker. At a more advanced competition, break the course into periods of 2 or 3 minutes.

CHALLENGE	POSSIBLE CAUSES	SOLUTIONS
DIFFICULTY IN ACHIEVING THE RIGHT SPEED FOR STEEPLECHASE	• Insufficient timing points	• To monitor your timing, measure the steeplechase course and work out where you should be at minute intervals. Use a stopwatch that beeps at minute intervals or an ordinary watch. If the minute point is just in front of a jump, however, do not look at your watch until after the fence.
	• Horse running away	• If you are going too fast because your horse is running away then you should do everything you can to pull up and retire.
	• Panic	• Trust your method and stay calm. Avoid going too fast – this depletes the horse's energy and increases the risks when jumping.
FEELING INSECURE IN THE STEEPLECHASE	• Lack of progression	• You will feel safer in your work if you progress gradually. Having established the normal speed for showjumping, you can then gradually begin to go a little faster over cross-country fences. Once you are comfortable doing this, you are ready to jump steeplechase fences of the same height. Then you can gradually increase the speed and attempt to jump standard steeplechase fences.
	• Riding too long	• To help your security, shorten your stirrups by approximately two holes. This allows your seat to stay behind your knee when you close your seat to the saddle over the top of a fence. It will keep you secure even if your horse brushes through a fence. You do not have to ride as short as a steeplechase jockey, but it can help to study photographs of them so you can see what you have to do.
FEELING FRIGHTENED	• Lack of progression	• Many riders will say that they need to be a little frightened to concentrate the mind and perform at their best. If you are more than a little frightened, however, then you should not be going across country. Your confidence will quickly return with progressive training and the right group of people to support you.
	• Past experiences	• After a bad experience it can be difficult to regain confidence. Analyse why the problem happened and ensure the same circumstances are not repeated.
	• Lack of control	• If your horse is out of control, the only sensible approach is to pull up. Do not risk hurting yourself or other people by riding a horse that you cannot control. Change your preparatory work and come back another day, possibly with a different bit and noseband. Do not just hope your horse will settle down. If necessary, take your horse to a professional for evaluation.

HORSE CHALLENGES

CHALLENGE	POSSIBLE CAUSES	SOLUTIONS
HORSE SLIPPING AND SLIDING	• Lack of appropriate studs	• Horses can cope with a remarkable range of conditions and terrains as long as they have suitable studs. It is important to get the balance right between using too few studs and too many, and between using ones that are too small or too big. This is because studs tend to create forces that pull the shoes off, and there is always a danger of a horse injuring himself with a prod from one of his own studs. Generally speaking, avoid sharp studs on the inside of the feet and use bigger studs in the hind than in the front feet.
	• Excessive speed	• A horse that stiffens up through fear or lack of athletic ability will stand a greater chance of slipping. The commonest cause of slipping, however, is going too fast for the conditions. You would not do it in a car, so do not do it on your horse. In difficult conditions, forget your watch and ride at a reduced speed.
NOT GOING FORWARDS	• Lack of progression	• You are not safe going across country unless your horse is in gear and riding forwards willingly. Most horses enjoy cross-country work and will maintain their willingness as long as there is a logical progression to their training and their work and they receive clear instructions from their rider.
	• Passive or restrictive riding	• If you are too passive or, worse still, restrictive through the rein, you may find that your horse quickly loses confidence. You need to trust your preparation, and go across country with enthusiasm to help keep your horse in gear. Have a more active warm-up, and keep the exercises simple for your horse.
OUT OF CONTROL/RUNNING AWAY	• Over-excitement	• If you are not in control, you must pull up. To help you do this, a pulley rein will usually be effective. Many horses run away because they are too excited, and a more gradual exposure to work will help you avoid this problem.
	• Fear	• If a horse is frightened, his instinctive response is flight. Find the source of the fear so that you can deal with it. Stop riding across country and return to showjumping and quiet schooling exercises.
	• Habit	• A horse may run away because he has done it in the past and enjoyed it. A change of bit and noseband should provide the solution. You will find that a horse quickly gets used to a stronger bit, so it is important not to use one too often. One of the best bridles to use is a double bridle because you can ride on the snaffle, only using the curb occasionally (see p.386).

CHALLENGE	POSSIBLE CAUSES	SOLUTIONS
LACKING IMPULSION	• Lacking calmness	• Many horses lose their calmness when galloping across country and the resulting tension inhibits impulsion and control. This is the greatest challenge in training a horse for cross country – to have him 100 per cent in gear without losing his calmness.
	• Lacking forwardness	• For a horse to be in gear he must think forwards. A more assertive ride may help, but if there is not an immediate improvement you should retire and work at this at home.
	• Lacking straightness	• When under pressure, some horses start relying on their stronger side, which makes them gallop and jump crookedly. This reduces their power and impulsion. Go back to flat work and basic exercises and focus on developing the horse evenly. When getting your horse fit, make sure you work on both canter leads (see p.83).
LOSING CONFIDENCE	• Being overstretched	• If a fence is too big or too wide, a horse will quickly lose confidence. Return to smaller fences. Consolidate training to restore your horse's confidence before moving on to larger fences again.
	• Discomfort	• Horses often lose confidence because of discomfort. This can be caused by the rider getting too far back in the saddle, a pinching saddle or bridle, a hollow outline, hitting fences, or tiredness. Ask someone to watch you and help identify the cause of the discomfort.
	• Slipping and sliding	• Slow down in difficult conditions and make sure you are using the right studs (see p.189).
TIREDNESS	• Lack of fitness	• A good fitness programme will mean that your horse is prepared to cope with slightly greater demands than he will face in a competition. If your horse is tired because of a lack of fitness then you risk injury to him as well as to yourself. In this situation you must pull up. If you are near the end of the course, it is very tempting to continue, but it takes only one fence to have a bad fall.
	• Excessive speed	• In the excitement of a competition, some riders lose their feel and go too fast, which quickly tires the horse. In training, you must establish methods of judging speed (see pp.266–67).
	• Illness	• Despite good preparation and good riding, your horse may tire because he is unwell. Be sensitive to abnormal behaviour and check his temperature, pulse, and respiration as a matter of habit. This should be on your list of things to do on competition days.

HORSE CHALLENGES

CHALLENGE	POSSIBLE CAUSES	SOLUTIONS
NOT LOOKING OR TAKING CARE	• Lack of fifth-leg training	• Safety is of prime importance. Your horse needs to be taught to look at what he is jumping and to take care of his rider and himself. In dressage and showjumping training, he should establish calmness, self-carriage, and the confidence to work things out for himself. In cross-country training, use of grids (with the rider maintaining a very light rein contact), and schooling over a wide variety of obstacles at slow speeds will help his fifth-leg training (see pp. 270–71).
	• Over riding	• Some horses do not take sufficient care because they are listening to a rider who is over riding. Do not look at cross-country riding as something demanding great strength. You must sit as still as possible, particularly when you are close to fences.
	• Over-excitement	• Calmer riding will help a horse that is over-excited, but if he does not improve, you should not go across country.
HITTING FENCES BEHIND	• Discomfort	• If a horse clears a fence with his front legs, and he is jumping normally, there should be no reason for him to hit a fence with his hind legs. The exceptions to this is if the horse is in pain through the back, or if the rider severely tightens the rein and sits heavily on the back of the saddle. If your horse is jumping abnormally then an examination by the veterinary surgeon is advised.
	• Rider restriction	• If you are restricting the horse with your position, you need to go back to jumping smaller fences at slower speeds. Re-establish your confidence, balance, and harmony.
STOPPING	• Loss of confidence	• As a horse loses confidence it is understandable that he will eventually stop and refuse to jump a fence. Avoid punishing your horse and, with the help of your coach, tackle the root problem early on.
	• Self-preservation	• Some horses may stop because they are in an impossible situation, possibly caused by a slip or by losing the right line. A good cross-country horse must have a strong sense of self-preservation and not launch himself blindly at any obstacle. Aggressive riding, which stops a horse jumping carefully, is dangerous. If you are frustrated, pull up and take time out.
	• Tiredness	• Horses may stop because they are tired. Try to pull up before your horse has to make this decision and remember that good preparation means finishing with your horse still able to do more.

CHALLENGE	POSSIBLE CAUSES	SOLUTIONS
HITTING FENCES IN FRONT	• Excessive speed	• Most horses will respect cross-country fences and will only give them an occasional tap. However, if you go too fast or if the horse is tired, collisions can be more serious. Ensure that you have the right speed for each type of fence (see p.267). The faster you go the less room there is for error, so take things slowly.
	• Tiredness	• If your horse is tired there is only one answer – you must pull up and come back another day with a fitter horse.
	• Interference by the rider	• A horse may hit fences in front because the rider makes sudden changes to the speed and their own weight just in front of the fence in an effort to get the right take-off point. This invariably has the reverse result, with the horse putting in a very short stride before take-off, getting close to the fence, and hitting it.
TOO SLOW	• Under riding	• Competitive riding requires going at the specified speed to avoid time penalties. This will require an active ride from you because of the many changes of direction and speed that a cross-country course demands. You need to keep a horse in gear throughout the course.
	• Poor line	• When walking the course, a rider needs to look at all possible lines over fences to see where time can be saved without compromising safety. The more time you spend slowing down in front of fences in order to do this, the slower your round will be.
	• Lack of controlled impulsion	• Having to fight with your horse to get control is exhausting and inefficient for both of you. The fastest and safest rounds are usually produced by the riders and horses who have the best basic training and who understand their roles in the partnership (see pp.272–73).
DISLIKE OF CROSS-COUNTRY FENCES	• Lack of preparation	• Many horses do not like cross-country fences because they have not had progressive training. Introduce your horse to cross-country work using small fences and at slower speeds. The most typical dislike is water fences – make an effort to find streams and shallow water to walk through at an early stage of training.
	• Discomfort	• If a horse's first experience of a particular type of fence is uncomfortable or frightening he will tend to associate this fence with these feelings thereafter. In addition, a horse that has foot or back pain will find the varied ground and drops of a cross-country course an unpleasant experience.

CHAPTER EIGHT

PHYSICAL PREPARATION OF THE HORSE

Exercising your horse effectively should
not only improve his performance and
delay the onset of fatigue, but maintain his
willingness and enthusiasm for work. This
chapter will show you how to devise an
efficient physical preparation programme,
tailor-made for the requirements of your
particular activity and for the specific needs
of your horse. For this you need to have an
understanding of basic equine physiology,
and of the relative roles of a horse's speed,
strength, spring, suppleness, and stamina.

Your programme will involve working
your horse at varying intensities and
evaluating his fitness over a period of
time. The horse's diet will also affect his
performance, so you should also devise
a suitable feeding programme.

YOUR HORSE'S FITNESS

Horses have to be fit enough to perform without getting tired. Each equestrian activity demands different proportions of strength, speed, spring, suppleness, and stamina, and will therefore require different training. Understanding how to train to achieve specific goals is the backbone of any fitness programme, and for this it is necessary to be aware of the difference between aerobic training (muscle use with oxygen) and anaerobic training (muscle use without oxygen).

A FIT AND HAPPY HORSE

The level of fitness required by a horse depends on the type of activity he is being trained for. While maximum fitness is not necessary for a horse competing at a low level, such a horse should be sufficiently fit to complete his work with ease. This will not only reduce the risk of injuries through tiredness and cut down on recovery times, but it will make work a more enjoyable experience for the horse. Fitness training is not only about attaining physical fitness, but also about keeping the horse in a good state of mind. Horses are not motivated by gold medals or glory, and it is difficult for them to understand why another circuit of the gallops is required. Therefore, because it is vital that we maintain the horse's enthusiasm, we have to be careful to avoid overstressing him or being too prescriptive about his training programme.

A horse will rarely cope with being regularly stressed to the maximum. Keep him happy by varying his work, by always finishing with him being willing and able to do a little more, by working in company, and by being quick to give extra rest days if appropriate. Be alert to signs that your horse is not feeling well, and be ready to reward or rest him at exactly

ANAEROBIC ACTIVITY Strenuous exercise that requires muscles to work without the use of oxygen for short periods of time is known as anaerobic activity. It takes place in showjumping at almost every fence, and, in dressage, during canter pirouettes, extensions, and piaffe.

A HORSE'S FITNESS REQUIREMENTS FOR EACH DISCIPLINE					
DISCIPLINE	STRENGTH	SPEED	SPRING	SUPPLENESS	STAMINA
DRESSAGE	25 per cent	5 per cent	30 per cent	30 per cent	10 per cent
SHOWJUMPING	25 per cent	10 per cent	35 per cent	25 per cent	5 per cent
CROSS COUNTRY	10 per cent	20 per cent	10 per cent	20 per cent	40 per cent

the right moment. The most significant factor in your horse's enjoyment is ensuring he is comfortable in his work. Good-quality work, in which your horse uses his back well, is a vital requirement for comfort and, therefore, for all types of fitness training.

TYPES OF FITNESS

There are several components to consider when assessing a horse's fitness: strength, speed, spring, suppleness, and stamina. These are all interlinked, and all exercise activities need to be designed to enhance each aspect to some extent. The percentage of time spent on each component depends on the particular discipline for which you are training (see chart, above).

This does not mean that any horse can be trained to suit any activity. Every horse has different physical limits, and individual physical potential is set at birth. Good training may allow a horse to realize this potential, but it cannot enable him to surpass it. Few horses, however, go even close to their physical limit, and preparation for each component can make a significant difference to the level eventually achieved.

• Strength is all about developing the muscles so that the horse can both carry the rider more easily and sit more on his quarters and hind legs to achieve a more advanced balance. The vast majority of dressage exercises build basic strength. Those that develop collection (see pp.156–57) specifically improve the weight-bearing power of the horse.

• Speed primarily describes the horse's ability to accelerate rapidly. No horse should be asked to work at his maximum speed for anything but the briefest periods of time or to go fast when he is tired. Nevertheless, in horse trials, a high cruising speed is required to achieve the minimum speeds in the steeplechase and cross-country phases.

• Spring is required in dressage for the regularly repeated period of suspension in trot or canter. In jumping, there is a huge demand for spring at the moment of take-off. Exercise should be aimed at developing elastic strength and quick

reactions from the muscles. Jumping is an essential part of training for spring in both dressage and jumping horses.

• Suppleness, or flexibility, is the key aim of the majority of exercises in dressage. Suppleness allows maximum use of all the joints. A combination of strength, speed, and spring creates the power that, when used within a supple frame, is called impulsion – the force that drives the horse forwards into an active, energetic way of going.

• Stamina is all about endurance and being able to keep going steadily for long periods, and it requires aerobic muscle function.

Showjumping and dressage demand strength, spring, and suppleness. Cross country demands a combination of speed, suppleness, and stamina. During eventing, a horse has also to compete in both dressage and cross-country phases, so he will need strength, spring, speed, suppleness, and stamina. Such a horse is the equivalent of a human decathlete – the perfect all-round athlete.

UNDERSTANDING PHYSIOLOGY

The horse is an extraordinary natural athlete with a cardio-vascular system that provides considerably higher aerobic power than it does in any other mammal of comparable body weight. There is a huge capacity for improved function of this system in response to increased work.

The significance of this cardiovascular system is apparent if we look at basic mammalian physiology. Contracting and relaxing muscles accomplish movement, and to produce the energy needed for this, nutrients are burnt with oxygen. The supplies of oxygen needed to service the muscles are carried by the blood, which is kept flowing by the heart. The process of using nutrients results in the production of carbon dioxide and other waste matter. These would eventually poison the cells if they were not removed, so the blood also acts as a waste collector. Carbon dioxide is taken to the lungs to be exhaled, and other wastes are taken to the kidneys to be expelled in the urine.

AEROBIC AND ANAEROBIC EXERCISE

The system of using oxygen to create energy is known as aerobic activity. It is highly efficient because it produces a low level of waste products. But when, during intense exertion, the blood cannot deliver enough oxygen quickly enough, the muscles can temporarily solve the energy crisis by breaking down nutrients without the use of oxygen. This is called anaerobic activity.

Anaerobic activity produces much larger amounts of lactic acid than aerobic activity, and, unless removed, this will stop the functioning of the muscles. Anaerobic function can only last continuously for approximately 2½ minutes. After a period of strenuous exercise demanding anaerobic function, the body will have an oxygen debt that can be paid back only with a period of rest. The more efficient the heart becomes, the less the anaerobic system will be needed and the quicker this period of recovery will be. As the heart muscle is worked, it becomes stronger and more efficient. So, training that develops the cardiovascular system will reduce the need for anaerobic energy production.

Dressage, showjumping, and eventing, however, all require anaerobic energy production, so it is important that the horse's body is able to work anaerobically as well. The horse has two main types of muscle fibre, which are specifically designed to work aerobically (slow twitch) or anaerobically (fast twitch). There is also a third type of muscle fibre that can be used either aerobically or anaerobically depending on how it is initially used. In addition, some scientists believe that some slow-twitch fibres will mimic the fast-twitch fibres if the horse is worked anaerobically initially. This means that a young horse will not fulfil his anaerobic potential unless anaerobic work is included in his training. This has particular significance for showjumping and dressage horses.

TRAINING PROGRAMMES

All physical training programmes have to be tailored to suit each horse and each activity. For example, a showjumping round lasts between 1 and 1½ minutes, and each jump involves intense physical effort. This bears comparison with a human sprinter, while a cross-country round lasts longer and is more equivalent to a middle-distance runner's event. A long-distance runner works primarily on developing oxygen capacity – aerobic function – in order to fuel the muscles for long-term stamina; the same applies to the preparation of an endurance horse. A sprinter primarily uses the anaerobic system, as do both showjumpers and dressage horses, which need a high proportion of anaerobic power to produce strength and spring. The cross-country horse needs to work anaerobically as well as aerobically because of the need for

changes of speed, brief intense jumping efforts requiring strength and spring, and for the times there is an oxygen debt.

It is important to learn which type of training is which: many people think they are working the horse aerobically when they are in fact working him anaerobically and putting him in a state of oxygen debt. A classic use of human anaerobic conditioning, for example, would be to sprint 100 m (100 yd) and then walk 300 m (330 yd), repeating the sequence up to nine times. For aerobic training you would reverse this, having longer periods of low-intensity work and shorter rest periods, such as running 300 m (330 yd) and then walking for 100 m (110 yd) before repeating the sequence. Although horses cannot be continually worked at the peak of their abilities in the way that some human athletes are, it is not efficient to just work aerobically using long, steady periods

of low-intensity work. Such low-intensity work may be required for the delicate temperaments of some horses but it is not the best way to develop the impulsion of a showjumping or dressage horse. Anaerobic training demands asking your horse for as much impulsion as possible over short periods separated by rests. Jumping grids, with rest breaks in between, is a good example of anaerobic training. On the flat, it is possible to vary your demands so that there are brief periods of intense effort followed by less strenuous work and reward.

The need to keep a horse calm and happy in his work will dictate how much you can ask. Aerobic training, such as hacking and low-intensity flat work, is particularly important for event horses, because he needs all types of fitness. His training has to be carefully planned. A canter programme (see p.329) can be tailored to condition both aerobic and anaerobic systems.

EXERCISE REQUIREMENTS

DISCIPLINE	ANAEROBIC	AEROBIC
SHOWJUMPING	70 per cent	30 per cent
DRESSAGE	60 per cent	40 per cent
CROSS COUNTRY	40 per cent	60 per cent

AEROBIC ACTIVITY In both cross-country and endurance riding, there are periods of less strenuous exercise, at slower speeds, which require muscle function with the use of oxygen – aerobic exercise. When you are planning a training programme, make sure you include regular periods of hacking.

FITNESS PROGRAMMES

The key to devising a successful fittening, or conditioning, programme is to tailor it to the individual needs of your horse and the facilities at your disposal. An interval-training programme allows you to train either anaerobically or aerobically, and gives you the flexibility to train different types of horses for different competitions. The speeds, the duration of work, the intervals, and the frequency of sessions can all be varied to produce your own 3- to 4-month programme.

PREPARATORY WORK

Before any serious cantering or galloping is done, your horse must be given sufficient time and work to develop core fitness. This is called legging-up because, as fitness increases, the main tendons of the forelegs will become stronger with an increased blood supply. This will normally take 4 to 7 weeks, depending on your horse's condition, but a fat horse that has never been made fit before may need double this time.

Begin your fitness programme by riding your horse in walk on level, firm ground, building up from 20 minutes to 1½ hours a day, and alternating every second day with lungeing, building up from 15 to 30 minutes. Lungeing will ensure your horse uses his back effectively. Then he can be ridden each day with periods of trotting and cantering introduced.

Start with 3-minute periods of trotting and cantering. Over a period of 2 to 3 weeks, increase to five 4-minute sessions of trot and canter. At the end of this period, your horse should be capable of hacking with ease for 2 hours with up to 30 minutes (spread over the ride) spent in trot or a slow canter.

INTERVAL TRAINING

In interval training, several short periods of work are alternated with brief recovery intervals. The horse is rarely worked at maximum intensity. There are usually only three

FAST WORK After 4 to 12 weeks of basic fittening, you can start slow cantering at 400 m/min (14.8 mph). Do this for 4 weeks before beginning to go faster. Over the next 4-week period, gradually build up to doing two or three 800-metre (½-mile) gallops at 650 m/min (24.1 mph). Working with your horse well balanced and going slightly uphill reduces the pressure on his forelegs.

SLOW WORK Long, slow work is of immense value in building up a horse's core fitness and stamina. It is useful to either walk on roads, or trot slowly uphill. You should also try to replicate the conditions of cross country by finding undulating ground to canter on.

or four periods of work in any interval training session, and the work rarely lasts for more than 30 to 35 minutes in total. This is a popular alternative to cantering for long periods as a means of getting an event horse fit, but all horses need to do legging-up and showjumpers need to do the first 6 weeks of a canter programme (see p. 329).

The main principles of interval work are:

• The body will adapt itself to the stress of the demands made upon it, provided it is given time. Therefore small but increased demands are repeatedly made upon it.

• The intervals are timed so that full recovery is not quite achieved before the next period of work is begun. This enhances the training effect.

• The work periods are designed to avoid maximum stress so that the respiratory, cardiovascular, and muscular systems are all gradually developed. This reduces the risk of injury.

• Interval training should not be used more than once every 3 or 4 days so that the horse's metabolism can return to normal, and any other training essentials put in place. If your horse is young or excitable, one session a week may be enough. Adjust your programme to suit your horse.

• Depending on what is deemed to be suitable for a particular horse, it is possible to structure the intervals of work and rest, and the intensity of the work, to specifically work the horse aerobically or anaerobically.

BASE PROGRAMME

Interval training is suitable only for a mature horse that has completed 4 to 8 weeks of basic fittening and conditioning work. A normal active warm-up session of approximately 30 minutes and a similar cool-down session must precede and follow every day's interval training. If you are preparing your horse for a novice three-day event, you will need approximately 8 to 16 weeks of interval training beforehand. As a rule of thumb, approximately 3.2 km (2 miles), broken up into two or three work periods, are used in the first interval training session. In each subsequent session, you can either add approximately 800 m (½ mile) per session, or increase the speed by about 10 per cent.

At the end of this interval-training programme, a horse should be easily capable of cantering at half speed for twice the total distance used in the steeplechase and cross-country phases of the three-day event, broken up into three work periods. To avoid injury before the competition, many trainers try to reduce the cantering to a minimum, with the result that the horse is only just fit enough on the day. Whatever the demand of the competition, a horse should be fit enough to do a little more than will be required. This means that the risk of injury during the competition will be reduced because the horse is not taken to his limits of strength, speed, and stamina.

The interval training must be structured to take account of your competition programme. So, for example, after a one-day event, it is normal to miss an interval-training session to allow the horse to recover. If a horse is doing many competitions these substitute for the interval training either in whole or in part.

TENDON INJURIES

The area between the knee and fetlock joints is the most susceptible to injury when a horse is travelling at speed. This is because the two main tendons that run behind the cannon bone are less elastic than muscles. If the tendons are overstretched, or directly damaged, there may be long-term consequences, and your horse is likely to be at continual risk of a further injury and lameness if he does faster work again. With a minor injury, the tendons become scarred and thickened. With a major injury, they become permanently bowed when they should be straight. To reduce the risk of injury, always protect the legs with boots or their equivalent, and make sure there is a long, slow progressive build up of work. It helps if you start off with a horse that has good conformation of the forelegs (see p. 377). Always check for pain, heat, or swelling in this area on a daily basis. At the first sign of a problem, rest your horse immediately and call your vet.

RECOVERY PERIODS

The recovery times used in interval training normally range from 1 to 4 minutes, depending on the individual horse and his stage of training. The rate of recovery after a work period is measured by assessing pulse and respiration rates (see box, right). The pulse can be assessed while the horse is working or when he is resting, but since a horse breathes in time with his canter stride, the true respiration rate can be assessed only when the horse has stopped cantering. The recovery time should be sufficient for pulse and respiration rates to come down to the right level before working again.

If the horse is working aerobically, then the rest periods will be shorter and the intensity of the work less demanding. If the horse is working anaerobically then the intensity of the work is greater and creates an oxygen debt (see p.322), so the rest periods are normally longer.

WORK PERIODS

Each work period in a training session normally ranges from 3 to 12 minutes, and the speeds achieved in each period should range from 400 m/min (14.8 mph) to 650 m/min (24.1 mph). Most of the work is done at 400 to 450 m/min (14.8 to 16.7 mph) but as the horse becomes fitter it can be

TEMPERATURE, PULSE, AND RESPIRATION

A horse's normal temperature (taken with a rectal thermometer for 2 minutes) is 38°C. During strong exertion it may rise to 40°C. If it is static or goes higher, the horse must be treated immediately by the vet. The normal pulse rate at rest is 36 to 44 beats per minute. For aerobic training it should be between 60 and 120; for anaerobic training it should be between 150 and 200. The pulse can be detected on the facial artery under the jawbone. Take a 15-second count and multiply by four for the rate per minute. It can also be taken during work with a heart-rate monitor attached to the horse. The normal respiration rate is 8 to 16 breaths per minute and should not exceed 100 per minute. Watch the flanks and count each combination of in and out as one. Count for 15 seconds and multiply by four.

increased to 500 m/min (18.5 mph) and eventually to 650 m/min (24.1 mph). For an event horse, the faster work is usually not needed until the last 2 or 3 weeks before an event. Horses can be worked up gentle hills, for which (depending on the gradient) you can reduce both speeds and distances by up to 20 per cent.

EVALUATING FITNESS

Keeping records of heart, respiration, and recovery rates can help in the evaluation of fitness, but since rates vary between individual horses you must first determine the norm for your horse. For a meaningful comparison, assessments should be made after the same amount of exercise and recovery intervals have been taken. One method is to assess rates every 2 weeks after cantering up the same hill. Take the rates after 1, 5, and 10 minutes of recovery. As fitness improves, the rates should drop. Bear in mind that false readings can occur: an excited horse will have a high pulse, and a horse that feels hot can respire very quickly. Try to establish a normal pattern for each individual horse in a given situation. It is also useful to compare training programmes and fitness at competitions season by season. Always assess the recovery rate of a horse at the end of a cross-country phase, for example, and compare it with previous competitions. You should also have your vet take blood tests at intervals during the year to check for deficiencies. In the end, it is the experienced eye of the trainer and the feel of the rider that are the best judges of a work programme.

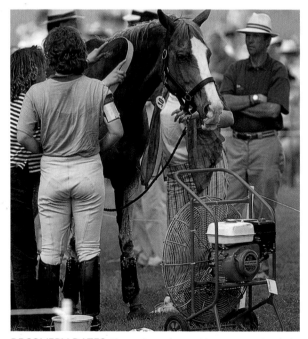

RECOVERY RATES If your horse has not been over-extended, he should be substantially recovered 5 minutes after completion of the cross-country phase and totally recovered after 10 minutes. If your horse has not recovered after 15 minutes, then veterinary advice should be sought.

UPHILL CANTER
Being able to canter slowly or to go faster up a gentle incline is of immense benefit in increasing the intensity of work while reducing the force on the forelegs.

OVER TRAINING

Horses can feel the strain of training, both mentally and physically, and signs of lethargy and ill health may indicate over training. Good observation on your part will allow changes to a programme before a slight strain develops into a major problem. A medium-term programme should be designed with the flexibility for these types of adjustments. A change of scenery and working with other horses can make a dramatic improvement, as can an extra few days off at the right time.

If a horse is uncomfortable in his work or he is in pain, it is often due to over training. If this goes unrecognized and untreated, it will almost certainly create an unwillingness to work. Research has shown that a horse can be given 2 to 3 weeks' rest without a significant decrease in fitness – this should persuade riders to make immediate use of rest periods at the first sign of any injury. When a horse is competing, there is often little need to do much serious canter work at home; once a horse has become fit, it is generally better to concentrate on the quality of the work rather than the quantity.

As with humans, a horse that is training hard is often more susceptible to viruses. Most viruses cannot be treated with antibiotics, and the only remedy is rest and the removal of stress. Viruses are an immense problem because, in the early stages, they may be undetectable. They may also remain latent for many months, only to reappear as the horse returns to strong work. A precise knowledge of your horse's behaviour and habits will be invaluable in detecting a problem.

A HAPPY HORSE No conditioning programme can be considered a success unless the horse is mentally as well as physically fit. Every horse should be treated as an individual with his own tailored programme.

CANTER PROGRAMME VARIABLES

The chart opposite outlines a canter programme leading to a one-star level three-day event. It would be suitable for a horse lacking a little in quality, and that has never been fit before. Work on non-cantering days, however, varies enormously with different horses and trainers. It will have a significant effect on the horse's mental state as well as on the programme itself. The type and personality of horse, and how recently he was last fit, will also have an influence on the canter programme. There is a fine line between a horse that is fit and fresh, and one that is fit and over the top. Excitable horses may need to be cantered slowly for long distances. Small Thoroughbred horses tend to become fit quite quickly, while a cold-blooded horse that has never been really fit will need longer preparation.

A CANTERING PROGRAMME BEFORE A THREE-DAY EVENT

This sample 15-week canter programme leading up to a one-star three-day event should be tailored to suit your horse and your circumstances. Initially, the programme concentrates on building stamina using slow cantering, and then gradually introduces faster periods of work. It is designed to work the horse aerobically and anaerobically. The cantering sessions should take place twice a week (**a** and **b**), with intervals of rest after each period of work. The horse must be warmed up for 20–30 minutes before and cooled down for the same period afterwards.

WEEK	1ST WORK PERIOD	REST	2ND WORK PERIOD	REST	3RD WORK PERIOD
1a	3 mins at 400 m/min (14.8 mph)	4 mins	4 mins at 400 m/min (14.8 mph)		
1b	3 mins at 450 m/min (16.7 mph)	4 mins	4 mins at 450 m/min (16.7 mph)		
2a	3 mins at 400 m/min (14.8 mph)	3 mins	3 mins at 400 m/min (14.8 mph)	3 mins	3 mins at 400 m/min (14.8 mph)
2b	3 mins at 450 m/min (16.7 mph)	3 mins	4 mins at 450 m/min (16.7 mph)	3 mins	3 mins at 450 m/min (16.7 mph)
3a	CROSS-COUNTRY SCHOOLING SESSION				
3b	3 mins at 450 m/min (16.7 mph)	3 mins	6 mins at 450 m/min (16.7 mph)	2 mins	3 mins at 450 m/min (16.7 mph)
4a	6 mins at 400 m/min (14.8 mph)	2 mins	8 mins at 400 m/min (14.8 mph)		
4b	SPARE SESSION OR CROSS-COUNTRY SCHOOLING				
5a	4 mins at 450 m/min (16.7 mph)	4 mins	4 mins at 500 m/min (18.5 mph)	5 mins	4 mins at 400 m/min (14.8 mph)
5b	8 mins at 400 m/min (14.8 mph)	2 mins	8 mins at 400 m/min (14.8 mph)		
6a	4 mins at 450 m/min (16.7 mph)	3 mins	4 mins at 500 m/m (18.5 mph)	4 mins	4 mins at 400 m/min (14.8 mph)
6b	ONE-DAY EVENT COMPETITION				
7a	REST AND REASSESS PROGRAMME AND GOALS				
7b	4 mins at 450 m/min (16.7 mph)	3 mins	4 mins at 550 m/min (20.4 mph)	3 mins	6 mins at 400 m/min (14.8 mph)
8a	8 mins at 400 m/min (14.8 mph)	2 mins	10 mins at 400 m/min (14.8 mph)		
8b	ONE-DAY EVENT COMPETITION				
9a	REST AND REASSESS				
9b	10 mins at 400 m/min (14.8 mph)	2 mins	10 mins at 400 m/min (14.8 mph)		
10a	6 mins at 450 m/min (16.7 mph)	3 mins	6 mins at 500 m/min (18.5 mph)	3 mins	6 mins at 400 m/min (14.8 mph)
10b	ONE-DAY EVENT COMPETITION				
11a	REST AND REASSESS				
11b	8 mins at 400 m/min (14.8 mph)	2 mins	10 mins at 400 m/min (14.8 mph)	2 mins	7 mins at 400 m/min (14.8 mph)
12a	4 mins at 500 m/min (18.5 mph)	3 mins	2 mins at 650 m/min (24.1 mph)	4 mins	4 mins at 500 m/min (18.5 mph)
12b	ONE-DAY EVENT COMPETITION PLUS STEEPLECHASE PRACTICE				
13a	REST AND REASSESS				
13b	SPARE SESSION/REST				
14a	2 mins at 550 m/min (20.4 mph)	2 mins	2 mins at 600 m/min (22.2 mph)		
14b	2 mins at 550 m/min (20.4 mph)	2 mins	2 mins at 600 m/min (22.2 mph)	3 mins	2 mins at 550 m/min (20.4 mph)
14c	2 mins at 550 m/min (20.4 mph)	2 mins	2 mins at 650 m/min (24.1 mph)		
15a	SPARE SESSION				
15b	THREE-DAY EVENT (NOVICE LEVEL) See exercise overview (pp.296–97)				

A FEEDING PROGRAMME

Your horse needs the right quantity and type of fuel to match the physical requirements of his activity. Providing the correct fluid intake plus good-quality hay, and feeding little and often, are the prinicples of any good feeding programme. As far as possible, you should replicate the horse's natural feeding habits and complement them by using concentrates tailored to supply the specific energy needs of your horse's competition work.

FEED LITTLE AND OFTEN

In a natural environment, a horse will spend about 60 per cent of his time grazing (see pp. 50–51). As far as possible, your feeding regime should reflect this: feed your horse as continuously as you can through the day. Frequent small meals are digested more efficiently than two large servings. The most important part of a horse's diet is good-quality, clean horse hay, because it provides both the fibre and the 12 per cent level of protein required by a horse. If you make this hay constantly available, a mature horse will probably eat 9–11 kg (20–25 lb) per day. This will not only meet his basic energy needs, but it will also make digestion easy and reduce the risk of colic. It will make his stomach feel pleasantly full, and take a fair amount of time to eat and so relieve boredom.

Hard feed, such as oats or nuts, satisfies only the first two requirements (fibre and protein), although it is necessary as work levels are increased. As a maximum, a horse should not have more than 1.8 kg (4 lb) of oats or 900 g (2 lb) of nuts at one time (ideally, even less), otherwise there is a greater likelihood both of colic and of the food passing through the body only partially digested.

REGULARITY AND QUANTITY

While humans have a strong desire for variety, it is better to give horses uniform feeds at strictly regular times. Regularity in feeding can increase efficiency in digestion and absorption of nutrients by as much as 40 per cent. A horse needs around 1.1 kg (2½ lb) of feed for every 45 kg (100 lb) of body weight. So a 450-kg (1,000-lb) horse needs 11 kg (25 lb) of hay and hard feed per day. As a general rule, feed a maximum of 450 g (1 lb) of hard feed for every 45 kg (100 lb) of body weight; if the hard feed is increased, the hay ration should be decreased by 300 g (⅔ lb) for every 450 g (1 lb) of hard feed. It is sensible to slightly underfeed rather than overfeed, otherwise your horse is likely to become too fresh.

DRESSAGE HORSE AT COMPETITION A dressage horse looks quite bulky, not because he is fat but because of his muscle development. Any feeding programme is sufficient if a horse maintains a consistent weight, has enough energy for his activity, and maintains a supple skin and a glossy coat.

WATER

Fifty per cent of a mature horse's body is water. Without sufficient fluid the horse's body cannot function; in particular, the blood would be unable to carry nutrients, the digestive system would fail, and the horse would starve. Water is the first essential of feeding, yet many horses slowly dehydrate because of dirty buckets and troughs, or periods without water. Under normal conditions a horse will require 36–55 litres (8–12 gallons) a day, with a greater demand if the weather is hot, and a lower demand if he is turned out on damp grass. Grass is about 80 per cent water and the natural food for a horse. When feeding dried food, such as hay and nuts, it is especially important to provide a constant supply of water close to the food. This applies throughout a competition and when travelling. The only time fluid intake should be limited is immediately after strong work before the horse has recovered.

Prepared nuts and pellets provide a convenient way of giving your horse precisely what he needs, or you can feed traditional oats with added salt. A working horse that sweats needs more salt than he will find in a diet of oats and hay, so add 50–60 g (1½–2 oz) of salt a day, spread throughout the feeds, or use a salt lick that is available to him at all times. Salt stimulates the secretion of saliva and is essential for body-fluid levels and blood quality. A lack of salt causes cramps. Another common cause of cramp is a sudden introduction of high-feed value concentrates, haylage, or alfalfa.

Generally speaking, a healthy horse does not need any of the minerals and vitamins offered in the various supplements. Excessive quantities of minerals will actually harm your horse, as can some vitamins. To make sure you give only the additives and supplements that are needed, have a blood test taken at regular intervals. In addition have stool samples analysed twice a year to see what worming programme is required.

ANAEROBIC OR AEROBIC FEEDING

For the horse participating in anaerobic activities, such as racing, withhold hay for 8 hours prior to a competition and give hard feed – 1.3–1.8 kg (3–4 lb) for a 450 kg (1,000 lb) horse – 2 to 3 hours before he does his fast work. This eliminates the bulkiness of a full belly of hay, which would slow the horse down, but provides the fuel necessary for anaerobic work. For showjumping, you would do almost the same but withhold a half to three-quarters of the hay.

For the horse who is going to do a full day's work, such as endurance work, give the normal hay ration (not alfalfa or haylage, which has too high a nutrient value to be fed at this time) the night before and throughout the day. Munching on grass or hay helps maintain the fuel stores. Withhold hard feed for 8 hours prior to the competition, and do not feed any during the event as this will divert some of the blood supply away from the muscles where it is most needed. For the cross-country horse, withhold both hay and hard feed for 4 hours prior to the competition and do not allow eating during the competition.

There should always be regular availability of fluids, and electrolytes should be used during travelling and at the competition, but only then. Electrolytes contain the minerals that the horse needs for normal body function. These get depleted by prolonged sweating and dehydration. Electrolytes can be added to water, which can be drunk straight after exercise, with added glucose to make it palatable.

TRAVELLING TO A COMPETITION

When you arrive at a competition, you want your horse to be in prime condition after the weeks of optimum feeding and training. Most horses travel well as long as they have had a pleasant introduction to travelling and are allowed to face at least partially backwards, rather than forwards. Partitions should come down no lower than the top of the horse's legs so that they can spread their legs to help their balance if required. The horse should wear travel boots or an equivalent protection on the legs that cover the area around the feet, the knees, and the back of the hock. Tail bandages are inadvisable because they can rub the sensitive skin under the tail or the bandage can slip and tighten. A simple tail guard is effective and safe. Before travelling, reduce hard feed by 25 per cent in the previous 12 hours. During a journey, good ventilation and regular checking of the horse is vital. Offer water regularly and small quantities of hay, but no hard feed. On long journeys, give the horse a maximum of 50 per cent of the usual quantities of hard feed. This is because the digestive process may be adversely affected by travelling.

CHAPTER NINE

PHYSICAL PREPARATION OF THE RIDER

Although riding does not require great strength, it does require good physical control and a certain amount of stamina. Riders at all levels will benefit from a regular programme of exercises away from the horse.

The specially designed exercises in this chapter relate directly to your position and effectiveness. Your aim is to be able to use each arm and leg independently, and to be equally efficient riding on either rein. You will find that by improving your posture, balance, suppleness, strength, stamina, and co-ordination, your riding ability will advance immeasurably. Working on your general fitness with aerobic exercise and maintaining a healthy lifestyle will also give you the energy to cope with the demands of riding.

FITNESS FOR RIDING

Being effective in the saddle requires physical fitness. You need good posture, balance, strength, and stamina to be secure in the saddle; suppleness to move in harmony with the horse; and co-ordination so that you can give effective aids.

The challenge is not just in achieving a good position, but also in being able to maintain this position for long periods of time. By doing a few exercises each week, you can greatly improve your fitness and, in turn, your riding ability.

PHYSICAL FITNESS

If you find it difficult to maintain a good position in the saddle, you may be prone to bad habits, such as tensing your legs and holding on with your hands. Even if you are able to practise your riding on a daily basis, you will still benefit from a programme of off-the-horse exercises aimed at strengthening the specific muscles that you use for riding. Exercise will not only improve your riding ability, but it will also make your riding safer because you will be more secure in the saddle.

IMPROVING YOUR SKILLS It is not easy to make improvements to your position when you are on the move in trot or canter. You can progress quickly, however, by doing a combination of regular riding and a series of exercises off the horse.

EXERCISING SAFELY

Before starting an exercise programme, minimize the risks by following a few rules: have a health check; always warm up and cool down; work within your capabilities; and always stop if you are in pain. Exercise little and often and vary your training activities so that you avoid continually putting stress on the same parts of your body. Always seek the advice of a coach to ensure that your work is safe and effective.

ASSESSING YOUR FITNESS

These exercises will help you assess your current level of physical fitness for riding. When you are in the saddle, you need to use both arms, both legs, and both sides of your body equally. You may find the exercises in this assessment difficult at first,

Posture Balance Suppleness
Co-
Strength ordination

but once you have recognized your weaker areas, you can greatly improve your ability by following a few specially designed exercises. Working at your core fitness (see pp.350–51) will also have a beneficial effect on your riding.

POSTURE
Can you easily stand with your heels, buttocks, shoulders, and the backs of your hands in contact with a wall? Your hips, shoulders, and hands should be evenly placed.

SUPPLENESS
Can you grasp your hands behind your back equally well with either arm going over your shoulders?

BALANCE
Can you easily balance on either leg, with the sole of your foot on the inside of the opposite thigh and your arms stretched upwards?

STRENGTH
Can you walk 6.4 km (4 miles) in 60 minutes, followed by five press-ups (leaving your knees on the floor) in 20 seconds, without strain?

CO-ORDINATION
Can you use both arms and hands almost equally well in simple co-ordination exercises? Try drawing an object, such as a star, with your right hand, and then repeat with your left hand and compare the results.

DEVELOPING GOOD POSTURE

Your form, or shape, in the saddle directly affects your riding ability. In all riding activities, the shape of your back should remain the same. A neutral alignment of the spine allows the joints to move freely and the muscles, which work the joints, to be in an efficient position to contract and relax. The exercises below and on pp. 338–39 will help you achieve a good posture and will develop the muscles around your spine so that you are able to maintain an effective position.

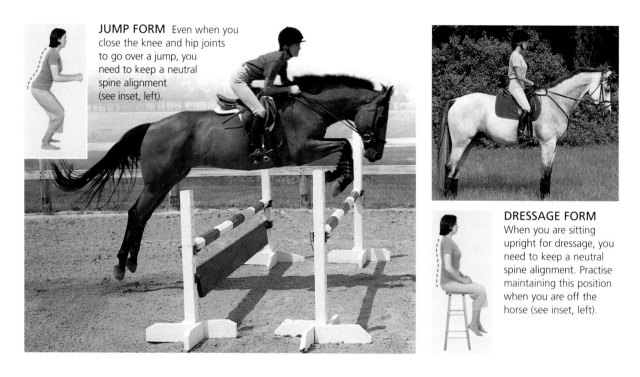

JUMP FORM Even when you close the knee and hip joints to go over a jump, you need to keep a neutral spine alignment (see inset, left).

DRESSAGE FORM When you are sitting upright for dressage, you need to keep a neutral spine alignment. Practise maintaining this position when you are off the horse (see inset, left).

SPINAL ALIGNMENT

Whether riding or exercising, the aim is to have your pelvis and spine in a neutral position. Lie on the floor with your knees bent. Rotate your pelvis so that the small of your back is touching the ground. Then rotate your pelvis the other way, arching your back. The neutral position is mid-way between these two extremes: there should be a small arch under the small of your back. Once you have achieved this, draw in your lower stomach as though you were pulling it towards your spine. Hold this for 10 seconds and repeat ten times. This alignment will give your lower back the required support for riding and daily life.

TUCKED UNDER   **ARCHED**   **ALIGNED**

SHOULDER OPENER This exercise (see left) releases tightness around the chest and allows the shoulders to come back. Stand in a doorway. Place both your forearms on the door frame with your elbows at shoulder level and your wrists in line with your elbows. Lean forwards gently. Hold for 5 seconds, rest, and repeat twice. Gradually build up to holding for up to 60 seconds.

Place your hands with palms facing upwards

Lie on the towel so that it lifts your spine

THORACIC STRETCH This exercise (see above) is particularly helpful if you have a stiff back. It helps correct the common riding fault of rounding the back and pushing the chin forwards. Lie down and place a rolled towel under the middle of your back. When comfortable, place your arms on the floor above your head. Hold this position for 30 seconds to 1 minute at a time. This is a passive stretch, so just allow it to happen. Then move the towel up a little and repeat. You can move it up another two levels towards your shoulders. Stop the exercise if you feel any discomfort.

Lumbar stretch: start position

Keep your shoulder blades and chin down

LUMBAR STRETCH This stretch loosens the lower part of your back as well as your lower abdomen. Lie face-down on the floor and place your hands under your shoulders, facing forwards (see inset, above right). Lift your chest and shoulders up, leaving your pelvis on the floor. This will stretch your lumbar vertebrae. Be careful not to push too hard: there is no need to straighten your arms.

Feel the stretch in your lower back

Support your weight on your arms

THE CLAM This exercise helps build strength around your buttocks, as well as your lower abdominals, which help maintain posture and prevent injury. Lie on your side with your lower arm supporting your head. Do not let your pelvis roll back – imagine there is a wall behind you. Bend your knees so that your thighs are at 90 degrees to your body and your lower legs are at 90 degrees to your thighs (see inset, right). Gently lift the top knee – keep your toes touching each other. Hold the position, then lower and repeat ten times on both sides. Rest and repeat a further ten times.

Start position

Keep your upper arm in front of you with the palm flat on the floor

Draw the stomach muscles in below the navel and pull them towards your spine

Rotate your knee upwards and hold

Keep your toes in contact with each other

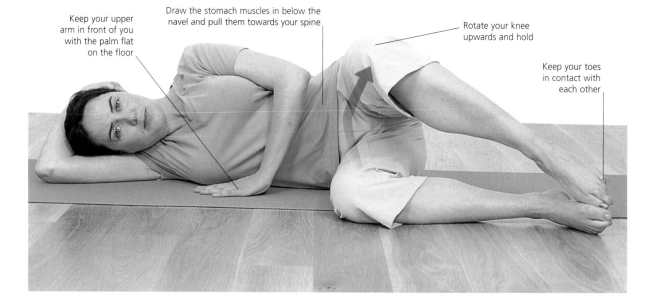

SIDEWAYS LEG LIFT This exercise works on the buttocks and lower abdominals. Start in the same start position as the clam (see inset, above right). Keep your legs bent and your pelvis aligned. Draw in the lower abdominals then straighten the top leg and lift it. You will feel this in your buttocks and on the inside of your leg. Keep the toes flexed towards your leg – this simulates the ankle position used in riding and will stretch the calf muscles. Repeat on other side.

Keep your leg straight. Hold the position for 5 seconds and then lower and repeat

Make sure your toes stay flexed

KNEE FALL-OUT This tones the muscles that support the spine. Lie with your knees bent and your feet flat on the floor (see inset, below). Keeping your spine neutrally aligned and your abdominal muscles pulled in, let one knee at a time fall out to the side. Keep the other leg and your body still – imagine there is a glass of water you are trying not to spill balanced on each side of your pelvis .

Start position

Gently lift your foot and return it to the ground

Place your hands on your pelvis

FOOT LIFT This exercise tones the abdominal muscles. Lie on your back with your knees bent and find your neutral spine alignment. Gently lift one foot up off the floor, bringing the knee back a little. Hold for 5 seconds and then lower. Repeat ten times with each leg. The main aim is to do this exercise without losing your neutral spine alignment: imagine an egg under the arch of your back, which should neither roll out nor break.

Straighten your leg and keep it at 45 degrees to the floor

STRAIGHT LEG LIFT This exercise strengthens the abdominal and thigh muscles to help you maintain a good posture in the saddle. Lie on your back with your legs bent and find your neutral spine alignment. Keeping the pelvis still, gently lift one foot up and then straighten the leg in the air. Bend your knee again before taking the foot back down. Repeat 10 times with each leg.

IMPROVING YOUR BALANCE

Being secure in the saddle is fundamental to riding, and for this you need to have a good sense of balance. Without it, you will find it difficult to move in harmony with the horse and to give him precisely controlled signals. The following exercises finely tune your body awareness so that you start to achieve good balance automatically. Before using equipment such as a balance board or a balance ball, try the exercises while standing on the floor or sitting on a stool

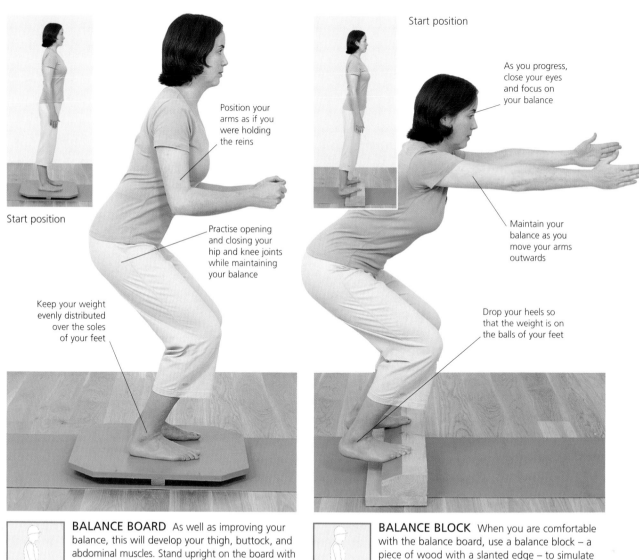

Start position

Position your arms as if you were holding the reins

Practise opening and closing your hip and knee joints while maintaining your balance

Keep your weight evenly distributed over the soles of your feet

Start position

As you progress, close your eyes and focus on your balance

Maintain your balance as you move your arms outwards

Drop your heels so that the weight is on the balls of your feet

BALANCE BOARD As well as improving your balance, this will develop your thigh, buttock, and abdominal muscles. Stand upright on the board with your feet apart (see inset, above). Practise lowering and raising your seat without tilting the board. Then, rotate the board so that the support runs from front to back and practise keeping an equal weight on each leg, just as you would in the saddle.

BALANCE BLOCK When you are comfortable with the balance board, use a balance block – a piece of wood with a slanted edge – to simulate the position of your feet in the stirrups. Stand upright (see inset, above), lower your seat, and stretch your arms out. Keep your posture and balance as you open and close your knee and hip joints. This will also strengthen your calf muscles.

BALANCE BALL The balance ball helps you develop body awareness and allows you to practise giving leg and rein aids without changing your balance. This exercise also strengthens the buttocks. Sitting on the ball, lift one foot. Hold for 5 seconds, then rest. Repeat 10 times with each leg. Try simulating a riding balance by taking both feet off the ground (see inset, below right).

Cross-country balance in action.

Stretch out your arms

Maintain a neutral spine alignment

Draw in the area below your navel towards your spine

Use a ball appropriate for your height

Riding position

Lift foot approximately 10 cm (4 in)

BECOMING MORE SUPPLE

Being flexible enough to move in harmony with the horse's back is important if your riding is to progress. Some riders do suppling exercises on horseback, but this can be dangerous because you do not have control over the horse. Carrying out gentle, progressive exercises on the floor will ensure that you do not overstretch yourself. Start off by holding a position for 5 to 10 seconds; as you become more supple, you will be able to maintain positions for longer.

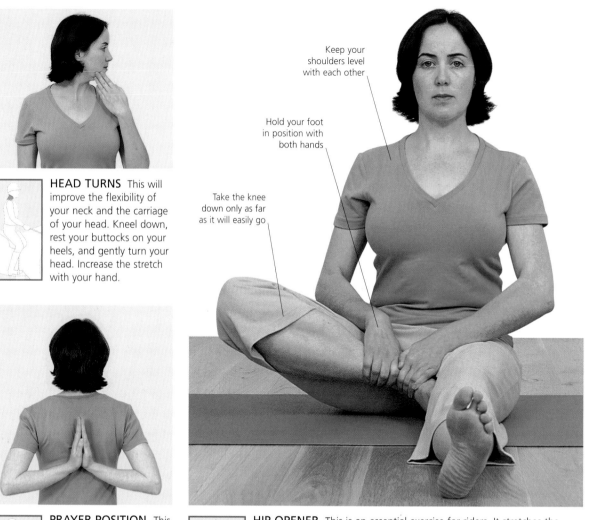

Keep your shoulders level with each other

Hold your foot in position with both hands

Take the knee down only as far as it will easily go

HEAD TURNS This will improve the flexibility of your neck and the carriage of your head. Kneel down, rest your buttocks on your heels, and gently turn your head. Increase the stretch with your hand.

PRAYER POSITION This exercise improves the joint mobility necessary for an allowing rein contact. Gently take one arm up behind the back and then the other, and touch your palms in a prayer position.

HIP OPENER This is an essential exercise for riders. It stretches the adductor muscles (on the inside of the thighs) and improves the flexibility of the hip joints, which is particularly important for rising trot. Sitting upright, straighten one leg out in front of you and place the other foot on the inside of the outstretched thigh. Gently push your knee down towards the floor without losing your neutral spine alignment. Hold this position and then repeat with the other leg. Try to get your knee a little closer to the floor each time you do this exercise.

SPINAL TWIST A stiff, tight lower back makes it difficult for a rider to go with the movement of the horse. This exercise helps to stretch the lower back. Start on your back with your knees bent and cross one knee over the other (see inset, right). Then, very gently allow the knees to fall to one side. If this is too difficult, start without crossing the legs and just let both knees gently roll to one side at a time. It is important to do both these exercises gently and slowly.

Start position

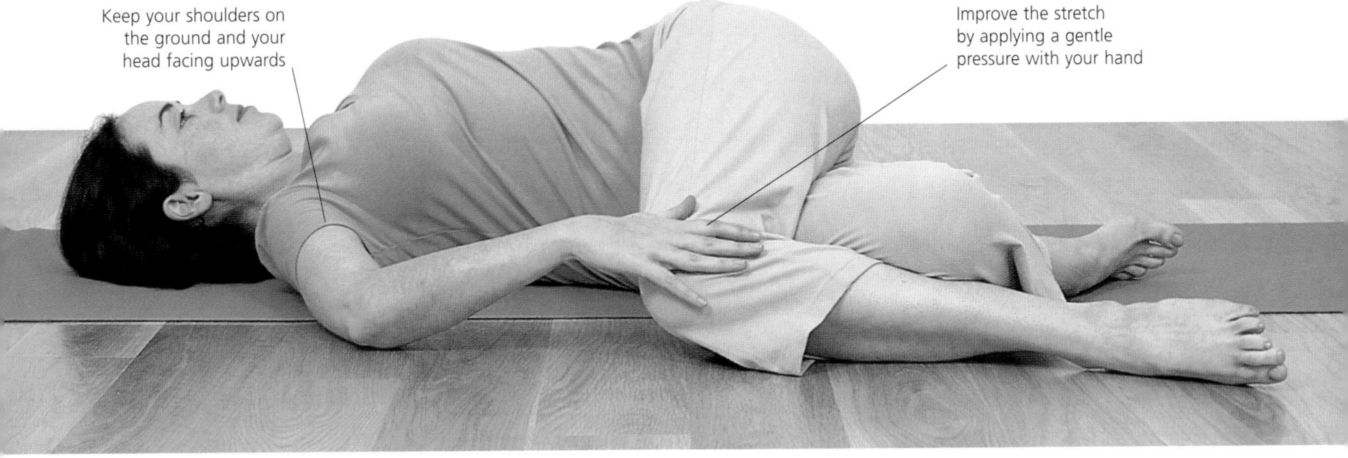

Keep your shoulders on the ground and your head facing upwards

Improve the stretch by applying a gentle pressure with your hand

DOUBLE KNEE FLEXION This exercise stretches the lower back muscles needed for moving with the horse, particularly in sitting trot. Lie on the floor and use your arms to gently pull both knees in towards your chest. Avoid rounding your back. Try this exercise with one knee at a time, keeping the other leg straight (see inset, right).

Pull gently so the base of your spine stays on the floor

Single-knee flexion

Leave your shoulders on the ground

Keep your feet relaxed – do not stretch your toes

HAMSTRING STRETCH

Flexible hamstrings will let you sit comfortably astride the horse and give leg aids easily. Lying on your back, bend one knee. Take hold of your thigh with your hands (see inset, right), or with a belt if you cannot reach that far. Gradually straighten your bent leg towards the ceiling. The base of your spine must stay on the floor and your spine should be kept aligned, so do not pull too hard.

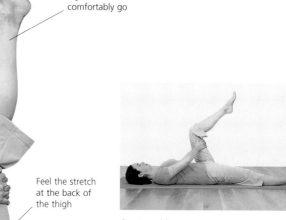

Gradually lift your leg as far as it will comfortably go

Start position

Support your leg with your arm

Feel the stretch at the back of the thigh

LEG STRETCH

This exercise strengthens your hamstrings and calves to help refine your leg and weight aids. When you can do the hamstring stretch, lie near a wall and hook a belt around one foot. Straighten your leg (see inset, right) and rest your arm on the ground. Allow your foot to fall gently against the wall.

Let your leg stretch out and rest against the wall

Start position

Start position

FIGURE-FOUR STRETCH This exercise stretches the buttocks and opens the hips. Lie on your back with your knees bent and rest one ankle on the opposite knee (see inset picture, far left). Take hold of the thigh under this knee, so that it is at 90 degrees to the body. Very gently draw your thigh in towards your chest. Repeat with the other leg.

Keep the base of your spine on the floor

Look straight ahead and keep your head up

Keep your shoulders level with each other

SIDEWAYS LUNGE This increases the flexibility of your inner thighs. Stand with your feet a stride apart (see inset, below). Move your right buttock down over your right foot until it touches the heel. Place your hands on your weight-bearing leg for balance. Keep your body and your feet facing forwards and your posture upright. Repeat the exercise with your other leg.

Feel the stretch in your inside thigh muscle

Start position

IMPROVING STRENGTH

You do not need great strength for riding but you do need to tone your muscles so that you are secure in the saddle and are able to give effective aids. You also need to have stamina so that you can sit for extended periods on horseback. The exercises for your arms will help you maintain a consistent rein contact, and the exercises for your legs will help you stay secure in the saddle. They will also help you develop your kick for emergency forwards (see p.27).

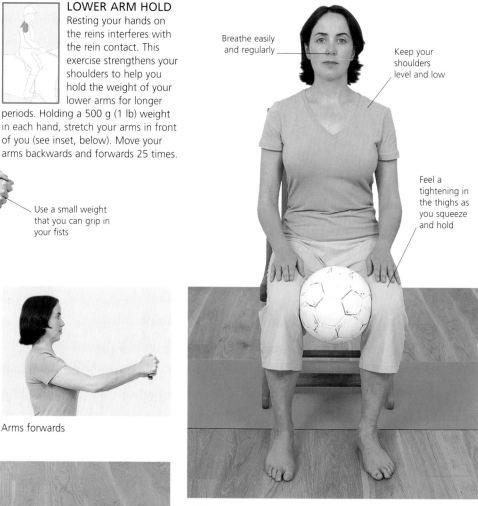

LOWER ARM HOLD
Resting your hands on the reins interferes with the rein contact. This exercise strengthens your shoulders to help you hold the weight of your lower arms for longer periods. Holding a 500 g (1 lb) weight in each hand, stretch your arms in front of you (see inset, below). Move your arms backwards and forwards 25 times.

Use a small weight that you can grip in your fists

Arms forwards

Breathe easily and regularly

Keep your shoulders level and low

Feel a tightening in the thighs as you squeeze and hold

BALL SQUEEZE Just by sitting on a horse, you place a strain on the inside thighs, so practising the ball squeeze is extremely valuable. Squeeze a standard football by approximately ½ cm (¼ in), but not too hard because you need to maintain your neutral spine alignment. Hold for 5 seconds and repeat up to 25 times. As a progression, use a bigger ball.

LEG KICK This exercise simulates using the leg against the horse's sides. It helps improve your leg aids by building up strength in the lower leg and in the buttocks, as well as helping your co-ordination. Hook a ring of elastic cord onto a stationary object and put the other end of the loop around your ankle. Simulate a kicking action from the knee joint, pulling against the tension of the elastic cord. Repeat this 25 times on each leg. To strengthen your inner thighs, try this exercise standing sideways, and this time moving your leg in towards the supporting leg (see inset, right).

Stamina is required for cross-country riding.

Sideways pull

Rest your hands on your hips

Let your weight rest on your right leg

Bring your lower leg inwards, just as you would use a leg aid

IMPROVING CO-ORDINATION

A good rider can use both legs equally well, and is able to ride effectively on both the left and the right rein. However, many riders are one-sided and, in turn, make their horses one-sided. Doing simple exercises that concentrate on your weaker side will help to correct this. You can also do specific co-ordination exercises, with your coach or a friend simulating the movement of the horse's head and neck, to improve your rein contact and rein aids.

BALL BOUNCING This exercise will quickly develop your less dominant arm and hand. Bounce a ball with your stronger arm, and then repeat with your weaker arm (see inset, below) until there is little difference between either side. Setting yourself goals to do a specific number of bounces without faltering will make your progress more obvious.

Repeat the exercise using the weaker arm.

FINGER CO-ORDINATION

This exercise will help with both holding the reins and giving rein aids. When you hold the reins you need to make a 90 degree angle between your palm and the first joint of the fingers. You then bring the rest of each finger around naturally, as though you were holding something fragile in the hand. This exercise has the same starting point but is more difficult because you flex each finger by itself until it is parallel with the palm, then bring it back to the other fingers. This should be done without moving the wrist. It is not easy, but it is the sort of control you need for holding the reins, particularly as you start using two reins, as with a double bridle.

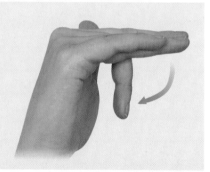

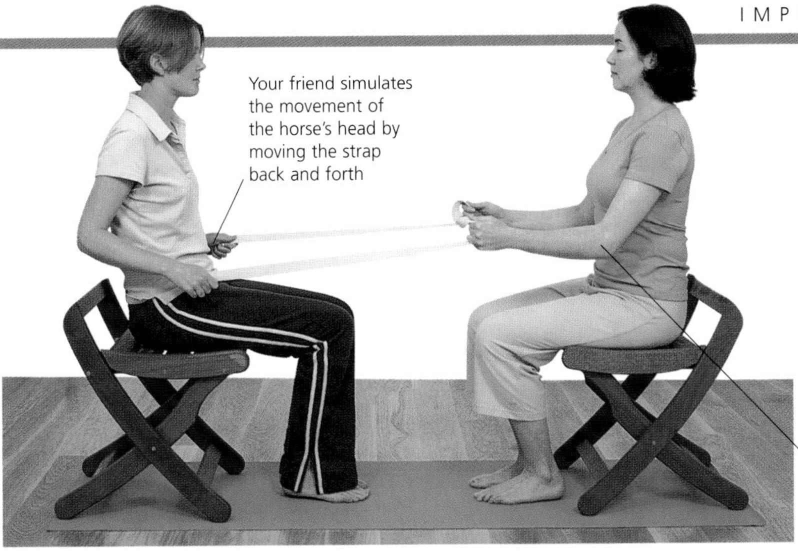

Your friend simulates the movement of the horse's head by moving the strap back and forth

REIN CONTACT This exercise will help you develop an allowing rein contact – one that is consistent, but not restricting. Ask a friend to hold a set of reins (or a material strap) as if they were attached to a horse, moving them backwards and forwards. Close your eyes and let your hands go with the movement of the reins, keeping the same weight on either side and ensuring you carry the weight of your lower arms.

Let your arms go with the movement of the reins

KICKING BACKWARDS

Most people can easily use their right leg by itself but not their left leg, and this exercise is designed to even out the imbalance. Stand diagonally in front of a mirror and, with your weaker leg, kick a ball backwards to the opposite wall. This simulates the movement used when giving a leg aid with your heel. The aim is to keep repeating the exercise as the ball bounces back to you. Try to do a set of 10 kicks before resting.

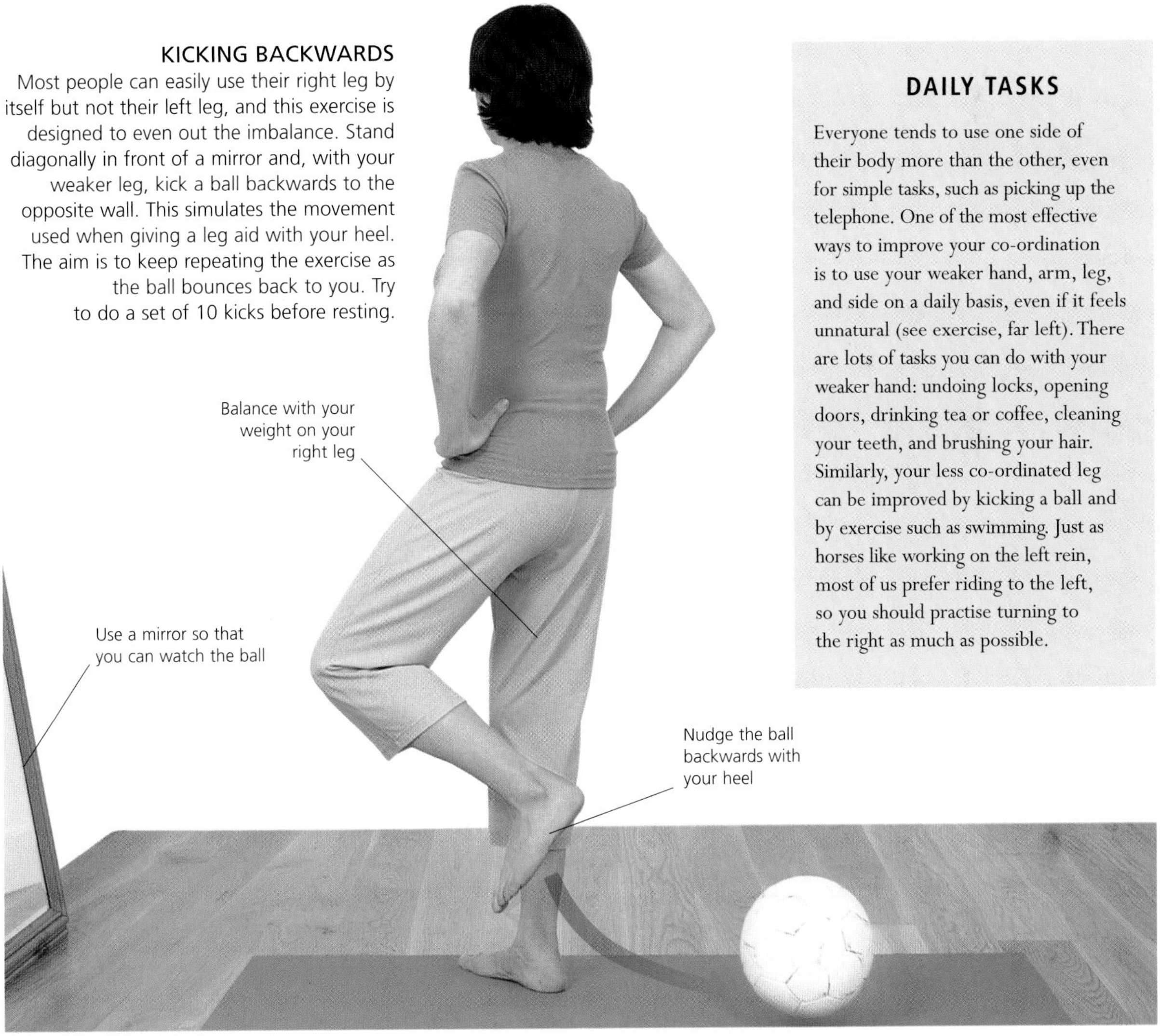

Balance with your weight on your right leg

Use a mirror so that you can watch the ball

Nudge the ball backwards with your heel

DAILY TASKS

Everyone tends to use one side of their body more than the other, even for simple tasks, such as picking up the telephone. One of the most effective ways to improve your co-ordination is to use your weaker hand, arm, leg, and side on a daily basis, even if it feels unnatural (see exercise, far left). There are lots of tasks you can do with your weaker hand: undoing locks, opening doors, drinking tea or coffee, cleaning your teeth, and brushing your hair. Similarly, your less co-ordinated leg can be improved by kicking a ball and by exercise such as swimming. Just as horses like working on the left rein, most of us prefer riding to the left, so you should practise turning to the right as much as possible.

DEVELOPING CORE FITNESS

As well as doing exercises specific to riding, it is important to maintain your general fitness and stamina so that you can maintain an effective position in the saddle over extended periods. For this you need to do regular aerobic exercise to develop your heart and lungs. Complement this aerobic programme with a range of exercises that develop both sides of your body. In addition, making improvements to your diet and your general lifestyle will give you the energy you need to keep up your training and to do all the physical tasks involved in horse management.

AEROBIC FITNESS

All riders will benefit from maintaining a good level of core fitness. Aerobic exercise improves the efficiency of the heart and lungs and increases the amount of oxygen in your blood, which helps your muscles work efficiently. As you get fitter, your pulse becomes slower because your heart is able to pump more blood around your body with each beat, and your lungs are better able to exchange oxygen for waste products in the blood. This gives you increased energy and stamina.

Aerobic exercise is low-intensity and rhythmic, and works major groups of muscles. Activities such as walking, cycling, swimming, rowing, and rollerblading are good examples. The key to effective aerobic exercise is to keep your pulse rate at an optimum level (see chart, below). If you walk, for example, you may need to walk at a faster pace than usual to reach this level, but at the same time you must not let your heart rate increase too much (by sprinting, for example). If you work your body intensively, you will quickly tire and are likely to do less exercise overall. So, work your body like you

AEROBIC EXERCISE
Jogging on a trampoline for 20 minutes at a time is an ideal exercise because it will increase your heart rate and tone your leg muscles without jarring your knee joints.

TARGET HEART RATE

Aerobic training involves increasing your heart rate to 70–85 per cent of its maximum. Burning fat requires an increase to only 50–60 per cent of your maximum heart rate. These levels depend on your age, so use the chart (right) to find your target level. For example, if you are aged 25, your aerobic training zone is 134–162 beats per minute. To measure your heart rate in beats per minute, find your pulse on your wrist or neck, count the beats for 15 seconds, then multiply this by four. Do this as you are exercising, since your heart rate will fall as soon as you stop. Alternatively, you can use an electronic heart monitor, which will give you a constant reading. Adjust the intensity of your exercise so that you stay in your target zone for the entire session.

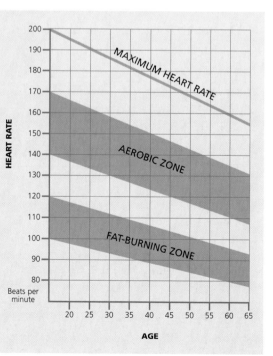

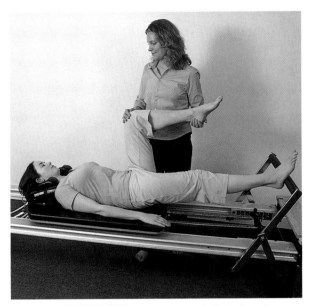

MUSCULAR EXERCISE Many gyms and physiotherapists are equipped with pilates machines. These are designed to strengthen core muscles, and they are excellent for improving posture, flexibility, and body awareness.

condition your horses – with periods of aerobic work followed by periods of rest – and always try to finish before you begin to feel very tired. Over-exertion will not benefit your heart or lungs, and can actually be dangerous to your health.

To get the benefit, you need to keep your heart rate in its aerobic zone for at least 20 minutes at a time. Aim for sessions of around 40 minutes, three or more times a week. Less intensive exercise is required for burning fat (see chart, left) and long walks are ideal.

A BALANCED EXERCISE PROGRAMME

As well as doing low-intensity aerobic exercise to develop your heart and lungs, improve your riding by increasing your strength and muscle tone. Most of the exercises that are good for your aerobic training will also help your general muscular tone and strength for riding. Any exercise you do should have low impact to prevent wear on the joints and should use both sides of the body and all the limbs as equally as possible – racquet sports, for example, mainly use one side of the body, so are not helpful for riders. Examples of suitable activities include walking, swimming, aqua aerobics, cycling, skiing, dance, basketball, and martial arts. Performing a variety of activities ensures that you use a wide variety of muscle groups, so try to alternate between any three of these sports. Yoga, pilates, and the Alexander Technique are all excellent for developing strength, posture, balance, and suppleness

without being stressful on your joints. Pilates, for example, helps build core stability of the pelvis and spine using techniques such as pelvic floor exercises. Choose one of these activities to complement your fitness training.

It is really important that you enjoy the sports you do. If you are not having fun, change the sport or the people you do it with. Whatever exercise you do, always take advice from a qualified instructor who understands equestrian sport and can ensure you are working at the right level.

STAYING HEALTHY

Exercise is not the only thing you need to pay attention to in your physical preparation. In competitive riding, people are becoming increasingly careful about what they eat and drink. There is an obvious practical reason for this: a horse will last longer and be able to perform better if he carries less weight. On the other hand, horses differ in their shape and size, and everyone should find a horse strong enough to carry their weight. However, a healthy diet has other benefits: it means that your energy levels will be better and that you are less prone to illness. Being exhausted or unwell will obviously be a set-back to your training. Leading a generally healthy lifestyle by eating well, getting enough sleep, being careful about your alcohol consumption, and not smoking, all contribute to a healthy mind and body. The aim is a balance that will allow you to achieve more and enjoy life to the full.

GETTING SPECIALIST HELP

There are many types of specialist who can help you plan an exercise regime. It is important that you go to someone who is experienced and qualified and who assesses you properly before you start a programme. The ideal specialist is someone who understands the demands of equestrian sport but who also has wide ranging expertise with a good overview of developments in suitable therapies and treatments.

There is an increasing number of personal trainers who are qualified in sports physiology and can give valuable help, but who are not qualified to treat injuries. A physiotherapist will not only be able to treat you if you have an existing injury, but is also able to assess your state of fitness and advise about suitable exercises to develop core stability of the spine and fitness of the muscular system. Joint injuries and displacements are also treated by chiropractors and osteopaths. Both involve manipulative treatment and it would be advisable to get a medical opinion before deciding on any course of action. Of course, once you have embarked on a fitness programme, you will become stronger and more flexible. You will be less likely to suffer injuries and will have less need for specialist help.

CHAPTER TEN

MENTAL PREPARATION OF THE RIDER

In equestrian sports, where the horse does most of the physical work, it is mental attitude that defines a rider's limits. All riders – from novice to elite – can greatly improve their performance by altering their attitude of mind.

In this chapter, you will learn practical ways to prepare for competitions, using techniques such as visualization and controlled breathing. You will also learn to concentrate on what motivates you, and to identify your long-term aims, so that you can set yourself goals and organize your time accordingly. Success comes from being positive, aspirational, and open-minded, but it also means keeping things in perspective, getting on with people, and, above all, enjoying yourself.

WHY MENTAL PREPARATION?

If you want to be a successful rider, improving your mental abilities is just as important as developing your physical abilities. Mental preparation will help you avoid being disorganized in your training or performing below your expectations in competitions. It will also enable you to harness a greater proportion of your brain power. There are six key components in mental preparation, and these should be an integral part of any competitor's training.

BENEFITING FROM MENTAL PREPARATION

There is often great resistance towards training the mind in the riding world. Many riders are reluctant to use mental preparation techniques because there is a belief that everyone has inherent mental strengths and weaknesses that cannot be changed. This is obviously untrue. Simply thinking positively or breathing more efficiently can have an immediate effect on your performance. Elite athletes from every sport continually emphasize the part that mental preparation plays in their success: the need to be sufficiently disciplined, motivated, committed, calm, and organized is crucial. Increasingly, coaches are building time into training schedules for mental preparation, and even hiring sports psychologists to work with their riders. Even for the novice rider, mental preparation is the easiest route to improvement on a daily basis.

MAKING TIME

Lack of time is another common reason given for not preparing mentally. Horse riding and management certainly is hugely time consuming but, as long as you are prepared to believe that mental preparation skills can be effective, you and your coach will make the time to practise them. For example, time spent doing mundane stable-management tasks can be used productively to practise concentration techniques, thinking positively, visualization, and other exercises. While you are out hacking, there is plenty of peaceful time to analyse your progress and sort out your training priorities.

LEARNING THE TECHNIQUES

In the past, coaches would shout such things as "Relax!" to their riders during a competition in an effort to improve their performances. In reality, such commands do not have the desired effect, particularly if the rider does not know how to respond effectively to them.

For example, being able to calm yourself down in a competition is not easy without having studied practical ways of doing so beforehand. In training, you need to practise relaxation techniques (see pp. 358–59) in the same way that you would practise riding exercises. Then you can make these techniques work for you in competitions.

ASSESSING YOURSELF

It is important to realize that it is possible to change your assumptions, as well as the way you think, and the way you react to particular situations: although our genes may predispose us to a certain pattern of behaviour, we need to build on that potential. The first step to making changes is to assess what are your main strengths and weaknesses. Read through the following list of questions. If your answer is "yes" to any of them, then you will benefit by improving your mental preparation – both in your riding and in your life.

HAVE YOU EVER...

- Lost your way in a dressage test or showjumping round?
- Become very nervous before a competition?
- Become angry after making a mistake?
- Made the same mistake repeatedly?
- Lacked confidence in your ability?

- Focused on all the negative aspects of your riding?
- Found it difficult to get motivated?
- Lost concentration?
- Failed to prepare for a competition sufficiently?
- Found it difficult to be disciplined in your weekly training?
- Performed well in training, but badly at the competition?

Mental preparation can be a valuable part of the armoury of every rider. Of course, it cannot be a substitute for technical ability: it must complement, not replace, your physical training.

THE AIMS OF MENTAL PREPARATION

Mental training can be divided up into six different areas, each of which you can concentrate on in turn. A truly accomplished rider will be proficient in all these areas, but it will take time to reach this level of accomplishment – just as it takes dedicated training to improve your riding skills.

• **Be Steady** – Being methodical and consistent is essential if you are to maintain a good relationship with your horse. You also need discipline to get up early each morning and stick to your timetable. Your aim is to work hard, and to be calm but persistent.

• **Be Simple** – A good rider will be driven by the need for logic and efficiency. Analysing complicated tasks and breaking them down into smaller parts will make them more manageable, as will defining vague tasks with more precision. Test out ideas and learn from your mistakes.

• **Be Positive** – You need to be constructive and optimistic. Realize the importance of working with others. Believe in yourself and focus on your abilities, not your shortcomings. Work from your strengths and always think forwards to your next goal.

• **Be Flexible** – To be the best, you have to be able to be creative and open-minded in your search for improvements. You need to look for more efficient progressions that will allow you to achieve more, and you must be prepared to think laterally. Always aim to find new, better ways of doing things.

• **Be Prepared** – The ability to plan ahead realistically is vital. From the start, you need to practise making decisions and taking control, so that eventually you are more ready and able to seize opportunities and be independent of your coach. In this way, you will always make the best of any opportunities you encounter

• **Be Human** – To cope with the ups and downs of competition life, you need to have respect for yourself and others. Developing your own individuality is an integral part of improving your performance. Accept life's diversity and unpredictability, and above all, enjoy yourself.

THE POWER OF THE MIND

The brain has enormous potential, which can be realized in a number of unique and unpredictable ways. It is an electrochemical powerhouse made up of billions of nerve cells, each capable of making and receiving several thousand contacts – a match-head's worth of your brain contains about eight billion connections. Once you understand how powerful your mind is, you will see why mental training can change your riding – and your life.

All of our actions are controlled by the brain, but most of the time we are not conscious of making any decisions. The unconscious mind is where most of your thoughts feelings, attitudes, and behaviours originate. An iceberg is a good analogy: the conscious mind is just the tip, with a vast amount of unconscious activity going on beneath the surface. However, you can consciously train your brain to be used in a more effective way.

You can exercise your brain just like any other part of your body. For instance, you can practise thinking rationally by solving problems that require rational thought – doing a crossword puzzle, for example, or thinking about how best to organize your finances. Such techniques will create and strengthen the connections between the cells used for this type of thought. This is true however old you are: ageing does not mean inevitable decline – although if you stop exercising your brain, it can lose much of its potential.

You can also change unconscious attitudes in the same way. For example, by actively trying to think positively on a daily basis, you will become predisposed to being positive in any situation. As a result, you will be able to achieve more, whereas a negative attitude will result in negative responses.

HORSE RIDING KEEPS YOU MENTALLY AND PHYSICALLY ACTIVE

GETTING STARTED

At the start of a mental preparation programme, there are two key areas to focus on. Firstly, you need to keep reassessing what motivates you, because your priorities and goals will change over time. Secondly, you must study the experiences of successful riders – this will give you ideas and inspiration. Use role-playing techniques to practise focusing on the mental attributes that these people possess. If you are able to think like a successful rider, you can become one.

MOTIVATING YOURSELF

Although we all recognize that it takes actions to achieve goals, it is difficult to remain consistently motivated. Unfortunately, few people are entirely self-motivated, but it would make an incredible difference if this were not so. As Kurt Hahn, the founding father of the outward bound schools, says, "We are all better than we know – if only we can be brought to realize this, we may never settle for anything less."

Motivation is all about individual needs and personalities. Different people are motivated by different things. For some, having a cause is enough; others are inspired by just watching top riders; and others do something simply because someone else said they could not. For many, it is all about the challenge of pushing themselves to the limit. Whatever it is that motivates you, the thing that underpins it all should be the possibility of achieving a personal best. The driving force behind the successful athlete's actions is not to be the best, but to be the best they can be.

STUDYING SUCCESS

Some riders take pride in reaching a certain level of riding expertise without any lessons, but this means that their knowledge is entirely limited to their own experience.

Those riders who actively seek out the champions and take every opportunity to study their methods will greatly accelerate their progress because they can use the sum of other people's experience. There is great value in studying champions at every level – not just those that have achieved

MASLOW'S HIERARCHY OF MOTIVES

In the 1950s, the American psychologist Abraham Maslow classified human motivation in a hierarchy ascending from basic biological needs to more complex psychological desires. The latter become motivators only after the more basic needs below them on the hierarchy have been satisfied. For example, when food and safety are difficult to ensure, the satisfaction of those needs will dominate a person's actions, with the result that learning or beauty will have little significance. On the other hand, if the lower needs are already satisfied, they will no longer be motivators.

There is a direct relationship between Maslow's hierarchy and the changing motives for your riding. Initially, horse riding will simply be a good sport – good for your health as well as fun to do, so long as you feel safe and enjoy being part of a riding group. As you become a better rider, you will increasingly be driven by your need to ride well and to understand all about riding. Then you may also start to think about doing things with a view to reaching the highest level in the future.

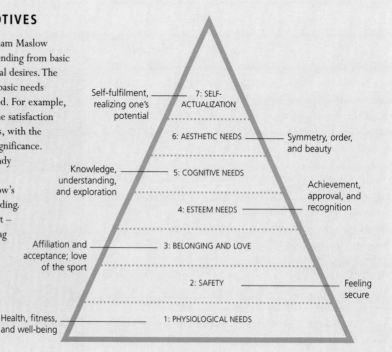

Self-fulfilment, realizing one's potential — 7: SELF-ACTUALIZATION

6: AESTHETIC NEEDS — Symmetry, order, and beauty

Knowledge, understanding, and exploration — 5: COGNITIVE NEEDS

4: ESTEEM NEEDS — Achievement, approval, and recognition

Affiliation and acceptance; love of the sport — 3: BELONGING AND LOVE

2: SAFETY — Feeling secure

Health, fitness, and well-being — 1: PHYSIOLOGICAL NEEDS

INSPIRATIONAL RIDERS By watching other riders, you can learn from both their successes and their mistakes. Go to shows and competitions. Try to watch the best and keep their image foremost in your mind – use them as your role models.

international status. Try to find role models who have similar characteristics and horses as you, and who ride at the same competitions as you do.

ROLE PLAYING AND MODELLING

We all play different roles in our work and daily lives, and in doing so we take on different qualities and characteristics. The way a person acts as a parent to his or her children, for example, is quite different from how they would behave in the company boardroom. You can harness this phenomenon for training purposes.

Role playing can be a very powerful tool in mental preparation, particularly in developing areas of weakness. Taking on a particular role can enable you to access a whole set of desirable qualities and attributes, whether you possess these in reality or not. Practise taking on different personas. You may wish to model yourself on someone you know well.

Recognizing that a friend has mastered a particular skill can help convince you that you too can develop the same attribute, given sufficient practice. Alternatively, you can invent your own characters. You can then bring a particular character to mind when you need to, for example, to think about how they would react to a particular situation. Eventually, their attributes can become a permanent feature of your own personality.

Choose a role model to suit the particular aspect of mental preparation you are focusing on (see p.355). At first, you will need to concentrate just on *doing* things – participating. This is where being steady and human comes in. Then you will look at doing things *well* – this is where being positive and simple count. Later, you will also be doing things with a view to the future – for this, you need to be flexible and prepared At any stage, role playing will help you to overcome areas of weakness:

• **Being Steady –** This is about being careful, disciplined, and persistent. The image of a banker works well as a role model. Alternatively, a competitor from a sport like long-distance running, rowing, or mountain climbing may be the right role model for you.

• **Being Simple –** This is about being rational and analytical. Imagining that you are a professor searching for answers and learning from mistakes, or a competitor from a precision sport like gymnastics, can help you to think like this.

• **Being Positive –** This is about having a constructive outlook on life. An army general is an ideal character to imagine here, because this role requires working together with other people in order to become stronger.

• **Being Flexible –** This is about being ready to adapt your ideas or approach in order to get the maximum result from the minimum effort. Imagine you are a wizard: finding a better idea can result in a magical performance.

• **Being Prepared –** This is about being able to deal with all eventualities and make effective decisions. A circus ringmaster could be your imagined character. The American golfer Tiger Woods is an inspiring role model.

• **Being Human –** This is about being able to empathize with others, as well as being able to keep problems in perspective. The image of a spirited and wise grandmother can help you with this attitude, or you may know someone like this personally. A famous role model, such as South Africa's Nelson Mandela, could also be effective.

BEING STEADY

Different riding activities have different physical and mental demands, and understanding what is required in each case will help you to take control and enhance your performance. Nerves and excitement may often ruin a potentially superb performance. Learning how to control your adrenaline levels with relaxation techniques, and training yourself to be able to concentrate on the task and to ignore distractions, can turn you into a winning competitor.

REDUCING YOUR AROUSAL LEVEL

Arousal is a term used by sports psychologists to describe levels of both physical and emotional alertness or activation in response to a particular situation. Strong emotions such as fear, anticipation, or anxiety cause the body to prepare either to run away or to face danger. The physical effects of this fight or flight mechanism are heightened adrenaline levels, pulse rate, and breathing.

Many riders think that the more aroused they are and the more adrenaline they have, the better their performance will be. However, while high arousal levels can increase determination, high adrenaline levels are actually counter-productive: they inhibit clear thinking, feel, and physical control. Even cross-country riding demands a cool head as over-excitement can lead to the taking of unnecessary risks. You can be over-aroused either because of worry about the competition or because you are excited. If worry is the cause, then progressive training and exposure to a competition environment will decrease your uncertainty and reduce the importance of the competition. It helps to try to slow everything down and deliberately smile and be proud of the fact that you have made it to the competition. If excitement is the cause, then use specific pre-competition routines to make everything normal, regular, and steady. Then, focus on the mechanics of your performance rather than what is going on around you. Surround yourself with a support team that is unemotional but dependable.

To be able to reduce arousal in competition, it is essential that you practise reducing excitement levels in training. Practise switching into a world that moves more slowly. You can create a bubble of calmness and security around you. There are two main strategies to relax: one is to use your

DEMANDS OF EACH DISCIPLINE

In any equestrian activity, there is an optimum level of arousal, with a depreciation in performance with either too much or too little arousal. This varies for each rider-and-horse combination and for each discipline (see diagram, right).

In dressage, for example, the rider needs to be well co-ordinated and in control of every movement. In this case, too much arousal can interfere. For showjumping, however, the rider needs to have a certain amount of physical energy to get the horse in gear. In cross country, where competitors brave formidable-looking obstacles at a fast pace, the optimum level is even higher.

One of the difficulties of riding is that sometimes a rider needs a different level of arousal from their horse. In showjumping against the clock, for example, the horse must be sufficiently calm to listen to the rider and jump athletically.

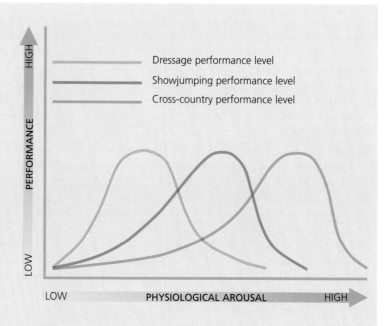

mind and imagination to relax your muscles, using meditation or role-playing techniques. The other way is to do the opposite: use your muscles to relax your mind. If you systematically tighten and relax all your main muscles you can induce physical relaxation which will be followed by mental relaxation. Focusing on your breathing will also immediately calm you down (see box, right) and lower your pulse.

INCREASING AROUSAL

When you become bored or lethargic, it is necessary to increase the level of arousal. If your horse also needs to be more energized then you should give a more vigorous warm-up than usual. Set yourself challenging performance goals, trying to produce a personal best in specific areas, and surround yourself with one or two people who you respect

" *WINNERS SUCCEED BY EFFORT NOT BY ACCIDENT* "

and who know your goals. They can have the task of cajoling and encouraging you to perform at your best and to help you feel a sense of anticipation and urgency. In addition, you can use positive trigger words such as "go" and "yes" and "do it" and "strong". Many people like to use personal stereos to listen to inspiring words or upbeat music.

IMPROVING CONCENTRATION

Lapses in concentration can undo all the good work that has gone into your training and preparation. It is easy to become distracted, both by external factors, such as words from spectators, or internal factors, such as thinking about receiving a prize as you ride into the ring when you should be thinking about the first exercise or fence.

Another typical internal distraction is thinking about hitting a fence or performing an inaccurate movement, and some riders concentrate on this to such an extent that they forget where they should be going next. This is particularly true during a showjumping round. In training, a rider needs to make it a habit always to think of the next step rather than to look backwards.

Both showjumping and dressage demand fairly short but continuous periods of concentration. The physical presence of the fences in showjumping tends to concentrate the mind very well. Dressage tests, on the other hand, do not have such mental props; and since a test is also two or three times

ABDOMINAL BREATHING

If you become stressed or agitated before a competition, practising abdominal breathing can help you feel calm. Put your hand in the centre of your abdomen below the bottom of your ribcage and breathe in. Your abdomen should expand and your hand should move outwards. Hold this for 2 seconds, then breathe out slowly by pulling in your abdominal muscles, pushing the air out of your lungs. Your hand should move inwards.

As you breathe like this, close your eyes and repeat a suitable trigger word like "stop" or "slow". You will find that your pulse rate lowers and you will feel calm. Do this ten times. With regular practice, you will find you can get the same effect in just three breaths. This exercise can become central to your method for relaxation. Use it to clear your mind before or during a training session.

longer than a showjumping round, they make greater demands on concentration. Get into the habit of analysing a test sheet as you would a course of fences – the end of one movement being the fence before the start of the next one. Then, see the movements as related distances in jumping, so that there is a continuous stream of concentration from one movement to the next. In addition, set yourself specific aims regarding the direction and speed for each movement.

Cross country demands long periods of continuous concentration. You cannot concentrate only on the fences because distances are far greater than in showjumping – every line around every corner is important if you are to save even a few metres and complete the cross-country course with the minimum effort in the required time. It is more effective to set specific performance goals, such as directional lines and minute markers.

For all equestrian activities, make concentration a specific goal. The easier riding is for you, the more likely you are to be distracted. It is therefore particularly important for more advanced riders to work on their concentration.

SIMPLIFYING YOUR TRAINING

Riding is a very time-consuming sport, and sometimes it is difficult to imagine how you will complete all your tasks in the time available. You need to be efficient and to organize your time effectively, and to do this you need to simplify your activities. If you identify your ultimate aim, and then plan ahead carefully, you can break everything down into manageable steps, and achieving your goals will not seem nearly as difficult as it might have first appeared.

LESS IS MORE

The phrase "less is more" might be something of a cliché, but encapsulated in these three words is a principle that, consistently applied, can make a very positive difference, not just to your training, but to your life in general. Making life less complicated, so that there is less effort and less waste, can turn an ordinary rider into a great rider. Aiming for simplicity and accuracy results in less change, less expense, and less stress, leaving you with more time and scope. For example, a general strategy to make less result in more should include buying just what you need, rather than what you want, or travelling when other people are not doing the same. The key is to prioritize.

There is nothing more important in your mental preparation than to aim for more simplicity and precision in your approach.

This is especially true in equestrian sports because of the interaction required with your horse. The simpler your communication system, the greater potential your horse will have because it will be easier and quicker to train him.

Make it a habit to reduce things down to their simplest forms. There are some riders who delight in using a whole series of different aids over several seconds to produce something as simple as a canter transition. Although the

BREAKING DOWN THE TASK Gridwork is one example of how a challenging exercise can be made manageable. This rider has simply to keep her balance, because her approach has been made with precision.

horse may understand and be very obedient to these aids, there are three main disadvantages. Firstly, while this series of aids is being given, it is not possible to give other aids – for instance, to change the direction or level of impulsion. Secondly, it makes it difficult for other riders when they ride that horse. And thirdly, it makes more advanced work difficult or impossible.

Being simple also means breaking down every advanced exercise into simple parts. There is a straightforward progression to every exercise. If the techniques are getting complicated or hard work then it is likely that there are some gaps in your progression. If you realize this and work from the basics, you will find that neither you nor your horse will find the exercises complicated and that you progress smoothly.

FINDING THE BEST SOLUTION

It is a fact that if you always do what you have always done, you will always get what you have always got. To improve performance, it is necessary to embrace changes and look for greater efficiency. As part of this process, you have to let a good idea give way to a better idea. This is not easy if you have worked hard to do something well over the years and

> ## "WINNERS ARE ACCURATE AND FOCUSED"

invested time in methods that you feel proud of and that have served you well. But you need to be unemotional, and to avoid letting your ego get in the way of a better way.

When you are training, actively try to find problems in your methods and exercises rather than just finding reasons why they are right. If, after honest appraisal, you cannot find things wrong with what you do, then it is likely your method is a good one; if, however, you work only from a list of positives, you are unlikely to reach a valid conclusion.

Searching for faults should not be an exercise in self-denigration: you should look at failure as part of a process that helps you to arrive at the right answer. Instead of trying to forget bad performances and mistakes, it is better to analyse them truthfully and constructively, so that you can perform more accurately next time. This attitude is of crucial importance for improving the quality of your training and for accelerating your progress.

Being efficient means finding methods that work for all the main equestrian activities. It is so difficult to foresee precisely what might happen in the future, so a flexible training base that leaves the door open for all activities is of enormous value. Hence the emphasis on establishing a basic riding position that can easily develop into a dressage or racing position, and the importance of establishing the constants (pp.122–23), which will allow a horse to be good at dressage as well as at jumping.

PRACTICE MAKES PERMANENT

The most obvious area in which there is a need to be precise and to do things well at an early stage is in practising your basic riding skills. If you rehearse physical actions, such as rising to the trot, over and over again, they become automatic: you no longer need consciously to put effort into them, and you do them without thinking. Some people refer to this phenomenon as muscle memory.

While such practice will make the action permanent, it will not make it good. Bad practice will simply establish bad habits. It always takes longer to correct bad habits than it does to establish good habits to begin with. Therefore, good-quality work from the beginning is vital for both you and your horse. Doing things well is normally easier than doing things badly, so the only extra resource required is a little more time at the start. This is important because you need to practise something until you no longer get it wrong, rather than practise it until you get it right at times.

STAYING FOCUSED

Being focused is a prerequisite for fulfilling potential, but many people talk about the need to be focused without realizing what it takes to do it. There are a number of essential ingredients to being focused, and if you are having problems with focus, the first step is to assess which are already in place and which must be added or improved.

Firstly, nothing can take the place of persistence. Talent will obviously not – the world is full of unsuccessful people with great talent. Education will not, because the world is also full of educated people whose lives stagnate. Persistence is of primary importance.

Secondly, being focused means being positive. You need to look forwards with self-belief. Thirdly, your focus needs to be refined by prioritizing your goals. It is not possible for even the most talented performer to do everything they wish to do, so choices have to be made. Some goals will have to be dropped while others may be given a longer time frame in order to focus on the priority. Your short-term focus will be improved if you also have a long-term goal.

GOAL SETTING

The pivotal skill of mental preparation is goal setting. Having something to aim for will motivate you, and you will feel a boost in your self-confidence when you achieve it. It will help you to decide what is important and what is not, so that you can organize your time accordingly. It will also help you to measure and evaluate your progress.

It is necessary to give goal setting a structure so that it includes the long-term aim, the intermediate goals, and the short-term action steps. The golden rule to remember is to plan backwards and execute forwards (see diagram, below). Having decided on your long-term aim (what might be achieved), you then work out the necessary intermediate goals (what could be achieved). Then you are in a position to list the various action steps (what should be achieved) to accomplish these goals.

The significant psychological advantage of this process is that, at each stage, the scale of the challenge is reduced. A good example of how this works was explained by British rower Steve Redgrave when aiming for his fourth gold medal in the Atlanta Olympics. "Times tend to improve by 4 seconds during an Olympic cycle. I calculate this involves an improvement of .0012 of a second for every hour spent training. That's one two-hundredths of the time it takes to blink an eye." So, in other words, Steve Redgrave scaled down the challenge by working out intermediate (and achievable) goals. In Atlanta, by simply completing his final action step – rowing 2,000 m (2,187 yd) – Steve Redgrave achieved his ultimate aim of winning a fourth gold medal. The point here is that if your goal-setting and action-steps programme is well planned, then eventually your long-term aim becomes just another action step.

If you fail to meet your goals, think of it as a useful lesson that you can use in modifying your training programme. Work out why things went wrong and how you can improve. Were you too stressed? Did you fail to warm up adequately? Or was the goal unrealistic in the first place?

If, on the other hand, you succeed, you can be justified in feeling pleased. Remember also that goals change over time, so if they are no longer working for you, do not be afraid to reprioritize.

PRIORITIZING

Equestrian sports potentially involve an enormous volume of information, techniques, and theories – not least because there are two participants, you and your horse. Also, the range of activities and the difference between novice and advanced levels are huge. Therefore the need to decide on priorities and simple structures is even more important than with most sports.

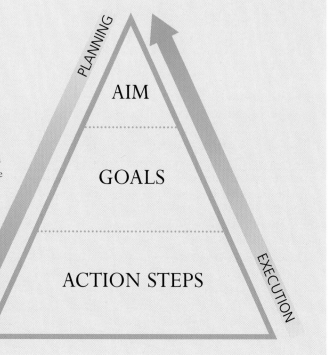

ACHIEVING YOUR ULTIMATE AIM

Having decided on your ultimate aim (to compete in the national championships, for example), you have to plan backwards, working out the goals that will lead to the aim and then the action steps that will lead to these goals. Your plan has to take everything into account, including your resources and your other commitments. In fact, one of your goals may be related to a reorganization of your commitments or to a fund-raising exercise.

When you execute your plans, you will start with the action steps, which will take you forwards to achieve the intermediate goals. Succeeding in these should eventually lead you to your ultimate aim. Of course, it will be much more satisfying if you make your long-term aim quite challenging, with no certainty of achieving it. The action steps, however, must be very achievable – then you will always be able to build on success.

To turn your goals into realities you must make them specific and quantifiable; agree them with your coach or partner and write them down. Include a time frame; and always double check that they are both essential and realistic.

PLANNING

AIM

GOALS

ACTION STEPS

EXECUTION

FORMING DAILY ACTION STEPS

Writing down the specific steps that you need to take each day will help you to define them precisely and – if you have lots of them – to prioritize them. Each action step should relate directly to specific goals – the examples here are all to do with the six components of mental preparation. Make sure they are manageable: there should never be any doubt about them being achievable. Put "I will" before each action step to emphasize your personal commitment to it.

1. BEING STEADY

- I will use the measuring tape to get the canter poles the right distance apart.

- I will get up at 6.00 am every day.

- I will buy a rule book at the main conference.

2. BEING HUMAN

- I will take deep breaths and smile inwardly before entering the competition arena.

- I will close my eyes and feel the movement of the horse.

- I will celebrate my birthday with my family on Tuesday.

3. BEING POSITIVE

- I will use serpentines and shoulder-in exercises to achieve straightness.

- I will ask a friend to stand and watch and give me support.

- I will write YES – CAN DO on the back of my hand.

4. BEING SIMPLE

- I will shorten my stirrups another hole for jumping.

- I will list my priorities for the week.

- I will get a friend to video tomorrow's ride so it can be analysed in slow motion.

5. BEING FLEXIBLE

- I will use yoga as well as circuit training for my physical preparation programme.

- I will study top riders jumping against the clock.

- I will do brainstorming on my finances next Monday.

6. BEING PREPARED

- I will compete at the National Championships at the intermediate level.

- I will sign up for a trainer's day.

- I will choose a new role-play category to work on each day.

In the short term, there is a type of prioritizing that can be very effective for those who feel swamped by the sheer number of tasks they have to tackle. Divide your tasks according to their level of importance and urgency. If a task is not important and not urgent then you should drop it and make no exceptions. If a task is not important but urgent you should try to delegate it; if it is important but not urgent you have the option of delaying it until later. Spend your time on tasks that are both important and urgent. Organizing your tasks like this will immediately simplify your life.

Whatever you prioritize in your riding training, it should always be something that will be of maximum use to you. For example, you can always keep the four components of the rider's position and effectiveness (see pp.100–101) at the forefront of your mind, because these are required at all levels and for all the main equestrian activities.

Similarly, the six aims of mental preparation (see p.355) should be a regular part of your overall programme, but these should be prioritized according to your needs.

MAKING TIME

In order to work smarter, and not just harder, it is important to structure your days so that you have sufficient time for the tasks you need to complete. Make up a timetable and allocate specific time periods for specific tasks. So many people become overwhelmed by everything they have to do that they jump from one task to another and actually end up doing less. By spending a solid hour on one task and rewarding yourself with a short break before tackling the next task, a huge amount can be achieved.

You may also wish to extend your normal timetable. It is worth noting that by finding an extra 2 hours a day you can create the equivalent of 13 extra working weeks a year, which is an extra 25 per cent. This could be done by getting up an hour earlier each day and staying on the job an hour longer. It is obviously important not to burn yourself out with excess work, but this is a good example of how a relatively small but regular increase in work can, over a long period, add up to a substantial amount.

STAYING POSITIVE

While all riders have slightly different aims, everyone can benefit from a positive approach. For example, many riders give up competing because they know someone who can ride better than they can. Instead, they should keep riding and set their own personal goals, rather than comparing their performance against others. With coaching and support you will grow in self-respect, confidence, and competence. The key is to be aspirational and to think positively.

KEEPING YOUR SELF-RESPECT

The huge downside to participating in sport is the sense of failure and lack of self worth if you do not do well in comparison with some others. This often results in active participants becoming armchair participants. You can avoid this in two main ways: first of all, by remembering that your overall self-esteem is more important than a particular performance or other people's expectations; and, secondly, by always putting your primary focus on your own performance and working to a personal best. This will both improve your performance and help you maintain your self-respect. The various marathon road races around the world are wonderful examples of events in which hundreds of thousands of runners seek to achieve a personal best; they participate in something in which everyone is a winner. As already mentioned, the point is not to be the best, but to do your best.

BEING ASPIRATIONAL

Many people question an approach to training that is primarily positive because they say that it gives people unrealistic expectations and that a culture of praise without criticism leads to a lowering of standards.

However, you need to have a balance between being over-idealistic and being negative. People tend to underestimate themselves because it is the safer thing to do. Why aspire to great achievements and risk disappointment when you can be more modest in your aims and therefore enjoy a better result

PERFORMING IN PUBLIC At competitions, riders are often faced with a huge audience, and this can be very daunting. Remember though, that the better you do, the more they will applaud – they are on your side. Some of them will have wanted to be in your place but lacked the persistence to get there – so put your mind on the task and enjoy your moment in the limelight.

as a bonus? Unfortunately this latter attitude will not stretch you enough to develop your ability. There are numerous examples of people with a positive attitude doing better than more talented people who limit themselves with a negative attitude. As a starting point, try not to think about problems but instead rename them as challenges. Subconsciously, most people react negatively to problems and positively to challenges. Winners love a challenge and know the importance of working from strengths and gradually expanding these strengths until the weaker areas are relatively small. Being in

"WINNERS KNOW THEY ARE ABLE"

a team is an advantage because team members can compensate for each other's limitations and together produce a better result. This is why the right horse for each rider is so important (see Chapter 11). It is also true that really successful riders are invariably those with the best support team, who do everything from helping to select the right horse to being a pair of eyes on the ground. This team will be supportive in times of stress, and will encourage, not condemn.

BELIEVING IN YOURSELF

The breaking of the four-minute-mile barrier by the British runner Roger Bannister in 1954 is a wonderful example of how simply having belief in your abilities can change everything. Bannister trained specifically for the challenge by setting goals for each quarter of the race, putting aside any negative thoughts of a barrier. He ran it in 3 minutes 59.4 seconds, and within 2 years most international milers were running under 4 minutes. What had changed was their belief in their ability. Their negative attitude had been made positive by Bannister's success.

The lesson to take from this is that negative thinking is frequently self-fulfilling. Everyone suffers from self-doubt from time to time. We ride into the arena and a voice in our head says, "Why am I doing this? It's too much." Instead you should think, "Well done, I've got here, wait for the bell." As you ride to a fence thinking, "Don't lean forwards," or, "I'm going too fast," try to rephrase your thought in a more positive way – "Shoulders back" and "Slow down". Do not worry about hitting a pole; focus on clearing it. Do not think about stopping; focus on moving forwards. Repetition of this technique is important if it is to become a good habit. Practise imagining positive experiences every day, and whenever a negative thought or picture enters your mind, replace it with its positive counterpart. Conjure up an image of your positive role model during moments of pressure or crisis to trigger the required positive qualities and to banish self-doubt.

A FLEXIBLE APPROACH

Although it is important to keep your riding techniques simple and consistent, small improvements can always be made in equipment and training. Truly great riders are open to new ideas and methods. They are proactive in that they look at the established way of doing things and consider whether it could be improved. When an innovative approach is combined with hard work, energy, and talent, you have the recipe for real success.

A BETTER IDEA

Over the years, sports change as competitors find better ways of doing things, and horse riding is no exception. In showjumping, a revolution happened almost 100 years ago when the Italian coach Captain Federico Caprilli invented "the forward seat", jumping the fence with the seat out of the saddle and the body inclined forwards. Up until then, all riders had jumped sitting in the saddle with an upright body or even leaning backwards. Although every showjumper now acknowledges the merits of Caprilli's balanced position, it took many years before it was universally adopted.

Otto Lorke, a German dressage trainer working between the 1920s and 1950s, had a similar effect on world dressage, although he achieved this with a large number of small changes rather than with one single change. He placed an emphasis on doing quality work in just a snaffle bridle before progressing, and rejected mechanical training. He

"WINNERS FIND A BETTER WAY"

also emphasized the importance of harmony – the ability to go with the horse's movement – above the shape of the rider. He showed that suppleness and lightness of rein contact were also vital. Those who adopted his methods include most of the influential riders and coaches in the dressage world – Willie Schulteis, Bubby Gunther, Joseph Neckermann, Harry Boldt, Herbert Reibein, and Reiner Klimke.

Such improvements to a best-practice model are obvious in the competition arena, but behind-the-scenes improvements – in stable management and types of equipment – can also make a significant contribution to performance. For example, the more natural stable management systems in Australia and New Zealand, where horses are given more freedom, including stables where they are free to walk out into a small, enclosed paddock or yard, and more natural feeding routines (see pp. 50–51), are increasingly regarded as best practice.

PRODUCING THE EDGE

It is common to describe an extraordinary performance by a horse and rider as magic. Of course, there is a method behind the performance: it is called magic only because the rider is a jump ahead of fellow competitors. The first step towards producing your own magic is to study these special performers.

In dressage, the best examples of this occur in the freestyle dressage test to music (kur), which is becoming increasingly popular. The movements and exercises used must be within the capabilities of your horse, but an imaginative rider can produce something that is original and capable of surprising the judges and audience. In showjumping, almost every round against the clock requires the rider to look at the course from all angles and find a route that is better than what is obvious. In cross country there is a similar requirement, with so many potential routes and different distances through combinations and related fences. When you walk the course, you need to look at all possibilities.

On a daily basis, be prepared in training to keep an open mind and experiment a little, looking for small gains in any area. These small gains will eventually give you your next personal best and possibly a major win. To understand the effect of each change, make only one alteration at a time if possible. If thinking creatively does not come naturally to you, then you just need to practise it. For example, try brainstorming several hypothetical ideas. For instance, what would the consequences be if humans had eyes in the back of their head, or could only walk sideways? This should get you into the way of thinking laterally and generating new ideas.

CREATIVE DRESSAGE
Freestyle dressage to music is a wonderful example of the need for creativity and imagination in riding, but it must be based on good-quality work. The horse can only produce high-level magic if he is exceptionally well trained. Here, Nadine Capellman from Germany and her horse Trannis form an inspirational team.

BEING PREPARED

It is said that luck is a combination of good preparation and opportunity. If you are prepared for all eventualities, you are more likely to make a success out of any opportunity that arises. This is especially true of equestrian sports because so much depends upon the attitude and performance of another – your horse. If you prepare yourself and your horse well, you will be ready to meet all the challenges that competition can provide, and you will create the opportunity for you to win.

BEING INDEPENDENT

When you are competing, whether in dressage, in the showjumping arena, or on the cross-country course, you cannot rely on instructions from your coach. If your preparation is good, it should allow you to be independent no matter what the situation. You should practise making your own decisions in training and regularly set up simulated competition situations.

As a beginner rider, you are almost totally dependent on your coach, but you should quickly be encouraged to take control of the warm-up and cool-down periods and then other small parts of the ride. In this way you can get used to making decisions and taking responsibility for your work. You will also find that your concentration level is generally much better if you have to take decisions rather than just wait to be directed.

You should also be actively involved in your own goal setting so that you can take ownership of your own training. This does not mean that the coach is opting out – on the contrary, giving responsibility to the rider is the sign of a good coach. Independent thinking is a vital part of creating and making the most of opportunity, but first there must be opportunities for the rider to be independent. As you learn to take informed decisions, you will also create an added dimension to your riding that is very satisfying.

MAKING DECISIONS

Being a step ahead is a prerequisite for good performance. It is often said that some people waste their lives in chasing dreams and thinking the impossible. However, if you know that life is not a rehearsal and are quite prepared to make tough decisions in order to seize the moment, then you can make the very best of a situation.

Initially, the choices you have to make can be small. Will it be the left rein or the right rein? Walk, trot, or canter? Light seat or seat in the saddle? Then, as an advanced rider, you make bigger choices. Which horse to buy? Which competitions to enter? Which coach to choose? As with all choices, deciding what not to do can be as difficult as deciding what you should do.

VISUALIZING THE COURSE Before you go into the arena, ride the course in your mind. This can significantly improve your reaction times and the ease of your performance, particularly with a jump-off course or a difficult related distance. You will need to have practised this technique in training.

CASE STUDY

THE PROBLEM:

On the drive to a show, Paul's car got a puncture. He missed his first competition and he knew that from then on, his weekend was going to get worse. At the second competition, his mother was late finishing plaiting his horse's mane. He felt angry with her because, as a result, he had hardly any time to get to the arena. The stewards shouted at him to come forwards and start, and his horse was not in a co-operative mood. He felt it was a disaster, especially as his fellow riders, Julie and Sinead, went so well.

That afternoon, as he was waiting to go into the arena, he decided to have one last practice jump. His horse tripped in the pit that had been created on the take-off side, and poles crashed in all directions. Paul kept thinking ahead to his round and dreading the six short strides in the course – he knew he would find them difficult. He was worried and tense, and all he could think about was the selectors who would be watching. During his round, he tried hard to slow down on the short six strides but his horse was not listening to him. They were on a half-stride and, before he knew it, the horse had stopped – just as Paul knew he would.

On the second day, in the big competition, he performed much worse than he had during training. He knew the selectors had written him off by then – they are so quick to point out weaknesses. And he had found it difficult to remember the course. People kept talking to him as he walked it, and he

was worried about whether his mother was tacking up his horse correctly. During his round, he over rode. A week ago he was the favourite to win, but on the day, he was not even placed. It was the same story as last year. His father would be furious.

COACH'S SOLUTIONS:

• Paul was favourite to win, so much of what he does must be good. He needs to recognize this and to work from his strengths.
• Most of his difficulties at the show were created by poor planning and by not remaining positive. Good planning and organization will get you to the show on time, even with a puncture, because you allow for the unexpected.
• The next step is to learn to remain calm. This would be a good opportunity to try role playing. Paul needs to identify with someone who is unemotional and disciplined.
• While at the show, Paul needs the support of people he can trust, such as his coach, who can help him keep his mind on his riding, not the other riders or the selectors.
• Paul must also learn to stay focused on what he has to do, not what he should not do. Visualization will help this positive focus and give him the chance to show his true talent in the ring.
• We need to talk about his goals and why he is riding – it should be for himself, not his father. If he can learn from his failures and look back on this and smile, he will find the future very exciting.

Other decisions you might face are to do with timing. For example, the timing of the aids and the timing of the stride to jump a fence, which is a special skill in itself. You also need to know when to start a new exercise or to change an exercise; when to rest, and when to ask for more. The ability to do this well comes from your own experience and from studying others.

VISUALIZATION TECHNIQUES

Many studies have shown that in physical terms, the human nervous system cannot distinguish between an actual experience and an experience imagined vividly and in detail. This is the reason why visualization works: you can prepare for situations that you are not able to practise in reality. Visualization is now commonly used in all sports as a standard approach to mental preparation — all you need is to be open to possibilities.

This technique has a huge variety of applications – you can use it to rehearse almost anything. Even as a novice rider, it is possible to benefit from visualizing something like the rising trot, because this will allow you to practise the movement in your mind. As you become more experienced, you can start

to visualize an introductory dressage test or course of fences. For more advanced riders, it is standard practice to do a mental rehearsal of a complete showjumping course or dressage test. In cross country, it is also helpful to visualize yourself in the safety position over a drop fence (see p.265).

> ## " WINNERS SEE SUCCESS AS A SCIENCE "

Visualization is particularly effective for exercises where everything happens very quickly, such as jump-offs against the clock or doing the sequence changes in a dressage test. It also allows continuous practice of difficult sequences, which you could not otherwise do without having a whole stable of horses at your disposal. In all cases, the more you can understand what is required and feel what is going on, the more effective the mental rehearsal will be.

A BALANCED APPROACH

In any sport, the focus needs to be on both the performer and the performance. Unfortunately, the development of the performer as a well-balanced human being often takes second place. If this happens, the performance will eventually suffer.

Whatever the competition level, all performers need to keep their sport in context. There is a time to be a success in your life and a time for your life to be a success. The balance between these two aims is of the greatest importance.

KEEPING A SENSE OF PROPORTION

If a life is entirely dependent on competitive success then disappointment is almost inevitable. Most people gradually realize, as they get older, that the real structure of their lives is centred around a loving core of family and friends rather than around money, possessions, and ambitions. A performer needs to achieve happily rather than achieve to be happy.

If there is one outstanding characteristic of those who participate successfully in sport it is that they enjoy themselves. So, if you are not getting much enjoyment from your horse riding, it is unlikely that you will progress quickly or stay in the sport. Others who are even more fortunate, actually love what they do, and it is true to say that if you love what you do nothing is tedious or hard work. The only surprising thing is that enjoyment is so often missed in mental preparation programmes. Unfortunately, so much emphasis is put on the things that we do wrong that many people are discouraged from participation. Instead, we should be more concerned about the things we do not do but that we could do. Giving yourself opportunities is, of course, a prerequisite for being a winner, but you will not succeed if you are not enjoying what you are doing.

The most typical reason for a lack of enjoyment is not having a balanced outlook. By developing a contented and secure life outside of your sport, you will normally find it easier to enjoy your sport. It can be a relatively minor thing, such as an overdemanding coach or unpleasant fellow competitors, that reduces your enjoyment. A brief analysis of what things please and displease you about your riding will quickly show you what things need to be changed. Any increase in enjoyment will help you to keep riding and to ride better.

As part of a balanced life, you also need to be able to relax. Horse riding should help most people relax, but many elite riders will need to do other things. Any activity that replenishes your energy and refreshes you can be considered relaxing. It may be something small like having a long bath or taking a day off to listen to music and see friends, or it may be something more active like walking or playing a different sport.

GETTING ON WITH PEOPLE

Research by the Carnegie Foundation, confirmed by the Stanford Research Institute, suggests that what determines a person's success is 15 per cent technical knowledge and 85 per cent the ability to manage yourself and deal with people.

Especially in the horse world, no one can remain in isolation. There are always people to deal with, whether they are fellow competitors, farriers, vets, coaches, or organizers. The basis for getting on with these people and getting the most out of each situation is to respect them, without losing

> ## " *WINNERS DELIGHT IN LIFE* "

your self-respect. You do this by being assertive rather than submissive or aggressive. Submissive behaviour is characterized by failing to stand up for your rights, or by standing up for them in such a way that others can easily disregard them. You express your thoughts in apologetic, over cautious, or self-effacing ways, or you fail to express yourself altogether. Aggressive behaviour is standing up for your rights in a way that violates the rights of another person. You express your thoughts in inappropriate ways, even though you may honestly believe the views to be right. If you are assertive, however, you will stand up for your rights in a way that does not violate another person's rights. You express your point of view but at the same time show that you understand the other person's position. These different types of behaviour can be summed up memorably by saying that the basis for assertive behaviour is thinking "I'm okay and you're okay," submissive behaviour is thinking "You're okay, but I'm not okay," and aggressive behaviour is thinking, "I'm okay but you're not okay."

When talking to other people, a key element of treating them with respect is to listen empathetically. This requires giving them time to say their piece and delaying any evaluation or judgment until you have heard all the story. It means using eye contact and both verbal and non-verbal encouragement as appropriate, saying, "I see," or, "I understand," and nodding and smiling. Watching the person's body language for clues to understand the full meaning of any communication will also be helpful. Horse people probably do this better than many others because they are used to reading a horse's body language.

If you combine these techniques with remaining broad minded and good humoured, then it is possible to get on with most people. This in turn helps you create the right support system. Performing at your best is so much easier if you are well supported. Everyone needs regular support from friends, family, coaches, sports scientists, sponsors, organizers, and the media. It is no coincidence that top riders always give maximum credit to their coaches.

PERFORMANCE BALANCES

Whatever you want to achieve in your sport, you will do it better if you have a balanced approach. The first and most important balance is between effort and delight. To succeed takes persistence and work, but the other side of the balance is about looking after yourself as a human being, making sure your emotional needs are taken care of, and that you create time for rest and personal development. This balance brings a harmony to your life that keeps you doing things.

The second balance is between doing more and doing less. A positive mental attitude encourages you to achieve more, to be confident and ambitious. This has to be balanced by the need to analyse and simplify things, and to look for priorities. The result of this balance is quality work.

The final balance is between possibilities and realities. Any performer will do better if they are creative, coming up with ideas for doing things more effectively. This has to be balanced by what is realistic. You have to consider your options and the resources and preparation required to achieve a successful outcome. Always do things with a view to the future.

THE BIGGER PICTURE   Horse riding is a great sport and one that permeates all areas of your life. The friends you make, the horses you ride, and the experiences you gain will stay with you for ever. Your successes and failures in competition are part of the bigger picture, not the whole picture.

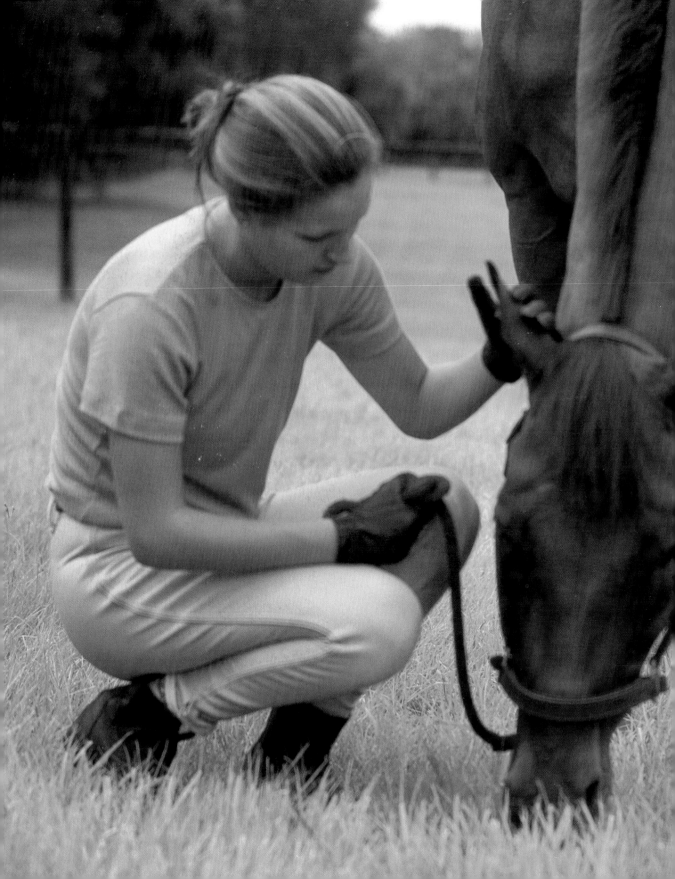

CHAPTER ELEVEN

BUILDING YOUR ULTIMATE TEAM

Finding the right horse is the starting point for successful riding, and you will need to know what to look for. The right horse could be a pony, a cob, a warmblood, or a Thoroughbred – so long as he has good sense, strength, and potential.

In addition to your horse, you will rely on other, human team members. Grooms, farriers, vets, organizers, associations, and coaches all form your network of support, with your choice of coach being of particular importance. An effective rider has to be a good team player and realize that each member of the team complements the others. Not only will this achieve extraordinary results, it can develop friendships that last a lifetime.

THE ULTIMATE HORSE

A horse that has the potential to become your ultimate horse will be the one that most suits you. Make sure you do your research before you buy. Horses come in many different sizes and shapes, but you will want the one you choose to be a pleasure to work with, and to have the right combination of good sense, strength, and potential. The aim is to find a horse with whom you can form a team whose value far exceeds the sum of its individuals.

BUYING A HORSE

Your ultimate horse might be bought at public auction, or from a private home, or from a dealer. Decide first on what type of horse you want and what type of work you want it to do. Then seek advice from a coach you trust or employ a reputable agent, because their knowledge and experience will be invaluable. It takes a special skill to be able to quickly assess a horse's ability and suitability, and it would be foolish not to make use of such people's wisdom.

The advantage of buying a horse at a public auction is that you know you are paying the market price, but the disadvantage is that there is normally a restricted time for trying out the horse and making up your mind. Buying privately gives you more time to make your assessment and test-ride the horse, but the asking price may be unrealistic and the vendor's riding facilities limited. In such cases, you may have to ask for the horse to be taken to a more suitable facility for you to assess him.

Buying from an established and reputable dealer gives the possibility of an after-sales service and an exchange if the horse proves unsuitable. Wherever you are purchasing your horse, the important thing is to do your homework and make full use of an agent and vet. You should do this even if you are looking at a fairly low-value horse, because the cumulative cost of keeping a horse over the years makes the purchase price relatively less important.

Horses with the potential to win advanced competitions or Olympic gold medals are hard to find, but if you discover a horse that has intelligence, strength, and potential, you will have found a special partner that may one day take you to unexpected achievement and glory.

INTELLIGENCE AND TEMPERAMENT

There is no doubt that your priority when choosing a horse suitable for general riding is that he should be sensible. The two things that most determine whether a horse is sensible are his basic nature and his intelligence; it is important to distinguish between the two. Unfortunately, slow-wittedness or lack of intelligence is often mistaken for good temperament.

Intelligent horses are desirable because they are far more likely to be quick to train, and to look after you in challenging situations, such as when jumping or riding across country. If an intelligent horse, however, is badly handled he is often more difficult to train because he is quick to think of evasions

VETTING YOUR HORSE

When you are considering buying a horse, always arrange a veterinary examination to check the horse's soundness and his suitability for a particular activity. Making an assessment is often not an exact science, but a matter of weighing up different factors. For instance, a horse that is not sound enough for the prolonged and intense physical demands of horse trials may still have a long and active life in pleasure riding or dressage. Just as with the many humans who cope with physical weaknesses, so it is possible, with good management, for horses with small ailments to work successfully and comfortably. An experienced vet who knows your sport therefore plays a key role in finding your ultimate horse.

and unusual reactions. For example, such a horse may quickly learn how to nap towards home or stop and rear, and he will soon learn what he can get away with.

On the other hand, slow-witted, passive horses tend to accept bad training practices and, regrettably, are used as examples to justify these methods. Horses like this are considered desirable for the beginner rider because their slowness makes them seem safe, but in reality their lack of responsiveness and engagement makes them a difficult ride and therefore unsuitable for the beginner.

A good temperament can be defined as a calm, willing, and sociable outlook, and this is what is required in a young horse. Such a nature is a prerequisite for easy training and for fulfilling a horse's physical potential, although, sadly, it is quite possible to ruin a good temperament with bad training. It is also possible to improve a horse's temperament, but only with skilful training, time, and patience. No matter how talented or beautiful a horse is, therefore, you should not consider buying him if he has an unwilling or difficult temperament. If, after you have bought your horse, he turns out not to be suitable for your needs, or you simply do not get on together, always be prepared to resell him to a more suitable home and look again.

ULTIMATE HORSE BIKO Karen O'Connor, riding for the United States Olympic team on her great horse Biko. As a 3-year-old, Biko's enormous potential was immediately evident.

STRENGTH

A horse's strength and the length of his working life stem from a combination of two things: good conformation and muscular strength. Some horses, such as quarter horses and sprinters, have a higher proportion of muscle that is suited to anaerobic exercise, such as dressage and showjumping. This results in a rounder, bulkier muscle shape and can produce great strength in the short term. Others, such as Arabs and ponies, have a higher proportion of muscle suited to aerobic exercise. This results in a flatter, leaner body shape and produces lower levels of strength over longer periods, hence the Arab's suitability for endurance riding. Good training can produce good muscle development, but when comparing horses, the ones that are natural athletes and have better conformation will have greater potential and durability.

A HORSE'S CONFORMATION

Conformation is related to function in the same way that a rider's position is related to their effectiveness. Breeding for specific physical characteristics that reflect fashion ideals but are unrelated to the use of the horse should be abhorred. The most important issue is whether a horse's build allows him

GOOD FEET

Having little height or width in the heel of the foot is a serious defect. Without this few horses remain sound because the navicular area is exposed to injury and there is particular risk of injury to the wings of the pedal bone. The front feet should be a pair at an angle of 54–58 degrees to the horizontal. A foot shaped like this will be able to disperse force evenly when it hits the ground, which reduces stress on the tendons, joints, and bones of the foreleg. Few horses have perfect feet, but a farrier can resolve some problems.

Any lack of symmetry in the feet will create additional strain on another part of the leg

With a good width of foot, line A will equal line B. Narrow feet tend to lead to soundness problems

On the front feet, the pastern should be at the same angle as the foot

HORSE MOVEMENT Showjumpers and dressage horses tend to make a round action with each step, with an obvious use of the hock and knee joints, whereas racehorses and Arabs, like this one pictured here, have a flatter, pendulum action.

to work well and efficiently. The key element of good conformation (see box, below) is overall proportion: everything should fit together in a balanced way.

Conformation is an important factor in soundness. Although there may appear to be exceptions – those horses with poor conformation that do work and stay sound – the experience of vets and of those who work horses in an intense way over many years suggests that some aspects of conformation are vital to ensure a long and useful working life.

The most important area is the front legs, from just below the knee to the ground, including the foot (see box, left). Tendon damage is the injury most commonly sustained by horses that have to gallop in their work, and longer tendons will be weaker. Therefore, the cannon bone should be short, so that the knee is close to the ground, and the main tendons between the knee and the fetlock joint should be correspondingly short. The width of the bone just above the

fetlock joint should be the same as it is just below the knee. Additional strain on the tendons can occur if the horse is back at the knee, which means that the foreleg appears to bend backwards, and be concave behind the line of the knee.

Sloping shoulders and a 90-degree angle at the hip joint (between the ilium/pelvis and the femur/thigh) will help the horse to make effective muscular use of his limbs. This, combined with his use of his back and his natural suppleness and way of going, will dictate whether or not a particular horse is a natural athlete.

A beautiful head with big eyes is often mentioned as a necessary requirement when choosing a horse, but in fact an ugly head bears no relationship to intelligence or personality. Despite this, many people insist on buying a horse with a beautiful head, so if you are looking for a cheaper horse, it may be a good option to choose one that does not have such a pretty face.

GOOD CONFORMATION

A horse with good conformation should fit into an imaginary square (see below). In addition, the vertical distance from the wither to the lowest part of the belly should equal the distance from this point to the ground. This ensures plenty of room for the heart and lungs to function. The knees and hocks should be close to the ground for short, strong tendons.

To minimize strain on the joints, all limbs should be straight. When viewed from the front, the pastern, cannon bone, and forearm should form a vertical line. Viewed from behind, there should be a vertical line from the point of buttock, through the hock, to the heel (see below). This will help the horse to move straight and thus reduce stress on the joints.

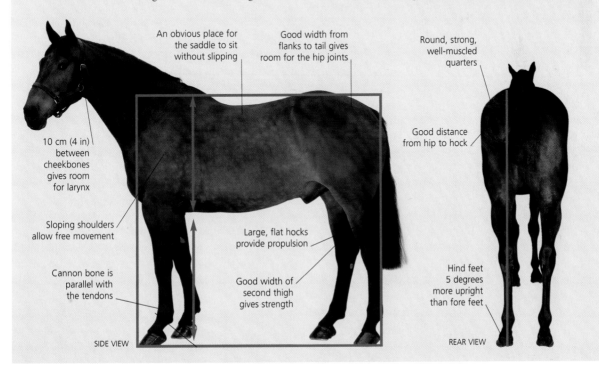

An obvious place for the saddle to sit without slipping

Good width from flanks to tail gives room for the hip joints

Round, strong, well-muscled quarters

10 cm (4 in) between cheekbones gives room for larynx

Good distance from hip to hock

Sloping shoulders allow free movement

Large, flat hocks provide propulsion

Cannon bone is parallel with the tendons

Good width of second thigh gives strength

Hind feet 5 degrees more upright than fore feet

SIDE VIEW

REAR VIEW

HUNTERS When looking for a hunter, temperament should be the priority. Then look for good feet, straight limbs, sloping shoulders, and big quarters. With these factors in place, the right training and feeding will produce an excellent equestrian partner.

COBS A cob is the ideal flexible family horse. At around 15 hands (1.5 m), they have great strength and can do everything from competition work to driving. The Welsh Cob (pictured below) and Morgan Horse are of this type and are utility horses.

THE HORSE FOR YOU

A horse's potential, or scope, dictates what activities he is able to do and to what level. Scope is affected by breeding or type, and the support or training the horse receives. With regard to breeding, horses are often described as cold-, warm-, or hotblooded. Coldbloods include the heavier and draught horses; hotbloods include the Thoroughbred and the Arab; and warmbloods are the result of breeding between coldbloods and Thoroughbreds. Increasingly, warmbloods are being bred directly from other warmbloods. These horses are widely known as sport horses because they are specifically bred for dressage, showjumping, and sometimes horse trials. Warmbloods can be divided into three groups according to their ability to carry weight: heavyweight – up to 118 kg (260 lb); middleweight – up to 102kg (225 lb); lightweight – up to 86 kg (190 lb).

All native ponies in the USA are originally from Great Britain, apart from Icelandic ponies, and there are no native breeds in France, Italy, or Germany. Natives, such as the Connemara and Welsh, probably have the most scope of all – they are hardy, but not lacking in ability. Adults who are small enough to ride ponies have a great advantage in that their costs will be considerably reduced: ponies need less intensive maintenance, they can often be worked without hind shoes, and they eat less than a big horse. Ponies are also tougher; they are less susceptible to sprained tendons, and will heal better without raised scars after cuts and grazes.

A cob is a type of small horse that can carry a heavier rider than a pony. The cob is possibly the most flexible and useful of all the horses for pleasure working. However, they are not built for speed, which generally precludes them from higher levels.

A horse's gender may also affect its scope. Stallions need knowledgeable handling and are not suitable for novice riders. Geldings (castrated stallions) are undoubtedly easier to manage. Mares are, generally speaking, cheaper to purchase, but you need to have sensitivity and awareness to manage them, especially when they are in season. By far the most influential factor in the scope, development, and value of any horse is the training and care that he receives. The humane and progressive training set out in this book will allow your horse to fulfil his potential, but it is a long-term project. To take a horse to advanced competition level requires immense dedication from riders and coaches, as well as from an extended back-up team.

OLYMPIC HORSE
Custom Made was discovered as a young horse. He showed potential with huge sense and strength, and found the perfect partner in David O'Connor, who won a gold medal at the 2000 Sydney Olympics on him.

THE ULTIMATE BACK-UP TEAM

The rider, horse, and coach form the core of any team, but the work of the farrier, groom, and vet keeps the show on the road, and a host of other people – including friends and family – play supporting roles that make special achievement and enjoyment possible. With the possible exception of the horse, there can be no stars in the team: if the team is to stay together, everyone must respect each other and understand their different responsibilities and roles.

FINDING AND KEEPING YOUR TEAM

When finding the professional members of your equestrian team, personal recommendations are always helpful. However, both farriers and vets belong to professional associations that can give you details of members working in your area. Successful farriers and vets are often reluctant to take on new clients, so it is an advantage to stable your horse at a commercial livery stable, which will have an existing back-up team that you can use. Grooms often advertise their availability in specialist equestrian magazines, and local pony clubs and riding clubs are both good sources of information, as well as being good training grounds for grooms.

In addition to the services of the farrier and the vet, you will occasionally need the help and support of other professionals. If your vet does not practise equine dentistry, for example, you will need a specialist to do this essential job

THE GROOM Whether you are your own groom or you have someone else looking after your horse, no one plays a bigger role in providing the safe and secure environment and the daily routine that a horse needs. A groom is in the best position to spot small changes in behaviour or health that require attention, and can also provide companionship for the horse.

of keeping your horse's mouth healthy and comfortable. You may also, at various times, need the services of an equine nutritionist, or the help of a physiotherapist or other specialist practitioner.

Once you have established a team, you need to keep it together. One of the keys to this is ensuring that all the team members can visualize the bigger picture — your long-term aims. It is also essential that their role in achieving these aims is recognized. It is worth recalling the story of the three men who were doing identical work in a marble quarry: when asked what they were doing, the first said, "I'm cutting marble," the second said, "I'm cutting marble for a column," and the third said, "I'm building a cathedral." This third man was the one most likely to remain motivated and committed to his work because he was acutely aware of its purpose. Team members who understand the overall aim, and who can respect and communicate with each other, are likely to keep together and to achieve the most.

SUPPORT NETWORK

Performing to the best of your ability is so much easier when you are well supported. Apart from your horse, your coach, and your team of key professionals, you need to be proactive in developing a wider support network. Family and friends can play a major role in this, especially in encouraging your motivation and discipline, such as on cold mornings and difficult days. They do not have to understand the technical details of riding, but they do need to understand your goals if they are to be supportive enough to make small changes in their lives to facilitate the achievement of your goals.

The same applies to people at your place of work or study. You will need their co-operation if you are to be able to stick to a timetable that takes into account your equestrian commitments. With a little luck you might also be able to use

THE FARRIER

"No foot, no horse," goes the old adage. You might add, "And no farrier, no foot." A farrier is a skilled craftsman who needs to visit your horse every 6 weeks or so to replace shoes or just to keep the feet trimmed and in good order. Different horses, and different activities and workloads, will require different types of shoe. In some cases, specially designed shoes are used to help remedy foot or balance problems.

some of these contacts for fundraising purposes. People like to be part of such a team: they feel good about supporting a worthy cause, about having an interest, and being part of the celebrations when you achieve success.

Your official equestrian association will be able to provide support if you are prepared to be involved in the association and give back in other ways. This is the strength of belonging to a vibrant organization. You will be able to make useful contacts and have access to everything from advice on coaches to details of special group visits to competitions or stables.

You may find it of great educational value to participate in training programmes for coaches or judges: it is surprising how useful it is for you, as a rider, to see yourself from the perspective of a coach or a judge.

THE VET

In many respects, the vet is the leader of the ancillary team because he will almost always be the person you call first when your horse is showing behavioural changes or needs treatment for any weaknesses or injuries. The vet will work with the rider and groom, and will know when to call in the physiotherapist or other specialist. It is essential that the vet is a good diagnostician — the veterinary assessment will determine the work of most of the other team members. He will look for pain, heat or swelling, and for any abnormalities in behaviour or way of going. Watching the horse in walk and trot, and then conducting a manual examination (possibly combined with the use of X-rays or thermal imaging) will help the vet to locate the precise site of any problem.

THE ULTIMATE COACH

When seeking out a coach, remember that, while internationally renowned trainers lead the competition world, it is more important to find someone who suits your individual needs. Also, you should never underestimate what you can learn from your horse – a well-trained horse can teach a great deal and is much sought after by those who wish to become better riders. Wise riders use every opportunity to learn so that they are eventually in a position to coach themselves.

IDENTIFYING YOUR COACH

Over the years there have been a number of great coaches who have advanced equestrian sports and introduced new and better techniques that, in time, have influenced all riders. A famous example is Bert De Nemethy, the late Hungarian coach of the USA showjumping team between 1955 and 1980. He was able to bring together his knowledge of classical dressage and the demands of international showjumping, and then apply his analytical mind to produce a systematic approach for the preparation of all showjumpers. He gave a generation of riders the belief and confidence to use his methods consistently.

Beware of being led astray by coaches whose ability to market themselves is superior to their methods. In justifying their particular method, they may say that there are many different, successful training approaches. In fact, what you need is best practice rather than something that just works. Studying what the very best coaches do at any level will be very helpful in assessing and choosing your own.

Your local coach may not have an international reputation, but this does not necessarily mean he or she cannot be better than an international guru. A good coach is trustworthy and

WORKING WITH YOUR COACH Every relationship between coach and student will be different, and will develop in different ways, but the best are two-way; a good coach will always learn something from his or her students.

welcoming, positive, simple and flexible in approach and, above all, a person with vision. Your trainer should be willing to identify with your difficulties, and understand that every student has special requirements, as well as special abilities that can be developed. If this description fits, then you have found a great coach.

LEARNING FROM YOUR HORSE

The consensus among top riders is that the horse is our best teacher. In analysing learning, research has continually shown that reading, hearing, or seeing something is only half as effective as feeling it. In other words, we remember best the things we actively experience.

Learning to ride is no exception: often it is not until riders have actually felt something that they can understand what is required. In this respect, a well-trained horse is invaluable: from such an animal you can learn what a new exercise should feel like, and you can begin to understand the relationship between the different exercises. Most importantly, you can learn about good timing and effective use of the aids. Many of the great riders have benefited from riding advanced horses trained by others.

The lessons you can learn from a young horse are very different: you learn about patience, the need to understand before taking action, and the importance of having a method and doing things correctly from the beginning. If you are a novice rider with good basics there is much to be said for learning both from an unspoilt young horse, with the help of your coach, and from a more advanced horse. But there is little value in riding a badly trained horse because this is only likely to give you bad habits.

LEARNING FROM A WIDER WORLD

The equestrian world is full of different training methods, so it is important that your influences are complementary. The Internet is a good resource. Books are invaluable, but beware of poor translations and older books espousing methods that apply to outdated standards of competition and equine care. Not all useful influences need be derived from equestrian sport: great coaches from other sports will have wisdom that crosses boundaries and can be crucial to your development. Best practice in areas such as mental and physical preparation, for example, can often be derived from those used in other sports.

Although it can be argued that the horse is still exploited by humans, we no longer accept the cruelty and misuse that has taken place in the past. We now recognize a need for a more humane and holistic approach to training, and this is at the heart of the training principles described in this book. There are huge benefits in this approach for you and your horse.

GREAT COACHES

Dr Reiner Klimke was a great German coach of the 1970s to 1990s, and his riding successes spanned many years. He was one of the fortunate elite who was influenced by Otto Lorke, who founded a dynasty of legendary German trainers, including Bubby Gunther, Willi Schultheis, Joseph Neckermann, Harry Boldt, and Herbert Rehbein. The qualities that made Dr Klimke a great coach were his passion to communicate and his love of horses. Here, riding his beloved Ahlerich, he epitomizes the coach who leads by example, and shows that good training can lead to a long life in equestrian sport.

BEING YOUR OWN COACH

Riders are primarily motivated not by rosettes and medals, but by feeling good about what they do and by the sheer satisfaction of performing well. The most satisfying thing a rider can do is to be self-sufficient, knowing that they are responsible for their own learning, and can approach it in an independent way. If you can do this, you can not only say that you had a good coach, but that you are now a good coach yourself. Ultimately, you have to make your own decisions, and in this respect are your own coach. If you can realize that, potentially, you are the very best coach you will ever have, you will be inspired to learn more.

GLOSSARY

A

ABOVE THE BIT When the horse carries his head high and well in front of the vertical as a result of not using his back and of accepting the rein contact.

ACCEPTANCE Acceptance refers to both the physical and mental acceptance by the horse of the rider's presence, weight, and leg, seat, and rein contacts, including basic language.

ACTION The way in which a horse moves. Straight action describes the limbs moving in a vertical plane (as opposed to moving the feet in or out during flight – known as dishing); round action is where the flight of the foot makes a circular shape, as in a dressage horse; flat action is where the foot stays a more consistent distance above the ground, as in a racehorse.

ADAPTATION *See* Training effect.

AEROBIC EXERCISE An activity level that utilizes a horse's capacity to supply oxygen to his cells. It occurs during work at relatively slow, steady rates and develops endurance. *See also* Anaerobic exercise.

AGAINST THE CLOCK A timed round in a showjumping competition. It either takes place in the first round (as in a speed class), or in later rounds, as in a timed round between all the competitors who have gone clear – known as a jump-off.

AIDS The ways through which a rider communicates or signals to a horse. The natural aids are the voice, legs, hands, seat, and bodyweight. The artificial aids are the whip and spurs.

AIRS ABOVE THE GROUND When the horse's forehand or both the forehand and the quarters come off the ground. They are not part of modern dressage competition, but are exhibition exercises, particularly at the Spanish Riding School in Vienna. Exercises include levade, courbette, and capriole.

ALLOWING Describes a rein contact that goes with the movement of the horse's mouth, rather than going ahead of or restricting it. *See also* Non-allowing rein.

ANAEROBIC EXERCISE Period of strenuous exercise demanding muscle function without oxygen. *See also* Aerobic exercise.

ANAEROBIC THRESHOLD The point, during work, beyond which a horse will begin to produce lactic acid in his muscles. *See also* Lactic acid.

ARENA (MANEGE, SCHOOL) An enclosure used for riding. Small arenas usually have an all-weather surface made of combinations of sand, clay, rubber, or synthetic materials; larger arenas are usually grass.

ASCENDING OXER A type of showjump where the front pole is lower than the rear pole.

AUSTRALIAN NOSEBAND *See* p.390.

AZOTURIA A condition characterized by muscle cramps. It occurs as a result of inappropriate feeding (especially overfeeding concentrates on rest days), combined with a lack of a progressive warm-up.

B

BACKING The process during a horse's training when a rider is put on the horse for the first time.

BALANCE The relative amount of weight on the horse's forelegs and hind legs and the consistency and stability with which that weight is carried. It also refers to the rider's weight distribution.

BANK A type of fence. In cross-country courses, banks range from a narrow type, which is jumped over, to the Irish bank, which is wide enough for the horse to jump onto and make a full stride before jumping off again. In showjumping, banks take the form of a variety of tables, between one to three strides wide.

BARS (OF THE MOUTH) The narrow gap between the incisor and molar teeth on which the bit sits. The bars are V-shaped and only covered by a thin layer of skin and tissue, so they are easily damaged.

BASCULE *See* Parabola.

BAUCHER HANGING SNAFFLE *See* p.384.

BITS Bits are used for communication and control, not for forcing a position of the head and neck. They can be divided into three main families: snaffles, curbs, and pelhams. The main action of a snaffle is on the tongue and bars of the mouth, while gag snaffles act upwards into the corners of the mouth. Curb bits and pelhams, which both have curb chains, act primarily on the tongue and lower jaw. A snaffle and curb used together create a double bridle (see p.386). A pelham is a combination of both a snaffle and a curb, with a single mouthpiece that sits in the same position as a snaffle. Most snaffles have a joint in the middle of the mouthpiece while curbs and pelhams are normally unjointed and straight or slightly curved. Bit mouthpieces are normally made of steel but various synthetic materials are used as well as rubber and copper.

FRENCH LINK SNAFFLE
The central plate spreads the load and makes direct contact on the tongue. A mild bit.

BAUCHER HANGING SNAFFLE
The mouthpiece is held upright, which helps prevent the tongue getting over the bit.

JOINTED EGGBUTT SNAFFLE
One of the two most commonly used snaffles for training and trained horses. A mild bit.

TWISTED JOINTED SNAFFLE
The mouthpiece is twisted, which gives a smaller bearing surface on the bars. A strong snaffle.

FIXED MOUTH CURB
The standard curb for a double bridle. The mouthpiece has a tongue groove.

RUGBY PELHAM
Designed to look like a double bridle and to be used with a double bridle headpiece.

VULCANITE PELHAM
A broad mouthpiece spreads the load on the tongue and bars of the mouth.

BEHIND THE BIT Describes a horse bringing his head back behind the vertical and shortening his neck in order to prevent normal rein contact from the rider. It is often the result of discomfort caused by sharp teeth or inappropriate use of strong bits or gadgets.

BELL BOOTS *See* Overreach boots.

BEND Referring to the lateral bend in the horse from the poll to the tail.

BETWEEN THE AIDS An alternative expression to on the bit and on the aids. It refers to the horse coming through his back, working as one connected physical unit, and accepting and understanding the basic aids through the leg and rein.

BITLESS BRIDLE Any of a variety of bridles that do not use a bit, but, instead, use pressure on the nose or jaw of the horse.

BONE The measurement around the leg just below the knee or hock. This measurement is one of the factors determining the horse's ability to carry weight.

BOUNCE FENCE Two fences placed between 3–5 m (9½–16 ft) apart, requiring the horse to take off for the second fence immediately after landing over the first fence without taking a stride. Another one or two fences are sometimes added to make a double or triple bounce. Bounce fences are often used at the start of many jumping grids and as a test in cross-country courses.

BOW HOCKED Describes a horse whose hocks point outwards so that the distance between the hocks

is greater than the distance between the fetlocks. It is the opposite of cow hocked where the hocks are very close together. Both are conformational defects that increase stress on the hocks and reduce their power.

BREASTPLATE A piece of equipment designed to prevent the saddle from slipping backwards. It is fitted around the horse's shoulders and chest and is attached directly to the saddle.

BREECHES Calf-length riding trousers worn with long boots.

BRIDLE *See* p.386.

BRIDOON A small-ring snaffle, commonly used as the snaffle bit of a double bridle.

BROKEN DOWN Describes a horse that has sustained severe damage to the tendons between the knee and fetlock joint. It particularly affects cross-country horses and racehorses, because galloping creates substantial forces in this area.

BROKEN-NECKED A horse whose neck is unnaturally flexed between the third and fifth vertebrae, rather than flexing naturally between the axis and atlas behind the poll. *See also* Flexion.

BRUSHING The action of one of the horse's feet striking his opposite foot or leg if he does not move straight. This can happen when riding on a circle or when a horse loses his balance. To protect the legs, brushing boots are often used on both front and hind legs, covering the area from just below the knee to just below the fetlock joint.

BULLFINCH A vertical fence, with light brush or birch sticking vertically out of the solid base. It is used in a cross-country course, and its origin is in a natural, cut and laid hedge.

C

CADENCE As a horse moves more efficiently with an increased level of impulsion, the period of time his feet stay on the ground (stance time) is reduced and the period of suspension increased. This emphasizes the rhythm of the pace and is often called cadence.

CALMNESS Refers to the need for the horse to be mentally calm in order to avoid the paralysing effect of mental tension, and to allow an unconstrained basis for all his work.

CANTER The pace between trot and gallop. It has three beats (outside hind, inside hind and outside fore together, inside fore) followed by a period of suspension.

CANTER PLANK OR POLE A solid plank or pole placed on the ground and used in place of a fence to practise the technical aspects of jumping. A plank is preferable to a pole because it cannot roll if trodden on and is therefore safer. *See also* Trotting plank.

CAPRIOLE A dressage movement where the horse kicks out with the hind legs, as though he was releasing the hind legs over a fence.

CAVALETTI A pole permanently fixed to either small blocks or X-shaped supports, which can be used for various jumping exercises. The X-type supports

SPANISH RIDING SCHOOL SNAFFLE
Also called the fulmer snaffle. The mouthpiece is held upright. There is an increased nutcracker action.

JOINTED CHEEK SNAFFLE
The long cheeks at the side help to improve steering, making it very suitable for young horses.

DUTCH GAG
Rein pressure on either of the two lower rings creates a gag action, lifting the mouthpiece upwards.

LOOSE-RING JOINTED SNAFFLE
One of the two most commonly used snaffles. It has a mild gag action.

D-RING JOINTED SNAFFLE
Also called a racing snaffle. Almost identical in use to the eggbutt snaffle.

STANDARD PELHAM
The mouthpiece should be slightly rounded to reduce pressure on the tongue.

KIMBLEWICK PELHAM
The straight mouthpiece with tongue groove increases pressure on the tongue.

JOINTED GAG
Rein pressure causes the mouthpiece to rise, putting pressure on the corners of the mouth.

are unsafe because of the risk of injury if a rider falls on to them. Cavaletti should never be placed on top of each other because they can cause a horse to fall.

CAVESSON NOSEBAND The standard noseband (*see* below).

CHAMBON A schooling gadget designed for use during lungeing work without a rider. A rounded strap or rope runs between the horse's forelegs to the poll and then to the bit. It encourages a horse to lower and lengthen the head and neck. It is particularly useful as part of a retraining programme for spoilt horses, but overuse of any gadget will tend to produce an unnatural way of going.

CHANGE OF CANTER LEAD Change of leading leg in canter. *See* Leading leg.

CHANGE OF REIN Change of direction in the arena or on a circle: from going around to the right to going around to the left, or vice versa.

CHAPS/HALF CHAPS Leather protection for the rider's legs, worn from the top of the thigh to the ankles (chaps) or from just below the knee to the ankle (half chaps). Half chaps permit the mobility of the joints that long riding boots often prevent.

CHIPPING IN A horse putting in one or two short strides before taking off for a jump.

COB A type of horse, rather than a breed, between 1.5–1.6 m (4 ft 9 in–5 ft 2 in), with the strength to carry between 77–90 kg (170–200 lbs).

COLDBLOOD Draught-type horse. When crossed with the Throroughbred (defined as a hot – or full – blood) they produce warmbloods, which are often called sport horses.

COLIC The term given to any restriction in the digestive process in the abdomen. Horses are prone to colic after changes to their natural diet of grass, and because they cannot vomit. Colic can cause extreme distress and is a common cause of death.

COLLECTION A variation of a pace, characterized by an increase of weight on the hind legs, combined with a slight lowering of the quarters, a raising of the head and neck, and a shorter stride.

COLT An uncastrated male horse up to 4 years old. *See also* Gelding.

COMBINATIONS In showjumping, a series of three fences separated by one or two strides. In cross country, there may be three to five fences separated by one to three strides or bounces.

COMING THROUGH THE BACK The process of having the horse's hind legs engaged, so that the chain of muscles can begin to lift his back and connect the horse as one athletic unit from the quarters to the poll. *See also* Engagement.

CONCENTRATES Foods consisting of high levels of carbohydrates, proteins and fats, including cereals, oats, barley, nuts, and mixes.

CONDITIONING The training of a horse to respond to a signal that is not instinctive. Responses to the main leg and rein aids are conditioned, while fleeing from danger is instinctive. Also describes the process of improving the horse's fitness and performance.

CONFORMATION The shape of the horse's body, as dictated by his skeleton and the relationship between the various parts. Conformation is a significant factor in soundness.

CONSTANTS The qualities constantly required in dressage, showjumping, and horse trials: acceptance, calmness, forwardness, straightness, and purity.

CONTACT The rider's leg and rein contacts.

COUNTER-CANTER A canter in which the leading leg is deliberately the outside foreleg, rather than the inside foreleg. Often used during training for flying changes and as a straightening exercise for the canter.

COUNTING STRIDES The process of being aware of the individual strides between fences or canter planks. The rider counts each stride as the leading leg comes to the ground.

COURBETTE A dressage movement where the horse leaps forwards in equal bounds from the hind legs, with the body staying at 45 degrees to the ground.

COW HOCKED *See* Bow hocked.

BRIDLES
The two classic bridles are the snaffle bridle and the double bridle. Both bridles are shown with cavesson nosebands. The noseband should be fitted two fingers distance below the protruding cheekbone. The headpiece of both bridles goes around the head behind the ears. It should be broad enough to spread the load of the weight of the bridle.

If your horse shakes his head and appears to be uncomfortable with the bridle it could be that the headstrap section of the noseband (which lies under the headpiece) is too narrow, with all the weight pressing on this narrow strap. Placing it on top of the headpiece will alleviate this problem.

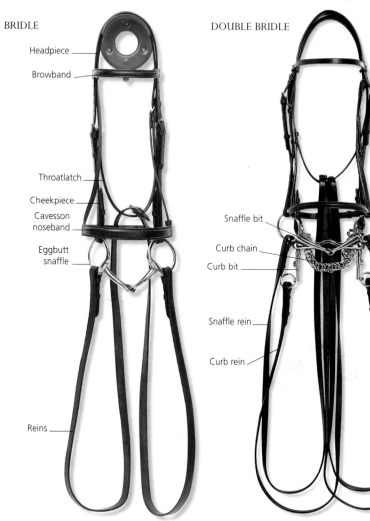

BRIDLE

Headpiece

Browband

Throatlatch

Cheekpiece

Cavesson noseband

Eggbutt snaffle

Reins

DOUBLE BRIDLE

Snaffle bit

Curb chain

Curb bit

Snaffle rein

Curb rein

CRAMPING BEHIND Describes a poor jumping style in which the horse fails to open up his hind legs behind him. Cramping increases the likelihood of the horse hitting the back pole of oxers.

CRIB-BITING A stable vice. The horse grabs hold of and chews any protruding material; it is often accompanied by windsucking. Usually caused by stress and an unsatisfactory environment, and it can damage the horse's incisor teeth.

CROSS BREEDING The crossing of one pure breed with another.

CROSS-REINS Two reins that run from the bit to the front of the withers and then cross over and attach to a roller or saddle approximately 30 cm (12 in) lower down. They are used while lungeing to introduce some weight to the horse's mouth without having the reins tight, and also to prevent too much bend in the neck to the inside or outside without falsely shortening the neck.

CURB BIT A bit with one mouthpiece, a curb chain, and two pairs of rings – one attached to the cheekpiece of the bridle, the lower pair attached to the reins. A curb is used with a snaffle (bridoon) of a double bridle. The curb chain prevents the curb from rotating more than 45 degrees and sliding up into the snaffle, causing discomfort. The curb is not intended to raise or lower the position of the horse's head. It allows the rider to use more refined aids, in the case of a trained horse, or to teach respect for the aids, in the case of a spoilt horse. *See* p. 384.

CURB CHAIN The chain that runs from one side of the curb bit to the other, behind the lower jaw, along the line of the chin groove.

D

D BOX The area used by the veterinary surgeon to inspect horses for soundness before the cross-country phase of a three-day event. It is also used for the 10-minute break to aid recovery and check equipment.

DEEP Getting too close to a fence on take-off.

DESENSITIZATION *See* Habituation.

DIAGONAL (IN RISING TROT) When the horse is in trot, his inside foreleg and outside hind leg move in a diagonal pair, as do his outside foreleg and his inside hind leg. The rider both rises and lowers in time with one pair of diagonals. You can change the diagonal you are rising on as appropriate.

DIRECTION The precise route you take, the rein you are on, and the bend that you have, depending on what exercise is being undertaken.

DIRECT REIN The normal, straight rein contact from the rider's hand to the horse's mouth, allowing the movement of the mouth. *See also* Indirect rein.

DISHING *See* Action.

DISMOUNT The action of getting off a horse, normally on the left-hand side.

DISUNITED Describes the canter when the front legs appear to have the correct canter lead but the hind legs are following the opposite lead. This gives the incorrect sequence for the pace: inside hind leg, outside hind and outside fore together, and finally the inside fore.

DOG LEG A jumping exercise demanding that the horse goes straight after landing over a fence and then makes a turn before going straight again to a second fence. This is different from a bending line which is on a curve from start to finish.

DOUBLE Two showjumping fences with a fixed distance between them.

DOUBLE BRIDLE *See* p. 386.

DRAW REINS *See* Running reins.

DRESSAGE SADDLE *See* p. 393.

DRESSAGE WHIP A stick, approximately 1.2 m (3½ ft) long, used to enhance understanding of the leg aids. *See also* Jumping whip

D-RING JOINTED SNAFFLE *See* p. 385.

DRIVING *See* Long reining.

DROP Any fence where the distance from the top of the fence to the ground on the landing side is greater than it is on the take-off side. Horses will land further away from a drop than with a normal fence, because the parabola of the jump lasts a little longer.

DROP NOSEBAND A type of noseband designed to discourage a horse from opening his mouth, crossing his jaw, and evading the bit. The front section fits above the bit, a hand's breath above the nostrils; the back section comes down underneath the bit and fastens at the back. When the horse opens his mouth, he draws the bit up into the corners of his mouth. *See* p. 390.

DROPPED BACK *See* Hollow back.

DUTCH GAG *See* p. 385.

E

ELECTROLYTES Simple inorganic compounds, including salt, which dissolve in water and are essential for many of the chemical processes in the body. They are given to the horse after prolonged sweating or loss of body fluids when competing or travelling.

ENDURANCE (LONG-DISTANCE) RIDING The sport of riding longer distances of between 20 –200 km (32 –322 miles) within set time periods, while keeping the horse in the best possible condition. Even with some of the longer rides it is possible to average 15 km/h (10 mph).

ENGAGEMENT When the hind legs are moving (engaging) in a way that allows the chain of muscles along the horse's length to lift his back and connect him from the quarters to the poll. When this happens, the horse is described as coming through his back. *See also* Coming through the back.

EQUITATION CLASS A jumping class judged on the performance of the rider rather than the performance of the horse.

EVADING THE BIT Any one of a number of actions that a horse may take to avoid accepting the bit, including crossing the jaw, opening the mouth, lifting the tongue, putting the tongue over the bit, or gripping the bit between his molar teeth.

EXTENSION One of the variations within a pace, characterized by maximum lengthening of the stride while maintaining the same tempo. Also pertains to the straightening of a joint as opposed to flexing (or closing) a joint.

F

FARRIER A person qualified to put shoes on a horse's feet, to take care of the health of the feet, and to ensure they are suitably balanced in relation to the action of the horse.

FAST TWITCH FIBRES Thick, glycogen-storing muscle fibres that accomplish vigorous exercise.

FAST WORK In racing, this describes working the horse for short periods close to or at his maximum speed. In horse trials, it describes working for short periods at three-quarter speed, well within the horse's maximum capability.

FATIGUE Any strain in the horse resulting in delayed adaptation and the horse's inability to respond. *See also* Training Effect.

FEEL Good feel allows the rider to do the right thing at the right time. It requires a combination of harmony with the movement of the horse and experience of how horses can and should feel to the rider.

FEEL A STRIDE *See* See a stride.

FEI Fédération Equestre Internationale (International Equestrian Federation), the international authority for equestrian affairs.

FIFTH-LEG TRAINING Training that encourages the horse to look at what he is jumping and take decisions to ensure the safety of both horse and rider.

FILLER Any of a huge range of wood or plastic decorative material used to fill gaps at the base of a showjumping fence.

FILLY A female horse under 4 years of age. After this time, they are called mares.

FITTENING The process through which a horse is made fit for a particular level of exercise.

FLASH NOSEBAND *See* p. 390.

FLEXIBILITY Describes both the physical suppleness and the mental ability to cope with different situations and activities. Both of these can be developed with good, progressive training.

FLEXION The natural bend between the atlas and axis vertebrae just behind the horse's poll. Forced flexion can stretch the ligaments here, causing discomfort and an unnatural flexion three, four, or five vertebrae down the neck (*see* broken-necked). Also describes the closing (as opposed to the extending) of any joint.

FLIGHT Describes the period of time when a horse's feet are off the ground. Also the name given to the period of time between take-off and landing over a fence.

FLYING CHANGE Change from one canter lead to the other canter lead during the period of suspension while maintaining canter. When a number of changes are made, with a fixed number of strides between each change, they are called sequence changes. The most difficult sequence is to change the canter lead at every stride.

FOAL A colt, gelding, or filly, up to a year old.

FOALSLIP A lightweight headcollar designed for a foal's head to allow leading and general handling. The foalslip should be removed when the foal is not being led or handled.

FORAGE Any food given to horses, including hay and concentrates.

FOREHAND The area in front of the saddle from the horse's shoulders to his head.

FOREQUARTERS *See* Forehand.

FORGING The striking of the horse's fore foot by the hind foot, making a sound like a hammer hitting metal. It occurs when the horse leaves the fore foot on the ground a little longer than normal, usually because of poor balance.

FORM The shape of the rider's position, including the posture of the spine and the position of the limbs.

FORWARD SEAT A term sometimes used to describe riding with the seat out of the saddle with a shorter length of stirrup than in dressage and a more closed angle at the knee and hip. It is also called two-point position, as opposed to three point where you sit on your seat and have some weight in both legs.

FORWARDNESS Refers to the horse going forwards willingly, responding to the rider's forwards aids.

FRESH Describes a horse that is feeling exuberant and behaving inattentively, usually through having had too little exercise.

G

GADGET Any piece of equipment, other than standard tack, that is used to elicit a specific response in training. Most gadgets work using either pulleys or pressure points. They include balancing reins, running reins, chambon, and overhead check reins. Gadgets do not form part of a progressive training programme, and they should be used only on a temporary basis and with the greatest care.

GAIT An alternative word for any of the paces (walk, trot, canter, and gallop), or variation (such as collected, working, and extended).

GALLOP A four-time pace, faster than the canter, with a period of suspension. The typical (transverse) gallop sequence is: outside hind, inside hind, outside fore, inside fore. If the hind legs are reversed (inside hind, outside hind, outside fore, inside fore) it is called a rotary gallop.

GELDING A castrated male horse.

GENERAL-PURPOSE SADDLE See p.393.

GETTING LEFT BEHIND Describes the action of restricting with the rein contact when jumping, which may also cause the rider to give the horse a jab in the mouth. In an extreme case, the rider also loses control of their weight, ending up sitting on the back of the saddle instead of keeping the majority of their weight through their legs.

GIRTH The strap that runs from one side of the saddle to the other and holds the saddle in place. It may be made of leather or webbing, sometimes with an elasticated insert. The term also refers to the circumference of the horse's body measured just behind the withers.

GIRTH GALLS Sores that appear just behind the elbows. They are caused by the friction of the girth on soft skin and can result in bad behaviour. If left untreated they can become infected.

GRAKLE *See* p.390.

GRAND PRIX In showjumping, the highest level of individual competition, with one Grand Prix class at each international show. In international dressage, it is the class between the Intermediate II level and the Grand Prix Special.

GREEN Describes a horse, normally young, that has started training but is still not established in his work.

GRIDS A series of jumps used to help develop a rider's jumping position and improve a horse's jumping technique. Training using grids is referred to as gridwork.

GRIDWORK *See* Grids.

GROUND LINES The use of a pole or small filler 50–75cm (20–30 in) in front of a fence to help prevent a horse getting too close to a fence before take-off and to help define the shape of a fence.

GYMNASTIC JUMPING Exercises, normally grids, that encourage a horse to jump more athletically and with greater spring.

H

HABITUATION The process of desensitization. For example, gradually exposing the horse to traffic or the leg contact so he no longer reacts adversely.

HACKING Pleasure riding done outside the arena.

HALF PASS A movement in dressage in which the horse goes forwards and sideways at the same time.

HALF-HALT An almost invisible, momentary, and co-ordinated use of the aids, used for getting the attention of the horse and improving his balance.

HALF-STRIDE DISTANCE A distance between fences that includes the equivalent of half a horse's stride – for example, three and a half strides. It requires the rider to either lengthen or shorten the stride slightly to achieve a good take-off point.

HALT *See* Square halt.

HALTER *See* Headcollar.

HAND The unit of measurement to describe the height of horses. One hand equals 10 cm (4 in). Most ponies are between 12 hands and 14 hands and most horses from 15 to 17 hands.

HANGING FORELEGS Describes the horse's failure to bring the shoulders, elbows, and knees forwards and to tuck up the legs while jumping. Also called dangling in front. A good horse will bring the knees up quickly: this is called snapping the knees.

HANGING TO HOME Describes a horse trying to head towards the stable or arena exit when ridden, or trying to avoid going away from the stable or arena exit. It denotes lack of acceptance and forwardness. It can eventually develop into napping. *See also* Napping.

HANGING SNAFFLE *See* Baucher hanging snaffle.

HARMONY The ability to go with, rather than follow or restrict, the movement of the horse. The rider's legs go with the horse's sides, the seat with the horse's back, and the hands with the horse's mouth.

HEAD TILTING When a horse rotates his head to one side from the poll, making one ear higher than the other. It usually occurs as the result of restriction through the rein (particularly when approaching a fence), or it may indicate discomfort in the mouth.

HEADCOLLAR A piece of bitless headwear used for leading a horse. It fits like a loose bridle.

HOLLOW (OR DIPPED) BACK A back that is concave: the result of the lowering of the vertebrae between the withers and the croup caused by lack of use or restricted use of the back. It is often exacerbated by age.

HOMEOPATHIC REMEDY A minute concentration of a substance – used to treat illness or injury – prepared in accordance with the homeopathic principle that like cures like.

HOT A horse that is excitable and free wheeling, being difficult to control and train to become calm. Often associated with Thoroughbreds.

HOTBLOOD The name given to Thoroughbred or Arab horses.

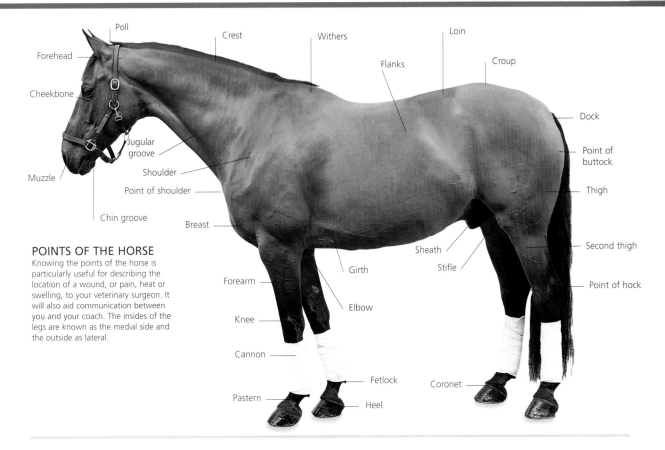

Poll

Forehead

Crest

Withers

Loin

Croup

Cheekbone

Flanks

Dock

Jugular groove

Point of buttock

Muzzle

Shoulder

Thigh

Point of shoulder

Chin groove

Breast

Second thigh

Sheath

Stifle

Forearm

Girth

Point of hock

Knee

Elbow

Cannon

Fetlock

Coronet

Pastern

Heel

POINTS OF THE HORSE

Knowing the points of the horse is particularly useful for describing the location of a wound, or pain, heat or swelling, to your veterinary surgeon. It will also aid communication between you and your coach. The insides of the legs are known as the medial side and the outside as lateral.

I

IMPULSION The combination of suppleness, strength, and spring, all achieved within a particular speed. An integral part of the horse being between the aids and coming through his back.

INCISORS The teeth at the front of the upper and lower jaws (six on each) that are used for cutting and pulling grass and hay.

INDEPENDENT SEAT A rider who has achieved a balanced position that does not require contact from the reins or leg in order to maintain the position is said to have an independent seat. It allows use of the limbs without disturbing the balance.

INDIRECT REIN Allowing rein contact made while the hands move over the neck or withers, breaking the straight line from the hand to the horse's mouth. See also Direct rein.

INDOOR SCHOOL An indoor arena.

INSIDE AND OUTSIDE Describes the direction of the bend of the horse, however slight. The hand, leg, and rein on the inside of the bend of the horse are therefore the inside hand, leg, and rein, and vice versa.

INTERVAL TRAINING A conditioning programme consisting of controlled periods of canter work separated by controlled intervals of rest, allowing partial recovery of the horse's resting pulse.

IRONS See Stirrups.

J

JODHPURS Ankle-length riding trousers worn with short (jodhpur) boots.

JOINTED EGGBUTT SNAFFLE See p. 384.

JUMPING SADDLE See p. 393.

JUMPING WHIP A short whip, approximately 60 cm (2 ft) long, used for jumping and general work.

JUMP-OFF See Against the clock.

K

KUR A freestyle dressage test to music.

L

LACTIC ACID A by-product of the breakdown of carbohydrates stored in the body, which restricts muscles if it is not removed. It is produced when there is insufficient oxygen supplied to muscle cells, such as during strenuous exercise.

LAME Describes the state in which the length, height, and weight of a horse's step is changed as a result of pain. When the same thing happens as a result of lack of suppleness or even development of both sides of the horse, it is usually called unlevel.

LATERAL WORK Dressage exercises in which the front and hind legs move on different tracks, such as in shoulder-in, travers, renvers, and half pass.

LEADING LEG The inside foreleg in canter that finishes each stride in front of the opposite foreleg. It is the last leg to leave the ground before the period of suspension. If the canter stride starts with the outside hind leg (first beat of canter), the inside hind and outside fore will follow next (second beat); the inside fore – the leading leg – then touches the ground (third beat). When the horse changes direction, the canter lead should also change.

LEATHERS Stirrup leathers. See Saddles p. 393.

LEFT REIN, RIGHT REIN See Inside and outside.

LEG YIELD The most basic of all lateral movements. The horse remains straight except for a slight bend at the poll. He goes forwards and sideways at the same time as his inside legs pass and cross in front of his outside legs.

LEGGING UP The first and longest phase of conditioning in which the mechanical frame of the horse, particularly the bones, joints, tendons, ligaments, and cartilage is strengthened throughout a 3 to 6 month period of aerobic conditioning over increasing distance.

LEG-UP Describes when a rider has assistance in mounting, by springing off an assistant's hand instead of the stirrup iron.

LEVADE A dressage movement where the horse remains stationary and brings the forehand off the ground, with his four legs bent and with a deep bending of the joints of the hind legs. The horse's body makes an angle of 45 degrees with the ground.

LIGAMENT Fibrous bands that attach the bones of the horse together.

LONG REINING (DRIVING) The horse is controlled from the ground by two long reins or ropes attached to the bit. The trainer walks approximately 4 m (13 ft) behind the horse.

LOOSE SCHOOLING/JUMPING The working of a horse without a rider or any equipment in an enclosed area, both with or without jumps. It is excellent for improving communication.

LUNGE CAVESSON A cavesson-type noseband fitted with rings to which a lunge rope is attached for the purpose of lungeing.

LUNGE WHIP *See* Lungeing.

LUNGEING Working the unridden horse on a circle by means of a long line, which is attached to the horse's head and held by the trainer. Also used with the ridden horse to help develop the rider's position without the rider having to control the horse. The trainer will also use a lunge whip, which is longer than a dressage whip and has a soft lash.

M

MANEGE *See* Arena.

MARE Female horse over 4 years of age.

MARTINGALE A piece of tack designed to prevent the horse's head from becoming excessively high. The most common is the running martingale: a strap that runs from the girth and then divides into two, each with a ring at the end; the rings run along the reins. The Irish martingale is simply a piece of leather about 25cm (9 in) long with a ring at each end. It joins the reins together under the horse's neck and so prevents them from coming over the horse's head.

MEXICAN GRAKLE *See* below.

MOLARS The back teeth in a horse's jaw (six on each side). The outside edge of the top jaw molars often becomes sharp and needs rasping by a veterinary surgeon or equine dental technician.

MONKEY STRAP A short strap attached to the front arch of the saddle and used as an extra support by novice riders.

MOUNT To get on to a horse. It can also refer to the horse itself.

MULTIBRIDLE (MICKLEM) The Micklem Multibridle is a combination of noseband, lunge cavesson, bitless bridle, and headcollar, developed by the author. It is based around the shape of a dropped noseband. It is designed to avoid pressure to the typical points of discomfort on a horse's head and also to avoid the need to change equipment.

N

NAPPING Describes when a horse continually turns towards home or refuses to go away from home. It denotes lack of acceptance and forwardness. *See also* Hanging to home.

NAPPY Describes a horse that has a tendency to nap. *See also* Napping.

NECK REINING Steering a horse with both reins in one hand. The horse moves in the direction the rider's hand is moved, responding to pressure on the neck by moving away from it. Neck reining is used in Western riding and in polo. It is also used for other activities where a free hand is required, such as leading another rider.

NECKSTRAP A strap that surrounds the horse's neck just in front of the withers. It is used as extra support by the rider.

NON-ALLOWING REIN A rein contact in which the hand does not go with the movement of the horse's mouth. This can come about as a fault, as a result of stiff hands, or intentionally, as in rein-back. Sometimes called a rein of opposition.

NUMNAH A type of soft pad used under the saddle to help produce an even-bearing surface and avoid pressure on the withers or spine.

O

ONE-DAY EVENT A type of horse trial, with the dressage, showjumping, and cross-country phases all on the same day. *See also* Three-day Event.

ON THE AIDS (ON THE BIT) *See* Between the aids.

OPENING UP BEHIND Describes a desirable jumping style in which, from the middle of the jump onwards, the hind legs are released, with the hip, stifle, and hock joints straightening out behind. When the hind legs do not straighten out properly, the horse is said to be cramping behind. *See also* Cramping behind.

OPEN REIN A rein moved away from the horse's neck to encourage the horse to move in that direction. It causes a slight increase in pressure on the opposite side of the horse's mouth, which he moves away from.

OUTLINE The shape of the horse from the poll to the tail. It is also sometimes called the topline, although

NOSEBANDS

Most nosebands are designed to discourage a horse from opening the mouth and evading the bit, but they should not be used as an excuse for using force or to cover up discomfort, resistance, or bad training. A well-trained horse can eventually be ridden in a loose cavesson noseband. Because a horse's top jaw is wider than his bottom jaw considerable discomfort inside the mouth can be caused by flash and standard grakle nosebands. Check in the rule book for approved nosebands.

DROP NOSEBAND
Ideal for early training. It comes into effect only when the horse opens his mouth.

FLASH NOSEBAND
The most popular noseband but often the most uncomfortable for the horse.

GRAKLE
Also called figure of eight. Its light weight makes it suitable for racing.

MEXICAN GRAKLE
More comfortable than a grakle or flash as the upper section is attached higher up the head.

AUSTRALIAN NOSEBAND
A wonderful noseband, reducing pressure on the tongue. This is appreciated by most young horses.

this is primarily a reference to the conformation of the horse rather than the shape he assumes in movement. When the horse goes with impulsion he is often described as having a round outline, particularly if he is worked with collection.

OUTSIDE *See* Inside and outside

OVERBENT When the face of the horse comes behind the vertical and the neck is shortened. Often associated with the use of overstrong bits or gadgets, and riding the horse from the hand instead of the leg.

OVERFACING Asking the horse to do an exercise that is too difficult for his stage of training or ability. The expression is most often used in relation to the size of a fence.

OVERGIRTH A girth that runs over the top of the saddle around the whole body of the horse. It is used as an extra girth for cross country and racing.

OVERREACH BOOTS Rubber, synthetic, or leather, bell-shaped boots that fit around the horse's pastern and cover the heels of the forefeet. They are designed to prevent injuries caused by the hind feet hitting the heels.

OVER RIDE Where the rider does too much or too little with their aids when riding, in relation to the needs of the horse.

OVERTRACKING Describes the hind foot landing beyond the print of the forefoot on the same side in walk and trot. This is also described as tracking up. In the collected paces the horse will not overtrack; the longer the step, as in extension, the greater the overtracking will be.

OXER A type of fence using two sets of poles. An ascending oxer is lower at the front than at the back, while a square oxer is the same height at the front as it is at the back.

OXYGEN DEBT When the intensity of work is such that the energy needs cannot be met by the use of oxygen and glycogen, the horse is said to have an oxygen debt. It is possible to temporarily fuel the muscles anaerobically, otherwise the horse must be rested. *See also* Anaerobic exercise.

P

PACES The steps of a horse, which include walk, trot, canter, and gallop.

PACING A trotting gait in which the horse moves the legs in lateral rather than the normal diagonal pairs. This is done deliberately in some types of harness racing. When a walk is hurried, or a horse is stiff in the back, he may also go very close to pacing.

PARABOLA The regular shape that a horse's centre of gravity makes when jumping. Also called the bascule. Usually, the shape of the first half of the jump and the second half of the jump will be identical.

PASSAGE A very collected trot with a prolonged period of suspension, the horse moving forwards

slowly. There should be an accentuated flexion of the knee and hocks, as in piaffe. *See also* Piaffe.

PELHAM A bit with a single mouthpiece, curb chain, and two sets of rings to which double reins can be attached. It is designed to combine the functions of curb and snaffle. *See* pp. 384–85.

PERIOD OF SUSPENSION The moment in trot and canter where all four feet are off the ground at the same time. Sometimes called a moment of suspension.

PIAFFE In dressage, a highly collected trot on the spot with a slightly prolonged period of suspension. The quarters are slightly lowered.

PIROUETTE When the hind legs stay in almost the same spot and the forehand moves around the hind end, either in collected walk or with a high degree of collection in canter. It can be performed for a quarter turn, half turn (demi-pirouette), or a whole circle.

PLACING PLANK/POLE Plank or pole used in front of a fence, normally out of trot, to help a horse and rider find an appropriate take-off point.

POINTS OF THE HORSE *See* p. 389.

PORT A raised section in the mouthpiece of some curbs and pelhams that presses on the roof of the mouth, designed to prevent the horse from placing the tongue over the bit.

POSITION TO THE INSIDE *See* Shoulder-in.

PRIX ST. GEORGE The introductory level of international FEI dressage test.

PROGRESSIVE LOADING Systematically exposing a horse to increasing exercise demands, with successive increments separated by recovery periods that allow for biological response and adaptation.

PROPRIOCEPTIVE SENSE The ability to be aware of the position and movement of the body and legs, even when they cannot be seen.

PUISSANCE A specialist showjumping competition for international horses only. It consists of a small number of fences over an extended number of rounds finishing with a triple bar and a wall approximately 2.2–2.3 m (7 ft 2 in–7 ft 5 in) high.

PURITY Refers to the naturalness and correctness of the paces, including both a natural and regularly repeated sequence of steps and period of suspension, and a natural outline and use of the horse's body, head, and neck.

Q

QUARTERS The part of the horse's body between the back of the saddle and the tail.

R

REARING The action of a horse taking the front legs off the ground and standing on straight hind legs. This is a resistance that can often be prevented by keeping a horse moving forwards.

REIN OF OPPOSITION *See* Non-allowing rein.

REIN-BACK Where the rider signals to the horse to walk backwards, moving his legs in diagonal pairs.

REINFORCEMENT The process of positive or negative reinforcements to encourage a desired behaviour. A positive reinforcement introduces a reward, such as a gentle pat on the neck or the offering of food; a negative reinforcement takes something away, such as the pressure of the leg or rein.

RELATED DISTANCES A specific distance of between three and ten strides between one showjump and the next.

RENVERS A dressage movement where the horse moves with his quarters to the outside and forehand to the inside, with the opposite bend to shoulder-in.

RESISTANCE A lack of acceptance of the bit and rein contact (shown in such reactions as the horse opening his mouth or grinding his teeth); a lack of willingness to go forwards; or a refusal to respond to the rider's aids.

RHYTHM The regularly repeated sequence of steps in walk, trot, and canter, with walk having four beats, trot two beats, and canter three beats.

RISING TROT *See* Diagonal (in rising trot).

ROLLER A wide strap that goes around the body of the horse. It is used instead of a saddle to attach side reins to when lungeing or when introducing the horse to the use of a saddle.

ROTARY GALLOP *See* Gallop.

ROUGHAGE Bulk, high-fibre foods, such as grass, hay, chaff, and straw.

RUGBY PELHAM *See* p. 384.

RUNNING AWAY The horse ignoring the rider's aids to slow down and, instead, going increasingly faster. To cure this, you must first find the reason for the horse running away.

RUNNING OUT When a horse avoids a fence by moving sideways to the left or right in order to go around it.

RUNNING REINS Separate reins forming a simple pulley. They run from the girth, either from just below the saddle flap on either side, or from between the horse's forelegs, up through the bit, and back to the rider's hands. They should be used with the greatest care as they frequently create an unnatural shape in the neck and prevent the horse truly connecting from the leg to the hand.

S

SADDLE *See* p. 393.

SADDLE SORE Any sore or damaged skin in the saddle area. It is caused by ill-fitting or dirty tack.

SCHOOL *See* Arena.

SCHOOL MOVEMENTS The exercises or movements formed from a combination of shapes – made up of straight lines and circles or parts of circles – which are used in the arena for the purpose of developing a horse's physical ability.

SCHOOLING WHIP See Dressage whip.

SEAT This refers to the way the rider's buttocks and the seat bones are placed in relation to the saddle. It also refers to the rider's position in the saddle for a particular activity, such as a dressage, a showjumping, and a cross-country seat. See also Independent seat.

SEE A STRIDE The rider's ability to find the right take-off point when jumping. It is the fundamental priority for effectiveness of the jumping rider if a horse is to jump to his maximum ability.

SELF-CARRIAGE When a horse does not seek the support of the rein contact, he is said to be in self-carriage. It is an often misapplied phrase because it is the horse that carries the rider, not the other way round. In many instances, the horse learns to lean on the rein because the rider gives him a rein contact to lean against.

SEQUENCE CHANGES See Flying change.

SERPENTINE A type of school movement where parts of circles are connected to each other, forming loops and S shapes, requiring the rider to keep changing direction and, therefore, rein.

SHOULDER FORE See Shoulder-in.

SHOULDER-IN The horse is bent to the inside and goes forwards with the forehand positioned to the inside in relation to the quarters. A smaller degree of this is called shoulder fore.

SHY Sudden movement away from an object. The horse may shy through fear of a stationary object or in response to unexpected movement, such as that of a bird suddenly flying into his path. Shying sometimes happens because of the horse's restricted vision. By putting a horse into shoulder-in position, away from the area that worries him, shying can often be avoided.

SIDE REINS Reins running from the girth or roller to the horse's mouth on both sides. These are used when training young horses and for lungeing work. They are used to introduce a rein contact and to control the bend of the horse's neck.

SITTING TROT The rider keeps the seat in the saddle during trot, as opposed to rising to the trot, where the rider allows the seat to rise out of the saddle and lower back again in time with the trot.

SNAFFLE The basic bit, consisting of a mouthpiece with a ring at each end to which single reins are attached. See p.384.

SNAP THE FORELEGS See Hanging forelegs.

SPEED The distance covered in a specific time, usually expressed as metres per minute or miles per hour.

SPEED CLASS See Against the clock.

SPEEDWORK See Fast work.

SPOOK See Shy.

SPURS An artificial aid: a metal or plastic attachment to the rider's heel used to back up the normal leg aids. The length of the spur is not as important as the shape at the end of the spur. They should not be capable of wounding a horse, and they should be worn only by an experienced rider who has a stable leg position.

SQUARE HALT A halt in which, when viewed from the side, the horse's two hind legs are perfectly in line and the two forelegs are perfectly in line. When training a young horse, it is more important that he is stationary, with weight on each leg. As his balance becomes more advanced, he will then naturally halt squarely.

STABLE VICES Any repetitive undesirable behaviours, such as crib-biting or windsucking, displayed by a horse in the stable or field.

STALLION A male horse, 4 years old or over, that has not been castrated.

STANDARDS See Wingstand.

STEEPLECHASE A type of fence made of birch with a sloping profile, which makes it very suitable for being jumped at speed. Steeplechase also describes a race over a course of this type of fence. In three-day eventing, there is a specific steeplechase section on the cross-country day.

STIRRUPS Consisting of the irons (in which the rider's feet rest) and the leather straps by which the irons are attached to the saddle.

STRAIGHTNESS Refers both to the equal and even development of both sides of the horse in each pace and to the precise positioning of the forehand, which together produce straightness.

STRAIN Immediate response to excessive demand, resulting in either fatigue or failure.

STRIDE Any one full sequence of the four legs of the horse. Each beat is referred to as a step. In trot there are two beats or two steps for one stride of trot. In canter there are three steps for each stride, and in walk there are four steps for each stride.

STUDS Metal pieces that are screwed to the horse's shoes to prevent him from slipping, for example, when jumping or riding cross country.

SUBMISSION This does not refer to subservience, but to the horse being willing, attentive, and confident in all aspects of his behaviour, and accepting a soft rein contact.

SUCCULENTS Fleshy foods, such as apples, given as a treat or added to feed to increase palatability.

SUPPLEMENTS Substances given in addition to a horse's basic feed for a specific purpose – to correct an imbalance or deficiency in the diet, to treat an illness, to add weight, to aid digestion, and so on. Supplements, which should be given strictly according to need, can include vitamins and minerals in concentrate form, salt-licks, electrolytes, and herbs.

SURCINGLE See Overgirth.

T

TEMPO The speed of the rhythm. It does not describe the speed at which the ground is covered but rather the speed of the steps.

TENDONS The dense cords of tissue that attach muscles to bone. In comparison to muscles, they are relatively inelastic. The main tendons are the deep flexor and the superficial flexor, which, combined with the suspensory ligament, are the most commonly damaged parts of a galloping horse. See also Broken down.

THOROUGHBRED Registered descendants of three sires (the Darley Arabian, the Brierly Turk, and the Godolphin Barb) of racehorse type, sometimes described as hotbloods.

THREE-DAY EVENT A type of horse trials at varying levels of difficulty, with a dressage phase, normally over 2 days, followed by a speed and endurance day (including roads and tracks, steeplechase, and cross country), and a final day of showjumping. See also One-day event.

TIED IN BELOW THE KNEE A conformational fault in which the width of the foreleg just below the knee is less than the width just above the fetlock joint. This fault places extra strain on the main tendons.

TIMING The rider has to time every aid and every transition accurately. In jumping, they also have to time every stride to produce a good take-off point.

TONGUE OVER THE BIT The tongue should normally lie under the bit. When there is excessive pressure on the tongue, the horse learns first to lift the tongue and then to place it over the bit. There are a number of attachments to stop the tongue getting over the bit, but with good training this should not happen.

TRACK Where you ride in the school. For example, the outside track is the area next to the arena fence. It also refers to the line followed by the hind legs and forelegs of the horse. In lateral work, the horse's front and hind legs go on different tracks.

TRAIL RIDING See Hacking.

TRAINING EFFECT (ADAPTATION) Physiological reaction to stress in which tissues (from hoof to bone to muscle) and body functions (from respiration to circulation to excretion) respond by adapting to achieve a greater level of capacity.

TRANSITION Used to describe both going from one pace to another, such as from walk to trot, and changing from one variation of pace to another, such as from collected trot to medium trot. The transitions can be either progressive, as above, or direct (sometimes called acute), such as going from walk to canter. Moving from walk to canter and then back to walk, is known as a simple change.

TRANSVERSE GALLOP *See* Gallop.

TRAVERS A dressage movement where the horse is bent to the inside, and goes forwards with the quarters positioned to the inside in relation to the forehand.

TROT A two-time pace, between walk and canter, in which the legs work in diagonal pairs, with each hind leg moving in unison with the foreleg on the opposite side.

TROTTING PLANK/POLE A series of three or four planks or poles placed in front of a fence that is approached in trot. They are used to help control the regularity of the trot and ensure a precise take-off point to the fence. *See also* Placing plank.

TURNBACK A showjumping term to denote a 180 degree turn back to a fence, often required in a jump-off against the clock.

TWISTED JOINTED SNAFFLE *See* p. 384.

U

UNLEVEL *See* Lame.

UPRIGHTS An alternative name for a vertical showjump. A type of narrow wingstand.

V

VARIABLES The variable components that are required for all riding activities – direction, speed, impulsion, balance, and timing.

VAULTING The sport of doing gymnastics on horseback, using a horse on the lunge and a vaulting roller that has supporting handles for the gymnast to hold while springing up onto the horse

VAULTING-ON Getting on a horse without using the stirrup or without the help of a leg-up, either with the horse standing still or in canter.

VOLTE A 6 m (20 ft) circle – the smallest circle ridden in dressage.

W

WALK A four-time pace, in which all four feet are moved separately in the following sequence: inside hind leg, inside foreleg, outside hind leg, and outside foreleg.

WARMBLOOD A type of horse derived from a combination of hotblood and coldblood lines. They are usually bred as sport horses.

WEAVING A stable vice caused by boredom and poor stable management: the horse moves his head and weight from side to side repeatedly, normally over the top of a door or gate.

WELS CAVESSON The type of lunge cavesson used at the Spanish Riding School. As with a drop noseband, it fits below the bit, which avoids squashing the sensitive tissue inside the horse's mouth between the outside edge of the teeth in the top jaw. As with a traditional lunge cavesson, it is positioned just below the protruding cheekbones.

WESTERN RIDING Used to describe any of a large number of activities, including trail riding, reining, cutting, and showing, using a Western saddle, which is deep and supportive, and is designed to be ridden with a long length of leg.

WINDSUCKING A stable vice in which the horse repeatedly sucks in air while crib-biting. *See also* Crib-biting.

WINGSTAND A wide support for the poles of a showjump, which also acts as a wing to discourage a horse from running out.

WOLF TEETH Small teeth very close to the first molar teeth that are present in some horses and can be very sensitive. As a general rule, they should be removed before introducing a bit to the mouth.

SADDLES

Whatever type of saddle you use, it should be comfortable for the horse. To make this possible it should not come into direct contact with the withers or any part of the spine. The weight of the rider should be spread as evenly as possible over the area that is in contact, and the saddle should sit as level as possible. It is often necessary to use separate pads under the saddle to achieve this, but these should not extend under the saddle flap so the width of the horse is not increased.

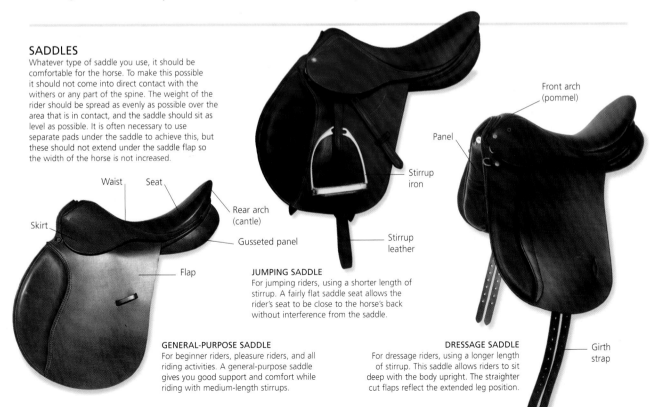

Waist · Seat · Rear arch (cantle) · Skirt · Gusseted panel · Flap · Stirrup iron · Stirrup leather · Front arch (pommel) · Panel · Girth strap

GENERAL-PURPOSE SADDLE
For beginner riders, pleasure riders, and all riding activities. A general-purpose saddle gives you good support and comfort while riding with medium-length stirrups.

JUMPING SADDLE
For jumping riders, using a shorter length of stirrup. A fairly flat saddle seat allows the rider's seat to be close to the horse's back without interference from the saddle.

DRESSAGE SADDLE
For dressage riders, using a longer length of stirrup. This saddle allows riders to sit deep with the body upright. The straighter cut flaps reflect the extended leg position.

INDEX

ACKNOWLEDGMENTS

Author's Acknowledgments
The author would like to thank the following
experts for their advice on this project: Consultants:
Brian Henry F.E.I. Course Designer; Ruth Magee
MPHTY, BSc, BA (Hons), Sports Sc, MISCP, MCSCP
for her advice on the Physical Preparation of the
Rider chapter; Dr Maureen Prendagast MVB, Cert
VR, Cert ES (orth) PhD, MRCVS for veterinary and
anatomical advice. Thanks also to British Dressage
and Fédération Equestre Internationale for
permission to use their dressage tests.

Packager's Acknowledgments
Studio Cactus would like to thank Kit Houghton and
Debbie Cook at Houghtons Horses Picture Library;
Richard Tibbetts, for his illustrations; Richard Dabb
at Dorling Kindersley for picture research; Maggie
Raynor; Musto Ltd (www.musto.co.uk), for the
loan of riding clothing; Calcutts and Sons, for the
loan of tack; Tredstep, for riding chaps, gaitors, and
footwear; and Brian and Aline Pilcher at Marine PR.

We would also like to thank the following for
allowing us to use their facilities during the
photoshoot: Hilda Hick and Sharon McClure at
Ashmore Equestrian Centre, Orlando, Florida;
Highlife Farms, Orlando, Florida; Clarcona
Horseman's Park, Orlando, Florida; Annacrivey
Stud, County Wicklow, Ireland; Hooze Farm,

Gloucestershire, England; Tim and Susan Phillips
at Ballinacoola Equestrian Park, County Wicklow,
Ireland; Audrey Magee; and Carol Bulmer.
Riding Models:
Lauren Ball, Addy Beattie, Lisette la Borde, Vicky
Brake, Jim Burger, Ruth Chadwick, Alexa Dix,
Katelyn Emberton, Leigh Emberton, Shawn Filley-
Fennessey, Mary Galloway, Christine Geever,
Jonie Griffin, Heidi Hamilton, Hilda Hick,
Bev Horvath, Blaine Horvath, Aidan Keogh,
Ruth Magee, Eric Martin, Sally Maxwell, Sarah
Micklem, Shonagh Stevens, Chase Todd, Ginny
Watts, Spencer Wilton, Diana Zaida

Thanks also to Laura Watson for design assistance;
Elizabeth Mallard-Shaw and Kate Green for editorial
and consultancy work; Jo Weeks for proofreading;
and Hilary Bird for compiling the index.

Picture Credits
Dorling Kindersley would like to thank the following
for their kind permission to reproduce their
photographs: (Abbreviations key: t:top, b:bottom,
r:right, l:left, c:centre)
**Photography by Kit Houghton
(www.houghtonshorses.com) except:**
Dorling Kindersley (www.dkimages.com):
51tr, 262br, 331br, 359tr, 377, 381tr, 386
Polyjumps (www.polyjumps.com): 190tl

Jacket:
Tony Parkes — Author photograph

Publisher's Note
The naming of any organization, product, or
treatment in this book does not imply endorsement
by the publisher and the omission of any such names
does not indicate disapproval. The publisher regrets
that it cannot accept any responsibility for acts or
omissions based on the information in this book.